World Conflicts
and
Confrontations

World Conflicts and Confrontations

Volume I
The Americas

Editor
Charles F. Bahmueller
Center for Civic Education

Project Editor
R. Kent Rasmussen

SALEM PRESS, INC.
Pasadena, California   Hackensack, New Jersey

Managing Editor: Christina J. Moose
Project Editor: R. Kent Rasmussen   *Production Editor:* Cynthia Beres
Research Supervisor: Jeffry Jensen   *Assistant Editor:* Andrea E. Miller
Copyediting: Douglas Long, Robert Michaels   *Research Assistant:* Jun Ohunki
Acquisitions Editor: Mark Rehn   *Graphics and Design:* James Hutson
Photograph Editor: Karrie Hyatt   *Layout:* William Zimmerman

Frontispiece: Tupac Amaru guerrillas, camouflaged in mud, move through a central Peruvian forest in a training exercise in early 1997, while awaiting the outcome of their movement's occupation of the Japanese embassy in Lima. (*Reuters/Mariana Bazo/Archive Photos*)

Library of Congress Cataloging-in-Publication Data

World conflicts and confrontations / editor, Charles F. Bahmueller; project editor, R. Kent Rasmussen.
   p. cm.
   Includes bibliographical references and index.
Contents: v. 1. The Americas — v. 2. Africa — v. 3. Asia and the Pacific — v. 4. Europe and the former Soviet Republics. Appendices.
   ISBN 0-89356-219-X (set : alk. paper). — ISBN 0-89356-220-3 (v. 1 : alk. paper). — ISBN 0-89356-221-1 (v. 2 : alk. paper). — ISBN 0-89356-222-X (v. 3 : alk. paper). — ISBN 0-89356-223-8 (v. 4 : alk. paper).
   1. World politics—1989-   . 2. Military history, Modern—20th century.   3. Low-intensity conflicts (Military science).   4. Violence—History—20th century.   5. Terrorism—History—20th century. 6. History, Local.   I. Bahmueller, Charles F. II. Rasmussen, R. Kent.

D860.W64   2000
909.82—dc21

99-33574
CIP

First Printing

Contents

Volume I

THE AMERICAS

Complete List of Contents

Volume I

Volume II

Volume III

Volume IV

Publisher's Note

World Conflicts and Confrontations is designed to meet the needs of middle and high school students and others seeking clear explanations of what has been going on in the world's many troubled countries. Each of its four volumes covers a major world region, identifying its "hot spots" and analyzing the most important of these in depth. Volume 1 covers the Americas and is divided into sections on North America, Central America, the Caribbean, and South America. Volume 2 covers Africa. Volume 3 covers Asia and the Pacific, with separate sections on the Middle East, the rest of Asia, and the Pacific Islands. Volume 4 covers Europe, with sections on Western Europe and Central and Eastern Europe, including the former Soviet republics in Asia. That volume also contains a selection of appendices.

The Editor's introduction, in volume 1, discusses the global dimensions of conflict, examining patterns and themes that connect conflict issues throughout the world. Each of the ten sections into which the four volumes are subdivided is introduced by an essay surveying the region as a whole. These regional survey essays explore regional patterns, analyzing why some countries within the regions have been more prone to conflict than have others.

The ten regional surveys are followed by a total of 104 essays on individual nations and four small groups of nations (Armenia and Azerbaijan, El Salvador and Honduras, the three Baltic republics, and the five former Soviet Central Asian republics). The 112 nations covered within these essays represent nearly two-thirds of the world's 175 sovereign nations and are home to perhaps 95 percent of the world's people. They have been selected for special coverage because of the intensity of their recent and current conflicts, as well as the significance of the roles they play in the world as a whole.

Each essay opens with a statement summarizing the most pressing problems of the country—or group of countries—followed by an analysis of the origins, nature, and history of these problems. Basic facts and statistics pertaining to each country are summarized in boxed profiles. The profiles list each country's common and official names, date of independence, former colonial rulers (if any), location, area, capital city, population size, official languages, major religions, gross domestic product, major exports, military budget, and number of military personnel.

Moreover, every essay (including the ten regional surveys) contains at least one map, a detailed time line of modern events, and a discussion of sources of further information, with special attention to the growing availability of the online resources of the World Wide Web. The three hundred photographs illustrating the set include many taken of events occurring while the project itself was underway.

Arranging articles by region offers several advantages. For example, readers primarily interested in a single region, such as South America, will appreciate finding all articles on that region grouped together, following an essay surveying the region as a whole. However, while geography provides the set's primary organizing principle, some adjustments have been made to accommodate political realties. For example, the Central Asian republics of the former Soviet Union are covered, not in the volume on Asia, but in the volume on Europe, given their close ties with other former Soviet republics within Europe. On the other hand, although Egypt is politically and culturally part of the Middle East, it is discussed in volume 2 because it is an equally integral part of the continent of Africa, to which it physically belongs.

The fact that the world is a complicated and constantly changing place has repeatedly been brought home to the editors of this project in their attempts to track events in the ever-changing world. While this set was being prepared for publication, not a single day passed without events in at least a dozen troubled countries making the news. Happily, not all this news has been bad. Some countries facing what appeared to be intractable conflicts when the project began now seem headed in more peaceful directions. Conversely, new troubles are brewing in other countries that recently appeared to be too stable to merit inclusion here. The unavoidable lesson from this is that the world changes so constantly and so rapidly that *any* reference work of this nature must be regarded as a work in progress. Nevertheless, every effort has been made to ensure that information here is as up to date as possible—particularly the information in time lines.

In addition to its essays on individual countries and regions, *World Conflicts and Confrontations* offers ten appendices to assist readers. A world perspective on the history of conflicts can be found in the World Time Line, which collects the most important events into one chronological stream. Another type of global perspective can be obtained in an appendix article on U.N. Peacekeeping Operations. It summarizes the history of U.N. efforts to foster world peace and offers brief entries on all U.N. peacekeeping missions since World War II. Explanations of basic terminology used throughout this set are offered in the glossary, written by the project's Editor.

Five other appendices are designed to direct readers to additional sources of up-to-date information on the world. The extensive bibliography at the end of volume 4 mainly comprises recently published books on world conflict issues. Most of its entries do not appear in the study notes for individual chapters, which focus more on materials relevant to the individual countries and regions. Another appendix summarizes information on news sources, in both print and broadcast media, that provide up-to-the-minute news on world affairs.

The embassies of many nations stand ready to provide persons interested in their countries with a wealth of information. All foreign embassies in the United States are listed in an appendix that provides their mailing addresses, phone and fax numbers, and, in many cases, Internet and Web site addresses. Similarly helpful are many of the international organizations listed in another appendix. It, too, offers addresses of many Web sites. Another appendix lists additional sites on the World Wide Web that provide information on world conflict areas.

Several features will help direct readers to the information they seek. In addition to the tables of contents in the front matter of each volume, lists of the countries discussed in individual essays are provided on the first page of each regional section. The map of the world's nations has seen scores of name changes in recent decades. For users uncertain of the current names of the countries in which they are interested, a list of current, former, and variant names of countries and regions can be found at the back of every volume. For readers interested in finding examples of conflict issues, a listing of essay topics arranged by conflict types can also be found at the back of every volume. Finally, a detailed index to the *entire* set appears in all four volumes. With entries on names, places, events, and issues, it should answer most questions readers may have about the content of the set and direct them to the information they seek. Readers should also remember that because the world is an increasingly interconnected place, many persons, countries, and events are discussed in more than one volume—another reason attention should be paid to the general index.

Reference works such as this would not be possible without the help of scholars from around the world. The seventy-three people who contributed articles to *World Conflicts and Confrontations* bring a wealth of knowledge and insights into the world to this project, and Salem's editors wish to extend their gratitude to them. We are especially grateful to Charles F. Bahmueller of Southern California's Center for Civil Education for serving as the project's Editor. In addition to the insights he brings as a political scientist who has worked closely with government officials and scholars from around the globe, Dr. Bahmueller has had extensive experience living and traveling abroad, particularly in the troubled Central and Eastern European nations, whose stories figure so prominently within these pages.

Contributors

Earl R. Andresen
University of Texas at Arlington

Debra D. Andrist
University of St. Thomas

Bryan Aubrey
Fairfield, Iowa

James A. Baer
Northern Virginia Community College

Charles F. Bahmueller
Center for Civic Education

Carl L. Bankston III
Tulane University

David Barratt
Chester, England

Alvin K. Benson
Brigham Young University

Milton Berman
University of Rochester

Karan A. Berryman
Andrew College

Cynthia A. Bily
Adrian College

Kevin J. Bochynski
Beverly, Massachusetts

Pegge Bochynski
Beverly, Massachusetts

Steve D. Boilard
Sacramento, California

Gordon L. Bowen
Mary Baldwin College

Fred Buchstein
John Carroll University

Peter E. Carr
Caribbean Historical & Genealogical Journal

Beau David Case
Ohio State University

Bernard A. Cook
Loyola University

Richard V. Damms
Mississippi State University

Margaret A. Dodson
Boise Independent Schools

Michael Shaw Findlay
California State University, Chico

Carol G. Fox
East Tennessee State University

Richard A. Fredland
Indiana University, Indianapolis

Robert F. Gorman
Southwest Texas State University

Daniel G. Graetzer
Seattle, Washington

Robert J. Griffiths
University of North Carolina at Greensboro

Johnpeter Horst Grill
Mississippi State University

Irwin Halfond
McKendree College

Obioma M. Iheduru
Fort Valley State University

Tseggai Isaac
University of Missouri, Rolla

Jeffry Jensen
Altadena, California

Masoud Kheirabadi
Marylhurst College

Grove Koger
Boise Public Library

Eugene Larson
Pierce College

Thomas T. Lewis
Mount Senario College

Lee Liu
Southwestern Oklahoma State University

Thomas McGeary
Champaign, Illinois

Paul Madden
Harden-Simmons University

Paul D. Mageli
Kenmore, New York

Cynthia Keppley Mahmood
University of Maine

Khalid Mahmood
Waterville, Maine

John S. Murray
Fairfax, Virginia

Alice Myers
Simon's Rock College

Joseph L. Nogee
University of Houston

Robert C. Oberst
Nebraska Wesleyan University

Ranee K. L. Panjabi
Memorial University of Newfoundland

Wayne Patterson
St. Norbert College

Contributors

Nis Petersen
Jersey City State College

Lela Phillips
Andrew College

G. R. Plitnik
Frostburg State University

John Powell
Pennsylvania State University, Erie

Victoria Price
Lamar University

P. S. Ramsey
Highland, Michigan

R. Kent Rasmussen
Thousand Oaks, California

Douglas W. Richmond
University of Texas at Arlington

Carl Rollyson
Baruch College

Joseph R. Rudolph, Jr.
Towson University

Rose Secrest
Signal Mountain, Tennessee

Roger Smith
Portland, Oregon

Michael Strada
West Virginia University
West Liberty State College

Susan A. Stussy
Neosho County Community College

John C. Super
West Virginia University

Robert D. Talbott
University of Northern Iowa

Leslie V. Tischauser
Prairie State College

Robert D. Ubriaco, Jr.
Spelman College

William T. Walker
Chestnut Hill College

George C. Y. Wang
George Washington University

Annita Marie Ward
Salem-Teikyo University

Samuel E. Watson III
Midwestern State University

Richard L. Wilson
University of Tennesse, Chattanooga

Lisa A. Wroble
Redford District Library

Robert Zaller
Drexel University

Introduction

The world is constantly in conflict. While this remark may seem commonplace, people often think peace has been restored once wars end. People tend to believe that peace reigned, if only for a short time, when World War II ended in 1945, when the Vietnam War was settled in 1975, and when the Persian Gulf War ended in 1991. The truth, however, is otherwise.

It has been said that "the fighting never stops." Violent confrontations among states (known as "countries," "nations," or "nation-states") or groups within them occur virtually continuously. The articles in these volumes describe and analyze a comprehensive range of actual and potential conflicts and their causes within and among the nations of the world. They deal with every large country and many smaller ones. In addition, continents and other regions have separate articles providing an overview of the area covered.

It has also been said that there are no "economic problems," "political problems," "social problems," and so on, but only *problems*. These problems have economic, political, and social aspects. In other words, these factors are all interrelated. They are not separate.

The same consideration is true of the principal causes of conflict in the world. Poverty, for example, plays some role in nearly every major conflict. It is uncommon to observe rich peoples violently fighting each other. Those with much to lose are less likely to risk its destruction than those with little or nothing to lose.

Social and economic causes of conflicts are generally closely related. This is readily apparent in many ethnic conflicts. Impoverished Indonesians, for example, blame their poverty on their Chinese neighbors, who control 70 percent of Indonesia's wealth. Idi Amin, the Ugandan dictator of the 1970's, expelled his country's entire population of East Indians because of jealousy over their accomplishments as traders. Thus, ethnic prejudice and economic problems interacted.

Ethnic Conflict. Perhaps the most common type of conflict in the world is ethnic conflict. Ethnic groups are either entire peoples (in some cases called "tribes") or fragments of a people, most of whom live elsewhere. Italian Americans or Greek Australians, for example, are ethnic groups related to peoples living in Italy and Greece. By contrast, the Zulu people of South Africa and the Ibo of Nigeria live almost entirely within their own countries.

Every inhabited continent has experienced some form of ethnic conflict. In some cases, conflict occurs between settlers from other places and indigenous inhabitants. For example, such conflicts have occurred in Brazil, in which Westernized settlers have been developing portions of the Amazon Basin in which Amerind societies have lived for centuries.

In other cases, ethnic enclaves—places inhabited entirely by members of one group—are surrounded by other groups. Where there is historic hostility between the two groups, conflict is easily ignited. For example, fighting between Armenia and Azerbaijan erupted in 1988 over the attempt of Nagorno-Karabakh, an Armenian enclave within Azerbaijan, to secede from Azerbaijan and join Armenia.

Most often, ethnic conflict occurs among groups that live among or near each other within a single country. Conflict among ethnic groups is quite common in Africa. In some cases, conflicts have resulted from arbitrarily drawn borders created under European colonial rule. Nigeria, for example, contains about 250 ethnic groups cast together in a single state by Great Britain. Tension among these groups led to a disastrous civil war in the late 1960's, when southeastern Nigeria's mainly Ibo people declared their independence to escape discrimination by Nigeria's ruling ethnic groups.

In Russia, the attempted secession of the Chechnya people during the 1990's cost thousands of civilian lives. Within Bulgaria, there has been tension between majority Bulgars and minority Turks—who constitute only 10 percent of the country's population—in part because of Bulgar memories of five centuries of harsh Turkish rule.

Ethnic conflict is common when members of one ethnic group migrate to another country. Turks migrated to Germany after World War II, for example, at the invitation of the German government to ease a German labor shortage. German law makes it nearly impossible for Turks to become citizens, and resident Turks have become targets for violent, right-wing youths. Similarly, conflicts have arisen in Great Britain between white Britons and nonwhite West Indians, Pakistanis, and Indians, who began settling in Britain during the 1950's.

In some cases minority groups may rule majority ethnicities. Fearing their safety under majority rule, such minorities may use violence to maintain their dominance. On the other hand, a majority people, feeling enslaved or exploited under minority rule, may rebel. Such circumstances have occurred in the Central African nations of Burundi and Rwanda. Massacres have been carried out by both majority Hutu and minority Tutsi since 1972. In 1994, when 500,000 Hutu and Tutsi were killed in Rwanda, the violence spilled over to neighboring Burundi. There, mass killings of Hutu were carried out by troops of that nation's minority Tutsi government. By the end of the 1990's, decades of intermittent mass slaughter had not been brought to a close. Instead, both camps prepared for further bloodshed.

In some countries, large minority communities have grown sufficiently to constitute majorities, thereby setting off conflicts within the former majority group. This occurred during the 1990's in Fiji, when the minority, which had emigrated from India, gained control of the government in free elections. In response, the army, dominated by ethnic Fiji islanders, overthrew the government, throwing the island into crisis.

Other causes of severe ethnic conflict, both past and present, are preferential policies. Biafra's war of secession from Nigeria began after the Ibo people, who had been highly successful in Nigeria based upon personal merit, found themselves discriminated against by preferential policies favoring other ethnic groups that had done less well.

A similarly bloody war has continued for decades in Sri Lanka between the Sinhalese majority and the Tamil minority. By the time the island achieved independence from the British during the 1950's, the Tamils had, through merit, scored gains out of proportion to their numbers in university admittance and government jobs. In 1956 the Sinhalese majority began seeking to further their interests by discriminating against Tamils with preferential policies. Violent resistance began during the 1950's and escalated during the 1980's and 1990's. Preferential polices elsewhere, such as in Malaysia and India, may breed future conflicts.

Language and Assimilation. Ethnic conflicts frequently involve language issues, since language is often a defining characteristic of ethnicity. In Belgium, language has been the central issue separating Dutch-speaking Flemings and French-speaking Walloons. The French-speaking portion of Canada has long been divided from the English-speaking majority. Political reforms appear to have worked sufficiently in Belgium to keep the country from disintegrating. However, emotions have continued to run high over language and culture issues in Canada. In the late 1990's it was unclear if the country would remain united.

In all cases of ethnic conflict, various ethnicities have not, for whatever reason, assimilated into united wholes, even though they may have lived together for centuries. The ethnic groups that make up Bosnia, formerly part of the communist state of Yugoslavia, are a case in point.

How does the United States compare with other countries in dealing with ethnic conflict? After experiencing great waves of immigration in the late nineteenth and early twentieth centuries, the United States was more successful than any other major—and nearly every minor—country in promoting harmony among ethnic groups. Much of its success can be attributed to its policy of assimilationism, which promoted the "Americanization" of immigrant children in the schools. The United States promotes a common language by requiring those who wish to become citizens to pass English-language tests. All public school children in the United States must learn English in order to graduate. In the past there were noticeable divides among the millions of Italians, Germans, Irish, Scandinavians, and members of other European immigrant groups. By the end of the twentieth century, however, most of them had assimilated into what has been called the American "melting pot."

This does not mean that the United States has been entirely successful in forming a homogenous domestic culture. First, African Americans were never part of the melting pot. Some degree of racial conflict has always been a fixture of American culture. Moreover, in the late twentieth century, increasing numbers of immigrants have come from non-European regions. While some assimilation has occurred, for a variety of reasons it is not clear that the traditional melting pot will absorb immigrants from non-Western civilizations.

Religious, Social, and Political Conflict. A second common factor in conflicts around the world is religion. Major religions appear to be more violent at certain phases of their development. Early Christians suffered persecution and martyrdom in ancient Rome. By the European Middle Ages, however, Christians were promoting the aggressive and bloody Crusades in the Middle East. Later wars between Protestant and Roman Catholic Christians caused numerous deaths in Western Europe. Even in the late twentieth century occasional apocalyptic forms of Christianity found themselves in conflict with the political order, as in the incident in Waco, Texas, between Branch Davidians and U.S. federal agents. However, the age of Christian holy wars is now past.

Hindu nationalists in India threaten war against Islamic Pakistan. India has also been the scene of vicious fighting between Hindus and those of the Sikh religion. A militant form of Islam practiced in the Middle East has been shown to be excessively prone to violence, as opposed to less strict versions of Islam practiced elsewhere. Middle Eastern Islamic groups with such names as "Party of God" have practiced terrorism against Israeli targets. During the 1980's and 1990's theocratic Iran embraced state-sponsored terrorism against the West in the name of religious truth.

A variety of sociopolitical factors promote conflict among nations. Old-fashioned power struggles are still a constant factor in international politics. Seeking to counter the rise of militant Islam led by Iran, secular Iraq launched an invasion of Iran in

1980. Pakistan and India—mutually alarmed by each other's hostility and capacity for building nuclear weapons—both tested nuclear weapons in 1998.

Totalitarian North Korea, seeking to threaten nearby Japan and South Korea and hoping for economic gain through foreign sales, developed increasingly dangerous missiles during the 1990's. Taiwan, fearing invasion by mainland China, imported arms and strengthened its military capacity. China, in retaliation, attempted to intimidate the Taiwanese by testing weapons in Taiwan's coastal waters.

Irredentism. Irredentism is an expression of the desire of people in one nation, or group, to recover territory they have lost to another nation or group. A well-known modern example is the Somali people of northeast Africa, whom European colonialism left fragmented among Somalia, Kenya, Ethiopia, and Djibouti. Unification of all Somali peoples under one flag has been a goal of Somali nationalists since the Somali Republic was created in 1960.

In Europe irredentism is well illustrated by the competition between Germany and France to control the Alsace-Lorraine region—now a territory in northeast France—along their mutual border. From 1870 to 1945 each country claimed it as an integral part of its own territory, and it became a focus of several large-scale wars.

Japan has demanded that Russia return its Kurile Islands, which the Soviet Union occupied after World War II. This ongoing Japanese-Russian dispute is an example of irredentist desires that could eventually lead to conflict. Similarly, China's desire that Taiwan again become part of its territory reflects irredentist ambitions that have already led to violence and threaten further hostilities in the future.

Irredentism plays a central role in the protracted, seemingly insoluble, conflict between Israelis and Arabs—especially Palestinians—in the Middle East. Clashes between Arabs and Jews living in what is now Israel occurred for decades before the end of World War II. It was, however, creation of the Jewish state of Israel in 1948 that marked a new, bloody, and as yet unresolved chapter of the conflict. The declaration of Israeli independence in 1948 was immediately followed by a war with neighboring Arab countries from which Israel emerged victorious in 1949.

The fate of millions of Palestinians who became refugees from their homeland became the focal point of Arab hostility toward the new state. Additional wars followed in 1956, 1967, and 1973. In each, Israel gained land, which it was later pressured to return in exchange for peace. An initial peace accord with Egypt, a principal Arab antagonist, was brokered by the United States in 1979.

A comprehensive peace was elusive, however, with ever-renewed campaigns of violence perpetrated by a number of Palestinian groups, especially the Palestine Liberation Organization (PLO), led by Yasir Arafat. Another American-sponsored peace agreement between the PLO and Israel was signed in Washington, D.C., in 1994. Continued terrorist acts by splinter groups hostile to the continued existence of Israel, as well as Israel's refusal to relinquish territory claimed by the Palestinians, made genuine peace difficult. When an interim agreement between the two sides was hammered out in late 1998, the world watched as an uncertain new future began to unfold. If and when a permanent peace could be achieved was a complete unknown.

Succession Problems. A special type of political problem common in nondemocratic countries is the succession problem. This refers to the question of who will take power from those in office—who will "succeed" them. In democracies, this problem is usually solved by elections. In hereditary monarchies, the children of the rulers—usually the oldest son—ascend the throne. Few such monarchies, however, remain today.

In nondemocracies succession crises often lead to political instability and violence. Scrambles for power often result when dictators die, unless they have named acceptable successors. The son of North Korean dictator Kim Il-sung, for example, succeeded his father without noticeable incident. In China, Chiang Jemin had been identified as successor when the aging leader Deng Xiaoping died in 1997.

However, when Soviet dictator Joseph Stalin died in 1953, competitors to succeed him barricaded themselves in their offices to protect themselves from arrest. In a meeting to settle the power question, they had the head of the secret police, Lavrenti Beria, seized and executed. Such violence is not unusual in nondemocratic governments.

Autocratic rulers are often deposed while in office. Kwame Nkrumah, the Ghanaian ruler of the 1950's and 1960's, declared himself "president for life" but was toppled from power while on a foreign trip. Assassination is a favorite method of ridding nondemocratic states of unpopular rulers. Occasionally this occurs in democracies, as it has in the United States, where Presidents Abraham Lincoln, James Garfield, William McKinley, and John F. Kennedy were assassinated.

In India, nationalist leader Mohandas Gandhi was shot by a Hindu extremist in 1958. Indian prime minister Indira Gandhi was murdered by her own bodyguards in 1984. Seven years later, her son Rajiv Gandhi, himself a former prime minister, was also assassinated. In 1995 Israeli prime minister Yitzhak Rabin was gunned down by an Israeli religious fanatic. However, removal of rulers through violence is far more common under authoritarian government.

Perhaps the most common means of ousting autocratic and sometimes democratic rulers is the coup, short for *coup d'état* (literally, a blow against the state). Coups are nonconstitutional changes of government leadership carried out either by force or the threat of force. Several kinds of coups occur. Some are attempts by the military to introduce modernization into their countries. Others are "radical" coups, in which revolutionary changes are imposed on society. "Guardian" coups, by contrast, are attempts by military groups to protect society from weak and unstable or incompetent civilian governments.

Some nations have endured numerous coups, most often undertaken by military officers. African nations have endured untold numbers of coups and attempted coups. Sudan may hold the record: In 1969 army colonel Gaafar Mohomed el-Nimeiri toppled Sudan's government by a coup. Sixteen years later he himself was finally overthrown, after twenty-four failed coup attempts.

In Europe, Greece was ruled by army colonels during the 1970's. South America's largest country, Brazil, has had a number of military governments established by coups. In 1982 its southern neighbor, Argentina, was ruled by a military committee, or junta, that came to power in a coup when it attacked and occupied the Falkland Islands governed by Great Britain. Many examples of crises in nondemocracies relating to succession questions will be observed in these volumes.

Economic Sources of Conflict. It has already been mentioned that economic factors often interact with other circumstances to generate conflict. Poverty is a frequent cause underlying violent struggles. In some cases, economic factors are related to power struggles. When Iraq invaded oil-rich Kuwait in 1990, for example, it sought the increased power that control of Kuwait's oil reserves would provide.

Historically, Japan's attempts to dominate East Asia, from its invasion of China and Korea during the 1930's to its attack on the U.S. military base in Pearl Harbor and occupation of Asian Pacific territories during the 1940's, were occasioned and justified by economic circumstances. Modern scholars argue over whether population increases will set off wars elsewhere through competition for economic survival or by less direct causes, such as nationalist hysteria among impoverished masses with little to lose.

Poverty has played a significant, though sometimes hidden, role in the seemingly endless struggles among ethnic groups in Africa. White South Africa fought against African majority rule for decades to preserve its own enviable standard of living. In South America indigenous peoples have struggled against settlers who destroy the environment upon which the original cultures depend. "Eco-pirates," as they have been dubbed, destroy the environment for gain, setting off choruses of complaint pointing to renewed confrontations. When economic depression brought industrialized Europe to its knees during the 1930's, war was not long in coming.

The role of these and a multitude of other economic factors—such as the desire for scarce raw materials or more favorable terms of trade—should not be overlooked in analyses of conflict. On the other hand, economic factors should not be exaggerated. Classical Marxism, for example, saw the struggle of rich and poor classes, together with technology, as the sole forces driving historical change.

Regionalism and Secessionism. Additional sources of violent conflict and political instability are regionalism and secessionism. Asia has been the scene of many instances of these problems. For example, Tibet's leader, the Dalai Lama, demands regional autonomy for his country within China only because full independence appears unattain-

able in the foreseeable future. Also, there is sentiment in independent Mongolia favoring union with the region of China known as Inner Mongolia.

Indonesia has similar problems with secessionism, aggravated by the fact that it is made up of scattered islands. The northwestern tip of Sumatra known as Aceh, for example, seeks autonomy to practice its own brand of Islam. Irian Jaya, a part of Indonesia in western New Guinea, has waged a violent struggle for independence, so far unsuccessfully. A bitter struggle for independence in the former Portuguese colony of East Timor has led to an international outcry against the Indonesian government's often brutal suppression of the rebels.

Other regions of the Pacific Rim have also experienced conflicts over secession that threaten to recur in the future. The southern part of New Guinea known as Papua has sought independence. In 1988 rebels on the nearby island of Bougainville declared the island's independence from Papua New Guinea and launched a guerrilla war.

In the Philippines a people known as the Moros, a Muslim minority in a predominantly Christian country, have been seeking autonomy since the 1960's. The government failed to gain complete control in battling with Muslim guerrillas. To deal with the Moros' aspirations the Philippine government established the Autonomous Region for Muslim Mindanao in 1990. However, few provinces of the region agreed to this arrangement.

The Indian subcontinent has seen grievous conflict over regional aspirations and secessionism. In the island nation of Sri Lanka, off India's southern coast, the Tamil people have used violent means to secure independence from the Sinhalese majority. Both sides have committed atrocities against non-combatants, including numerous cold-blooded massacres. In some instances, surrendering combatants have been killed.

Equally serious for India and Pakistan have been the secessionist aspirations of Kashmir. This dispute might escalate into nuclear war at some future time. Apart from its troubles in its northwest, India has long suffered from endemic regionalism among its numerous language groups. India's constitution recognizes some fifteen regional languages, each of which has at least 5 million speakers. The country also faces periodic violence in the Punjab, an area dominated by members of the Sikh religion, who seek to protect their holy sites and religious freedoms. Efforts at a peaceful settlement have been undermined by divisions among moderate and radical Sikh factions.

In Africa the peace and stability of Ethiopia have been disturbed by disputes over regional self-determination. The worst of these, the war with Eritrean rebels, was settled when Eritrea was established as an independent country. Nevertheless, serious regional problems remain. Ethiopia's political parties tend to divide along regional lines. Government attempts to cope with these aspirations through arrangements for regional autonomy within a federal system have met only limited success.

In Ethiopia's western neighbor, Sudan, conflict has raged intermittently since the 1950's between the Muslim north and the Christian south. More than 1.5 million people have died, and no peace is in sight. On Africa's east coast, racial and ethnic tensions involving the autonomy of the island of Zanzibar have been constant features since it joined Tanzania in 1964. In 1993, for example, Zanzibar unilaterally joined the Organization of the Islamic Conference, thereby violating the Tanzanian national constitution.

In Western Europe regional conflicts and tensions have been common. Regionalism in Scotland, Wales, and Northern Ireland has long been a fact of British national political life. A further example of Western European regionalism is found in Italy, where northern Italians created the Lombardy League to protest the constant drain of their resources to the impoverished south. The League proposes to secede and form an independent country.

Organized Crime and Corruption. Large-scale organized crime and corruption are both forces that corrode the power of the state and may lead to conflict and political instability. Organized crime exists in every inhabited continent and in every major country. By its nature, organized crime generates conflict. Because it is criminal it is intolerable to the state. For this reason, criminals often attempt to bribe public officials to avoid open conflict. Organized crime is a factor in the politics of many countries, especially those in Central and Eastern Europe. In Italy one reason for the popularity of the Lombardy League lies in northern resentment of the role of the Sicilian-based Mafia in national politics.

Bribery and other corrupt practices play a significant role in most of the emerging world. Corruption is a serious problem in China and India, and permeates governments in African countries such as Nigeria. Drug trafficking in Latin America has promoted government corruption throughout much of the region. Observers point to compromised police and judiciary in many Latin countries. In Mexico the brother of a former president was accused of accepting tens of millions of dollars in bribes. Even in the United States, police have been convicted of accepting drug money. Some former federal prosecutors make lucrative livings as defense attorneys for drug lords. The widespread existence of corruption makes internal conflict inevitable whenever forces supporting the rule of law assert themselves.

Border Conflicts. Disputes over national borders, including sovereignty over islands, are another frequent cause of conflict. In the Americas, Honduras and El Salvador are still arguing over a border dispute more than one century old. Ecuador has had border issues with several neighbors that dismembered its former territory, which was far larger than at present. Until 1998 Ecuador had a simmering dispute with Peru over a forty-eight-mile strip of jungle territory. That dispute erupted into a four-day war in 1981, with more fighting in 1995 and 1996.

Argentina and Great Britain have long argued about who rightfully owns the Falkland Islands, known to Argentina as the Malvinas. Ongoing talks between the countries, interrupted in 1982 by the Argentine invasion of the islands, have resumed. Although the two nations are unlikely ever to agree on the status of the islands, especially after the discovery that significant oil deposits may lie in the Falklands' waters, it seems equally unlikely that Argentina will again resort to force.

In Asia China claims various of the Spratly Islands, some of which are also claimed by Vietnam, Malaysia, and other nations. Above all, China claims that the island of Taiwan is a renegade Chinese province with no right to independence. Severe tensions over the issue, including the threat of force, may continue for the foreseeable future. Although the United States agrees that Taiwan is a Chinese province, it is involved in these tensions because it is committed to defending Taiwan from the use of force to change its autonomous status.

China also has border disputes with its western neighbors. Ongoing disagreements over its boundaries concern remote mountain territory along its border with India and other remote lands along its border with Russia. China also has a dispute with Outer Mongolia over China's rule of Inner Mongolia.

Elsewhere in Asia, chronic and potentially lethal border disputes simmer unresolved. The most important of these is the dispute between India and Pakistan over Kashmir and Jammu, territories that border both countries. The Kashmir issue has led to horrific bloodshed in recent decades, with the Indian army charged by both neutral observers and Pakistan with numerous human rights violations. Since both India and Pakistan have developed nuclear weapons, a catastrophic collision over this seemingly insolvable issue cannot be ruled out.

Finally, Africa has long been the home of border disputes. Among the most significant is Eritrea's claim to islands in the Red Sea also claimed by Yemen. Eritrea's borders with Ethiopia are also unsettled. The nation fought a war of independence during the 1970's and 1980's against Ethiopia. In achieving its independence, however, Eritrea deprived Ethiopia of its only seaports. Ethiopia seeks secure access to the sea for trade. In another part of the African continent, Mali's claims for territory also claimed by Burkina Faso holds the potential for open conflict.

Transitions from Autocracy. Bitter conflicts often lie under the surface in autocratic countries, suppressed by the heavy hand of authority. However, when authority weakens, those conflicts come to the surface. The South American country of Chile, for example, was ruled from 1973 until 1990 by a military dictatorship led by General Augusto Pinochet. By the end of the 1980's most Chileans opposed Pinochet's regime, voting against him when he sought approval in a referendum for another term. Pinochet also had his supporters, however, since he had wrested power from a leftist regime and his economic policies had succeeded.

Once Pinochet left power, public fury at the gross human rights abuses under his dictatorial rule came to the surface. Chilean society was split between Pinochet's supporters and detractors. When Pinochet assumed the office of senator for life in 1998, fistfights broke out among legislators.

Later that same year, when Pinochet was arrested in London, England, for human rights abuses after Spain requested his extradition, riots broke out in Santiago, the Chilean capital. How long Chilean society would be rent from long years of dictatorship was unknown. It appeared likely, however, that enough of this social division would be directed into legal and political channels to preserve the nation's stability.

South Africa presents a similar, if more fragile, case. When the white apartheid regime controlled by the Afrikaner minority relinquished power during the 1990's, deep social conflicts emerged. For example, a significant portion of the nation's black African youths remained uneducated after spending years boycotting schools run by the old regime. This was just one of several reasons Africans were unprepared to enter a modern economy. Another was that the apartheid regime had systematically degraded African education and blocked roads to advancement. Long after apartheid was abolished, impoverished black youths represented a potentially explosive social problem of the first magnitude.

Conflict between the wealthy white minority and the nonwhite majority had already simmered before majority rule began. Afterward it emerged in full force. Some of this conflict took the form of violent crime, as millions of the country's dispossessed ceased fearing authority but also lacked moral education. Untold numbers of individuals and groups on both sides had been bred into violence under the old regime and had difficulty adjusting to the new situation. Terrible crimes had been committed under the apartheid government, often at its direction. Opponents of the regime who had violently opposed it languished in prisons. A government commission was established that was empowered to grant amnesty to those on both sides who came forward and confessed their crimes. This was a positive step toward reconciliation, but it could not stop the seemingly endless wave of criminal violence. Nor could it bring white extremists into the fold of reconciliation. Authoritarianism had left the country with a cloudy future.

Former Soviet Union. The situations in former communist countries presented more instances of the difficulties awaiting states attempting a transition from dictatorship to democracy. Most of these countries had been components of the Soviet Union or its satellites. A few were independent communist countries, such as Yugoslavia and Albania.

A key problem facing many of these nations is that they have little or no pre-Soviet democratic experience on which to fall back. The rapid and drastic change from communism to democracy left many people confused. Many were also disillusioned when their expectations of a quick and easy road from poverty were dashed.

A number of these states also found themselves in a moral vacuum. Marxism was dead, but other value systems, such as religion, were slow to replace it. In Russia, for example, people lacked moral direction. In these circumstances, organized crime quickly spread. Criminal gangs became a problem even in strongly Roman Catholic countries, such as Poland and Lithuania.

Everywhere economic and political problems stemming from a totalitarian past interacted to create real and potential strife. Under communism, all large industry, most of it poorly managed, was owned by the state. When governments tried to sell the least profitable of these industries to private investors, there were no buyers. Workers such as miners, steel workers, and other public employees were left unpaid by governments unable to collect taxes. If they printed more money and paid these state employees, ruinous inflation resulted. In the meantime, people suffered.

In Russia many men turned to alcohol abuse. In the freezing northern winters, large numbers suffered, especially the elderly. The result in populous Russia was a deeply troubled society. Moreover, the world worried that some of the country's twenty thousand nuclear weapons might be sold by a corrupt and impoverished military to potentially dangerous countries.

Another widespread problem affected the states of the former Soviet Union. When the Soviet Union was ruled by Joseph Stalin, whole groups of people were removed from their homelands as punishment for resistance and forcibly relocated to the frozen tundra of Siberia or to some equally inhospitable region. When the Soviet Union collapsed at the close of 1991, some of these people who had not returned to their homelands now wished to do so. Conflict with those who had taken their places was inevitable.

Allied to the problems of displaced peoples are those created by the migration under the Soviet

Union of some 25 million Russians to Soviet countries outside their native land. When the Soviet Union collapsed, countries with large numbers of these Russian nationals, such as the Baltic and Central Asian republics, became self-governing. Once members of the dominant nationality, these Russians became despised minorities. In Latvia, for example, most Russians were not citizens of the newly established republic, did not speak Latvian, and were socially separated from Latvians. They constituted more than 30 percent of the population.

A similar situation occurred in Estonia, where some border towns were more than 90 percent Russian. Other significant Russian minorities were found in Ukraine and in several of the Central Asian republics. Fears within Russia for the well-being of their fellow Russians in these other nations are a potential source of future conflict.

Former Soviet Satellites. Conditions in the former Soviet satellites vary greatly from country to country. After German reunification, eastern Germany's economic difficulties were eased by the relative wealth of western Germany. Factory workers in Poland and the Czech Republic faced hard times as inefficient state industries were sold off and layoffs occurred. Slovakia, once united with its Czech neighbors as Czechoslovakia, fared worse, as economic conditions deteriorated and political violence sometimes took the form of bombings at political rallies. Critics warned that if Slovakia was to become a member of international European bodies, including the North Atlantic Treaty Organization (NATO), such practices would have to be curbed.

In a number of countries of the former Soviet orbit, the transition to postcommunist governments has been complicated by the existence of massive secret police files. These files have made reconciliation more difficult between those who supported the communist states and those who suffered repression under them. If the files are opened, individuals can see which of their neighbors spied on them or denounced them to the secret police. If the files are not opened, suspicions might linger and individual rights to an open government might be denied.

Perhaps the most dramatic example of the potential for violence after communism is that of former Yugoslavia. That patchwork nation of separate nationalities was never in the Soviet orbit. Its independence was skillfully maintained by its long-time leader, Josip Broz, more widely known as Tito. After Tito died, Yugoslav national sentiment, fading communist ideology, and a central Yugoslav army that was dominated by Serbia could no longer keep the component countries together. Yugoslavia broke apart.

While prosperous Slovenia achieved its independence with relative ease, Serbia, Croatia, and Bosnia Herzegovina became involved in one of Europe's most violent struggles since World War II. In this case, nationalism mixed with religious intolerance. Fighting began in 1992 and lasted until late 1995. Croatia fought for, and achieved, independence. Serbia, seeking an enlarged territory that would include its nationals living outside its historical boundaries, practiced a vicious form of "ethnic cleansing" against Bosnian Muslims. The Serbs forced many of these Muslims, who had lived amicably with Serbs and Croats for many years, to become refugees and murdered many others. The previously peaceful multiethnic city of Sarajevo, picturesque site of the 1984 Winter Olympics, was reduced to rubble. Concentration camps became death camps for the first time in Europe since the days of Stalin and Adolf Hitler.

In 1998 ethnic Albanians in the southern Serbian region of Kosovo protested oppression by the Serb government by demanding independence. The Serbian military was accused of extensive human rights violations in putting down the rebellion. Serbia was threatened with military action by NATO forces if such rights violations continued.

Civilizational Conflicts. Another form of conflict has been defined by Samuel Huntington, a professor at Harvard University. In *The Clash of Civilizations and the Remaking of World Order* (1996), he argues that the world can be divided into a number of separate civilizations, which often conflict with each other. For example, he distinguishes Western civilization, which developed in the western half of the Roman Empire, from Orthodox civilization, which developed in the Eastern Roman Empire. Western civilization separated religious authority from political power, a division that eventually led to the separation of church and state.

By contrast, Eastern civilization more nearly combined religious authority and political power,

leading to a much different kind of society. Moreover, the West went though stages of development—the Renaissance, Reformation, and Enlightenment—unknown in nations that adhere to Eastern Orthodoxy, principally Greek and Russian Orthodox churches. Other principal civilizations in Huntington's analysis include Japanese, Chinese, Islamic, Hindu, and Hispanic.

Huntington's civilizational theory is controversial. He interprets certain conflicts among nations as forms of the clash of civilizations. One example during the 1990's was the fighting in the former Yugoslavia. One side was led by Serbia, an offshoot of Orthodox civilization, which battled both Muslims in Bosnia and Croats from Roman Catholic Croatia. In this view, the support consistently given to Serbia by Russia, center of Orthodox civilization, and to Muslims by Islamic forces illustrates the cohesion of civilizations and the conflicts among them.

Civilizational conflicts have something in common with ethnic conflict, since they nearly always involve solidarity among members of similar ethnicities. Thus, Russia's military assistance to Serbia in the Kosovo crisis in 1998 can be seen as a civilizational conflict, since the dominant Orthodox nation assisted another Orthodox nation in the face of military threats from NATO forces, all part of Western civilization. Russia and Serbia are both ethnically Slavic.

Huntington foresees the possibility of many more civilizational clashes in the future, especially between Islam and the West, and, possibly, between Chinese civilization and its Pacific neighbors. In this view, the question of whether Japan will remain allied with the West, led by the United States, or join China may prove crucial to what happens in the future.

Conclusion. The world remains the scene of wars and insurgencies, potential conflicts, and fragile peace. There are reasons for humanity to fear the future. New and terrible weapons of mass destruction have been developed. Atomic bombs can be carried in suitcases. Surface-to-air missiles able to bring down jetliners can be fired by a single person. Nerve gas and deadly biological agents have been produced in vast quantities.

Some of these weapons could find their way into the hands of irresponsible governments and terrorist groups. Some already have. Iraqi dictator

Saddam Hussein gassed his own people and threatened Israel with mass murder. A Japanese cult unleased deadly nerve gas in the Tokyo subway system. Religious zealots bombed the World Trade Center in New York and the Metro in Paris. Nuclear weapons are spreading. The world remains a dangerous place.

However, reason for hope remains. There are forces at work to prevent catastrophes. World organizations such as the United Nations, regional alliances such as NATO, ad hoc groups and individual nations, including the world's only remaining superpower, the United States, turn massive resources to the task of countering destructive forces. In addition, literacy is spreading. Awareness of the necessity for international cooperation is on the rise. Missile defenses may soon be able to protect exposed nations from the most malignant armed predators.

The global situation is therefore mixed, torn between the possibility of relative harmony, economic progress, and possibly even undreamt-of wonders on the one hand, and inexhaustible human malevolence and the dark side of technology on the other.

Charles F. Bahmueller

North America

Modern conflicts in North America have their origins in both the distant past and recent developments. Historically, the most serious international conflicts were wars over land and natural resources, such as silver, fish, and animal furs. American Indians and Europeans fought each other as they sought to preserve and extend their control over North America. Conflicts continued after the independence of the United States, Mexico, and Canada, and led to threats, treaties, and several wars. At the same time, struggles took place within countries over resources and political power. As the countries grew during the late nineteenth and twentieth centuries, domestic conflicts overshadowed international ones. New social and economic problems heightened old tensions and created new ones. Regional inequalities, population growth, industrialization and labor organization, ethnic and race relations, political struggles, and social issues have all led to conflict in all three North American nations.

Articles in This Section

The North American continent is composed of three large nations: Canada, the United States, and Mexico. Canada, the northernmost of the countries, covers 3,849,653 square miles and had a population of 30,387,300 in 1997. The United States, Canada's southern neighbor, is 3,717,792 square miles in size and had a population of 270,958,700 as of 1997. The southernmost of the three North American nations, Mexico, covers 761,602 square miles and, as of 1997, had a population of 97,563,400.

European Colonialism. Long before the arrival of Europeans in North America in the sixteenth century, American Indians fought to further their interests. In their desire for trade, tribute, and political power, they fought among themselves, forming armies and using weapons to defeat their enemies. The Aztec state of central Mexico in the fifteenth and early sixteenth centuries is a promi-

nent example of the organized use of violence to promote political ends. Less well known conflicts occurred in most parts of the continent as Native Americans sought to protect or extend their influence.

With the arrival of Europeans, conflicts increased in number and magnitude. In their efforts to establish colonies, the Spanish, French, and English changed the face of the continent. Conflicts among American Indians continued— and in some cases accelerated—but paled in comparison to the European threat. The relationship between American Indians and Europeans was often marred by war and exploitation. Africans forced into slavery and brought to North America suffered the same abuse. African Americans, African Mexicans, and the much smaller African Canadian population suffered under the new colonial regimes.

Colonial expansion also led to conflict. Wars among the Spanish, French, English, and Dutch led to gains and losses of territory and trade routes. With the independence of the former colonies, territorial claims continued to cause instability and, in some cases, war. The United States benefitted the most. With the Louisiana Purchase in 1803, the annexation of Texas in 1845, and lands gained

Although Canada has generally allied with the United States in its foreign policy, it departed from the United States in recognizing communist Cuba; here Canadian prime minister Pierre Trudeau (left) is seen conferring with Cuban president Fidel Castro (right), whom the United States has shunned, during a visit to Cuba. Mexico has also long recognized Castro's government. (AP/Wide World Photos)

from the Mexican-American War of 1846-1848, it became a country that stretched from the Atlantic Ocean to the Pacific Ocean.

The United States and Canada, after several early problems, have had a much more peaceful relationship than the United States and Mexico. During the American Revolution and the War of 1812, border conflicts and invasions harmed U.S. and British relations; so did Confederate efforts to involve Canada in the U.S. Civil War. These conflicts evoked fear in Canada but did not permanently damage Canadian-U.S. relations.

Armed Conflict. Direct military conflicts among the three countries of North America do not currently represent a threat to continental stability, although recognition of the power of the United States continues to influence Mexican and Canadian foreign policy. Past violence has given way to compromise and shared interests in maintaining peaceful relations. This is especially important given the long borders shared by the countries and the increasing economic integration of North America. Increased integration has meant that money, people, and technology are moving back and forth across borders at a fast pace. Discussion and compromise help solve problems.

Internal conflicts within the countries have led to more violence than the wars between them. Mexico suffered from the War of the Reform (1857-1861) in much the same way that the United States suffered from its own Civil War (1861-1865). In the early twentieth century Mexico experienced another great civil conflict, the Revolution of 1910-1917, a conflict that left a trail of violence into the 1920's.

Canadian history has been more peaceful. The Rebellions of 1837 in Upper (Ontario) and Lower (Quebec) Canada left few casualties. The same was true of the Red River Rebellion in 1869-1870 and the Northwest Rebellion in 1885. With a small population spread over a large territory and a tradition of political compromise, Canada's internal history has been relatively harmonious.

As the twentieth century unfolded, each country adjusted to change in its own way. There were, however, periods when they all experienced unrest. During the 1960's and early 1970's, radical political groups rebelled against their governments. Students challenged traditional cultural values and public policies with massive demonstrations, which were at times stopped by police force. Ethnic and racial unrest gained momentum during the 1960's, especially in the United States, where African Americans, Latinos, American Indians, and Asian Americans challenged the authority of those in power. Many feared that revolution would overthrow the government. In Quebec, Canada, changes were so far-reaching that the term "Quiet Revolution" has been used to describe them. Revolution did not take place, but violent confrontations did occur.

Current issues of violence and confrontation have their origins during the 1960's and earlier time periods. The unique history of individuals, groups, and institutions makes it difficult to summarize the important issues for all of North America. There are, however, some comparative themes

GREENLAND

CANADA

Vancouver

Seattle

Quebec

Ottawa ★ Montreal

Boston

Minneapolis

San Francisco

Denver

Chicago

Detroit

New York

Philadelphia

UNITED STATES

Washington ★
D.C.

Los Angeles

Oklahoma City

San Diego

Atlantic

Ocean

Waco

New
Orleans

Monterrey

Gulf

of

Mexico

Miami

BAHAMAS

MEXICO

Pacific

Guadalajara

Mexico
City ★

DOMINICAN
REPUBLIC

CUBA

Ocean

Oaxaca

JAMAICA

HAITI

Puerto
Rico

BELIZE

GUATEMALA

HONDURAS

Caribbean   Sea

EL SALVADOR

NICARAGUA

VENEZUELA

COSTA RICA

North America

PANAMA

COLOMBIA

and problems whose study may help provide an understanding of both North America as a whole and the individual countries.

Regional Inequalities. As long as there are regional differences in income, health, education, nutrition, and housing, regions will influence politics in North America. Some of the regions, such as the Great Chihuahuan Desert, the Rocky Mountains, and the Great Plains, span borders. Concern over environmental problems has led to an appreciation of the continental scope of regions. More often, regions are discussed in the context of individual countries.

In Mexico the southern states of Oaxaca and Chiapas, with their large Indian populations, have traditionally been the poorest in the country. The northern states of Baja California, Sonora, and Chihuahua that border the United States have been wealthier, although incomes are far lower than in the United States. Between north and south is Mexico City, the dominant force in the country. Mexican regional inequalities are deep, partly the result of a lack of a commitment to overcome them and partly the result of a slower rate of industrialization.

The United States has its own history of regional differences. The New England states contrast with the Deep South, the Mid-Atlantic states with the Midwest, the Southwest with the Northwest. In recent history, the poverty of the Appalachian region, especially states such as Kentucky and West Virginia, led to increased federal aid.

The politics of regions is stronger in Canada than in the United States and Mexico. The Atlantic provinces of Newfoundland, New Brunswick, and Nova Scotia demand recognition of their economic problems. British Columbia in the far West is oriented toward the Pacific and the Asian markets. French-speaking Quebec demands more autonomy. National politics in Canada is a delicate balancing act among the conflicting interests of these and other regions.

Population. Population increases provide one of the keys to explaining the differences among the three North American countries. This is a controversial topic because of disagreement about the consequences of population change. Despite the disagreement, there is evidence to prove that population size, rates of increase, and density, or numbers of people per square mile, are helpful in explaining conflict.

The Mexican population has grown the fastest in North America, creating many problems for the country. From 1950 to 1990 the Mexican population increased from 25,791,017 to 81,249,645, an increase of more than 300 percent. During the same period the U.S. population increased by less than 100 percent, from 151,325,798 to 248,718,301. The Canadian population increased from 14,009,429 to 26,994,045, about the same rate as in the United States.

An increase or decrease of population influences employment, health, education, and immigration. A rapid increase in population without a corresponding increase in economic opportunity has caused tensions in all three countries, but especially in Mexico.

Industrialization and Labor Organization. Agriculture dominated the economic history of all three countries until the late nineteenth century, when factories became increasingly common. The United States industrialized the fastest, followed by Canada and then Mexico.

As industrialization progressed, workers organized to defend and promote their interests. Individually, they had little power against the new corporations, which were often protected by law. Workers soon found, however, that they had more strength as members of workers' groups. Thus labor conflict grew and eventually clashed with the new corporations. Many incidents of labor conflict have occurred in each country. In the United States, the Haymarket Square strike (1886) in Chicago and the Homestead Strike (1892) outside Pittsburgh signaled a new era of labor violence. During the Cananea strike (1906) in Sonora, Mexico, the government and foreign interests joined to repress striking workers. In Canada the Winnipeg strike (1919) is remembered as the coming-of-age of organized labor.

Labor conflicts continue in North America, but they are not as disruptive as in the past. Mexico may encounter the most difficulties in the future because of its slower rate of industrialization.

In the twentieth century, the most industrialized countries enjoyed the highest quality of life. Per capita gross national product figures (the total of goods and services divided by the number of people) demonstrate the extreme differences in North America. In 1990 per capita income reached US$22,380 in the United States, US$15,640 in Canada, and US$2,580 in Mexico. In a global context, Mexico has a large, dynamic economy, but compared to its North American neighbors, it is poor. The poverty forces many Mexicans to migrate to the United States in search of employment. They contribute to economic development and at the same time place new demands on the educational and health systems of the United States.

Another difficulty for labor is the reorganization and globalization of production and distribution. International corporations, often called transnationals, produce and distribute their products in

Masked Zapatista rebels gather at a rally in Chiapas, the center of Mexico's most intense conflict. (AP/Wide World Photos)

North America

1519	Spanish occupation of Mexico begins.
1607	British settlement begins with founding of Jamestown, Virginia.
1608	French settlement begins with founding of Quebec City.
1756-1763	France and Great Britain fight for control of Canada in French and Indian, or Seven Years', War.
1763	France cedes most of its North American possessions to Great Britain at conclusion of war.
1776	(July 4) Britain's thirteen Atlantic seaboard colonies declare their independence.
1783	Britain recognizes independence of United States.
1803	United States purchases Louisiana Territory from France.
1821	Mexico gains independence from Spain.
1836	Revolt of American settlers in Texas against Mexican rule makes Texas independent.
1845	United States annexes Texas.
1846	Mexican-American War begins.
1848	Under treaty ending Mexican-American War, Mexico cedes almost half of its territory to United States.
1857-1861	War of Reform embroils Mexico in civil war.
1861-1865	Northern and Southern states fight in U.S. Civil War.
1864-1867	France attempts to rule Mexico through puppet emperor Maximilian.
1867	Constitution Act, formerly British North America Act, creates Dominion of Canada.
1898	U.S. victory over Spain in Spanish-American War expands U.S. influence in Caribbean and Pacific.
1910	Mexican Revolution begins.
1914	(Aug.) Canada enters World War I in support of Great Britain.
1917	Mexican constitution is signed in Querétaro.
1917	(Apr.) United States enters World War I against Germany.
1929	(Oct. 29) Wall Street stock market crash helps trigger Great Depression.
1939	(Sept.) Canada enters World War II in support of Britain.
1941	(Dec. 7) Japanese attack on Pearl Harbor brings United States into World War II.
1943	(June) American sailors attack Mexican Americans in Los Angeles's Zoot-Suit riots.
1945	(Aug. 14) World War II ends with unconditional surrender of Japan.
1948	(Apr. 30) Organization of American States is formed.
1954	United States deports Mexicans under "Operation Wetback."
1960	"Quiet Revolution" begins in Quebec.
1962	(Oct.) United States confronts Soviet Union in Cuban Missile Crisis.

1963	(Nov. 22) U.S. president John F. Kennedy is assassinated.
1964	(Aug.) Gulf of Tonkin leads to escalation of U.S. involvement in Vietnam War.
1965	(Feb. 21) Malcolm X is assassinated in New York.
1965	(Aug.) Riot in Los Angeles's Watts district is first of series of racially motivated summer rioting in major U.S. cities.
1968	Founding of Parti Québecois increases momentum for Quebec's separatism.
1968	(Apr. 4) Martin Luther King, Jr., is assassinated in Memphis, Tennessee.
1968	(Oct.) Mexican police kill hundreds of students demonstrating during Mexico City Olympics.
1974	(Aug. 8) U.S. president Richard Nixon resigns.
1976	Montreal Olympic Games are interrupted by violence.
1976	Large oil deposits are discovered in Mexico.
1980	(May) Racially motivated rioting leaves eighteen dead and many injured in Miami, Florida.
1989	Canada and United States sign Free Trade Act.
1989	(Mar. 24) Massive oil spill from *Exxon Valdez* oil tanker off Alaska increases concern about environment.
1992	(Apr.) Racially motivated rioting in Los Angeles leaves fifty-eight dead and widespread destruction.
1992	(Dec. 17) Leaders of Canada, Mexico, and United States sign North American Free Trade Agreement (NAFTA).
1993	(Feb. 26) Terrorist bombing of New York City's World Trade Center kills six people.
1994	Zapatistas initiate guerrilla war in Chiapas, Mexico.
1994	(Jan. 1) NAFTA goes into effect.
1994	(Mar.) Mexican presidential candidate Luis Donaldo Colosio is assassinated.
1995	(Apr. 19) Terrorist bomb kills 169 people in Oklahoma City federal building.
1998	Drug violence increases in Mexican border cities.
1998	(Aug. 7) Nearly simultaneous explosions of terrorist bombs kill and injure thousands at U.S. embassies in Kenya and Tanzania.
1998	(Nov.) Members of British Columbia's Nisg'a nation vote to ratify treaty with federal government that will give them title to their land and partial independence from provincial and national law; critics charge treaty may promote balkanization of Canada.
1998	(Dec. 19) House of Representatives votes two articles of impeachment against President Clinton, charging him with committing perjury and obstructing justice.
1999	(Mar. 4) President Zedillo proposes that Mexico adopt U.S. system of nominating presidential candidates through state primaries—a change that would end tradition of presidents' selecting their own successors.
1999	(Feb. 12) U.S. Senate votes decisively to acquit Clinton.

many different countries. Organized labor in the United States and Canada, fearful of losing jobs to lower-paid workers in Mexico and elsewhere, is trying to adjust to the realities of the global economy.

Ethnic and Racial Conflict. European colonization of North America created new tensions and set the pattern for racial inequality. Europeans held positions of power over American Indians and enslaved Africans. In central Mexico, Indian societies continued to exist alongside Spanish ones. This was partly because of the size of the Indian population and partly because of protective Spanish legislation. In the English colonies, Indians quickly lost their lands and independence. In the French colonies, Indians participated in trade and commerce, at times profiting from this activity. In the end, however, they fell under the control of the French.

Mexican Indians still suffer from discrimination and poverty. Clustered mainly in southern states, they are primarily rural and have limited access to education and health care. Violence and hostility continue to disrupt Mexican life. Most noticeable is the conflict between Indians and federal troops in the southernmost state of Chiapas. This conflict, which had its origins in the increasing poverty and exploitation of the region's Indians, erupted in widespread disorder on January 1, 1994.

In the United States and Canada, the number of Indians is much smaller, but their condition is essentially the same. Poverty and isolation make life difficult. A major change in recent years is a growing appreciation of Native American culture and the contributions Indians have made to North American life.

Africans in North America have their own history of poverty and oppression. Slavery existed in all three countries but only emerged as a widespread labor system in the United States. Even after the abolition of slavery, laws and social practices prevented African Americans from full participation in political and economic life. Only through struggle, some of it violent, have they managed to improve their condition.

Immigrants have also experienced discrimination. Different languages, dress styles, and social customs at times provoked a harsh reaction. Chinese and Japanese immigrants in all three countries suffered from physical and legal attacks beginning in the late nineteenth century. Recent immigrants from Southeast Asia and Latin America face their own problems in adjusting to life in the United States and Canada. Mexico also has large numbers of immigrants, most of them refugees who have escaped from political conflict in Central America.

Political Struggles. Canada and the United States have had a long-standing commitment to the exercise of power through constitutional rule. The particular form of this commitment has differed between the two countries, but it has been a part of their political history. Both countries are democratic and allow protest and reform. In other words, the citizens of both countries, through the vote and through political parties and other organizations, can influence politics.

Despite its democratic tradition, political violence affects the United States. The Civil Rights and Black Power movements during the 1950's and 1960's challenged traditional politics. Urban violence, although not a form of formal protest, has also threatened political stability. Riots in Los Angeles, Detroit, Miami, and other cities reveal some of the frustrations in the political system.

Canada lacks a tradition of widespread racial violence and urban riots. The most violent threats to constitutional authority in Canada erupted in the late 1960's with the Front de Libération du Québec, which argued that violent means were acceptable to change the government. This led to the implementation of the War Measures Act of 1914, which gives the government extraordinary power to deal with internal crises involving violence. Since that time, there has been little organized political violence in Canada.

Mexico has struggled unsuccessfully to develop an open, democratic system. More authoritarian and personalistic, the rules of the Mexican system have not favored the individual citizen. In contrast to the citizens of the United States and Canada, most Mexicans have not been able to influence politics. Beginning during the 1980's, however, Mexican politics entered a new period. Reforms of the political system, especially those that favor the rights of the citizen, promise a different future for Mexican politics.

In recent years terrorism has emerged as a new threat to the political stability of the continent. Unpredictable but usually carefully planned and executed, terrorism caught civil and military authorities off guard. By the late 1960's all three countries had experienced attacks against governments and businesses. Terrorists blew up buildings and kidnapped wealthy individuals. In extreme cases, terrorism took the form of "skyjackings," or the commandeering of an airplane in flight. Another form of terrorism known as environmental terrorism also appeared. Groups committed to environmental causes used violence or the threat of violence in hopes of protecting the environment. By the late 1990's Canada and the United States had experienced this type of violence.

As terrorism became more internationalized during the 1970's and 1980's, the focus of threats and attacks was clearly the United States. Mexico and Canada lived with occasional internal threats but rarely had to contend with attacks against their citizens in foreign countries. The United States, because of its power, politics, and wide visibility throughout the world, was singled out by terrorists. By the end of the 1990's terrorism was recognized as more of a threat to the security of the United States than traditional military conflicts.

The flow of arms, many of them manufactured in the United States, contributes to the violence. Canada has had a successful policy of gun control that has helped curtail internal violence. Mexico has been less successful but by the end of the 1990's had implemented more stringent inspections at its northern border to prevent the illegal importation of weapons. The widespread availability of weapons makes terrorism more difficult to control.

Social Issues. The concept of "social" issues encompasses many problems: poverty, illiteracy, drug addiction, crime, and minority rights, to mention only a few. Conflict and confrontation are associated with all of these problems. Recent attention has focused on the rights of minorities, acquired immunodeficiency syndrome (AIDS), youth violence, and the status of women and children. The changing status of women helps to illustrate broader patterns of change. Historically, laws and customs have relegated women to an inferior position in all three countries, making them dependent on fathers and husbands. Restrictions existed at many levels, from owning property to voting. Women suffered partly because of their inferior legal status. For them, much of the twentieth century was a struggle to improve their position.

The legal rights that women have achieved have not eliminated the problem of domestic violence. Most commonly directed against women and children, it was a hidden issue in the past. Efforts to stop domestic violence increased with the rise of the women's movement.

Domestic violence is of widespread concern in the United States and Canada and is gradually becoming a national issue in Mexico. Previously, women in cases of rape or battery suffered from legal systems that discriminated against them, weakened their cases, and often tried to make them accomplices instead of victims. Canada has perhaps gone the furthest in legally defending the rights of women, spelled out in the Canadian Charter of Rights and Freedoms (1982). Both the United States and Canada have created new institutions and support systems for women and children. Large cities and small towns have shelters for abuse victims, and social agencies provide counseling directed at reducing domestic conflict.

Women in Mexico have had a more difficult time in securing their rights. Mexican culture, traditionally described as patriarchal, or dominated by male authority, relegated women to an inferior position of power. Mexican laws confirmed the prevailing customs, limiting women's rights in the courts. This is beginning to change.

Two important changes have altered the roles of women in Mexico. First, as more men migrated to the United States, women assumed more responsibilities for the welfare of families. Women worked at more jobs and at the same time continued to maintain their households. Second, women started to work in factories, particularly those known as *maquiladoras*. These are special assembly plants first built along the border with the United States but now found throughout Mexico. In the large border cities of Tijuana and Ciudad Juárez, the factories are staffed mainly by women. These women often work in unsafe surroundings and receive very low wages. In addition, many have been assaulted or murdered on their way to and from work.

The plight of children in Mexico is a major problem. Estimates of the number of homeless children in Mexico vary, but most agree that the numbers are large, perhaps as many as five million. More than a problem of law, the problems of Mexican children result from population increases and the slow rate of economic growth. Families, especially those in urban areas, have grown faster than their abilities to provide support for their children. Children thus leave home to create a life for themselves on the streets. These street children, living by begging, stealing, and their wits, are far more common in Mexico than in the United States and Canada. They represent a major social challenge for Mexico.

John C. Super

For Further Study

Two brief introductions to North American history that include maps are Eric Homberger, *The Penguin Historical Atlas of North America* (1995), and Colin McEvedy, *The Penguin Atlas of North American History to 1870* (1988). More detailed studies that emphasize recent developments are James W. Russell, *After the Fifth Sun: Class and Race in North America* (1994), and Robert L. Earle and John D. Wirth (eds.), *Identities in North America: The Search for Community* (1995). For a comprehensive reference consult the four-volume work edited by Frank N. Magill, *Great Events from History: North American Series* (1997).

Two general introductions to Canada are Wayne C. Thompson, *Canada: 1997* (1997), and J. M. Bumstead, *The Peoples of Canada* (1992). Michael C. Meyer and William L. Sherman, *The Course of Mexican History* (1995), and Tom Barry (ed.), *Mexico: A Country Guide* (1992), provide similar introductions to Mexico. For general surveys of the United States, see Alan Brinkely, *The Unfinished Nation: A Concise History of the American People* (1997), and Robert James Maddox (ed.), *American History* (1999). Two surveys of foreign policy that emphasize the second half of the twentieth century are Lester D. Langley, *Mexico and the United States: The Fragile Relationship* (1991), and Robert Bothwell, *Canada and the United States: The Politics of Partnership* (1992).

Canada

Canada has two significant internal problems that have produced violence and remain possible sources of even more disruptive future conflicts. Quebec separatism has exploded into small-scale bombing and kidnapping. It led to the imposition of martial law in Montreal in 1970 and still threatens the integrity of the Canadian federation. Increasingly vigorous demands for effective self-government on the part of the native peoples of Canada have also proved difficult to accommodate. In addition, disputes over fishing rights off the Atlantic and Pacific coasts have at times resulted in serious confrontations with foreign powers.

The roots of current Canadian conflicts lie deep within the nation's past. Two different, and often hostile, European populations settled the land, conquered and exploited the native peoples, and dominated the country's social and political life. The French were the first to arrive; the British came after Great Britain's conquest of New France during the 1760's. They were joined by American loyalists who abandoned the United States when it attained its independence from Britain in 1783.

Fear of the military power of the United States after the U.S. Civil War (1861-1865) led the British government to seek to unify its scattered remaining North American colonies. The British parliament passed the British North America Act of 1867. It served as the Canadian constitution until 1982, establishing a confederation uniting Britain's North American colonies into a single dominion. Although the British North America Act defined the division of powers and functions between the provinces and the federal government, sources of friction remained, especially between predominantly French-speaking Quebec and the rest of the country.

Quebec History. The belief held by the overwhelming majority of Quebecers that Quebec is different from the rest of Canada is based on the distinctive history and culture of the province. Discovered by French explorers in the sixteenth

Profile of Canada

Official name: Canada
Independent since: 1867
Former colonial ruler: Great Britain
Location: northern North America
Area: 3,849,653 square miles
Capital: Ottawa
Population: 30,387,300 (1997 est.)
Official languages: English; French
Major religions: Roman Catholicism; Protestantism
Gross domestic product: US$721 billion (1996 est.)
Major exports: machinery and transport equipment; food, feed, beverages, and tobacco; petroleum and energy products; forestry products
Military budget: US$9 billion (1995-1996)
Military personnel: 61,000 (1997)

Note: Monetary figures rendered as "US$" are U.S. equivalents of values in local currencies.

century, Quebec was organized as a French colony during the following century. Almost from its beginning, relations were hostile between the French and the English colonies to the south. Border raids between the two areas, which often involved the use of Indian allies by both sides, were common. The Seven Years' War (also known as the French and Indian War), between the French and the English ended with the British conquest of Quebec and the cession of Canada to Great Britain in 1763.

Afterward Britain undertook to rule a settler population whose language, religion, and traditions of law and government differed from that of Britain. Hoping to win the loyalty of the inhabitants, the British government passed the Quebec Act of 1774. It promised continuation of French civil law and traditional practices in the new colony and guaranteed the special privileges and freedoms of the Roman Catholic Church.

Historians have estimated that fewer than 10,000 French immigrants migrated to Canada between 1608 and 1763. By that latter date, the region's population had grown to some 65,000. Over the next two centuries little additional French immigration occurred. However, an exceptionally high birthrate ensured that the French language and culture would survive, despite heavy English immigration into Quebec and large-scale French migration from Quebec to the United States. Canada's 1991 census counted more than 6 million French speakers, 90 percent of whom lived in Quebec.

Meanwhile, English-speaking settlers gained control of the government, commerce, and industry of Quebec and dominated Montreal, the province's largest city and financial center. The region's French-speaking people tended to live in rural areas, where the Roman Catholic Church controlled education and social welfare. The Church encouraged a defensive attitude toward the rest of society, asserting that the French Canadians had a God-given duty to preserve their French and Roman Catholic culture from corruption by the modern world.

"Quiet Revolution." Dramatic changes in politics and society began with the victory of the Liberal Party and election of Jean Lesage as premier of Quebec in 1960. Pledged to institute major reforms, Lesage's government enacted measures that became known as the "Quiet Revolution" because of their far-reaching impact on both Quebec and Canada.

The reformers set out to bring Quebec into the modern age by secularizing the educational system of the province. They also reduced the role of the Roman Catholic Church and encouraged Quebecers to study subjects that would prepare them for active roles in an industrial society. The reformers challenged the control of Quebec commerce and industry by English-speaking Canadians and Americans. Their slogan was *Maîtres chez nous* (masters in our own house). They nationalized key public utilities, bringing them under the control of the provincial government, and appointed French Canadians to run them. They provided financial support for French Canadian investors to help them compete with outside enterprises. They enacted innovative social welfare legislation and organized a new ministry of cultural affairs to support French Canadian cultural endeavors.

Population changes worried many Quebecers. Although 80 percent of Quebec's residents spoke French, the language seemed destined to decline within the province, as it already had in the rest of Canada. The birthrate among Canadian French speakers was falling so low that the total number of French speakers was declining. Immigrants into the province—who arrived in increasing numbers—chose to send their children to English-language schools. The situation in Montreal was particularly worrisome. Many English-speaking residents never bothered to learn French. Most of those fluent in both French and English were of French, not British, descent.

The success of the "Quiet Revolution" increased pride in the accomplishments of French-speaking Quebecers, and reinforced the idea that the province's unique culture deserved special government protection. Worries over the future of the French language and culture were shared by both those Quebecers proud to be Canadians and those who thought Quebec should be a separate nation. Jean Lesage claimed that since Quebec was the only province with a French majority, it needed special powers over language and immigration to preserve the French culture of its inhabitants.

Quebec Nationalism. Meanwhile, other Quebecers demanded a greater measure of independence from the national government. René Lévesque, who had been a cabinet minister in Lesage's government, left the Liberal Party. In 1968 he helped found the Parti Québécois (PQ), which demanded that Quebec become a sovereign nation. In the 1970 provincial election, the PQ won 23 percent of

René Lévesque, leader of the Quebec separatist movement during the 1970's. (Library of Congress)

Canadian national unity supporters at a rally in Hull, Quebec, on the eve of the October, 1995, referendum on Quebec secession. (AP/Wide World Photos)

the vote, demonstrating the increased popularity of the idea of Quebec sovereignty. Some young Quebecers rejected peaceful political methods and joined the Front for the Liberation of Quebec (FLQ), which claimed that only a violent revolution could bring independence for Quebec.

In the late 1960's the FLQ began a campaign of bombings, around Montreal. In October, 1970, they kidnapped James Cross, the British trade commissioner in Montreal, and Pierre Laporte, a cabinet minister. Robert Bourassa, leader of the Liberal Party who had become premier of Quebec that year, called on the federal government for help. Canadian prime minister Pierre Trudeau then declared martial law, suspended civil liberties throughout the country, and sent the army into Quebec.

Laporte was later found murdered, but Cross was rescued alive. More than four hundred people were arbitrarily arrested, only twenty of whom would later stand trial and be convicted, including two found guilty of Laporte's murder. Although many Quebecers resented the arbitrary nature of Trudeau's action, most condemned the FLQ, which soon ceased to exist.

Similar acts of terrorism did not happen again. However, the idea of Quebec separatism was far from dead. To reduce its appeal, Prime Minister Trudeau and the national Liberal Party adopted a policy of bilingualism. To ensure that French Canadians would feel at home everywhere in Canada, all federal agencies were to conduct business in both the French and English languages. The provincial governments were encouraged to do the same.

In 1974 Bourassa and the Quebec Liberal Party moved to reassure Quebec nationalists by passing a law declaring French the official language of Quebec. They hoped the move would not offend English speakers, but the law satisfied neither French nor English.

In 1976 the Parti Québécois won control of Quebec's legislature promising to hold a referendum in which the entire province could vote on independence. Premier René Lévesque waited four years before holding the referendum, however. He used the long interval to demonstrate that his party could effectively govern the province in the interest of its French-speaking inhabitants.

The following year the PQ government passed a Charter of the French Language that made French the sole language of debate in the legislature. It also banned English-language signs on commercial buildings and called for the use of French in all businesses in Quebec. The law also tried to solve the problem of immigration by forcing children of parents whose native language was not English to attend French-language schools.

In May, 1980, Lévesque finally held his long-promised referendum, asking the voters to authorize the government to negotiate the secession of Quebec from Canada while continuing economic association with the country. The PQ had difficulty refuting the argument that independence for Quebec would cause economic hardship for its people.

Opposition to the independence move was led by Liberal Party members of the national parliament from Quebec, especially Prime Minister Trudeau and his minister of justice, Jean Chrétien. To the shock of the PQ the referendum was decisively defeated: 60 percent opposed independence, against 40 percent who favored it. Polls indicated that more than half the French-speaking voters rejected independence. Separatism was defeated, but Quebec nationalism would continue to complicate attempts to define the Canadian constitution.

Canadian Political Leaders

Lucien Bouchard (1938-   ): Leader of Bloc Québécois in Canadian national Parliament (1991-1996); premier of Quebec and chairman of Parti Québécois (1996-   ).

Robert Bourassa (1933-1996): Leader of Quebec Liberal Party who tried to combine support for Canadian federalism while promoting Quebec's cultural autonomy; premier of Quebec (1970-1976, 1985-1994).

Jean Chrétien (1934-   ): Prime minister of Canada (1993-   ) and leader of Liberal Party; opponent of Quebec secession in 1993.

Elijah Harper (1949-   ): Ojibwa-Cree Indian who was the first Indian to win a seat in the Manitoba legislature; his veto helped defeat the Meech Lake Accord in 1990.

Jean Lesage (1912-1980): Leader of Quebec Liberal Party and premier of Quebec (1960-1966) who helped transform the province through his "Quiet Revolution."

René Lévesque (1922-1987): Leader of Quebec separatist movement and founder of Parti Québécois; premier of Quebec (1976-1985).

Brian Mulroney (1939-   ): Leader of Progressive Conservative Party of Canada and prime minister of Canada (1984-1993) who tried to solve problem of Quebec through the Meech Lake and Charlottetown Accords.

Jacques Parizeau (1930-   ): Active separatist; as premier of Quebec (1994-1995) resigned when 1995 referendum failed to support secession.

Pierre Trudeau (1919-   ): Prime minister of Canada (1968-1979, 1980-1984); leader of the national Liberal Party who opposed Quebec separatism.

Constitutional Crises. In 1982 Canada's basic constitution was still the 1867 British North America Act, which had established the confederation. As an act of the British parliament, it could be amended only by Parliament in London. Although the British parliament routinely endorsed Canadian requests for changes in the law, many Canadians deeply disliked having to ask a foreign body to change their own constitution. Prime Minister Pierre Trudeau wanted to transfer this power to Canada. He also proposed adding a Charter of Rights and Freedoms, something lacking in the 1867 act.

Trudeau desired to pass his Canada Act with the consent of all Canadians, but this proved difficult. Native Canadians sought recognition of their own claims, so a clause was added to the Canada Act that vaguely affirmed their existing and original rights.

Leaders of the provincial governments pressed for greater powers for their own legislatures. They received important concessions—especially one that allowed provinces to pass laws going against provisions of the Charter—on the condition that they reviewed such acts every five years. Every province but Quebec accepted the revised text of the act.

Quebec premier Lévesque particularly objected to the guarantee of minority-language rights designed to protect the use of French in the rest of Canada because it would also protect the use of English in Quebec, interfering with the PQ's laws restricting that language. The formula for amending the act made it impossible for any one province

Canadian prime minister Jean Chrétien arriving in Vancouver, British Columbia, in November, 1997, for an economic conference with leaders of Pacific Rim nations. (AP/Wide World Photos)

to exercise a veto, something Lévesque insisted Quebec needed. Trudeau went ahead without Quebec and the new constitution became effective in April, 1982.

Two more attempts would be made to find a compromise acceptable to Quebec that would secure its consent to the constitution. The defeat of the PQ by the Liberal Party and the reelection of Robert Bourassa in 1985 as Quebec's premier put a believer in federalism in charge of the province. Meanwhile, control of the federal government had passed to the Progressive Conservative Party led by Brian Mulroney, who hoped to succeed where Trudeau had failed.

Meech Lake Accord. In 1987 Mulroney and the premiers of all Canadian provinces agreed to amendments to the constitution proposed by Bourassa. Known as the Meech Lake Accord—after the town north of Ottawa where the premiers met—the agreement called for recognition of Quebec as a "distinct society," entitled to protect and promote French culture within Quebec. The accord provided that future changes to the constitution would require the consent of all ten provinces. Bourassa insisted that these were the minimum requirements for Quebec to accept the Canadian constitution.

To become Canadian law, the Meech Lake Accord required the consent of all ten legislatures by June 23, 1990. Opposition soon surfaced. Some Canadians objected to the expansion of Quebec's powers, especially the vagueness of what was meant by a "distinct society." They feared that this provision might permit achievement of independence by Quebec without the consent of the rest of Canada.

The agreement also ran into strong opposition from Native Canadian peoples. They objected to granting a special position to Quebec's French-speaking people while ignoring their own demands for self-government. Eventually, the federal parliament and eight provincial parliaments passed the accord. The government of Manitoba had delayed action while requesting modifications to the accord. When the Meech Lake Accord came up for consideration in Manitoba, it was so late in the province's legislative session that the issue could be discussed only with the unanimous consent of all members to waive normal rules of procedure. Elijah Harper, an Ojibwa-Cree Indian member of the Manitoba legislature, refused his consent nine times, effectively vetoing the accord.

Charlottetown Agreement. In 1992 Mulroney tried again to achieve a constitutional compromise. He called for a meeting in Charlottetown, Prince Edward Island, where the original agreement to form a Canadian confederation had been reached. This time representatives of Native Canadian groups participated. The Charlottetown Agreement tried to provide something for everyone. The constitution would contain a "Canada clause" to balance the Quebec "distinct society" clause; there would be further discussion of native self-government; the Canadian senate would be reformed along lines demanded by groups in western Canada; the powers of provincial legislatures over matters that had been joint federal-provincial areas would be increased.

Because it tried to satisfy so many groups, the Charlottetown Agreement provided targets for attack by those who found a specific provision objectionable. Trudeau campaigned in Quebec against the agreement, claiming it granted too many concessions to Quebec nationalists. The Parti Québécois rejected it, charging that it granted too few concessions to Quebec. In a national referendum held in the fall of 1992 the country decisively rejected the agreement by a 54-46 percent margin.

The failure of two attempts to secure a special place for Quebec in the Canadian confederation gave new momentum for the separatist cause. In September, 1994, the Parti Québécois won back control of the Quebec legislature and Jacques Parizeau became premier, promising to hold yet another referendum. The October, 1995, vote attracted some five million Quebecers, about 93 percent of the electorate, who narrowly rejected secession by just over 1 percent; 50.6 percent voted no, 49.4 percent voted yes. Some 60 percent of French-speaking residents voted for independence, but large majorities in Montreal and in other English-speaking and immigrant districts voted against it. Cree Indian and Inuit areas in northern Quebec also voted against independence. Infuriated by the results, Parizeau resigned as premier, bitterly attacking Quebec's ethnic minorities, whom he blamed for the defeat of the measure.

After two failed referendums and two failed agreements among Quebec and the other provinces, it was unclear what arrangements might sat-

Canada

1534	Jacques Cartier lands on Gaspé Peninsula, where he claims region for France.
1608	Quebec City is founded.
1663	New France is proclaimed a royal French province.
1756-1763	British and French fight in Seven Years', or French and Indian, War.
1763	Treaty of Paris cedes New France to Great Britain.
1774	Quebec Act confirms freedom of religion and French civil law for inhabitants of Quebec.
1783	Immigration of British Loyalists from newly independent United States begins.
1867	British North America Act establishes Canadian Confederation.
1960	Jean Lesage is elected premier of Quebec and leads "Quiet Revolution."
1968-1979	Pierre Trudeau serves as prime minister of Canada.
1968	René Lévesque helps found Parti Québécois (PQ).
1970	(Oct.) Members of the Front for the Liberation of Quebec (FLQ) kidnap a British trade representative and a provincial cabinet minister.
1974	French is declared Quebec's official language.
1975	James Bay and Northern Quebec Agreement settles land claims of Cree and Inuit peoples.
1976	Parti Québécois wins control of Quebec's parliament; René Lévesque becomes provincial premier.
1980-1984	Trudeau again serves as prime minister.
1980	(May) Voters reject proposal to have Quebec government negotiate sovereignty for the province.
1982	(Apr.) Canada adopts its own constitution, which replaces British North America Act.
1987	Prime Minister Brian Mulroney and provincial premiers propose Meech Lake Accord, which is to give Quebec a special status.
1988	National Parliament approves free trade agreement with United States.
1990	Meech Lake Accord fails.
1990	(May) Quebec, Ontario, and New York State police invade Mohawk reserve and close its casinos.
1990	(July) Mohawk militants begin long standoff with Quebec police and national army.
1992	Charlottetown Agreement on position of Quebec in Canadian federation is defeated in national referendum.
1992	Federal government agree to turn over jurisdiction for Mohawk policing, social services, education, and cultural activities to local Mohawk communities.
1994	(Sept.) Parti Québécois wins back control of Quebec legislature and Jacques Parizeau becomes premier.
1995	Canadian vessels seize Spanish fishing boat, precipitating international incident with Spain.
1995	(Oct.) Quebec voters narrowly reject proposal to seek independence.
1997	(Sept.) Prime Minister Jean Chrétien calls meeting of provincial premiers that Quebec refuses to attend.

1998	(Jan.) Canadian minister of Indian Affairs formally apologizes to country's Indian and Inuit peoples for past government policies.
1998	(Jan. 7) Federal government issues statement of reconciliation to Native Canadians for past government programs that hurt their interests.
1998	(Feb. 17) Government releases controversial data on race collected in 1996 census; figures show that 11.2 percent of population consider themselves members of visible minorities.
1998	(Mar. 2) Daniel Johnson, leader of Quebec's opposition Liberal Party, resigns, conceding that his party cannot beat Parti Québécois in provincial elections.
1998	(Mar. 22) Killing of two members of Tsuu T'ina Nation in shootout with Royal Canadian Mounted Police officer provokes anger among Native Canadian communities throughout Canada.
1998	(Aug. 20) Supreme Court of Canada rules that Quebec cannot secede without first negotiating terms with other provinces and federal government.
1998	(Sept. 21) Hundreds of U.S. farmers block North Dakota rail line at Canadian border as part of growing U.S. protests again rising imports of Canadian agricultural products.
1998	(Nov.) Members of Nisg'a nation in British Columbia vote to ratify treaty with federal government that will give them title to their land and partial independence from provincial and national law; critics charge treaty may promote balkanization of Canada.
1998	(Nov. 30) Parti Québécois wins provincial elections, retaining control of Quebec's government with slightly reduced parliamentary majority.
1999	(Apr. 1) Eastern portion of Northwest Territories becomes the new territory of Nunavut, whose native Inuit people are given a large measure of sovereignty.

isfy Quebec's sense of its own uniqueness and at the same time be acceptable to the rest of Canada. The PQ threatened to hold yet another referendum on separation. When Prime Minister Jean Chrétien called a meeting of the premiers of all ten provinces for September, 1997, Quebec refused to attend.

"First Nations." The native peoples of Canada, the Indian tribes and the Inuit (the name the Eskimo prefer which translates as "the people") have become increasingly assertive in pressing demands for special treatment. They can truthfully assert that they were the first people to arrive in Canada—long before any French or English appeared in the country.

During the seventeenth and eighteenth centuries, European colonial powers signed treaties with the Indian tribes that recognized them as sovereign entities. In the nineteenth century, however, Canada treated the native peoples as inferior dependents. They were crowded onto reserves that were

a small part of their original land claims. Native children were sent to government-run schools in which they were forbidden to speak their own languages and were forcibly assimilated into European culture. At the same time Quebec's French-speaking people were beginning to demand consideration as a special group, Canada's native peoples were beginning to challenge the loss of their ancestral lands and their arbitrary and paternalistic treatment by the government of Canada.

Within every province of Canada native groups have demanded full reconsideration of their claims. Some of their claims have been based on actual treaties, others on original occupancy—the right to own and use their own ancestral lands. Where Native Canadian demands have been ignored, they have begun forceful, sometimes violent actions to press their cases. Native Canadian tribes in British Columbia have blockaded logging roads to protest what they see as invasions of their territory. Coastal tribes have insisted that the resources of rivers and the sea are included in their claims, setting off many disputes over fishing rights.

The Cree and Inuit of northern Quebec were the first Native Canadians to succeed in pursuing their claims. They faced extensive flooding of their traditional hunting and trapping areas after Quebec's government began a hydroelectric project whose dams would divert rivers flowing into James Bay. Quebec refused to recognize any native land claims until a legal injunction obtained by the Cree halted construction.

In 1975 the Canadian and Quebec governments and the native groups signed the James Bay and Northern Quebec Agreement, the first land claim settlement in modern Canadian history. The Cree and Inuit received compensation of $225 million to be paid over twenty-five years for surrendering their land claims. They also received title to the land around their villages and exclusive hunting, fishing, and trapping rights over a larger area. The communities concerned also received rights to local self-government.

The Iroquois. Among the most militant of Canada's Indian groups are the Six Nations that constitute the League of the Iroquois, especially the Mohawk, who make up nearly two-thirds of Canada's Iroquois population. The Iroquois came to Canada from the south during the eighteenth century. Most arrived after the American Revolutionary War (1775-1783), in which they had sided with the British and suffered at the hands of the victorious Americans. Modern Iroquois argue that they came to Canada as sovereign nations allied to the British crown. The land they were granted in Quebec and Ontario was a reward for their loyalty and recognized their independent status. Neither the provincial governments of Quebec and Ontario nor the Canadian federal government have been willing fully to honor Iroquois claims. The clash of beliefs has resulted in angry confrontations.

The Mohawk. Violence erupted within Mohawk Quebec communities in 1988 and 1990. One Mohawk reserve straddles the United States-Canadian border and is ideally located for moving cigarettes and alcohol into Canada without the consent of the Canadian authorities. The Canadian government calls this activity smuggling; the Mohawks call it exercising their sovereign rights.

Police raids in 1988 failed to halt the practice and led the Mohawk to block the Mercier Bridge,

a major link between the south shore of the St. Lawrence River and the city of Montreal. Younger Mohawks formed a Warrior Society to protect gambling casinos set up on the reserve in defiance of the traditional tribal authorities. In 1990 a civil war broke out. Arson, bombing, and the killing of two Mohawks finally led to the invasion of the reserve by Quebec, Ontario, and New York State police, and closure of the casinos in May, 1990.

The Warrior Society won more widespread acceptance among Indians for its role in another confrontation at a different reserve later that year. To prevent the expansion of a golf course onto land the Mohawk claimed, the Warriors joined local Mohawks in setting barricades around the disputed area. A raid in July, 1990, by more than one hundred Quebec police resulted in the death by gunfire of one policeman and the retreat of the rest. The police then set up barriers around the reserve, the Mohawks near Montreal again blocked the bridge into the city, and, to show their solidarity with the Mohawks, Indian groups across Canada set up road blocks near their own reserves. After a seventy-eight-day standoff, the Canadian government sent in its army, put down the rebellion, and reopened the Mercier Bridge.

The violent events of 1990 brought the problems of Native Canadians to national attention. One result was a 1992 agreement between the federal government and the Mohawks to turn over jurisdiction for policing, social services, education, and cultural activities to the local communities. Other native groups have seen progress in resolving land claims and in achieving expanded opportunities for self-government. However, at best, such advances have been achieved in areas of local control and fail to meet the demands of those who insist on full sovereignty. In January, 1998, to signal that times had changed and to reduce the probability of more confrontations and violence, the Canadian minister of Indian Affairs formally apologized to the country's Indian and Inuit peoples for past government policies that had tried to destroy native cultures.

International Confrontations. The geographical position of Canada between the United States and the former Soviet Union meant that any war breaking out between the two superpowers would necessarily involve Canada. To protect itself, Canada closely cooperated with the United States in military matters. Canada helped set up a joint defense command for North America and an early-warning radar system in the North. It also joined the United States and Western European nations in the North Atlantic Treaty Organization (NATO). The dissolution of the Soviet Union in 1991 greatly reduced Canadian fears of a major international conflict.

Contests for control of the fishing regions off both the Atlantic and Pacific Coasts have occurred throughout Canadian history. As stocks of fish declined in the late twentieth century, tensions arose among nations competing to catch them. Decreasing harvests of cod in Canada's Atlantic coastal waters, for example, led to a confrontation between Canada and Spain in 1995, when Canadian patrol vessels seized a Spanish fishing boat accused of using illegal fishing practices. Spain sent its own patrol boats to the area to protect its fishermen. Open violence was prevented by a formal agreement worked out with the help of the United Nations. Disagreements over managing declining stocks of Pacific salmon led to a forcible blockade of United States shipping by Canadian fishing boats in an effort to compel Alaskan canneries to reduce their production. Again, peaceful negotiation defused the crisis, but future confrontations seem likely.

Until the middle of the twentieth century, when Quebecers and native peoples began to assert themselves, few Canadians were aware of the serious problems that existed in these areas. Earnest efforts to respond to Indian and Inuit complaints continue with the hope of avoiding the violent conflicts that marred the past. How to satisfy Quebec without destroying the Canadian confederation is a more difficult problem because of the increasing support for independence among Quebecers and the stiffening opposition to providing a special position for Quebec throughout the rest of Canada.

Milton Berman

For Further Study

Canadian Politics in the 1990s (4th ed. 1995), edited by Michael S. Whittington and Glen Williams, contains twenty-one articles by scholars ana-

lyzing the major domestic and international political and social issues in Canada. Louis Balthazar's *French-Canadian Civilization* (2d ed. 1996) surveys the political, cultural, and economic developments that transformed Quebec into a politically active society determined to preserve its unique French-derived identity. Jonathan Lemco, *Turmoil in the Peaceable Kingdom: The Quebec Sovereignty Movement and Its Implications for Canada and the United States* (1994) is a pessimistic analysis of the long-term consequences for Canada, the United States, and Quebec itself, of the province's possible secession from Canada. Robert A. Young, *The Secession of Quebec and the Future of Canada* (1995) assumes a Quebec secession can be carried out peacefully, but he is equally pessimistic about its possible consequences.

Olive Patricia Dickason, *Canada's First Nations: A History of the Founding Peoples from Earliest Times* (1992) describes the Canadian Indian and Inuit experience from the first migration from Asia to 1990, stressing how Indians and Inuit have struggled to control their own destiny. Alan D. McMillan, *Native Peoples and Cultures of Canada: An Anthropological Overview* (2d ed. 1995), covers the same time span and analyzes the cultural factors that influence current conflicts between native peoples and other Canadians over land titles and self-government. Essays collected by Bruce Morrison and C. Roderick Wilson in *Native Peoples: The Canadian Experience* (2d ed. 1995) describe the efforts of the original inhabitants of Canada to reject paternalistic domination by the central government and reestablish control over their own lives. Menno Boldt, *Surviving as Indians: The Challenge of Self-Government* (1993) is a provocative critique of Indian, as well as federal and provincial political leaders for not doing enough to end Indian dependency, revitalize Indian cultures, and encourage increased self-sufficiency while remaining within the Canadian mainstream.

Younger readers will find much useful information in two general surveys of the land, people, history, and government of Canada: Guek-Cheng Pang, *Canada* (1994) and John F. Grabowski, *Canada* (1998).

Mexico

Many problems threaten the domestic stability of Mexico. Increasing mass opposition to the ruling Institutionalized Revolutionary Party (PRI) has generated considerable conflict both within the government and against it. An insurrection in the southern state of Chiapas has provoked numerous armed clashes with authorities. While the Chiapas revolt was the most serious issue of the late 1990's, severe economic problems that originated during the early 1980's have led to a dramatic fall in living standards for the country as a whole. Moreover, many Mexicans have suffered as a result of the activities of drug traffickers who have aggravated Mexico's relations with its powerful neighbor to the north, the United States.

The northernmost of the Western Hemisphere Latin American republics, Mexico shares a 1,500-mile-long border with the United States in the North American continent. Its position next to the powerful and wealthy United States has provided opportunities as well as problems for Mexico. While the U.S. economy provides technology and markets to Mexico, many Mexicans cannot find work within their own country.

Early History. A variety of societies ruled Mexico before Spain began occupying the region in 1519. The Olmecs, Maya, and Aztecs all developed brilliant civilizations noted for their advanced arts and sciences, monumental architecture, and large-scale political systems. During the colonial period, which lasted three centuries, Spanish administrators assumed that all problems had legal solutions.

In their efforts to create a new society in Mexico, the Spanish government and its partner, the Roman Catholic Church, permitted a measure of continuity with the indigenous past. Local officials administered Mexico through the indigenous institutions, wherever such existing customs and practices did not conflict with the demands of church and state. However, the Indian peoples had been stripped of tribal protection with little individual freedom.

After Mexico declared its independence in 1821 under the leadership of Agustín de Iturbide, various governments began to remove the strong ties that had formerly bound church and state together. However, Mexico's new rulers could not agree upon a political philosophy under which to govern the country. The 1835 revolt of American settlers in Texas symbolized Mexico's failings, not only to grant its citizens reasonable amounts of local self-rule, but also its inability to colonize its northern territories.

Mexico's catastrophic defeat in the Mexican-American War of 1846-1848 motivated the country's liberal faction to blame clerics for this national humiliation. Under the Treaty of Guadalupe Hidalgo, which ended the war, Mexico ceded half its national territory to the United States. Although the liberals successfully resisted French occupation of Mexico during the 1860's, they could not generate economic growth or political order.

Dictatorship and Revolution. From 1876 to 1911 an impressive army general, Porfirio Díaz, controlled Mexico's government. Through strong authoritarian rule and rapid economic growth, Mexico seemed finally to have discovered a formula for successful development. Díaz encouraged foreign investments and promoted industrial growth. For the first time federal police (the *federales*) had jurisdiction over local law enforcement officials. Railroads linked the entire country together, and a prosperous middle class arose. For the first time since the 1820's, Mexico enjoyed friendly relations with the United States. Fiscal stability and a solid national currency, the peso, gave Mexico a great deal of pride.

From 1911 to 1937 the Mexican government, however, shifted its emphasis as part of a reform effort. A violent civil war that began in 1911 caused later governments to promote land redistribution and the unionization of workers. At the same time momentum grew to restrict the activities of foreign investors. These changes in economic policy resulted in Mexico's having chilly relations with the United States and European nations. Particularly important was a new constitution in 1917 that empowered the Mexican government to own all mineral wealth, as well as the right to nationalize land or businesses in the name of collective need.

In 1937 the Mexican government began establishing policies that continued to the end of the twentieth century. During the Great Depression, President Lázaro Cárdenas's government emphasized industrialization and slowly curtailed a strong anticlerical movement in the country.

Relations with the United States improved during and after World War II. The government paid less attention to the needs of peasants and workers. Gradual modifications of the 1917 constitution eventually ended land reform during the 1990's. The authoritarian texture of government modified slowly, beginning with a shocking massacre of students demonstrating during the Olympics in 1968 that resulted in a gradual democratization.

Relations with the United States. Friction between the United States and Mexico has been largely a product of rising illegal immigration of Mexicans seeking employment in the United States. Mexican migration to the United States has grown consistently over three decades. More than 260,000 Mexicans settled in the United States during the 1960's. That number rose to more than 2 million during the 1980's. By the 1990's about 315,000 Mexi-

cans were entering the United States every year. This rate projected to a total of about 3.2 million people for the decade. By 1996 at least 7 million Mexicans had moved to the United States permanently. Of these, about 2.3 million were regarded as "undocumented" because they lack legal immigration papers.

The Mexican government has been reluctant to respond to complaints from the United States for several reasons. Mexicans working in the United States send an estimated US$2.5 billion to their families in Mexico every year. That figure is equivalent to about 5 percent of Mexico's total export income. Even more significantly, it accounts for about 57 percent of the foreign exchange income that Mexico realizes through direct foreign investment.

The Mexican government objected strongly when the United States began enforcing its border controls more effectively to reduce the numbers of Mexicans crossing into the United States. A 1986 law that legalized many undocumented workers also reduced illegal cross-border traffic by permitting many workers to bring their families to the United States legally.

Chiapas Insurgency. Mexico has more than two hundred separate indigenous ethnic groups, whose members speak more than fifty difference

Profile of Mexico

Official name: United Mexican States

Independent since: 1821

Former colonial ruler: Spain

Location: North America, between United States and Central America

Area: 761,602 square miles

Capital: Mexico City

Population: 97,563,400 (1997 est.)

Official language: Spanish

Major religion: Roman Catholicism

Gross domestic product: US$777.3 billion (1996 est.)

Major exports: machinery and transport equipment; petroleum; agricultural goods

Military budget: US$1.56 billion (1997 est.)

Military personnel: 175,000 (1997)

Note: Monetary figures rendered as "US$" are U.S. equivalents of values in local currencies.

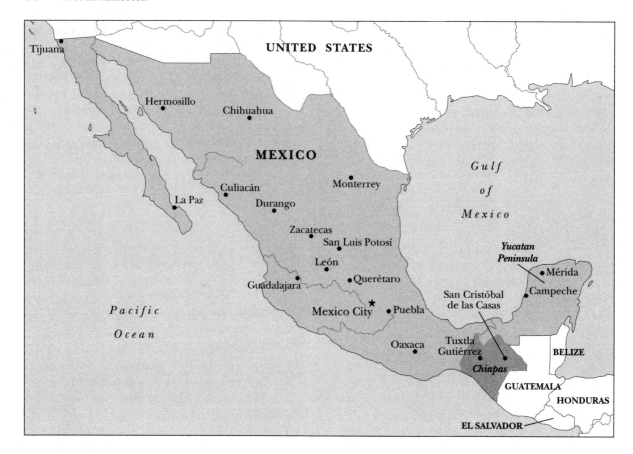

languages. Within Mexico, Native American peoples have often been regarded as obstacles to national unity and economic development. Many Mexicans are concerned about the dangers of the country being fragmented by this cultural diversity. For this reason, as well as others, Mexico's Indian societies have suffered from widespread discrimination.

Language has not been the only barrier to Indians enjoying greater economic progress. They have long endured the unequal policies of a ruling white and mestizo (white-Indian mixture) elite. For example, Indians have often been denied bank loans to develop their own businesses.

With a large native Maya population, the southern state of Chiapas has one of the large concentrations of indigenous peoples in Mexico. These people have long been dominated by white and mestizo rulers and landowners. Despite differences among themselves, the elites have remained cohesive, adaptive, and able to survive outside events. Most of the state's governors have been prosperous landowners whose government policies have favored the development of large-scale commercial agriculture. Government efforts to improve the grim lot of Chiapas's highland Indians and lowland laborers and renters have been minimal. The state's government has been bogged down by corruption and compromised by the needs of big landowners. Issues of peonage and inequitable ownership of land that caused protests during the late nineteenth century have remained.

During the 1990's Chiapas approached a crisis. As its Indian peoples began creating their own organizations, a rapid increase in their numbers raised popular demands for land and food. Illiteracy stood at 30 percent, more than double the national average. High rates of alcoholism and malnutrition compounded social problems.

A cultural problem peculiar to Chiapas has been the unusually large number of its residents who have converted from Roman Catholicism to Protestant faiths. Often expelled from their communities for refusing to take part in religious fiestas and other Catholic traditions, many of these new Protestants have resettled in cities such as San Cristóbal de las Casas. Many of Chiapas's Protestants have been beaten, killed, or had their houses burned down by local authorities.

The policies of Governor Patrocinio González have also fueled discontent throughout Chiapas. After assuming office in 1988, González could take credit for several accomplishments. Under his administration the state built more roads and highways than under any governor in a quarter of a century. His administration also strung many more electrical power lines than any previous administration had. He also punished new arrivals who were illegally clearing forests in eastern Chiapas.

However, González's foes contended that his failures outweighed his successes. Taking a hard line against Indians who complained about social conditions, he modified state law so that protesters could be classified as "terrorists" and "delinquents." When more than three hundred peasants marched to Chiapas's state capital, Tuxtla Gutiérrez, to demand land reform in early 1990, González's government betrayed them. Authorities told the marchers that González would talk to them at the airport. When the marchers reached the airport, seven hundred police officers gassed and clubbed them.

González blamed teachers and leftist priests for inciting the antigovernment protesters. In September, 1991, he jailed a Roman Catholic priest for encouraging rebellion. Thousands of Catholics protested. Human rights abuses in the state mounted. Leaders of peasant organizations were murdered, and Indian farmers were jailed. The governor allowed state police to help ranchers clear out Indian squatters trying to pursue their claims to land.

Others protested against rigged elections for municipal leaders. The August, 1991, elections in Chiapas resulted in the PRI winning an unlikely 100 percent of the votes in fifty municipalities.

Chiapas Revolt and National Politics. As early as 1987 the Chiapas government began monitoring armed groups, whose existence had been an open secret for years. But Chiapas villagers continued to whisper about nighttime training sessions in caves and jungle hideouts. In 1989 government intelligence officers reported their discovery of a crude weapons factory. In May, 1993, government soldiers discovered a rebel training camp. In response, the national government ordered an emergency aid package for Chiapas. The government wanted to cover up signs of rebel activity in order to assure passage of the North American Free Trade Agreement (NAFTA) and ensure the ruling party's victory in the presidential election scheduled for August, 1994.

The government strategy collapsed when Chiapas's Zapatista National Liberation Army attacked San Cristóbal de las Casas and several other towns on the first day of 1994. Fighting between government troops and rebels continued for weeks in the hills surrounding San Cristóbal. Fears of rebel attacks spread in January, as electrical towers were downed in two states. Police in Mexico City beefed

Luis Colosio in front of a portrait of President Carlos Salinas de Gortari in November, 1993. Colosio was considered the leading contender to succeed Gortari but was assassinated four months later. (AP/Wide World Photos)

up patrols outside banks, public buildings, the subway, and the airport.

In a display of support for the Chiapas rebels, thousands of workers, peasants, and students marched on Mexico City on January 7. They demanded an end to government use of military force to quell the uprising. Former Chiapas governor Patrocinio González, recently elevated to head the interior ministry in the national government, was forced to resign on January 10. He became the first major political casualty of the uprising that shocked Mexico.

Faced with a continuing rebellion that drew international attention to charges of human rights abuses in Mexico, President Carlos Salinas appointed Jorge Carpizo to the interior ministry. Carpizo enjoyed a reputation for evenhandedness and respect for the law. Salinas had earlier made Carpizo head of a national human rights commission after a politically motivated shooting of a crusading lawyer. Later, as attorney general, Carpizo had denounced corruption and fraud within his own office and that of the Federal Judicial Police.

Carpizo's appointment to the interior ministry was significant, as it gave him responsibility for supervising the 1994 presidential elections. With him in charge, there appeared to be a real opportunity for PRI opponents who favored more open and democratic elections.

Meanwhile, saddled with the worst crisis of his political career, President Salinas also named his close friend Manuel Camacho Solis to head a new Commission for Peace and Reconciliation in Chiapas. A former Mexico City mayor, Camacho Solis immediately had trouble obtaining a cease-fire agreement from Chiapas's rebel leaders, who were suspicious of Salinas's peace initiative.

Nevertheless, rebels began sending secret messages to Camacho Solis through Bishop Samuel Ruiz, the leader of the archdiocese of San Cristóbal who was trusted by Zapatista leaders. After the rebels seized the governor of Chiapas, Camacho Solis praised the rebels for their apparent willingness to spare the man's life. Camacho Solis also promised the rebels that government troops would remain in their garrisons as a sign of the government's good will. Despite his promise, small towns in remote parts of Chiapas were soon filled with government tanks, artillery, and armored personnel carriers as soldiers remained on alert.

Zapatista Movement. Rafael Guillen Vicente emerged as the leader of the Zapatista rebels. Guillen was a thirty-seven-year-old philosophy instructor who had graduated with high honors from the National Autonomous University in Mexico City before earning a master's degree at the Sorbonne in Paris. He taught at the University of Nicaragua during the rule of its Marxist Sardinista regime. Known as Comandante Marcos, Guillen became a colorful spokesman for the Chiapas insurrection.

The demands of the Zapatista guerrillas were extensive. Many rebels cited the government's free trade agreement with the United States and Canada as a major grievance. President Salinas's policy of privatizing state-owned businesses was also a serious issue.

Rebels also objected strongly to Salinas's revising the national constitution to foster capitalism in the countryside by allowing peasants, for the first time since 1917, to sell commonly held farmland. Another fundamental grievance was the government's curtailment of land redistribution. The rebels considered these moves unacceptable departures from the ways in which Maya lands had been collectively owned since before Spanish colonizers arrived in the sixteenth century. The rebels feared that their poverty would inevitably lead individual landowners to sell their small plots to wealthier Mexican farmers or, worse still, to American, Canadian, or European agribusiness conglomerates.

Another problem in Chiapas was the government's withdrawal of subsidies for coffee farmers. This change in policy devastated the state when coffee prices collapsed in 1989. With this in mind, the rebels demanded land, work, food, housing, education, liberty, democracy, and peace as well as justice.

Peace Negotiations. Discussions to resolve the Chiapas crisis had an encouraging beginning. In mid-January, 1994, Bishop Ruiz began serving as mediator between rebel leaders and the government. Camacho Solis proposed an amnesty and promised that the peace talks would lead to the "political recomposition" of Chiapas, immediate changes in the state's judicial system, and eventual solutions to the problems found in indigenous communities.

However, the government stopped short of recognizing the rebels as a "belligerent force," as the guerrillas demanded. Rebel leaders sought to

Forty-five victims of the Acteal massacre were buried in a mass funeral ceremony on Christmas Day in 1997. (AP/Wide World Photos)

broaden the talks by inviting representatives of Mexico's political parties to be observers. In an effort to win the guerrillas' trust, Camacho Solis journeyed to the heart of rebel territory, where he visited the town of Guadalupe Tepayac to seek the release of a retired army general and former governor, whom the Zapatistas had held captive for six weeks. Camacho Solis even let himself be searched by Zapatistas and shook hands with two heavily armed and uniformed rebels when they delivered up their prisoner. He also listened silently as townspeople shouted their unbridled support for the rebels. Meanwhile, the guerrillas' demands began to moderate and they dropped their insistence that Salinas resign immediately.

The peace talks that began on February 21 quickly became a battlefield for the hearts and minds of people across Mexico. Under a signed accord, the government agreed to hold a special session of congress to enact electoral reforms before the August, 1994, presidential election. President Salinas's representatives offered to enact a national law that would, for the first time, outlaw discrimination against Indians and be enforced by a new office created to prosecute discrimination cases. The proposed new federal law was to protect Indian autonomy in such matters as family, business, land, and farming. Improved health and education services were also part of the proposed agreement. Other promised reforms included bilingual education in Spanish and Indian languages. The rebels were also to enjoy an amnesty.

Despite these promises, the Mexican government limited its concessions to Chiapas and refused to install a transitional national government. The negotiators decided that local governments should serve indigenous communities more directly and that the Chiapas state legislature should have increased Indian representation. The impoverished state would also enjoy more roads, new housing projects, and expanded electrical power service. In addition, it was to have redesigned judicial districts with judges trained to respect indigenous cultures. Finally, a new criminal law for the state was to outlaw the practice of expelling people from indigenous communities.

Failure of Peace Negotiations. The unprecedented concessions made by the government to the rebels eventually failed. A right-wing group threatened to burn the cathedral in San Cristóbal de las Casas if Bishop Ruiz did not resign, even though the bishop denied having a personal role in guerrilla military activities. However, Ruiz argued that the Zapatista campaign was just—a point of view that infuriated conservative entrepreneurs and ranchers.

The Zapatistas themselves dealt a major blow to the peace process by flatly rejecting the March agreements. Even more stunning was the sudden resignation of Camacho Solis as peace envoy. He blamed Ernesto Zedillo, PRI's new presidential candidate, for blocking his efforts to launch a new peace initiative. Zedillo had criticized publicly the peace process. Bishop Ruiz announced shortly afterward that he was resigning as a mediator in the negotiations.

In the aftermath of the stalled negotiations tensions mounted. Worried authorities in Chiapas arrested more than one hundred squatters who had taken over several ranches. Landowners in Chiapas complained that four hundred other ranches had been occupied by landless peasants or guerrillas. At least nineteen ranch owners had been kidnapped and forced to sign papers agreeing to surrender their properties. The guerrillas kept some farmers captive for weeks, forcing them to earn their freedom by teaching the militants how to their operate tractors and other farm equipment.

Worried about the renewal of fighting, President Salinas ordered Mexican army troops to return to the positions they had held on January 12—the day the government ordered a cease-fire as part of the plan to lure the rebels back to the negotiating table. However, the rebel movement had not caught on as its leaders had hoped. The populace did not rise up in arms, and the PRI remained firmly in power. Facing thirty thousand government troops, the rebels were at a strong military disadvantage.

After Zedillo was elected, in a sudden departure from his efforts to restart peace talks with the Zapatistas, he suddenly sent three thousand soldiers and police officers into the rebel strongholds in early February, 1995. More than a dozen alleged rebels were arrested. Zedillo had ordered the seizure of the rebel leadership. Soldiers and police met little resistance. Tens of thousands of supporters of the leftist Democratic Revolutionary Party marched into the capital's main plaza to demand an end to hostilities. But the conservative opposition National Action Party, as well as Zedillo's PRI, strongly endorsed the government's decision to use force against the rebels. Eight days after the assault, Zedillo vowed not to let the rebels gain the upper hand again.

Zedillo proved unable to resolve the crisis. Perhaps his worst mistake was naming a hardliner, Emilio Chuayffet, to the ministry of interior. Not long afterward, human rights groups and journalists based in Chiapas warned anyone who would listen that death squads associated with the PRI were carrying

Zapatista rebel leader Marcos in 1996. (AP/Wide World Photos)

Members of the Zapatista National Liberation Army wear ski masks to hide their identities as they head for peace talks in San Cristobal de las Casas in November, 1998. (AP/Wide World Photos)

out a terror campaign against supporters of the rebels in Chiapas. Still, complex negotiations finally resulted in the February, 1996, signing of the San Andres Accords on Indigenous Rights and Culture. Zedillo, however, set these agreements aside rather than support their enactment into federal constitutional law.

Not surprisingly, the rebels walked away from talks with federal officials in September, 1996, after the government withdrew its approval of two key items in the San Andres Accords. The government balked on provisions that would have allowed Indians to expropriate land, to elect representatives, and to decide issues by traditional methods of consensus instead of direct votes. Zedillo then encouraged the Mexican congress to decide on the issue, hoping the Zapatistas could not reject a publicly supported proposal.

These tensions resulted in the Acteal massacre on December 22, 1997. Several Chiapas villages

declared themselves separate from the government in April, 1996, citing negotiated but unratified peace accords calling for indigenous autonomy. The delicate truce between the government and the rebels soon began to disintegrate as killings, burning of homes, and forced expulsions of Indians took place. Finally, gunmen attacked the Chiapas highland village of Acteal and murdered women and children praying in a small clapboard Roman Catholic church. Nearly all were members of an independent peasant group which sympathized with the Zapatistas. In all, nine men, twenty-one women, fourteen children, and an infant, all unarmed civilians, had been shot in cold blood and finished off with machetes.

More than six hours would pass before police would take action, which consisted of cleaning the site and digging mass graves. Amid an international outcry, dozens of arrests were made and the former governor resigned, along with the minister

Mexico

1519	Spain begins conquest of Mexico.
1821	(Feb. 24) Mexico declares its independence from Spain.
1846-1848	United States wins Mexican-American War and takes control of California and most of what will become the American Southwest.
1862	(May 5) Mexican troops turn back French invasion force on date later celebrated as Cinco de Mayo.
1890's	Protests and reform campaigns begin in Chiapas.
1910	(Nov.) Mexican Revolution begins.
1911	(May 25) President Porfirio Díaz goes into exile.
1911	(Nov. 6) Francisco Madero becomes president of Mexico.
1914	U.S. Marines occupy Mexico's chief port, Vera Cruz, to control customs collections.
1917	Revolutionary national constitution is adopted.
1938	(Mar.) Mexican government nationalizes all foreign-owned oil properties in country.
1982	Government devalues peso three times.
1985	(Sept. 19) Earthquake devastates Mexico City.
1987	(Dec.) Currency falls to rate of 2,300 pesos to one U.S. dollar.
1988	(July) Patrocinio González becomes governor of Chiapas.
1988	(July 6) Carlos Salinas is elected president of Mexico.
1990	(Mar.) Hundreds of Chiapas peasants march on state capital to demand land reform.
1991	(Aug.) PRI claims to have won 100 percent of votes in fifty Chiapas municipalities.
1991	(Sept.) Governor of Chiapas jails a Roman Catholic priest for encouraging rebellion.
1993	(May) Government soldiers find Zapatista training camp in Chiapas.
1994	(Jan. 1) Chiapas revolt begins.
1994	(Jan. 1) Zapatista rebels attack San Cristóbal and other Chiapas towns.
1994	(Jan. 7) Students, workers, and peasants march in Mexico City in support of Zapatista rebels.
1994	(Jan. 10) Interior minister Patrocinio González resigns from cabinet.
1994	(Feb. 21) Peace talks begin in Chiapas.
1994	(Mar. 23) Presidential candidate Luis Donaldo Colosio is assassinated.
1994	(Aug.) Ernesto Zedillo is elected president of Mexico.
1994	(Dec.) New government peso devaluation triggers economic and financial crisis.
1995	(Feb.) President Zedillo sends army into rebel areas of Chiapas.
1995	(Sept.) Tijuana police commander Ernesto Ibarra is one of many attorney general agents assassinated throughout Mexico.
1996	(Feb.) San Andres Accords on Indigenous Rights and Culture is signed.

1996	(Mar.) U.S. drug czar Barry McCaffrey meets with Mexican officials to discuss drug policies.
1996	(Sept.) Chiapas rebels break off talks with federal government.
1997	(Feb.) General Jesús Gutiérrez Rebollo, head of Mexico's antidrug campaign, is jailed.
1997	(May) Government's antidrug czar is revealed to be on payroll of Mexico's leading drug smuggler.
1997	(Dec. 22) Progovernment vigilantes massacre villagers in Acteal, Chiapas, with support of state police.
1998	(Jan. 7) Chiapas governor Julio Cesar Ruiz Ferro resigns.
1998	(Jan. 28) Chiapas leftist leader Rubicel Ruiz Gamboa is killed outside his home in Tuxtla Gutierrez.
1998	(Feb.) National government expels four foreigners working in Chiapas.
1998	(Feb. 26) U.S. president Bill Clinton's administration issues report "certifying" Mexico's efforts to combat drug traffic, despite strong contrary findings by U.S. Drug Enforcement Agency.
1998	(Feb. 28) European and Canadian human rights observers complete two-week fact-finding visit to Chiapas.
1998	(Mar. 14) President Zedillo proposes constitutional and legislative reforms to improve conditions in Chiapas, drawing on unimplemented San Andres Accords approved in early 1996.
1998	(May 11) Government deports forty Italian human rights observers visiting Chiapas.
1998	(May 18) U.S. Treasury and Justice Departments announce indictment of three Mexican banks and 130 individual Mexicans for drug-money laundering.
1998	(June 10) New violence between Zapatistas and government forces erupts in El Bosque and other Chiapas towns.
1998	(July) Government reports awarding of US$3,900 to each family of victims of Acteal massacre.
1998	(July 5) PRI victories in Chihuahua and Durango gubernatorial elections help strengthen party.
1998	(Nov. 20) Representatives of national congress meet with members of Zapatista National Liberation Army in effort to resume official peace negotiations.
1999	(Jan.-Feb.) Number of undocumented migrants passing through Mexico from Central America surges because of devastation caused by Hurricane Mitch.
1999	(Jan. 21) Raul Salinas, brother of former president Carlos Salinas, is convicted of arranging murder of political leader José Francisco Ruiz Massieu in 1994.
1999	(Mar. 4) President Zedillo proposes that Mexico adopt U.S. system of nominating presidential candidates through state primaries—a change that would end tradition of presidents' selecting their own successors.
1999	(Aug. 1) PRI begins Mexico's first-ever primary election campaign to nominate the party's presidential candidate on November 7.

of interior. The attorney general's office reported in March, 1998, that a progovernment vigilante group had plotted the Acteal massacre for more than two months. State police helped the attackers by transporting weapons in police vehicles.

New Economic Problems. Beginning in 1982 Mexico began to suffer an intense economic as well as political crisis. A worldwide oil glut that appeared in the spring of 1981 triggered a catastrophic fiscal crisis. Excessive amounts of oil were being produced throughout the world which forced a sudden drop in Mexican revenues. At that point Mexican president José López Portillo might have stopped borrowing money, but he refused. In addition, the price of Mexican commodities such as silver, coffee, and copper also plunged. Nevertheless, the government continued to spend money freely. The federal deficit increased to 14.2 percent of the gross national product, up from 7.6 percent in 1980. Attempting to maintain the peso when it became seriously overvalued was also a mistake because extra borrowing increased the national debt by US$20 billion in less than a year.

The financial crisis struck with full fury when López Portillo devalued the peso three times in 1982. A few weeks after claiming that he would "defend the value of the peso like a dog," López Portillo authorized the first devaluation in February, 1982. Once López Portillo selected Miguel de la Madrid, head of the Planning and Budgeting ministry, to succeed him in late 1981, deficits grew after de la Madrid began giving in to cabinet officials in order to enhance his presidential campaign. The central bank had nearly run out of reserves and the government allowed the peso to float.

These devaluations provoked mass social unrest. They raised the cost of imports and increased the consumer price index by almost 100 percent. When the scarcity of U.S. dollars made it almost impossible for firms to buy machinery that would have allowed them to switch production to use more local materials, Mexican companies began to lay off employees. The Mexican government teetered on the verge of bankruptcy and requested postponement of debt payments.

The financial crisis only accelerated under President de la Madrid. Mexicans were shocked when the peso fell from 150 to the dollar and then to 380 during the summer of 1985. By late 1986 pesos were being exchanged for dollars at a rate of 800 to 1. The next year was worse: By December, 1987, the exchange rate shot up to 2,300 pesos to 1 U.S. dollar. To make matters worse, the foreign debt increased almost in proportion.

Growing Social Tensions. Mexico's growing economic and fiscal crisis fostered the emergence of social hostilities during the September, 1985, earthquakes that devastated Mexico City. From local police to cabinet ministers, many government officials revealed themselves as corrupt, inept, and more concerned with exercising power rather than rescue and recovery. Agencies at all levels were unprepared to deal with the scale of the natural disaster confronting them. The real heroes of the emergency proved to be volunteers, who triumphed over both physical and governmental obstacles. Although the government tried to justify its poor response to the disaster, anger spread among the public.

President de la Madrid managed to lessen the possibility of social conflict by establishing a National Solidarity Program, which replaced many of the broader social programs and improved many local communities. The government offered direct negotiations to new and independent labor, peasant, and middle class groups over social issues as well as selected benefits. De la Madrid also initiated a new policy of privatizing the economy—selling off government-owned enterprises to local businesses—and reducing government expenditures.

The 1988 presidential elections represented a severe challenge to the government. The PRI's declining electoral support during the 1960's and 1970's can be attributed to the increasingly urban nature of Mexican society. Opposition parties attracted supporters from the masses and the middle class that had previously supported the PRI.

After being declared winner of the election, President Carlos Salinas met the challenge of public anger by modernizing the electoral process and neutralizing traditional groups within the PRI that had opposed reforms. Salinas gained much support by vastly accelerating the privatization policy and the Solidarity program. New investments poured in, creating many jobs.

New Crises. Nevertheless, crises soon developed under the Salinas regime that encouraged social conflict. Problems of income inequality and unemployment remained as serious issues. Many businesses in Mexico sought U.S. investment, although they actually belonged to drug traffickers.

Rumors circulated that Raul Salinas, the president's brother, was in league with well-known drug lord Juan Garcia Abrego, who helped him conduct a campaign of intimidation and wiretapping in order to ensure his brother's election in 1988. In 1995 Swiss authorities confirmed that Raul had amassed US$100 million in suspected drug money. Meanwhile, he awaited trial on charges of masterminding the murder of a senior Mexican politician, José Francisco Ruiz Massieu, his and Carlos's former brother-in-law.

These events were almost as unsettling as the 1994 assassination of Luis Donald Colosio, the popular PRI presidential candidate. Attempts to explain Colosio's death angered the public. First the government said the death was the work of a lone gunman, then a plot was said to have been uncovered, then the plot was denied.

Currency Crisis. Certainly the greatest threat to domestic peace and tranquility was the December, 1994, announcement that Mexico had devalued its currency. It appeared to be a necessary step that was long overdue because President Salinas was spending and borrowing large sums of money before the 1994 presidential election in order to ensure that Ernesto Zedillo would be elected to succeed him.

Mexico's foreign currency reserves dwindled from a high of US$30 billion to a low of only US$6 billion. In the wake of the North American Free Trade Agreement (NAFTA), imports shot up rapidly, far more than exports. Even before Zedillo took over, Mexico did not have enough to pay its obligations or to sustain the peso's value against the dollar. Prodded by Salinas, the Bank of Mexico had issued more than US$40 billion in short-term debt, mainly in treasury bonds known as *tesobonos* that matured in only a year. Because the government provided little warning about the devaluation and concealed its weak financial reserves, investors lost confidence and huge sums of capital left Mexico quickly.

Severe social problems quickly resulted from the 1994 devaluation. Even before the crisis hit, more than 13 million of the country's 91 million inhabitants were living in extreme poverty. At least 18 million suffered from malnutrition, and more than 45 million were earning less than ten dollars a day. Wage rises fell increasingly far behind price rises. At least 40 million persons lived in substandard conditions.

In an effort to combat poverty by reducing the birth rate, government hospitals frequently pressured women to accept tubal ligations or intrauterine devices after giving birth. At the same time, the economy made increasing use of child labor. Millions of children earned money by washing windshields of passing cars or by selling fruit and gum to supplement dwindling family incomes.

Conditions worsened from 1995 to 1996, when an estimated 65 percent of Mexico's families were classified as poor—a condition defined as living on less than ten dollars a day. In southern states such as Guerrero, two-thirds of the people lived in one or two-room shacks without running water, gas, or electricity. Only one Mexican in ten owned a telephone. By May, 1996, 2 million people lost their jobs and purchasing power fell by 25 percent.

Under these strains, the national banking system nearly collapsed. Interest rates shot up and 20 percent of persons holding bank loans defaulted. The government bailed out nine troubled banks and seized six others. During this deep recession, the national currency lost another 54 percent of its value. The national economy shrank 6.9 percent in 1995—the biggest contraction since the Great Depression.

On top of these problems, the Zedillo administration imposed an austerity program that called for rises in sales taxes and gasoline and electricity prices. These measures were severely criticized by the overwhelming majority of the nation's citizens. Meanwhile, Mexico's foreign debt increased by US$22 billion for a total of US$160 billion.

The harsh decline in living standards generated several violent confrontations. On May 31, 1996, for example, a group of mostly women and children from Monterrey stopped a freight train, unhooked three cars loaded with imported corn, and carried off fifty tons of grain. Police who tried to halt the looting were stoned.

During the spring of 1995 poor peasants from rural areas began converging daily at the main square in Mexico City to demonstrate in support of the Zapatista rebels in Chiapas, as well as to denounce economic problems. To the chant of "people can't take it anymore, the people are rising up," about five thousand demonstrators marched to Los Pinos, the residence of Mexico's president.

Shortly afterward, on May 1, tens of thousands of workers called for Zedillo's resignation, instead of staging their traditional May Day march of solidarity in support of the regime. Labor leaders stated that they made their decision because Mexico's economic woes left workers with little to celebrate. Many demonstrators gestured obscenely and shouted curses at the president. A similar May Day protest took place a year later.

Rising Crime. Crime became another signal that Mexico's social stability was threatened. Many of the growing numbers of girls and boys who worked on the streets came from one-parent or dysfunctional families, among whom drug addiction or alcoholism were common. In addition to the low esteem exhibited by these young people, many became criminals. In Mexico City, for example, armed robberies increased by 35 percent within a year after the peso devaluation. Many crimes were committed by children as young as ten. An average of fifty-eight carjackings took place each day.

From 1993 to the end of 1995, the number of crimes rose from 360 to 550, more than 43 percent of which were violent offenses. In January, 1996, more than a dozen banks were robbed. Assailants armed with machine guns often raided businesses, killing anyone who got in their way. Robberies in taxicabs became so common that the U.S. embassy recommended that visitors to Mexico City use only cabs associated with their hotels. Foreigners became favorite targets of kidnappers and murderers. Eight in ten criminal suspects were never apprehended. It soon appeared that the police themselves were often the worst criminals. One commander and a group of state police even attempted to carjack, in broad daylight, an automobile driven by the president's eldest son.

Drug Trafficking. As long as the United States remains rich and Mexico poor, their thousands of miles of shared border is likely to foster problems. Clearly the Mexican drug trade has concerned the U.S. government more than any other issue between the two countries. Mexican traffickers first began with low-level production and distribution of heroin and marijuana. Later they allied with Colombians when U.S. agents blocked the latters' south Florida entry routes. Then Mexican groups bought the cocaine for their own profit and generated a booming trade in methamphetamine. Mexican mafias buy the chemicals, produce methamphetamine, and ship it across the U.S. border.

By the early 1990's, Mexican drug cartels threatened the United States more than Colombian producers. More ominously, Mexican drug traffickers gained enormous influence over Mexico's political and judicial systems. Drugs became tied to several high-profile assassinations, while Mexican financial institutions appeared vulnerable to money-laundering schemes.

In response, U.S. president Bill Clinton's administration worked out various plans to cooperate with the Zedillo regime to restrain the drug trade. U.S. drug czar Barry McCaffrey and his delegation met with Zedillo, his attorney general, and other Mexican officials in March, 1996. In response, Mexican lawmakers introduced a bill to fight money laundering and indicated that they might strengthen the bill to meet U.S. concerns. More difficult was whether or not Mexico would extradite its citizens for trial in the United States.

The U.S. delegation with Barry McCaffrey carried the names of suspected drug kingpins. Both countries also attempted to plan the training of Mexican soldiers in the United States on antidrug patrols. Proposed military cooperation grew out of a trip to Mexico City made in 1995 by Defense Secretary William Perry. However, a furor developed when Perry said the United States also might consider joint exercises with Mexico's military.

Over several years, drug traffickers have stepped up their efforts to buy off Mexico's law enforcement agencies. Shortly after Tijuana police commander Ernesto Ibarra publicly stated that some Mexican officials had become "servants" of the drug gangs in September, 1995, he was assassinated. Ibarra was one of more than forty attorney-general agents killed in the line of duty from 1995 to late 1996. Mexican agents describe such deaths as part of the sacrifices they make while combatting drug traffickers. Mexico's attorney general acknowledged that drug-related corruption remained a problem in his office. He claimed in January, 1997, that public confidence in his agency had fallen so low that it was pointless to give speeches promising better days.

The drug issue soon became acrimonious. By early 1997 the U.S. government obtained considerable evidence that Raul Salinas and other high-ranking Mexican politicians were more closely tied to narcotics traffickers than had been previously believed. U.S. prosecutors jailed a former Mexican deputy attorney general, Mario Ruiz Massieu, when he was arrested for a currency violation. He had carried US$9 million in cash to a Newark, New Jersey, airport on his way to Spain.

General Jesús Gutiérrez Rebollo was arrested in February as Zedillo defended his use of the military to combat drugs, despite warnings that the military could become as corrupt as other law enforcement agencies. In May, 1997, it was revealed that Mexico's antidrug czar was on the payroll of Mexico's most powerful drug smuggler.

Douglas W. Richmond

For Further Study

Thomas Benjamin's *A Rich Land, A Poor People: Politics and Society in Modern Chiapas* (1989) is a comprehensive history of modern Chiapas that focuses on the long line of governors since the 1890's. Jan Rus's chapters in *Everyday Forms of State Formation, Revolution and the Negotiation of Rule in Modern Mexico* (1994), edited by Gilbert M. Joseph and Daniel Nugent, focuses upon basic social and political forces within Chiapas. Joseph and Nugent's book offers an original framework for understanding the formation of the Mexican government. Frank Cancian and Peter H. Brown, "Who is Rebelling in Chiapas?," *Cultural Survival Quarterly* (1994), is a masterful analysis of the racial and ethnic forces that resulted in insurrection. The summer 1994 edition of *AKWE:KON Journal*, published as *Chiapas: Challenging History* (1994) contains twelve articles that present indigenous points of view, as well as the social process that has caused such desperation.

Susan Kaufman Purcell and Luis Rubio, editors, *Mexico Under Zedillo* (1998) examines the political dilemmas created by the Chiapas guerrilla movement, as well as the crucial question of how political parties cope with ongoing social change. Stephen D. Morris, *Political Reformism in Mexico: An Overview of Contemporary Politics* (1995), explores the history of Mexico's one-party regime to weather crises. Elena Poniatowska's *Nothing, Nobody: The Voices of the Mexico City Earthquake* (1995) is a compelling account of the 1985 Mexico City earthquakes seen through the eyes of its victims.

Douglas W. Richmond, "Crisis in Mexico: Luis Echeverría and López Portillo, 1970-1982," *Journal of Third World Studies* (1988), discusses the socioeconomic origins of the 1982 crisis. Maria Lorena Cook, Kevin J. Middlebrook, and Juan Molina Horcasitas, editors, *The Politics of Economic Restructuring: State-Society Relations and Regime Change in Mexico* (1994) provides timely and detailed analyses of economic reform and its effect upon society during the Salinas regime. A remarkable documentary, "The Last Zapatistas" (1996) emphasizes Mexican legislation that privatizes traditionally communal lands.

United States

By the early 1990's the United States bestrode the world like a colossus. The breakup of the Soviet Union had ended the Cold War, leaving the United States the only superpower. It appeared that the twentieth century had truly become "America's Century"—a term coined decades earlier by journalist Henry Luce. Political leaders such as President George Bush spoke of a "New World Order"—a change that seemed on the road to fulfillment with the allied victory over Iraq in the Gulf War. Moreover, the capitalist U.S. economy was the envy, and often the model, of much of the world. The U.S. economy was admired not only because of the spectacular failure of communism, but because of a severe financial crisis and recession that began in Asia in 1997. Despite the hopeful future of the United States, there remained, however, issues that continued to trouble many Americans. These concerns, both domestic and foreign in nature, were sometimes real, sometimes potential, sometimes perhaps only imagined. Warranted or not, they caused unease among some Americans as the millennium approached its end.

A democratic republic since its founding in the late eighteenth century, the United States is a North American nation bordered to the north by Canada and to the south by Mexico. The oldest forty-eight of its fifty states are physically connected in the region known as the continental United States. Hawaii is an island state in the mid-Pacific Ocean. The state of Alaska is on the North American continent but is physically separated from the other mainland states by western Canadian.

The United States is governed under a federal system in which power is shared between the central national government and the individual states. The national, or federal, government, is organized in three branches. Its legislative branch contains the two houses of Congress; the executive branch is centered on the office of the presidency; and the judicial branch contains a hierarchical court system that reaches up to the Supreme Court. The three branches' headquarters, along with numerous government agencies, are located in the nation's capital, the city of Washington, which makes up the federal District of Columbia (D.C.).

The United States is a land of vast geological and geographical contrasts, with rugged mountains and extensive deserts, dense forests and high plains. Temperatures vary widely throughout the country, but are generally neither so cold nor so hot as to limit human activities. Generally moderate weather conditions have combined with great natural wealth (in the form of minerals, forests, fertile lands, and extensive waterways), as well as the creative endeavors of more than 250 million citizens to make the United States the world's premier economic power.

Past and Present. Many of the issues causing anxiety and concern at the end of the twentieth century had deep roots in American history. These issues included the challenge of assimilating minorities and new immigrants into the cultural and social mainstream, the proper role of religion in society, and the supposed decline of traditional moral values, as well as the associated issues of abortion, illicit drugs, and criminal violence. Other issues included disagreement over the proper scope and responsibilities of government, the purported failures of elected representatives, and the inefficiencies and abuses of government bureaucracies, as well as U.S. relations with the wider world. All these issues could be traced back to earlier eras.

Immigration. The United States is a nation of

immigrants. Even the ancestors of modern Native Americans immigrated from Asia long ago. The Spanish established the first European settlements in North America in the sixteenth century. However, it was Great Britain that provided the dominant cultural influence during the colonial era. The British introduced the English language, which became the language of the majority of the American population.

Through much of American history immigrants were welcomed cordially, reflecting a nation of vast lands and sparse population. There were, however, exceptions. Irish Catholics faced discrimination in the mid-nineteenth century, as did immigrants from Japan and China. During the 1920's the United States significantly reduced the number of immigrants it would accept.

During the 1960's U.S. immigration laws were revised, allowing additional legal immigration from Asia and elsewhere. By the 1990's, however, particularly in border states such as California and Texas, where many new immigrants were settling, there was often friction between the older and the newer immigrants. Two overlapping issues evolved from the newer immigration. First, although many recent immigrants were in the country legally, many were not. Many American citizens expressed the fear that their nation's borders were being overrun.

American resentment against illegal immigrants arose from two objections. First, they clearly violated U.S. immigration laws. Second, many were seen as taking jobs away from American citizens, raising U.S. taxes because of their dependence on government welfare and medical aid, or adding to the crime rate—a matter of central concern to many Americans. Politicians responded by passing laws that increased the policing powers of the federal Immigration and Naturalization Service. The federal government erected more imposing barriers to keep out illegal immigrants and hired more guards along the Mexican border. These programs had only partial success.

Americans also developed fears about the increasing numbers of legal immigrants. Descendants of earlier immigrants—typically those of European extraction—feared that new immigrants from Asia, Latin America, and the Middle East could not blend into a culture and society built on English and European roots.

Multiculturalism. The Civil Rights movement of the 1960's made that era one of the most crucial decades in U.S. history. The changes it produced contributed to increased public awareness of the contributions made by African Americans, Native Americans, women, and other long overlooked minorities to the American mosaic. These were valuable and necessary correctives to the traditional history of the country; American society was clearly the better for it.

However, these correctives to historical views were controversial. The newer immigration, both legal and illegal, compounded public concerns. Some people argued that a common core of what it was to be an American was being weakened, if not lost, and that a unified American society was in danger of giving way to disparate and antagonistic groups, each clamoring for its own rights, recognition, and redress—often at the expense of the whole.

Many people believed there was, or at least should be, something definable as "American." An increasingly multicultural America was a challenge, perhaps a danger. Some observers argued

Profile of the United States

Official name: United States of America
Independent since: 1776
Former colonial ruler: Great Britain
Location: North America, between Canada and Mexico
Area: 3,717,792 square miles
Capital: Washington, D.C.
Population: 270,958,700 (1997 est.)
Official language: (none)
Major religions: Protestantism; Roman Catholicism
Gross domestic product: $8.1109 trillion (1997 est.)
Major exports: machinery and transport equipment; chemicals and related parts; food and live animals; scientific and precision equipment
Military budget: $267.2 billion (1997 est.)
Military personnel: 1,447,600 (1997)

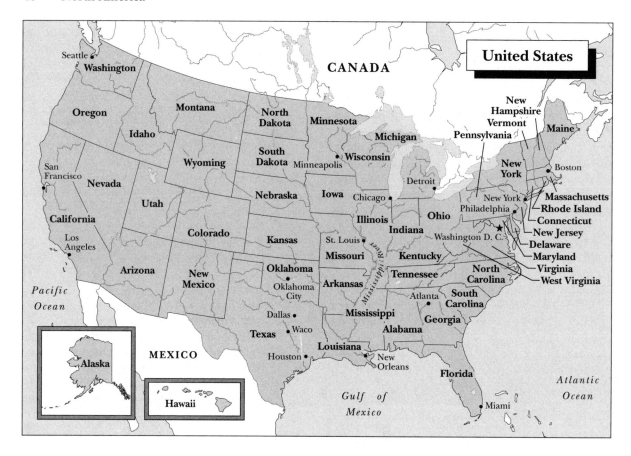

that instead of strengthening American society by giving equal recognition to the many cultures it comprised, multiculturalism might lead to a tribalized society, in which each group went its own way.

By the end of the 1990's there was a backlash against what was considered to be excessive attention to multiculturalism. Government programs, many of which had originated as a result of the upheavals of the 1960's, such as affirmative action and bilingual education, came under increasing attack. Affirmative action had initially been instituted during the 1960's to provide easier access to education, jobs, and government contracts for African Americans, who had been deprived of equal opportunity through slavery, legal segregation, and racism. In time, affirmative action was applied to all groups deemed to be "underrepresented minorities," including women.

Despite a multiplicity of languages spoken by the numerous new immigrants, in practice bilingual education meant the use of the Spanish language as part of the education process, primar-

ily because Hispanics were often the largest non-English-speaking minorities in individual communities.

The state of California is often seen as a bellwether of the nation's future. In the mid-1990's its electorate voted to end both affirmative action and bilingual education in public schools. These decisions caused considerable anguish and anger within minority and immigrant communities, whose members saw the majority's decision as a manifestation of cultural racism. Whether these differences would lead to violence was uncertain, but if the Black Power movement of the 1960's was any predictor, violent incidents were at least a possibility.

Native Americans. America's original minority group members were Native Americans, also known as American Indians. Both names are misleading: Indians are not from the Indies—which their original European discoverer, Christopher Columbus, thought he had discovered—and they are not, strictly speaking, "native" to North Amer-

United States

1492	(Oct. 12) Christopher Columbus reaches Western Hemisphere.
1607	First British settlement is established at Jamestown, Virginia.
1620	English Pilgrims settle at Plymouth, Massachusetts.
1776	(July 4) Continental Congress declares independence.
1783	Revolutionary War ends, and Britain recognizes U.S. independence.
1787	Constitution is drafted in Philadelphia.
1789	Constitution is adopted; George Washington becomes first president of new federal government.
1812-1814	United States fights war with Great Britain.
1820	Missouri Compromise establishes principle of parity between new slave and free states.
1828	Andrew Jackson's election inaugurates Age of Common Man.
1850	Compromise of 1850 permits expansion of slavery.
1860	Abraham Lincoln is elected president.
1861-1865	Civil War separates Northern and Southern states.
1898	United States defeats Spain in Spanish-American War and acquires Puerto Rico and the Philippines.
1901-1909	Theodore Roosevelt's presidency coincides with Progressive movement.
1913-1921	Woodrow Wilson is president.
1917	(Apr.) United States enters World War I against Germany.
1924	Congressional legislation makes all American Indians U.S. citizens.
1929	(Oct. 29) Stock market crash begins Great Depression.
1933	Inauguration of President Franklin D. Roosevelt launches New Deal.
1939	(Sept. 1) World War II begins in Europe.
1941	(Dec. 7) Japanese bombing of Pearl Harbor brings United States into world war.
1945	(Aug.) United States drops atomic bombs on Hiroshima and Nagasaki, Japan, ending war.
1949	Soviet Union blockades land access of Western nations to Berlin.
1949	(Apr.) United States helps found North Atlantic Treaty Organization (NATO).
1950-1953	United States fights in Korean War.
1954	(May 17) U.S. Supreme Court declares segregation in public schools illegal.
1955	Civil Rights movement begins in earnest with Montgomery, Alabama, bus boycott.
1962	(Oct.) United States confronts Soviet Union in Cuban Missile Crisis.
1963	César Chávez founds United Farm Worker Association.
1963	(Nov. 22) President John F. Kennedy is assassinated.
1964	Congress passes sweeping Civil Rights Act.

(continued)

1965	President Lyndon B. Johnson escalates war in Vietnam.
1968	Arab oil embargo.
1968	(Apr. 4) Martin Luther King, Jr., is assassinated.
1968	(June 6) Robert F. Kennedy is assassinated.
1968	(July) American Indian Movement is founded.
1973	(Jan. 22) U.S. Supreme Court's *Roe v. Wade* decision legalizes most abortions.
1974	(Aug. 9) President Richard M. Nixon resigns because of his involvement in Watergate coverup.
1975	(Mar. 29) Last U.S. troops leave Vietnam.
1979	(Nov. 4) Iranian students seize U.S. embassy in Tehran, taking many Americans hostage.
1980	(Nov.) Ronald Reagan is elected president.
1989	(Dec.) United States invades Panama and takes latter's president Manuel Noriega prisoner.
1991	(Jan.) United States leads international war against Iraq.
1991	(Dec. 31) Soviet Union's collapse ends Cold War.
1992	(Nov.) Bill Clinton is elected president.
1993	(Feb. 26) Terrorist bomb kills six people and injures a thousand more at New York's World Trade Center complex.
1993	(Apr. 19) Eighty people are killed in fire when federal law enforcement officials attempt to take Branch Davidian complex in Waco, Texas.
1995	(Apr. 19) Bombing of Oklahoma City federal building kills 169 people.
1998	(Jan. 8) Federal court convicts Ramzi Ahmed Yousef for his role in 1993 bombing of World Trade Center.
1998	(Jan. 29) Bomb kills security guard at Birmingham, Alabama, abortion clinic.
1998	(June 6) New York State invokes death penalty for first time since reauthorizing it in 1995.
1998	(Aug. 7) Terrorist bombs explode next to U.S. embassy buildings in Kenya and Tanzania.
1998	(Aug. 20) U.S. warplanes fire missiles at suspected terrorist sites in Afghanistan and Sudan.
1998	(Aug. 27) Suspects in bombings of U.S. embassies in East Africa are arraigned in New York.
1998	(Sept. 21) Hundreds of U.S. farmers block North Dakota rail line at Canadian border as part of growing U.S. protests again rising imports of Canadian agricultural products.
1998	(Oct. 7) Federal grand jury in New York City indicts four suspects connected with August bombings of U.S. embassies in East Africa.
1998	(July 17) United States opposes U.N. General Assembly vote in favor of treaty to create permanent war-crimes tribunal.
1998	(Nov. 3) Democratic Party scores gains in House of Representatives and holds even in Senate and in gubernatorial elections, despite Republican Party efforts to discredit President Clinton in midterm elections.
1998	(Nov. 4) Federal grand jury in New York City indicts Osama bin Laden, a Saudi Arabian millionaire, charging him with responsibility in August bombing attacks on U.S. embassies in Kenya and Tanzania.

1998	(Nov. 6) House Speak Newt Gingrich announces his resignation from Congress after Republican Party's unexpected losses in national elections.
1998	(Dec. 19) House of Representatives votes two articles of impeachment against President Clinton, charging him with committing perjury and obstructing justice.
1999	(Jan. 7) Clinton's impeachment trial opens in Senate; (Feb. 12) Senate votes to acquit Clinton.
1999	(Apr.-July) U.S. forces lead NATO air attacks on Yugoslavia military positions until Slobodan Milosevic's government agrees to withdraw from Kosovo province.
1999	(May 7) U.S. missile hits Chinese embassy in Belgrade, Yugoslavia, causing major rift in U.S.-China relations.

ica. Like all "Americans," Native Americans originally came from somewhere else.

For much of American history, Native Americans were perceived as savages who should either be made to accept Christianity and European culture or be eliminated through war, disease, or forced expulsion. In the nineteenth century, many Native American communities were driven across the Mississippi River into federal lands known as Indian Territory, part of the later state of Oklahoma.

The federal government's general policy was to treat Native American communities as sovereign peoples, or nations. Treaties established formal relationships between the individual tribes and the U.S. government. Almost all of the treaties were one-sided. Eventually most Indian nations were driven onto reservations, lands not deemed valuable by the country's new majority—Americans of European descent. Eventually, approximately 250 reservations were scattered throughout the United States. In 1924 those Native Americans who were not already U.S. citizens were granted citizenship, ending a long piece-meal process of incorporating Indians into the American mainstream. At the same time, however, the change created something akin to dual citizenship for many Native Americans.

During the 1960's and 1970's, Native Americans joined the wider Civil Rights movement by demanding recognition of their special problems and redress. Violence occasionally resulted from confrontations between Native American activists and government authorities over such issues as titles to land, broken treaty promises, and demands for

change, particularly in the upper Midwest and up-state New York.

In the Northwest, Native Americans defied state and federal authorities by pressing their historical right to fish in federally protected areas that had been established for conservation purposes. During the 1990's, some tribes came into conflict with the state and federal government over demands that they had the right, as sovereign nations, to establish unrestricted gambling casinos that violated state and federal gaming laws.

There also was discord among Native Americans themselves, particularly in the development of their limited reservation lands. Conflicts arose over whether it was permissible to use reservation lands to enrich individual Indians, while only incidently enriching tribes as a whole, through mining or other activities. Some Indian activists argued that tribal lands should remain relatively undeveloped to help preserve traditional cultures under siege. Occasionally, violence arose among factions.

After centuries of Native American degradation, deprivation, exploitation, and poverty, there was as dramatic reversal in public perceptions of Native Americans as moral victims, rather than savages. Nevertheless, most Americans remained relatively unconcerned about continued Native American problems. In the late 1990's it seemed unlikely that Indian demands, or even occasional threats, would seriously disrupt the general national tranquility.

Drugs. American fears of foreign immigration were closely tied to growing problems relating to illegal drugs, such as marijuana, cocaine, and heroin. The use and sale of illegal drugs were central public concerns because of their connection to issues of crime and welfare dependency. Drug use also tied into the broader public issue of societal moral decline.

Mind-altering drugs of various types have long been part of civilization. Through history different societies and groups have banned some drugs and accepted others, depending upon changing cultural contexts. In the United States, for example, consumption of alcoholic beverages has generally been legal and considered socially acceptable, except during the era of federal Prohibition during the 1920's. Smoking tobacco was also long accepted, and smokers were often considered icons of maturity and sophistication. However, although smoking tobacco has remained legal, it was losing public acceptance by the 1990's. California again led the way in the United States by outlawing smoking in all restaurants and bars.

Many other drugs, however, remained largely outside the legal pale for most Americans. The use of substances such as marijuana, cocaine, and heroin has been associated in the public mind with African Americans, jazz music, and antisocial behavior in general. The 1960's was a watershed era for changing public perceptions of drug use. During that decade many people—particularly young members of the so-called "counterculture"—used recreational drugs. Drug use spread from the inner city to suburbs and college campuses.

By the end of the century various illegal drugs had their ups and downs. Lysergic acid diethylamide (LSD) went out of fashion, but use of methamphetamines became increasingly popular. As cocaine came in, marijuana dropped, then increased in popularity. As fashions changed, however, illegal drug use in various forms continued. There were growing fears that drug use was increasing among the very young, even those in grade school.

The profitability of the drug trade was linked to both consumption and production. Antidrug policies attempted to attack both foreign suppliers and domestic users. In general, drug users were arrested and incarcerated. Sale and distribution of illegal drugs had a marked impact on the level of crime and violence within the United States. However, most of the violence it generated was confined to the individuals and gangs directly involved in the trade.

By the late 1990's so many persons had been jailed for drug possession and dealing in the United States that one clear consequence of the drug problem was a major increase in prisons and associated costs. Some critics of American antidrug policies have argued for the legalization, or at least decriminalization, of so-called "soft" drugs, such as marijuana.

Many of the illegal drugs consumed in the United States—particularly cocaine and marijuana—are produced in Latin America. The United States government has tried working with numerous Latin American governments to destroy and to cut off the entry of illegal drugs, but results have been less than satisfactory. Indeed, antidrug campaigns have possibly even contributed to the chronic social and political destabilization of Colombia and other Latin American nations, while increasing U.S. tensions with Mexico.

Because many drugs reaching the United States have passed through Mexico, the U.S. government has constantly encouraged—demanded—Mexican authorities do more to stop the traffic. Strained relations between the two nations took a turn for the worse in 1998. Under the code name "Casablanca," the U.S. Treasury Department entrapped a number of Mexican financial institutions, accusing of them laundering drug money. Because neither the U.S. State Department nor the Mexican government was told about the Treasury Department operation beforehand, the government of Mexico was most distressed.

At the end of the twentieth century illegal drug use was a great concern to the wider public and to most elected politicians. Much of the violent crime in the United States was associated with illegal drugs; however, the financial costs associated with illegal substances were probably less than those associated with such legal drugs as nicotine and alcohol.

Whether the danger to American society of illegal drugs was increasing or decreasing in the late 1990's was difficult to ascertain. Nevertheless, the issue remained rooted in the public consciousness, associated with both societal decline and acts of violence.

Religion and Moral Decline. Religion and traditional Judeo-Christian morality have played a central role in American history. Even at the end of the twentieth century many Americans continued to describe themselves as religious believers—if not always practitioners. Commentators and pundits frequently noted that among the world's major industrial nations, the people of the United States seemed to be the most serious about religion.

At the same time, a number of Americans feared that the country was straying from its Judeo-Christian religious roots. They also feared that fewer and fewer Americans were believers, much less worshipers. As a consequence, many feared that the nation's "one nation under God" principle was in the process of being lost.

Modern concern about religion, like other concerns, was partially rooted in the past. Religion in America has historically meant Protestant Christianity, even though Jews were among the earliest colonists and the country's former Spanish and French territories have long been home to many Roman Catholics. Paradoxically, many of the nation's original Founders—such as Thomas Jefferson and Benjamin Franklin—were not particularly religious, at least not by orthodox standards.

The concept of the separation of church from state was firmly established in the United States by the early nineteenth century. Nevertheless, the United States was largely a Protestant Christian country well into the twentieth century. Nineteenth century Irish and German Roman Catholic immigrants faced strong discrimination, as did Jewish immigrants in the early twentieth century. However, by the end of the twentieth century many other religions—particularly Islam—were also represented in American society. The growing cacophony among so many competing religions caused uncertainty for some Americans who feared their country was becoming a land of strangers.

The religious experience in the United States has taken on varied forms. These have included various manifestations of Christian Fundamentalism. By the late twentieth century manifestations of Christian Fundamentalism could be found in all regions of the country, particularly in rural areas and in the South. The so-called "old time religion" often remained a brake on multicultural modernity—not only in theological matters, but in social, moral, and familial issues.

The U.S. role as an international police force holds out a potential for trouble at home. Here Southern Californians express their opposition to the government of Iraq in late 1998. (Michele Burgess)

Abortion. In the last quarter of the twentieth century the issue of abortion became a major flashpoint for religious conservatives. Legalized in 1973 by the U.S. Supreme Court's *Roe v. Wade* decision, the right of a woman to chose to have an abortion became a benchmark in the women's movement. Although public opinion polls consistently indicated that a significant majority of Americans supported abortion rights, a sizable minority did not, objecting on theological and moral grounds.

Coinciding with religious conservativism, opposition to abortion was strongest in rural areas and in the South. It was also opposed by many Republican Party office holders, whose positions reflected the wishes of their constituents. In response to increasing pressure, much of it from the Religious Right, new restrictions were being placed on abortions for minors during the 1990's, and late-term abortions were coming increasingly under attack.

Resolution of such a volatile issue as abortion was seemingly impossible. The theological and accompanying moral beliefs of opponents to abortion made compromise improbable. For many in the other camp abortion was seen as a symbol for feminine rights and women's liberation. Opposition to abortion has generally been peaceful, if often strident. However, occasional acts of violence, planned and unplanned, have occurred. For example, in 1998, the bombing of an abortion clinic in Alabama sparked a long search for the perpetrator. In addition to abortion clinic bombings, some antiabortion activists drenched abortion clinics in foul-smelling acid, forcing them to close down temporarily.

Crises of Political Leadership. Another lasting legacy of the 1960's that continued to resonate through the years was a loss of public respect for politicians and the political process. President John F. Kennedy's numerous sexual liaisons came to light only in later years. Nevertheless, they inflicted damage to American faith in the president as moral leader. This faith was even more seriously eroded during President Bill Clinton's second term, when he faced impeachment and the humiliating official and public scrutiny into his sexual misbehavior.

During the late 1960's President Lyndon B. Johnson's Vietnam War policy, with its often less-than-forthright explanations and justifications, alienated many Americans, especially the young. The presidency of Richard M. Nixon was seriously tarnished by his involvement in the Watergate Scandal—the result of the failed cover-up of an inept break-in at the Democratic Party's headquarters in the Watergate building during his 1972 election campaign. Several senior members of his administration went to jail and Nixon himself was forced to resign to avoid impeachment and possible removal from office. Nixon's successor, Gerald Ford, then compromised his own administration by too quickly pardoning Nixon.

Ford was defeated by Jimmy Carter in the 1976 presidential election. Carter was perceived by some as bumbling and incompetent, particularly in economic matters and in his Middle East policies. President Ronald Reagan followed Carter and was credited with restoring positive leadership qualities to the office, but his second term was burdened by increasing federal deficits and the so-called Iran-Contra scandal, which involved charges of illegal arms deals in the Middle East and Central America.

As leader of the so-called Free World, Reagan's successor, George Bush, presided over the fall of Germany's Berlin Wall, the symbolic event which signified the end of the Cold War. He also led an allied coalition to victory over Iraq in the Persian Gulf War. However, the defeated Iraqi leader, Saddam Hussein, held on to power while Bush's credibility at home was lessened when he raised federal taxes after having earlier pledged not to do so.

In 1992 Bill Clinton was elected in reaction to Bush's perceived failures, but Clinton frequently vacillated over specific policies. Several of his senior advisors were indicted for corruption, and Clinton's own reputation for honesty and morality was tainted because of numerous accusations of sexual misconduct. As a result, Clinton was impeached by the House of Representatives on December 19, 1998. His Senate trial resulted in an acquittal on February 12, 1999, and he was not removed from office. While most Americans agreed that the president had displayed poor moral judgement in his personal life, they did not believe that he had at any time endangered the security of the nation in doing so. Clinton's impeachment, however, stimulated much public discussion about the perceived moral degradation of American values.

Meanwhile, the federal Congress had also suffered a loss of public esteem. Whether Congress was under the control of the Democrats, as it was through the decades following the Great Depression of the 1930's, or under the Republicans, who took control in 1994, the public's attitude was that its members were corrupt. Many Americans believed that members of Congress focused mainly on their own reelection or were incompetent to deal with the real issues facing the country.

Public distrust of government activism was symbolized by the election of Ronald Reagan, by Bill Clinton's claim that he was a "New Democrat," by the Republican takeover of Congress in 1994, and by the partisan voting that took place during Clinton's impeachment. For many Americans Franklin D. Roosevelt's New Deal revolution of the 1930's and the promises of Lyndon B. Johnson's Great Society of the 1960's no longer seemed as relevant as they had in the past.

Distrust of government and politicians also extended to the state and local levels. In some states, such as California, voters endorsed term limits in reaction to the so-called career politicians and their failures. Many voters abandoned the major political parties, effectively weakening the two-party political system which had endured since the beginning of the republic. Some people saw the decline of major parties as a positive development, but others predicted that it boded the breakup of the political consensus under which America had become the world's foremost nation. Perhaps the greatest danger to American society and American democracy was not a revolution, violent or otherwise, but growing cynicism toward, and alienation from, the political process.

Reaction on the Right. Through much of the twentieth century, and particularly since the New Deal of the 1930's, political liberalism was the dominant ideology in America, and government, particularly the federal government, was the chosen vehicle for improving society through various government programs. This belief was particularly held by members of the Democratic Party, which controlled Congress from Franklin D. Roosevelt's first administration to 1994 (except briefly in the early 1950's).

Even a Republican such as Richard Nixon made use of the federal government in pushing social and economic reform, such as the creation of the Environmental Protection Agency and instituting wage and price controls. However, by the 1980's liberalism was no longer unchallenged. The winds of change symbolically began with Senator Barry Goldwater's 1964 presidential candidacy, but the conservative revival was mainly associated with Ronald Reagan. By the end of the century both major political parties had turned to the political right, the Republicans more than the Democrats.

The terms "conservative" or "the Right" have many meanings. The Republican Party contains both economic and social conservatives. Advocates of conservatism have wanted to reduce the scope and size of government by limiting government activity and involvement in the economy. Conservatives want to reduce taxes and allow greater opportunities for private initiative. Social conservatives have been oriented toward what were often called "family values." To them, the most important issues confronting the country are abortion, higher divorce rates, increased crime (especially by juveniles), and a general turning away from what has been considered the traditional religious morality which has supposedly made America the nation it is.

A few turned their backs on the political process entirely. Throughout American history there have been individuals and groups who have refused to operate comfortably within the prevailing consensus: During the 1840's David Henry Thoreau went to jail rather than pay taxes to support what he considered to be an unjust war with Mexico. Members of the Church of Jesus Christ of Latter-day Saints (Mormons) moved outside of what was then the territorial United States to pursue their religious goals. Proslavery southerners attempted forcibly to secede from the Union. Vigilantism was common in the west in the late nineteenth century. Civil rights advocates during the 1950's and 1960's refused to obey what they considered unjust laws.

If antigovernment activities can be pinpointed on a political spectrum, then it might be argued that opponents of the Vietnam War during the late 1960's and early 1970's who burned their draft cards and battled police in the streets or radical conservationists who spiked redwood trees and demolished power transmission lines were on the Left. Theodore Kaczynski, the so-called Unabomber, who was arrested in 1996 and later sentenced to life in prison for sending lethal bombs through the mail, perversely represented this tradition. However, at the end of the twentieth century this rejection of the government and the majority soci-

Neo-Nazis march through Coeur d'Alene, Idaho, in July, 1998, ignoring the jeers of antiracists lining the streets. (AP/Wide World Photos)

ety became particularly associated with the radical right.

During the 1990's armed militia groups were to be found in various parts of the United States—especially in rural areas of the South, West, and Northwest. They opposed federal tax policy and government environmental protection regulations. Some of them feared their right to keep guns and other weapons might be restricted. Others were simply opposed to *any* government control or oversight in their lives. One amorphous militia movement known as the Freemen circumvented the monetary system by issuing their own "comptroller warrants" and placing liens against the property of those whom they perceived as enemies.

A group of Freemen in Montana held off federal agents for eighty-one days in 1996 before surrendering; several were later convicted of racketeer-

ing. In 1998 members of a secessionist group known as the Republic of Texas were arrested and charged with scheming to assassinate President Clinton through the bizarre technique of using a cigarette lighter modified to shoot cactus needles coated with such toxins as anthrax or HIV.

Many militia groups were inspired by racist attitudes. The Ku Klux Klan, which had begun in the South after the Civil War, was still a lingering presence, though less visible than in the past. Newer white supremacy groups, such as the Aryan Nations, who in small numbers marched to accompanying jeers in Coeur d'Alene, Idaho, and the Aryan Brotherhood, a faction found in prisons, sometimes resorted to verbal and physical violence. In 1998, thirty years after the death of Martin Luther King, Jr., three young white men brutally murdered an African American in the small Texas town of

Jarvis by dragging him behind a pickup truck. America's history of racial violence had not yet ended.

Other extremist groups followed religious visions. These included David Koresh's Branch Davidians in Waco, Texas, whose compound was destroyed with considerable loss of life in a confrontation with federal authorities in 1993. Another group was a small sect called Heaven's Gate, whose members committed group suicide in Southern California in early 1997. They hoped to achieve the "Next Level," a transcendent state among extra-terrestrial aliens, a New Age religious phenomenon. The mass suicides brought back references to the 1978 tragedy of the Reverend Jim Jones and Jonestown, Guyana, where hundreds of

cultists also committed suicide. By the end of the 1990's, many Americans predicted that other forms of religious extremism would emerge, perhaps to be accompanied by violence and death.

Whatever the motives and concerns of members of those groups, weapons and violence frequently played a role in their actions. An example was a shooting that took place at Idaho's Ruby Ridge in 1992, when several people, including a small child, died. Even more infamous was the bombing of a federal office building in Oklahoma City in 1995. In that incident 169 persons, including many young children, lost their lives. Timothy McVeigh and an accomplice were later convicted of perpetrating the crime, and McVeigh was sentenced to death.

Memorial service held in front of Oklahoma City's Alfred P. Murrah Federal Building sixteen days after it was destroyed by a terrorist bomb on April 19, 1995. (AP/Wide World Photos)

Police and emergency vehicles line up in front of New York City's World Trade Center after a bomb exploded in an underground parking garage on February 26, 1993. (AP/Wide World Photos)

The gun was becoming a divisive symbol in American society, setting those who defended firearms as constitutionally guaranteed and necessary for survival in a damaged society against those who believed that guns were among the primary causes of that damage.

International Insecurity. The Berlin Wall raised by the communist regime of East Germany in 1961 to keep its citizens from escaping to the capitalist West became the most notorious symbol of the Cold War. That wall came down in 1989, and the Soviet Union collapsed two years later. In a climate of near-euphoria, expressions of great hopes and optimism throughout the Western world became common, and a New World Order was envisioned.

The Cold War had ended in a decisive victory for the United States, the West, liberal democracy, and for market-oriented capitalism. Many predicted that a stable and progressive world would be the result, an "end of history," at least history as defined by the clashing of social and political ideologies, as one writer expressed it.

In retrospect, there was much naïve optimism about the world's future. During the 1990's the world remained a difficult place—as American involvement in the Middle East's Persian Gulf War, as well as conflicts in Haiti, Bosnia, Somalia, and elsewhere indicated. The Cold War's old "iron curtain" may have fallen, but in the interdependent world of the late twentieth century it was no longer possible for the United States to retreat behind the vast oceans and distances as many Americans probably wished.

The 1993 bombing of New York City's World Trade Center by Islamic fundamentalists from the Middle East established the vulnerability of Americans, even at home within the United States.

Abroad, terrorist violence was more than just a possibility. In August, 1998, several hundred persons died in coordinated bombings of the American embassies in the East African nations of Kenya and Tanzania. A terrorist camp in Afghanistan and a supposed chemical weapons factory in Sudan were quickly targeted by American missiles.

Many commentators predicted that international terrorism would only increase in future years, possibly through the actions of rogue nations such as Iraq, Iran, or North Korea. Perhaps equally dangerous were the actions of individuals or small, ideologically driven groups using nuclear or biological weapons—such as had occurred in Japan.

As the twentieth century drew to a close, the threat of nuclear warfare was renewed when both India and its archrival, Pakistan, successfully tested nuclear weapons. Major new international conflicts similar to the century's two world wars or the Cold War seemed unlikely. The ideologies of fascism and communism had become marginalized. Nevertheless, there remained other causes that might yet drive peoples into acts of great violence. In an increasingly interconnected world, even the United States was not immune.

Conclusion. In the two centuries since its founding the United States has become the world's leading power. Its economy is the most productive, its political system—though imperfect—is stable, and it generally guarantees equal rights for all its citizens. Few places on the globe enjoy greater freedoms, opportunities, or prosperity. However, the promises of the nation's founding document, the 1776 Declaration of Independence, remain incompletely fulfilled. Despite the successes of the Civil Rights movement, racism and discrimination still continued. The nation's poor still suffer, not only economically but also from greater crime, more disease, and substandard educational opportunities. Many Americans have become disaffected, and a few have resorted to violence in their anger and frustration. Although the United States is the world's only superpower, it is no less vulnerable than any nation to human-induced terrorism and to environmental disasters.

Nevertheless, the United States remains like a city on a hill—as a Puritan divine claimed three hundred years ago. Compared to the crises of many other nations, those faced by America might be considered minimal. It remains a nation which, despite many anxieties and concerns, is privileged beyond the dreams and hopes of most others.

Eugene Larson

For Further Study

Among many fine narrative histories of the United States are *A Nation of Nations* (1990) by James West Davidson and others, and *The American Promise* (1998) by James L. Roark and others. The excellent *Oxford History of the United States* includes three volumes that stand out for their coverage of crucial periods of the nation's history: Robert Middlekauff's *The Glorious Cause: The American Revolution, 1763-1789* (1982), James M. McPherson's *Battle Cry of Freedom: The Civil War Era* (1988), and James T. Patterson's *Grand Expectations: The United States, 1945-1974* (1996). *The Dictionary of American History* (rev. ed. 1961) is a multivolume reference source that includes summaries of major events of the nation's past. Statistical information can be obtained from *Historical Statistics of the United States, Colonial Times to 1970* (1975) and *Statistical Abstract of the United States, 1996* (1996).

For the more recent past, William L. O'Neill's *Coming Apart: An Informal History of America in the 1960's* (1971), and George C. Herring's *America's Longest War: The United States and Vietnam, 1950-1975* (1986) are excellent. Gary Wills, *Reagan's America: Innocents at Home* (1987) is provocative. Sanford J. Unger, *Fresh Blood: The New American Immigrants* (1995) discusses recent immigration, and the rise of the Right is covered in Dan Balz and Ronald Brownstein, *Storming the Gates: Protest Politics and the Republican Revival* (1996), and in Kevin Phillips, *Boiling Point: Democrats, Republicans and the Decline of the Middle Class Prosperity* (1993). For an optimistic prediction about the post-Cold War world, see Francis Fukuyama, *The End of History and the Last Man* (1992). For a much broader perspective, a brilliant interpretation of the world's winners and losers is David S. Landes, *The Wealth and Poverty of Nations* (1998).

Extensive resources are available on the Web. Among them are "American Memory: Historical Collection from the National Digital Library Program" (http://rs6.loc.gov/amhome. html) and "Historical Text Archive" (http://www.msstate.edu/Archives/History).

Caribbean

From the Bahaman beach where Christopher Columbus first landed in 1492 to Pope John Paul II's visit to communist Cuba in 1998, the Caribbean region has had a long and tumultuous history that belies its sleepy tropical image. After its islands were claimed by European nations, they saw their original peoples exterminated, carried the burden of slavery and uprisings, and threw off colonial rule—only to find that political freedom sometimes only brought its dictators closer to home. The massive influx of African slaves during the seventeenth and eighteenth centuries forever changed the composition of the population, giving the region a rich cultural tradition that is at once like and unlike anything else in the world. Tragically, ongoing political and ethnic upheaval is also a part of that legacy.

Articles in This Section

The Caribbean region is a large branch of the North Atlantic Ocean separating North and South America that is enclosed by Central America in the west and the Antilles Islands on the east. Its numerous islands, also historically known as the West Indies, are the upper tips of a submerged chain of volcanic mountains that form a two-thousand-mile-long breakwater that separates the Caribbean from the main part of the Atlantic.

The region contains thirteen independent and mostly tiny nations: Antigua and Barbuda, the Bahamas, Barbados, Cuba, Dominica, Dominican Republic, Grenada, Haiti, Jamaica, St. Kitts and Nevis, St. Lucia, St. Vincent and the Grenadines, and Trinidad and Tobago. There are also thirteen dependencies—territories ruled by other countries. These include Guadeloupe and Martinique (administered by France); Aruba, Curaçao, and Netherlands Antilles (administered by the Netherlands); British Virgin Islands, Cayman Islands, Montserrat, and Turks and Caicos Islands (administered by Great Britain); and Navassa Island and Puerto Rico (administered by the United States).

Exploration and Colonization. The Caribbean Islands were the first areas of the Western Hemisphere, or New World, found and permanently colonized by European explorers. In the five centuries following Columbus's first voyage, Denmark, Great Britain, France, Spain, Portugal, the Netherlands, and the United States have all claimed Caribbean islands. Centuries of colonization have had a distinctive impact on the ethnic composition of the islands. The surviving remnants of the islands' original peoples mixed with European settlers and slaves imported from Africa to create diverse cultures.

By 1993 estimates, more than 60 percent of the people living in the Caribbean are of black African or mixed African and European descent. Thirty-five percent are European. Most of these are people of Spanish descent who live in Cuba, the Dominican Republic, and Puerto Rico. The remaining 5 percent are of East Asian descent. Most of them live in Trinidad and Tobago. The peoples of Haiti and the remaining islands are predominantly of African descent.

Languages spoken in the Caribbean vary as much as the cultures. Although English is the re-

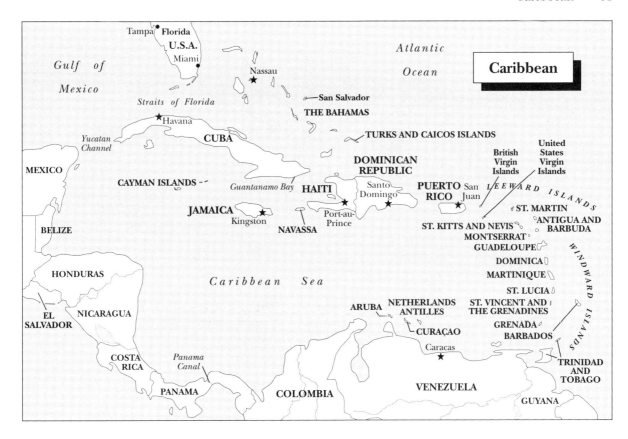

gion's predominant tongue, the people of Cuba, Haiti, and a few other countries continue to speak the Spanish and French of their early colonizers. In addition, many islanders speak regional dialects that linguists call patois. This term was originally applied to the bastardized French spoken by colonized peoples, but it has come to apply to any local blend of native and imported languages.

Caribbean identity remains a problem. The region and its islands are known by a variety of names. The most common name for the region, the West Indies, was coined by Columbus, who believed he had discovered islands off the coast of India. In France and Spain, the islands were called Antilles. Variants on this name have included the Greater Antilles (the large islands of Cuba, Jamaica, Hispaniola, and Puerto Rico in the west of the chain) and the Lesser Antilles (the smaller islands to the east). Some of them are also known as the French Antilles and the Netherlands Antilles.

The Lesser Antilles (also known as the Caribbees) are divided into Windward Islands and Leeward Islands. "Windward" and "Leeward" refer to

the position of the islands relative to the northeast trade winds, with the Windward Islands receiving the brunt of the trade winds in the east, and the Leewards situated at a somewhat more sheltered position to the west.

Early History. Before 1492 two main ethnic groups populated most of the Caribbean islands: Arawaks and Caribs. They are believed to have originated in the northern regions of South America. Barbados and many other, smaller islands were not permanently inhabited by anyone at that time. Estimates of the Caribbean's late fifteenth century population vary greatly, but it is generally accepted that there may have been between one million and five million people in the region when Columbus arrived.

Most native Caribbean peoples lived on the large island, called Hispaniola by Spanish explorers, that is divided between Haiti and the Dominican Republic. Arawaks cultivated crops using the slash-and-burn method that is still responsible for much of the environmental degradation in the region. The Caribs were a more warlike people.

The few descendants of Caribs who resisted European assimilation now live on a reservation in Dominica.

Following the arrival of Columbus, the Caribbean became the launching point for the European expansion into the North and South American continents. By the middle of the sixteenth century, Spain's discovery of Mexico and Peru, a smallpox epidemic, the ravages of Dutch English and French pirates, and the destructive power of earthquakes had combined to reduce the native population of the Caribbean islands to about 30,000 people.

As the European colonies expanded, they became important sources of revenue for their home countries. Plantation agriculture in the islands generated great wealth from its production and sale of crops such as sugar, cotton, and tobacco. Planta-

Statue of Christopher Columbus in Santo Domingo, the capital of the Dominican Republic. (Tim Gibson)

tion agriculture needed large numbers of workers, so vast numbers of Africans were imported to the Caribbean as slaves during the eighteenth century. Their arrive made white Europeans an increasingly small minority. After Great Britain abolished slavery through its empire during the 1830's, the Caribbean colonies turned to importing indentured workers from India, China, and the East Indies. These new arrivals added even greater diversity to the hybrid culture of the islands.

Independence. The largest and most heavily populated Caribbean islands were the first to shed their European rulers. France's richest Caribbean colony, St. Domingue, occupied the western portion of the island of Hispaniola. It was the world's leading sugar producer during the mid-eighteenth century. However, its wealth came at the expense of exploiting a captive workforce. More than a million slaves in the colony died from oppressive working conditions and disease during that same time.

The brutal conditions on St. Domingue provoked a successful slave uprising led by Pierre Toussaint L'Ouverture and Jean-Jacques Dessalines in 1804. Afterward St. Domingue reverted to its original Arawak name, Haiti, when it became the second independent nation (after the United States) in the Western Hemisphere, as well as the world's first black-ruled republic.

The new nation of Haiti almost immediately tried to conquer the entire island of Hispaniola by overrunning the Spanish colony in the eastern portion of the island. Haiti succeeded in 1822. Ironically, this meant that when the Dominican Republic declared independence in 1844, it did so not from a European overlord, but from its Caribbean neighbor.

Independence for the island of Cuba came much later, as a result of the Spanish-American War of 1898, when Cuban rebels sided with the United States against Spain. After defeating Spain, U.S. forces occupied the island until 1902, when Cuba became an independent nation. The Platt Amendment to the Treaty of Paris (which had ended the war in December, 1898) gave the United States continuing authority to intervene in Cuban affairs, which it did several times over the next twenty years. Although U.S. president Franklin D. Roosevelt repealed the Platt Amendment in 1934, the

Caribbean

1492	(Oct.) Christopher Columbus lands on Caribbean islands, which he claims for Spain.
1697	Treaty of Ryswick grants Haiti to France.
1717	Great Britain assumes military and civil control of Bahamas.
1763	St. Vincent is taken by the British.
1789	French Revolution inspires slave revolt in Haiti.
1797	Turks and Caicos Islands come under jurisdiction of Bahaman government.
1804	Haitian slaves revolt; Jean Jacque Dessalines proclaims Haitian independence.
1814	Great Britain takes possession of St. Lucia.
1822	Haiti takes control of neighboring Santo Domingo.
1834	Slavery is abolished in British colonies.
1844	Dominican Republic declares its independence from Haiti.
1860	Barbuda is annexed to Antigua.
1888	Trinidad and Tobago are united as a British Crown Colony.
1898	United States defeats Spain in Spanish-American War and takes possession of Puerto Rico.
1902	Cuba gains independence after four years of U.S. occupation.
1917	Puerto Ricans are made U.S. citizens.
1948	(Apr. 30) Organization of American States (OAS) is formed.
1952	Puerto Rico becomes self-governing commonwealth of United States.
1954	Batista is reelected president of Cuba in questionable election.
1957	François Duvalier ("Papa Doc") begins rule by decree in Haiti.
1958	Federation of West Indies is established by Great Britain.
1959	Fidel Castro takes control of Cuban government.
1960	Castro declares Cuba a socialist country.
1961	United States severs diplomatic relations with Cuba.
1961	U.S.-backed Cuban exiles attempt invasion at Cuba's Bay of Pigs.
1961	Jamaica and Trinidad and Tobago withdraw from Federation of West Indies.
1962	Jamaica and Trinidad and Tobago become independent.
1962	Great Britain limits immigration from its Caribbean colonies.
1962	(Oct.) United States and Soviet Union face off in Cuban Missile Crisis.
1966	Barbados gains independence from Great Britain.
1968	Caribbean Free Trade Area (CARIFTA) is established.
1969	Anguilla rebels against St. Kitts and Nevis and becomes British dependency.
1971	Haitian president Duvalier dies and is succeeded by his son, Jean-Claude ("Baby Doc").

(continued)

1973	Caribbean Community and Common Market (CARICOM) replaces CARIFTA.
1973	(July 10) Bahamas become independent.
1974	(Feb. 7) Grenada becomes independent.
1978	(Nov. 3) Dominica becomes independent.
1979	Coup installs Marxist government in Grenada.
1979	(Feb. 22) St. Lucia becomes independent.
1979	(Oct. 27) St. Vincent and the Grenadines become independent.
1981	Antigua and Barbuda gain independence from Great Britain.
1983	St. Kitts and Nevis gain independence from Great Britain.
1983	United States invades Grenada, accompanied by token forces from other Caribbean nations.
1986	President Jean-Claude Duvalier flees Haiti.
1990	Jean-Bertrand Aristide wins presidential election in Haiti.
1991	Aristide goes into exile following coup.
1993	Puerto Rican referendum maintains U.S. commonwealth status.
1994	Aristide returns to power in Haiti with U.S. aid.
1995	First meeting of Association of Caribbean States is held.
1996	U.S. Maritime and Overflight Agreement goes into effect.
1996	President Clinton signs Cuban Liberty and Democracy Act (Helms-Burton Act).
1997	Eruption of Soufriere Hills volcano in Montserrat devastates two-thirds of island.
1998	Pope John Paul II visits Cuba.
1998	(July-Aug.) Cuban president Fidel Castro pays state visits to Jamaica, Barbados, Grenada, and Dominican Republic.
1998	(Sept.) Hurricane Georges devastates Caribbean region from Leeward Islands to Gulf Coast of United States, hitting Hispaniola especially hard.
1999	(Jan. 11) Haitian president Rene Preval announces his intention to rule by decree in attempt to break stalemate with parliament.
1999	(Jan. 18) New National Party wins all fifteen parliamentary seats in Grenada elections, and Keith Mitchell remains prime minister.
1999	(Jan. 20) Barbados Labour Party wins largest majority in national history, and Prime Minister Owen Arthur continues to hold his post.

United States afterward continued to maintain a large naval base in Guantanamo Bay, on the eastern tip of the island.

Nationalism in the British colonies dates back to the 1938 labor riots in Jamaica and the eastern Caribbean, which led to the establishment of self-government and voting rights throughout the region during the next two decades. Jamaica became fully independent in 1962, as did Trinidad and Tobago (neighboring islands united in one country). Barbados followed in 1966. The Bahamas progressed to internal self-rule under the British during the 1960's and then to independence in 1973. By the late 1960's, six more colonies became "associated states" of Great Britain, which meant they were internally self-governing in all matters except defense and foreign affairs. These six colonies became independent shortly thereafter: Grenada (1974), Dominica (1978), St. Lucia (1979), St. Vincent and the Grenadines (1979), Antigua and Barbuda (1981), and St. Kitts and Nevis (1983).

In 1998 five official British dependent territories remained in the Caribbean region: Anguilla, the Cayman Islands, the British Virgin islands, Montserrat, and the Turks and Caicos Islands. Bermuda, a small island group north of the Caribbean, also remained a British dependency.

Despite winning independence, most former Caribbean colonies have elected to keep the British monarch their official head of state. In these nations, the British queen is represented by governor generals, who open the local parliaments, sign legislation, and formalize government decisions on the advice of the local prime ministers. In 1998, however, Barbados became the first former British colony in the Caribbean to abolish its connection with the British monarchy. Jamaica was expected to follow its example. For the remainder of the nations, however, maintaining a connection with the British monarchy has been an important means of remaining culturally distinct from the nearby United States.

The Dependencies. The Netherlands Antilles and Aruba are internally self-governing states, but they rely on the Dutch for defense and foreign affairs. In 1986 Aruba withdrew from the Netherlands Antilles to become an autonomous member of the Kingdom of the Netherlands. Both the Netherlands Antilles and Aruba have resisted full independence.

The islands of Guadeloupe and Martinique (known also as the French Antilles) have also chosen assimilation over autonomy. They are "overseas departments" of France—which means they have the same legal status as France's mainland departments. Such dependency is not without its detractors. In December, 1959, there was anti-French rioting in Fort-de-France, Martinique. Pro-France parties managed to hold office throughout the 1960's and 1970's, but those favoring autonomy made up a large minority. By the 1990's, the islands' independence movement had waned, but a militant proindependence minority remains active.

The island of Puerto Rico has chosen a different path. A U.S. territory since 1898, when Spain ceded it to the United States after the Spanish-American War, Puerto Rico was officially designated a "commonwealth" in 1952. Residents of Puerto Rico are U.S. citizens; however, they do not pay federal income tax and cannot vote in national elections. In a 1993 referendum, 48.4 percent of Puerto Rican voters opted to retain their commonwealth status. Another 46.2 percent chose statehood, and the remainder voted for complete independence from the United States.

Economic Unity. There have been many attempts to organize the islands of the Caribbean into regional economic and political organizations. The West Indies Federation was, for example, an attempt by Great Britain to unite its ten Caribbean colonies in one political grouping to prepare them for collective independence in 1958. The federation offered free movement of labor among the islands, as well as certain trade advantages from economic union.

In 1961 Jamaicans voted to withdraw from the West Indies Federation. Its people were worried that their more impoverished island neighbors would migrate to Jamaica and deplete their bauxite-based economy. Trinidad and Tobago left the federation shortly afterward. Without total cooperation of all the British colonies, the federation lasted only until 1962. At the time, experts attributed this failure to the strong nationalistic identities among the islands, especially after so many centuries of colonial rule.

As each Caribbean island became independent, it initially was most concerned with maintaining its own internal stability. As these nations have grown accustomed to independence, however, their need for combining their strengths has gradually tempered their resistance to pan-national organizations. In 1968 Antigua, Barbados, Trinidad and Tobago, and the South American nation of Guyana (formerly British Guiana) established the Caribbean Free Trade area (CARIFTA). It was designed to provide a wider market for industrial products. Anguilla, Dominica, Grenada, Jamaica, Montserrat, St. Lucia, St. Kitts and Nevis, and St. Vincent and the Grenadines joined it later that year. In addition, the Caribbean Regional Development Bank was established in 1969 to make loans to encourage industry.

By 1973 Barbados, Guyana, Jamaica, and Trinidad and Tobago had left CARIFTA to form a customs union known as the Caribbean Community and Common Market (CARICOM). This new union provided for internal free trade and common tariff rates on goods produced outside the union. It also worked toward creating more uniform fiscal, monetary, and other economic policies. By 1975 all the original members of CARIFTA had joined CARICOM.

During the 1990's CARICOM negotiated preferential trade arrangements with Colombia and Venezuela, providing nonreciprocal access to the markets of the both countries. Haiti—which never had a British colonial connection—joined CARICOM in 1997. Its acceptance as a member reversed the union's earlier policy of accepting only the smallest Caribbean nations. The CARICOM nations are also considering a strategic alliance with the Central American Common Market (CACM). Such a union holds out the potential for a regional free-trade zone containing sixty million consumers.

Changes in the world marketplace pose risks to the region. For example, bananas are a major Caribbean export crop. They account for 50 to 60 percent of the export earnings of the Windward Islands alone. The numbers are even higher in Dominica and St. Lucia. Almost 90 percent of their agricultural earnings come from bananas, and 50 percent of their work forces are employed in banana cultivation.

The survival of entire island economies depends on their continued access to the European Union (EU) under favorable postcolonial guidelines. This preferential treatment has come under legal challenge from Latin America growers in Ecuador, Honduras, Mexico and Guatemala, backed by multinational enterprises based in the United States. In March, 1997, a World Trade Organization Dispute Panel determined that the EU's banana import regime violated open trading rules, causing widespread concern in the region.

This concern is not unfounded. The collapse of the Caribbean banana industry would create high rates of unemployment. Such a occurrence might encourage growers to turn to the only other cash crop suitable for the hilly, nonarable land in most of the eastern Caribbean—marijuana.

Economic diversification holds out the most likely solution to Caribbean economic problems.

Some islands look to service industries to end their reliance on agriculture. The Cayman Islands, for example, have developed offshore banking. Jamaica has become an important data processing center, and St. Lucia is hoping to become a key transshipment center for trade between South America and North America. In addition, the United States, Canada, and Mexico are considering extending the North American Free Trade Agreement (NAFTA) to include Caribbean and Central American countries by the year 2005.

Drug Trafficking. The global strategic importance of the Caribbean became obvious during World War II, when the United States established military bases on several islands not directly under its control, such as Jamaica, Antigua, St. Lucia, and Trinidad. Because of its close proximity to the Caribbean, the United States has maintained a strong presence in the region. Radio and television transmissions, industry ties, trade agreements, and a growing tourist industry have forged social, economic and cultural links between the United States and its small island neighbors.

Toward the end of the twentieth century, narcotics traffic in the Caribbean region became big business. It gave rise to increased violence, corruption, and political regimes known as "narco-democracies." The islands have also provided convenient locations for transferring shipments of South American-produced cocaine and a Caribbean strain of marijuana that commands high prices in the United States. According to some estimates, 40 percent of all South American cocaine and heroin destined for the United States moves through the Caribbean. In 1996 the U.S. government identified Aruba, the Netherlands Antilles, the Bahamas, the Dominican Republic, Haiti, and Jamaica as major drug-transit countries.

Since 1996 the U.S. Maritime and Overflight Agreement (known also as the Ship Rider Agreement) has empowered the U.S. Coast Guard, U.S. Navy, and other U.S. law enforcement agencies to conduct land and maritime searches, seize contraband drugs, and arrest suspected drug traffickers *within* the territories of Caribbean countries that have signed the agreement. The agreement has also permitted U.S. aircraft to fly over Caribbean countries and make suspicious aircraft land in those countries.

By November, 1996, at least ten Caribbean countries had signed on to some version of the agreement with the United States. Critics claim that the Ship Rider Agreement is not simply a tool of drug enforcement, but an attempt by the United States to reduce the sovereignty of Caribbean island nations. The agreement has also caused some dissention within the Caribbean community. After Jamaica and Barbados refused to signed the original arrangement, they were offered versions that intruded less on their territorial sovereignty.

Political Stresses and Strains. Other potential regional problems include the possible secession of Barbuda from Antigua, ongoing political turmoil in Jamaica, and disputes between Trinidad and Tobago and Venezuela over fishing and oil rights in their overlapping coastal waters. Some factions in Puerto Rico continue to press for U.S. statehood, while others seek complete independence from the United States. Environmental degradation and overpopulation also contribute to the general instability of the Caribbean region.

Haiti remains a particularly troubled spot. An internationally monitored election in 1990 failed to bring peace to the troubled nation. The nation's first democratically elected president, Jean-Bertrand Aristide, was forced to flee to the United States in September, 1991. The following month, the Organization of American States (OAS) called for a voluntary embargo on some trade with Haiti. However, the neighboring Dominican Republic ignored the embargo, and other countries did not effectively enforce it.

With Operation Restore Hope, the United States moved into Haiti in September, 1994, to restore President Aristide to power. U.S. forces remained long enough to oversee the 1995 election of Aristide's successor, Rene Preval, then turned the task over to United Nations peacekeepers. The peacekeeping mission lasted two and a half years, during which Canadian and Pakistani troops trained a new Haitian national police force to replace the corrupt and repressive army. Nevertheless, Haiti's future remained uncertain. The Haitian economy is the poorest in the Americas. Its narcotics traffic is on the rise, and President Preval's inability to establish a stable government has frozen an estimated US$142 million in international relief loans.

Dominican Republic drug police examine a hole made by a bomb hurled into the compound of the National Drug Control Directorate headquarters. (AP/Wide World Photos)

Cuba and the United States. Perhaps the greatest threat to political stability in the Caribbean region is the ongoing standoff between the United States and Cuba. Since Fidel Castro assumed power in 1959 and established a socialist government, the United States has been uneasy about having a communist nation so close to its shores. The United States severed diplomatic relations with Cuba in 1961. Since then a rigid trade embargo has prevented U.S. companies from doing business with the communist nation.

In 1996 the U.S. Congress passed the Cuban Liberty and Democracy Act (also known as the Helms-Burton Act), which was designed to extend and tighten the U.S. embargo against Cuba, with the ultimate goal of bringing down the Castro regime. Canada and Mexico immediately prepared counterlegislation as an "antidote" to the Helms-Burton measure and considered challenging the U.S. law under provisions of NAFTA. Helms-Burton was also condemned by the OAS, the Rio Group, and CARICOM.

Cuba, meanwhile, has strengthened its economic ties with other Caribbean islands. Castro participated in the first Association of Caribbean States (ACS) in 1995 and hosted the second meeting in 1996. That same year, Cuba had free-trade negotiations with Trinidad and Tobago and established an embassy in Port of Spain, Trinidad. During that time, Cuba also reestablished diplomatic relations with Grenada and the Dominican Repub-

lic. Although Cuba had not yet joined CARICOM, that body's individual member nations have negotiated trade alliances with Cuba. Cuba also had the prospect of a trade agreement with the European Union (EU).

The United States has officially linked the possibility of its normalizing relations with Cuba to Cuba's establishment of a democratic government. By 1998 the tide appeared to be turning in Cuba's favor. In March of that year U.S. president Bill Clinton relaxed the U.S. trade embargo on Cuba to permit direct charter flights to the island nation, to expedite sales of medical supplies, and to allow Cuban Americans to send money to their relatives in Cuba. In 1998 Congress considered two bills that would increase U.S. humanitarian aid to Cuba through religious groups and the Red Cross. Sof-

At the end of Pope John Paul II's five-day visit to Cuba in early 1998, he celebrated a mass in Havana's Plaza of the Revolution, where he called for the creation of a new Cuban society offering "peace, justice, and freedom," while warning of the dangers of capitalism. Here the pope is being greeted by Cuban president Fidel Castro (left). (AP/Wide World Photos)

tened U.S. attitudes toward Cuba have been attributed, in part, to a visit by Pope John Paul II to Cuba in 1997. That visit showed the world that there was more to the island nation than Fidel Castro's communist dictatorship.

P. S. Ramsey

For Further Study

An excellent overview of the Caribbean region can be found in Jan Rogozinski's *A Brief History of the Caribbean* (1992). *The Caribbean: The Genesis of a Fragmented Nationalism* (1978), by Franklin W. Knight, deals primarily with the social and economic development of the region. Other useful books include Neil E. Sealey's *Caribbean World: A Complete Geography* (1994) and *The Caribbean in the Wider World, 1492-1992: A Regional Geography* (1992), by Bonham C. Richardson. For more information on the era of exploration and colonialism see *The British in the Caribbean* (1972), by Cyril Hamshere.

To learn more about the impact of the slave trade on the Caribbean nations, see Michael Mullin's *Africa in America: Slave Acculturation and Resistance in the American South and the British Caribbean, 1736-1831* (1993), Herbert S. Klein's *African Slavery in Latin America and the Caribbean* (1988), and *Caribbean Slave Society and Economy: A Student Reader* (1994), edited by Hilary Beckles and Verene Shepherd.

Good studies of relations between the United States and Caribbean island nations are Jenny Pearce's *Under the Eagle: U.S. Intervention in Central American and the Caribbean* (1982), Raymond Carroll's *The Caribbean: Issues in U.S. Relations* (1984), and *The Caribbean: New Dynamics in Trade and Political Economy* (1995), edited by Anthony T. Bryan. For an interesting perspective on the Caribbean's future, see *Caribbean Public Policy: Regional, Cultural, and Socioeconomic Issues for the Twenty-first Century* (1998) edited by Jean-Pierre Chardon.

Cuba

The largest island in the Caribbean, Cuba broke from the Spanish Empire comparatively late, only to begin its independence as a client state of the nearby United States. Until Fidel Castro's communist revolution succeeded, Cuba suffered from corrupt, arbitrary dictatorships and political violence. Having no plan when he came to power in 1959, Castro developed a pragmatic approach to governing. Over the following decade he transformed Cuba into a socialist state. After freeing Cuba of economic dependence on the United States, however, he made Cuba dependent upon the Soviet Union. With the breakup of the Soviet Union during the 1990's and a shift to market economies by Cuba's former Communist bloc trading partners, Cuba's economy declined drastically. Under Castro's rule, many Cubans have disliked his policies, but there has been no organized opposition of any importance. Leaving the island has been the chief form of opposition, and hundreds of thousands of Cubans have fled—primarily to the United States. During the 1990's some internal opposition to Castro emerged, but the government's extensive system of surveillance continued to make organized opposition dangerous.

The northern most and largest island of the Greater Antilles, Cuba is only eighty miles southeast of Key West, Florida. The island has two main mountain ranges: the Sierra Maestra, which runs parallel to the south coast, and a line of low mountains along the north coast. The mountains occupy only a quarter of the land mass and are neither high nor continuous. The climate is subtropical, but the trade winds, which blow year long, provide relief from the heat.

Cuba is strategically located at the Atlantic Ocean's entrance to the Gulf of Mexico. During its long period under Spanish colonial rule Cuba controlled the sealanes to New Spain (Mexico) and the Isthmus of Panama. After Cuba became independent at the beginning of the twentieth century, its nearness to the United States was a major factor in its economic growth.

Colonial Period. Cuba was one of the islands discovered by Christopher Columbus during his first voyage of discovery to the New World in 1492. The island contained little to attract Spanish interest. It had little gold, and its native population was small and ill-suited for labor. First and foremost, the island was a way station on the route to the mainland. It thus became an important base for fleets sailing between the New World and Spain. Spain built great fortifications to protect the port city of Havana on the north coast and made that city the base for the naval fleet protecting Spanish colonies in the New World.

Spain did little to develop Cuba economically until the nineteenth century. After losing most of the rest of its American empire during the first decades of that century, Spain paid much greater attention to Cuba. Sugar production dominated Cuba's economy and utilized ever greater numbers of African slaves at a time when other nations were abolishing slavery. After the middle of the century the United States began investing in the Cuban sugar industry and infrastructure. American investments became the most powerful element in the island's economy.

Several times during the nineteenth century Cubans attempted unsuccessfully to rebel against Spain. In 1898 the United States intervened in a Cuban rebellion after the battleship U.S.S. *Maine* mysteriously blew up in Havana harbor. As a result of the Spanish-American War that followed this incident, Cuba became nominally independent.

However, the United States exercised a protectorate over it.

U.S. Occupation of Cuba. Many Cuban patriots did not want the United States to intervene in their affairs. They feared, with reason, that the United States would dictate the formation of their new government, even though the U.S. Congress had forbidden U.S. annexation of Cuba. To U.S. president William McKinley, however, it was unthinkable to withdraw U.S. troops from Cuba without providing for the new nation's law and order and democratic government.

In 1899 the United States set up a military government over Cuba under the leadership of General Leonard Wood. Wood disarmed the civilian population by paying off the soldiers who had fought against Spain. He also established a new civil administration, created a court system, and built roads, telephone lines, and schools—which were staffed by Cuban teachers trained in the United States.

U.S. medical researchers discovered the cause of yellow fever, which had long devastated Cuba, and virtually eradicated the disease from the island. The United States conducted the first Cuban census, and the U.S. Army selected Cuban delegates to a convention that wrote a new constitution for the country. The constitution created a centralized government, separated church and state, and incorporated elements of an American law, the Platt Amendment, which gave the United States the right to intervene in Cuban affairs. A treaty between the two nations concluded in 1903 included the same provisions.

The Platt Amendment gave the United States the right to intervene to preserve Cuba's independence and to oversee maintenance of a Cuban government adequate to protect life, property, and individual liberty. Cuba was forbidden to contract debts beyond its ability to repay, and it was barred from making treaties that might impair its sovereignty. The Platt Amendment also provided for the United States

to lease Guantanamo Bay, on the eastern tip of Cuba, as a naval base. Moreover, it prohibited Cuba from claiming the Isle of Pines; however, that island was later returned to Cuba.

Early Years of Independence. In 1902 Tomas Estrada Palma became the first president of Cuba. Prospects for the new nation appeared to be bright. Unlike most other Spanish American nations, Cuba had no serious racial problems, no church-state disputes, no rigid caste system, and no great postwar economic decline. Moreover, the United States was buying Cuban products and investing capital for economic growth.

Nevertheless, trouble developed almost immediately. Rampant factionalism caused not by ideology but by public pressure to secure government jobs developed. The new national congress behaved irresponsibly, concerning itself too much with patronage and paying bonuses to soldiers. A negative political character prevailed from the beginning. When Estrada Palma was reelected president in 1905, members of the Liberal Party charged that the elections were fraudulent and boycotted the polls. In 1906 the Liberals revolted. Unable to handle the situation, Estrada Palma appealed to U.S. president Theodore Roosevelt for help. Roosevelt sent a mission under Secretary of War William H. Taft to reconcile the factions. Estrada Palma resigned and retired to his farm. He died in

---

Profile of Cuba

Official name: Republic of Cuba
Independent since: 1898
Former colonial ruler: Spain
Location: off southern tip of Florida
Area: 42,803 square miles
Capital: Havana
Population: 10,999,000 (1997 est.)
Official language: Spanish
Major religion: Roman Catholicism
Gross domestic product: US$16.2 billion (1996)
Major exports: sugar; minerals and concentrates; fish products; tobacco
Military budget: US$700 million (1997)
Military personnel: 60,000 (1997)

Note: Monetary figures rendered as "US$" are U.S. equivalents of values in local currencies.

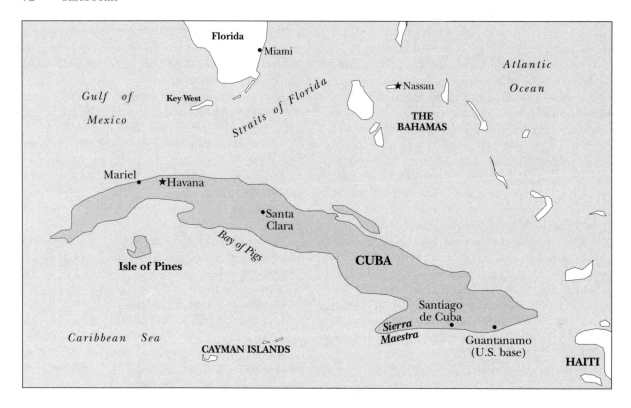

poverty a few years later. His precedent of dying poor was one no future president followed.

When Taft's mission failed to accomplish its job, President Roosevelt sent the U.S. Army to Cuba to set up a new administration under Charles E. Magoon. Magoon controlled Cuba for two years, training Cuban administrators, decreeing necessary laws that the Cuban congress had neglected to pass, and distributing political jobs to both Liberals and Moderate Party members. Instead of winning public support, however, Magoon was accused of extravagance, dishonesty, favoritism, and tyranny. His real problem was that he was closely identified with U.S. control of Cuba.

Meanwhile, U.S. investing was leading to American companies owning a majority of Cuba's sugarcane estates and refineries. As land prices increased, many Cubans sold their lands to U.S. investors and ended up as seasonal laborers on the large estates, where they worked only during the annual three-month harvest period. Growing unemployment and underemployment came to characterize the Cuban economy, especially in the rural areas. Neither the U.S. investors nor Cuban politicians showed any concern.

In 1908 the United States presided over a new presidential election and turned the government back to Cubans. Many elected officials seemed to be interested mostly in making money and staying in power. The presidents controlled the army and used it to rig elections. Few politicians or intellectuals openly expressed concern for the masses or for the economic domination of the economy by the United States.

World War I and Its Aftermath. During World War I and into the immediate postwar years, the Cuban sugar industry boomed and new investments poured into the country. This era became known as the "dance of the millions." Much of the new wealth was used for extravagant homes, luxuries, or gambling. Once again the United States intervened in Cuban politics to put down a revolt by the Liberals, who claimed that the election of 1916 was fraudulent. The U.S. Marines stayed in the country until World War I ended.

By the election of 1920 the "dance of the millions" was over. Many remaining Cuban landowners were bankrupt. Virtually all Cuban banks had failed, and rural laborers were unemployed. The government had disintegrated to the point it could not even stage an election, so many Cuban politicians invited U.S. general Enoch Crowder to supervise the election. However, Crowder could do little to prevent the Cuban army from driving voters away from the polls and stealing ballot boxes. Despite these problems, a presidential candidate believed to be a reformer was declared the winner of the election. However, no real changes took place. The same patterns of corruption, failure to do anything for the masses, and manipulation of voting continued. Nevertheless, prosperity began to return as postwar disruptions subsided.

During the 1920's the direct impact of Americans in Cuba became obvious to all. American tourists discovered Cuba as a winter playground that offered legal gambling and prostitution. American gangsters moved in as well. The prosperity that had returned by the time of the elections of 1924 disappeared with the onset of the Great Depression in 1929. The defects of the Cuban economy and society could no longer be ignored.

President Gerado Machado, who had been in power since 1924, was blamed for the ills of the nation. His answer to increasing opposition was imposition of dictatorial government. He imposed censorship, had suspected political opponents beaten, shot prisoners, made arbitrary arrests, and closed the university. The situation degenerated into general urban and rural violence.

Rise of Batista. This time U.S. intervention was not military. Instead of sending the Marines, President Franklin D. Roosevelt sent a diplomat, Sumner Wells. The politicians and military leaders to whom Wells talked were willing to see Machado go. A massive outbreak of revolutionary violence and a general strike in 1933 led to the removal of Machado. Although many Cubans approved, the change was brought by U.S. intervention.

Fulgencio Batista when he was head of Cuba's armed forces in 1933. (AP/Wide World Photos)

Cuban president Fidel Castro addressing the United Nations General Assembly in September, 1960. (United Nations)

A provisional government approved by Wells was overthrown almost immediately by Fulgencio Batista, a Cuban army sergeant. Batista held real power until the election of 1944, but until 1940 he ruled through seven figureheads. Batista undertook many reforms that improved conditions for the masses. Labor unions were organized; education was encouraged; women got the right to vote; and the press was given more freedom. Legislation was also passed to improve working conditions, protect against accidents, and provide for old age care.

Batista made himself president in 1940. He presided over a nation prosperous because of World War II and U.S. aid. Nickel and magnesium mining developed by U.S. capital had became an important part of the economy. By 1944 Batista was so confident of his control over the country that he did not rig the presidential election. However, his own candidate lost to a reformer, and he went into exile.

The next two Cuban presidents were also reputed to be reformers, but again no real changes took place. Indeed, things got worse. Communists who had been denied a role in the government set out to control labor unions and raised the level of political violence throughout the country until near anarchy prevailed. Despite this political chaos, the period was one of prosperity. U.S. sugar purchases and tourism provided wealth for the upper classes. Cubans were able to buy back most of the sugar estates from Americans, but U.S. investments still dominated public utilities, mines, light industry, and distributing businesses. Meanwhile, the Cuban masses, still ignored by the government, lived in poverty.

In 1952 former president Batista returned to Cuba and declared his candidacy for president.

However, he did not wait for the election to seize power again. After making himself president again, he moved to suppress all opposition. To the mass of Cuba's people, the United States was the cause of all of their problems and Batista was the tool of the United States. Conditions in Cuba became ripe for real revolution.

Rise of Fidel Castro. Fidel Castro was the son of a wealthy landowner in northwestern Cuba. As a young man he began to associate with communists and other revolutionaries throughout the Western Hemisphere, including the United States. His brother Raul and his close associate, the Argentine doctor Ernesto (Che) Guevara, were communists. Castro saw himself as a leftist reformer and did not declare himself a communist until he came to power.

Castro's political career began when he entered the University of Havana in 1945 and became involved in violent political activities. In 1947 he participated in an unsuccessful attempt by university students to overthrow the dictator Rafael Trujillo in the Dominican Republic. He was a follower of the reformer Eddie Chibas, a popular radio personality, and a member of the reform Orthodoxo Party.

On July 26, 1953, Castro led a small group of workers in an attack on the Moncada army barracks near Santiago de Cuba. He hoped to spark a rebellion, but it did not happen. Castro and all of his followers were captured or killed. At his ensuing trial Castro delivered his "History Will Absolve Me" speech, which would help make him world famous.

While in prison Castro developed a strategy to bring down Batista's government. After he was released in a general amnesty granted by Batista in 1955, he went to Mexico. There he met Che Guevara, who became his second in command. In November, 1956, he returned to Cuba with eighty-two followers, including Che and his brother Raul. They intended to coordinate their landing in Oriente Province with an uprising in Santiago. However, their plans were betrayed. Castro and a few of his men narrowly escaped into the Sierra Maestra. There they waged guerrilla war against the government and repeatedly defeated troops sent to capture them.

In February of 1957 Castro gave an interview to Herbert Matthews, a well-known reporter for *The New York Times*. Matthew's article gave Castro credi-bility as a political leader in the United States, while helping to spread the word among Cubans that Castro was alive and still in revolt.

By ordering his men to treat the peasants well and to pay for everything they took, Castro gained the sympathy and help of Cuba's rural population. As he became better known, more followers joined him. Urban resistance, especially in Havana, became common, and Cuba was in a full fledged civil war. Batista's brutal repression alienated both Cubans and the United States.

In mid-1958 the United States ended its support of Batista, and the Cuban middle class turned against him. Some elements of the Roman Catholic Church also opposed the regime, and support for Castro continued to grow. Batista launched an all-out attack against the guerrilla forces. When it failed his regime was doomed. Castro's guerrillas marched triumphantly into Havana on January 1, 1959. A week later Castro himself entered the city as a revolutionary hero.

Castro's Revolution. In the first four years of Castro's regime, his revolution consolidated its political position, began to socialize the economy, and set a new pattern of foreign relations. Castro and his lieutenants decided parliamentary democracy was inappropriate for Cuba at that time. The Fundamental Law, decreed in February, 1959, gave legislative power to the executive, that is Castro. As prime minister, and later secretary of the Communist Party, Castro held decisive posts in the government and in the party.

Castro moved the revolution left to accomplish his goals, which included land reform, income redistribution, agricultural diversification, and economic independence from the United States. His first program designed to benefit the masses was a massive education program that virtually eliminated illiteracy for the first time in the history of Cuba. Housing was greatly improved and a government health care system was started for the rural areas.

The radical economic program and the concentration of political power in the Twenty-sixth of July Movement alienated much of the middle class. Moderates and anticommunists were purged from the government, and Castro turned increasingly to the Communist Party. Realizing that conflict with the United States was almost inevitable, Castro turned to the Soviet Union for support.

Cuba

1492	Christopher Columbus discovers Cuba.
1589	Havana becomes capital.
1762-1764	Great Britain occupies Cuba.
1791-1795	Emigration from Caribbean islands to Cuba.
1848	United States tries to buy Cuba.
1850-1851	Unsuccessful invasions to liberate Cuba.
1868-1878	Terrible Ten Year War.
1890	United States grants preferential tariffs to Cuban sugar.
1892	Jose Marti founds Cuban Revolutionary Party.
1895-1898	Second Cuban insurrection.
1898	United States defeats Spain in Spanish-American War, and Cuba becomes nominally independent.
1899-1902	United States occupies Cuba.
1902	Cuba's first president is elected.
1906-1908	Liberal rebellion and U.S. intervention.
1915-1920	"Dance of the millions."
1920	General Crowder's mission.
1933	Fulgencio Batista takes over government in coup.
1940	Fulgencio Batista y Zaldivar is elected president of Cuba.
1944	Batista goes into exile.
1952	Batista again seizes power.
1953	(July 26) Fidel Castro launches revolution.
1959	(Jan. 1) Castro occupies Havana and takes power.
1961	(Jan.) Diplomatic relations with United States are severed.
1961	(Apr. 15) Invasion attempt by Cuban exiles supported by United States is crushed at Bay of Pigs.
1962	(Oct.) United States forces Soviet Union to withdraw missiles it is installing in Cuba.
1966-1971	200,00 Cubans flee to United States.
1967	Che Guevara is killed in Bolivia.
1968	Remaining private enterprises are nationalized.
1975	Cuban combat troops are sent to Angola.
1976	New constitution is promulgated.
1977	Cuba and United States establish limited relations.
1985	United States begins Radio Martí broadcasts.
1991	Unemployment increases, as well as food, gasoline, and everyday necessity shortages.

1992	Castro encourages tourism, medical treatment for foreigners, and sale of medicine for hard currency.
1992	Emigration to United states is increased with help of corrupt Cuban officials.
1998	(Jan.) Pope John Paul II visits Cuba; during his visit he calls for release of political prisoners and for greater freedom.
1998	(Jan. 27) Guatemala restores diplomatic relations with Cuba.
1998	(Feb. 2) Castro publicly rejects proposal of Cuban American organization that humanitarian aid be sent to Cuba.
1998	(Feb. 7) Haiti reopens its embassy in Havana.
1998	(Feb. 12) Government announces it will free at least two hundred prisoners, including some political prisoners, on humanitarian grounds.
1998	(Feb. 24) New national assembly reelects Castro to new five-year term as president.
1998	(Mar. 6) More than fifty U.S. business executives visit Cuba to explore trade and investment possibilities.
1998	(Mar. 20) U.S. president Bill Clinton's administration announces easing of restrictions on cash remittances and travel to Cuba; Castro cautiously praises U.S. policy shift.
1998	(Apr. 26) Canadian prime minister Jean Chretien visits Cuba and discusses human rights issues and foreign investment with Castro.
1998	(July 29-Sept. 5) Castro pays state visits to four Caribbean nations, Brazil, and South Africa.
1999	(Jan. 1) Cuba celebrates fortieth anniversary of revolution.
1999	(Jan. 5) U.S. president Bill Clinton announces easing of trade restrictions on Cuba but rejects proposal of bipartisan Senate group to review U.S. policy toward Cuba.

Cuban relations with the United States deteriorated. In 1960 Castro confiscated U.S. holdings. In retaliation U.S. president Dwight D. Eisenhower broke relations with Cuba and withdrew permission for Cuba to export a previously agreed-upon quota of sugar to the United States at a price higher than the world market price. Eisenhower also banned all U.S. exports to Cuba. This ban became a permanent part of U.S. policy toward Cuba. All formal relations between the countries were severed in January, 1961.

Bay of Pigs Invasion. As relations between the two nations grew worse, the U.S. Central Intelligence Agency (CIA) began to finance Cuban exile groups and provide military training for anti-Castro groups. Plans for an invasion of Cuba begun in the Eisenhower administration were approved by John F. Kennedy shortly after he became president of the United States in early 1961. On April 15 of

that year, the exile army invaded Cuba at the Bay of Pigs. The expedition was a fiasco. Not only was there no uprising in Cuba to support it, but Castro's victory over the invaders enhanced his prestige and provided an impetus for even more radical reconstruction of the Cuban economy and society.

After the Bay of Pigs invasion the Soviet Union greatly increased military and economic assistance to Cuba. Its assistance included military airplanes and missiles capable of delivering atomic weapons to most of the United States. President Kennedy determined that these were offensive weapons. On October 22, 1962, he ordered a quarantine on all offensive weapons bound for Cuba and demanded the removal of all Soviet missiles from the island. As a result of his ultimatum, the world came close to nuclear war.

A compromise was reached between the United States and the Soviet Union whereby the missiles were removed in return for a pledge that the United States would not attack Cuba and would remove its own missiles from bases in Turkey. Castro himself was not consulted during the U.S.-Soviet negotiations, leaving him furious with the Soviets. The U.S.-Soviet agreement demonstrated that Cuba had exchanged American for Soviet domination.

Revolution and Reform. Castro's program of redistributing income to the rural and urban masses achieved considerable success during the first three years of his revolution. Wages were raised, purchasing power increased, and unemployment and underemployment virtually disappeared. Government-sponsored changes were greater in the rural areas than in the cities by design. The revolutionary government wanted to reverse urban growth by inducing more people to live in the countryside.

Land reform began with the first Agrarian Reform Law of 1959. All private holdings including those of the Castro family in excess of stated limits were expropriated and put into state farms. Eighty-five percent of Cuban farms were nationalized.

Later all farms were nationalized. The law was administered by the Institute of Agrarian Reform.

The government nationalized foreign companies starting with the unpopular telephone system owned by U.S. investors. After relations with the United States were broken, American oil refineries, sugar mills, and public utilities were taken over by the government. Banks, urban housing, and Cuban-owned businesses followed.

A long-range problem developed with the redistribution of income. Since Cuba could no longer import consumer goods and food from the United States, increases in purchasing power caused severe shortages, especially of meat. The overkilling of cattle for beef made the situation worse. As a result, the government instituted rationing in 1962, and it became a part of Cuban life. The agricultural diversification and the industrialization programs contributed to the problem.

In an attempt to make Cuba more self-sufficient, the government transferred land used for sugarcane to other food crops. This policy had little success, however, and had the effect of causing sugarcane production to fall drastically. The indus-

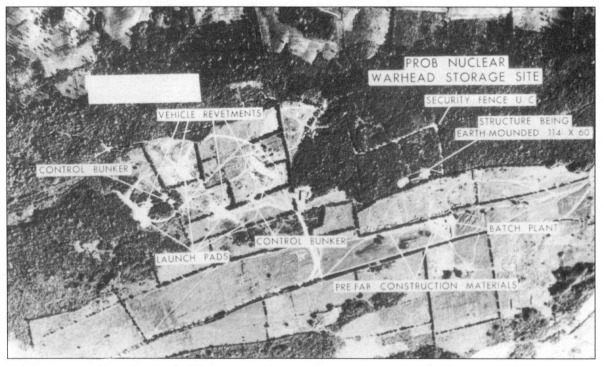

U.S. aerial reconnaissance photograph of the Soviet missile bases in Cuba whose installation precipitated the Cuban Missile Crisis in October, 1962. (National Archives)

On July 26, 1998, the forty-fifth anniversary of launching his rebellion, President Castro addresses his supporters in Santiago, Cuba. (AP/Wide World Photos)

trialization program immediately ran into trouble and was dropped, causing wastage of limited economic resources.

Economic Problems. After 1961 the economy suffered because of the inability of the government to organize, plan, and administer the economy efficiently. Castro himself contributed to the problem by personally interfering with plans developed by the bureaucracy and by instituting projects he favored without reference to central plans. Cuba put a large portion of its resources into building factories, roads, and other improvements, but poor planning wasted much of these investments. Many projects were never finished or were not maintained and fell into disrepair.

In 1963 Castro decided to reemphasize sugarcane production. He hoped that increased sugar sales would provide enough earnings to finance industrialization. He announced a goal of ten million tons of sugar in the 1970 harvest. Meeting that

goal was to be a measure of the success of the revolution. Sugar production was disappointing after 1962, however. Much of the best cane land had been diverted to other crops, and new cane had not been planted. Sugar mills fell into disrepair. Equipment and manpower were badly managed, and transportation was grossly inadequate. Resources and manpower were diverted to the 1970 harvest and caused disruption and turmoil through the economy.

Not only did the 1970 harvest fail to reach the goal of ten million tons, the efforts to meet that goal did extensive damage to the economy. The eight and one half million tons harvested virtually ruined the sugar industry. Equipment broke down under the work load and sugar lands were exhausted. Harvests in the following years were poor.

Meanwhile, in 1965 Che Guevara introduced moral incentives in place of material incentives into the national ethic. The "new socialists" were to be motivated to work up to their capacity for the betterment of society, rather than for the material reward they personally received. Although the plan was introduced several times for brief periods, it never worked. Castro complained about the lazy workers. Productivity was low and absenteeism from the workplace was high.

In 1966 Castro permitted Che Guevara to go to Bolivia to assist in organizing that country's socialist revolution. In less than a year Guevara was hunted down by Bolivian authorities and killed. Not only was Cuba's Bolivian project a failure, it antagonized other Latin American nations and the United states who opposed the Cuban policy of "exporting revolution."

Revolution Institutionalized. Cuba's sugar program had been Castro's own idea. Its failure thus cost him some of his prestige. That failure was the most severe setback suffered by the revolution. Castro addressed the Cuban people and publicly acknowledged his mistakes. He reemphasized that sacrifice and hardships lay ahead, reintroduced moral incentive, and vowed that the revolution would go on.

Castro promised changes, and during the next five years he delivered them. He depersonalized the government and institutionalized the revolution. More power was delegated to a new executive committee and greater decision-making power was given to the bureaucracy. A socialist constitution, adopted in 1976, provided for a pyramid of elective bodies. At the bottom were popularly elected municipal assemblies that chose delegates to provincial assemblies and the national assembly.

Most of the delegates to these assemblies were Communist Party members, who constituted a minority of the citizens. Nonparty citizens still had almost no participation in government. However, Castro remained president of the Council of State, first secretary of the Communist Party, and head of the national government.

Severe economic problems remained, and Cuba continued to be dependent upon its sugar crops. Cuba attempted to produce the items it could no longer import, but lack of professional management, quality control, and labor discipline resulted in poor quality and low productivity.

Although Cuba already owed the Soviet Union US$10 billion During the 1980's, it borrowed another US$7 billion from Western countries. Con-

sidering Cuba's total resources, this debt load was enormous, and Cuba has been unable to meet its repayment obligations.

Increasingly dissatisfied with food shortages and rationing, Cubans saw no end to their dreary life. Younger people were especially unwilling to continue to sacrifice as Castro called for them to do. Many attempted to enter foreign embassies in Havana to escape from the country.

After an incident at the Peruvian embassy, Castro angrily said that any Cuban who wanted to leave the country could do so from the port of Mariel. Approximately 125,000 people quickly left for the United States. Afterward the U.S. government began to rethink its open door policy for immigration.

Changing World Conditions. After Ronald Reagan was elected president of the United States in 1980, he tightened the economic blockade of Cuba. In 1985 the U.S. government launched Radio Martí to broadcast anticommunist propaganda into Cuba. Relations between Cuba and the United States deteriorated further. However, relations between Cuba and the Soviet Union also grew worse. Castro found his nation increasingly isolated both politically and economically.

Cuba's economy suffered an almost fatal blow with the breakup of the Soviet Union. In 1990 the Communist bloc nations began moving into a market economy and demanded payment in hard currency for its goods. Cuba lost its sugar market in the Soviet Union and no longer could import inexpensive Soviet oil. Perhaps the biggest blow, however, was Cuba's loss of a Soviet subsidy that had reached as much as US$5 million a day.

Persistent economic problems, lack of consumer goods, food shortages, rationing, and the rise of a new population that lacks the older generations' respect for Castro have all created discontent. Opposition to Castro can be seen in graffiti on the walls of Havana and in passive resistance. Because of fear and the extensive security fores, no organized opposition has appeared and in the late 1990's it seemed unlikely that it would appear.

A mass exodus of Cubans, mostly to the United States, began in the early years of the revolution and became greater after 1990. Although Castro has to contend with fewer discontented citizens as a result of the exodus, he has also had to pay an economic price with the loss of a major part of

Cuba's professional and managerial classes, as well as a large number of young people who have been the majority of those fleeing the country. Despite growing opposition and continuing economic problems, Castro has retained power while refusing to move toward a market economy or a more democratic government.

Robert D. Talbott

For Further Study

A handy general reference source on the country is Jaime Suchlicki's *Historical Dictionary of Cuba* (1988) in Scarecrow Press's Latin American Historical Dictionary series. Suchlicki is also the author of *Cuba: From Columbus to Castro and Beyond* (1997), which pays particular attention to the post-Cold War years and Cuba's tense relationship with the United States. There are numerous works on Castro and his revolution. Many are biased, either for or against him, but a fine objective work is Robert R. Quirk's *Fidel Castro* (1993). Georgie Anne Geyer's *Guerrilla Prince: The Untold Story of Fidel Castro* (1991) draws on numerous interviews and published sources to describe Castro. *Cuban Communism* (1977), edited by Irving Louis Horowitz, is a collection of essays on all aspects of Cuban communism by fifteen prominent scholars. *Cuba After the Cold War* (1993), edited by Carmelo Meso-Lago, collects ten essays by noted scholars on the Cuban economy after the breakup of the Soviet Union. Jorge F. Perez Lopez edited a collection of essays in *Cuba at the Crossroads* (1994) on various topics including labor, the Communist Party, party congresses, tourism, biotechnology, and economic policy. Accounts of Cubans who have fled Cuba are collected in Lorrin Philipson and Rafael Llerena's *Freedom Flights: Cuban Refugees Talk About Life Under Castro and How They Fled His Regime* (1980).

Haiti

About 75 percent of Haiti's people live below the threshold of absolute poverty. A small elite has always owned most of Haiti's land and other resources, and a rigid caste system has promoted conflict and bitter resentment. In political viewpoints, the population is polarized between a right wing that supports free-market capitalism and a left wing that desires land reform and socialism. Although independent since 1804, Haiti has never had a constitutional system that the majority of its citizens consider legitimate. Its turbulent history has included many brutal dictators, violent seizures of power by the military, great corruption, and military interventions by the United States. The 1991 overthrow of the country's first freely elected president, Jean-Bertrand Aristide, was followed by a flood of refugees trying to flee the country. Motivated primarily by the refugee problem, the United States sponsored Aristide's return to the island in 1994. With the withdrawal of U.S. troops, there were some signs of greater political stability, but the persistent economic problems appeared almost intractable.

Haiti occupies the western third of the Caribbean island of Hispaniola. The remainder of the island forms the Dominican Republic. Located between Cuba and Puerto Rico in the West Indies, Haiti has a mountainous terrain, and its very name comes from an Arawak Indian word meaning land of mountains. Tropical forests in the northern mountains receive about eighty inches of rain each year, but less than half of that amount falls along the southern coast. Destructive hurricanes often strike the island between June and October.

With more than 6.6 million people, Haiti is one of the most densely populated countries of the Western Hemisphere. The majority of its people struggle to earn their livelihoods in agriculture, and 80 percent of the people live in rural areas. The typical Haitian farmer has a small plot of less than two acres in size; however, about a fourth of the rural population owns no land at all. Some farmers cultivate land so steep that they must anchor themselves with ropes to keep from sliding down hills. With its eroding soil and unproductive methods of cultivation, Haiti must import about a quarter of its food. Haiti's leading export item is coffee. Its other major food crops include rice, beans, sugarcane, cocoa, and bananas.

Because of its limited domestic market, Haiti's relatively few manufacturing industries generally produce goods for export to developed countries. Most large factories are located in the area around the capital city, Port-au-Prince. There American and other foreign companies take advantage of cheap labor, weak labor unions, minimal taxes, and lax environmental regulations. These factories use materials made abroad to assemble a variety of products, such as electronic equipment, clothing, and pharmaceutical goods. For example, Haiti is a major supplier of baseballs used in the United States. Throughout the country, many Haitians work in traditional craft industries such as woodcarving and sewing.

At least 95 percent of Haitians are descendants of Africans, who were originally brought to the island as slaves. Traditionally, Haiti has had a class system that has been related to skin complexion. Descendants of slaves with dark skins make up the country's large lower class. The country's aristocracy, less than 5 percent of the people, comprises lighter-skinned Haitians of mixed European and African ancestry. They are known as the "colored elite," or "mulattos." In the twentieth century, especially after the "Black Revolution" of 1946, a small "black elite" managed to gain political power and relative affluence.

With a few notable exceptions, wealthy Haitians are not especially affluent by the standards of other countries. Although Haiti has a small middle class composed of shopkeepers, teachers, and lawyers, few citizens have opportunities to enter this class.

French is the official language of the country. Most Haitians, however, actually speak a language called Haitian Creole. It is a mixture of older French combined with African expressions and words borrowed from Spanish and English. To most Creole speakers, French is as alien a language as Russian. An educated elite constituting only about 10 percent of the total population, are proud that they are fluent in the standard French language.

The majority of Haitians practice a folk religion called Voodoo (from *Vaudun*, meaning gods). It is a varied blend of African and Christian beliefs. Originating in Dahomey (now Benin) and other regions of West Africa, Voodoo recognizes the powers of numerous deities and spirits (usually called *loa*) and ranks the Christian God the highest of the deities. Voodoo adherents practice a variety of religious ceremonies, including animal sacrifice. They often experience ecstatic trances which are believed to be caused by spirit possession. Most Haitians undergo Roman Catholic baptism, but about 10 percent belong to Protestant churches.

Early History. The Italian navigator Christopher Columbus first landed on Hispaniola on December 6, 1492, while exploring for Spain. He named the island Española, for "Spanish Island." Columbus attempted to establish Fort Navidad on the northern coast of Haiti. However, the Spaniards who stayed at the fort were apparently killed by local Arawak Indians.

Within fifty years of Columbus's arrival, the entire indigenous population of Hispaniola, estimated at 100,000 Arawaks, had fallen victims to a combination of disease and oppression. The Spanish increasingly used African slaves to work on large sugar plantations, which were concentrated on the eastern part of the island—a region known as Santo Domingo. By the seventeenth century, French settlers had gained a foothold in the western third of the island. It was recognized as a French colony in the Treaty of Ryswick of 1697.

The French colony, initially known as St. Domingue, prospered during the eighteenth century. On the eve of the French Revolution in 1789, about half a million slaves of African ancestry were working on plantations. Although slaves had some protection under the Black Code of 1685, they were treated as harshly there as elsewhere. Colonial society became highly stratified into rigid social classes. About 40,000 French aristocrats held the positions of political power. They owned about two-thirds of the land and slaves. Approximately 25,000 mulattos owned the remaining third of the land and slaves. Perhaps 4,000 middle-class and poor whites owned shops or worked as overseers, mechanics, or soldiers. The rest of the people were African slaves.

Revolution and Independence. The French Revolution's slogan of "liberty, equality, fraternity" was interpreted differently by each of the social classes of St. Domingue. The aristocrats demanded and received more local autonomy. The mulattos were primarily interested in the right of all free males to vote. In 1791 more than 100,000 slaves, demanding their freedom, rebelled in the north-

Profile of Haiti

Official name: Republic of Haiti
Independent since: 1804
Former colonial ruler: France
Location: western part of island of Hispaniola
Area: 10,714 square miles
Capital: Port-au-Prince
Population: 6,611,400 (1997 est.)
Official language: French (Haitian Creole is unofficial)
Major religions: Roman Catholicism; Protestantism
Gross domestic product: US$6.8 billion (1996 est.)
Major exports: light manufactures; handicrafts; coffee; essential oils

Note: Monetary figures rendered as "US$" are U.S. equivalents of values in local currencies.

ern part of the island. An educated former slave, Pierre Toussaint L'Ouverture emerged as the most charismatic of the leaders. Winning control of the entire island by 1801, Toussaint abolished slavery and proclaimed himself governor-general for life.

In 1802 the French ruler Napoleon Bonaparte sent a large army to restore French authority and announced a return of slavery. French officers lured Toussaint into a trap, and the black leader died in a French prison the next year. However, his two lieutenants, Jean-Jacques Dessalines and Henri Christophe, continued the insurrection. With the help of yellow fever, they eventually defeated the French invaders. In 1804 Dessalines proclaimed independence for the western part of the island, giving it the Arawak name of Haiti. Haiti thereby became the first independent nation of Latin America.

Lacking the prerequisites for constitutional government, Haiti was soon torn by insurrection and civil war. Dessalines proclaimed himself emperor in 1804 but was killed by mulatto rebels two years later. Spain regained control of the eastern part of the island in 1809. Henri Christophe proclaimed himself the king of northern Haiti in 1811, while an educated mulatto, Alexandre Pétion, became

president of an unstable republic in the south. Jean-Pierre Boyer, a French-educated mulatto was proclaimed president following Pétion's death in 1818. Within two years he united the entire island under his control. To pay for his large army and fortresses, Boyer took out large loans from creditors in France and elsewhere.

In 1844 the Spanish-oriented eastern part of the island revolted and adopted its present name: the Dominican Republic. Boyer's weakened government was soon overthrown. Through the next seventy years, a succession of thirty-two different men ruled Haiti. Elections were dishonest and often ignored. New constitutions were frequently approved and then repudiated. Most of the rulers were tyrannical military commanders who seized power, and most of them were either assassinated or removed in coups. Haiti saw little economic development, and large landowners continued to dominate the economy. Meanwhile, Haiti's foreign debt continued to grow.

U.S. Occupation, 1915-1934. In 1915 President Jean Sam became the sixth Haitian president to die a violent death in four years. Faced with this disorder, U.S. president Woodrow Wilson ordered the Marines to take control of the country. Wilson insisted that the general disorder in Haiti threatened American life and investments. He also warned that the Haitian debt might cause a European country to intervene militarily. Wilson was continuing a U.S. policy known as the Roosevelt Corollary to the Monroe Doctrine. Under that doctrine, the United States was prepared to use force to prevent European nations from carving out new spheres of influence in the Western Hemisphere.

During the U.S. occupation, an American military high commission exercised police powers throughout Haiti. It installed a series of puppet presidents, supervised the training of a professional army and police force, and controlled Haiti's finances and foreign

Haitian Political Leaders

Pierre Toussaint L'Ouverture (1746-1803): Leader of the slave insurrection, he controlled the region by 1797. He was eventually captured and died in a French prison.

Jean-Jacques Dessalines (c. 1758-1806): Former slave who succeeded Toussaint-L'Ouverture as ruler of Haiti. He defeated the French invaders and was crowned emperor as Jacques I, only to be assassinated later.

François Duvalier (1907-1971): Medical doctor and Voodoo devotee who presided over a despotic and corrupt regime from 1957 until his death. His Tontons Macoutes kept Haitians in a constant state of fear.

Jean-Claude Duvalier (1951-   ): The son of Papa Doc, the younger Duvalier proclaimed himself "president for life" in 1971. He moderated the dictatorial practices of his father, but public demonstrations against his rule forced him into exile in 1986.

Jean-Bertrand Aristide (1953-   ): Radical priest who was expelled from the Catholic Church because of his revolutionary teaching. He became Haiti's first freely elected president in 1991. Forced into exile after a bloody coup, he returned with U.S. support in 1994.

trade. The people of Haiti had almost no voice in the administration of the government. Although a new constitution was adopted in 1918, a promised presidential election was repeatedly postponed. The U.S. occupation force did little to promote industrial development, and the administration opposed the idea of land reform. Very limited progress took place in the building of needed schools, hospitals, roads, and sanitation facilities. In 1922 a large U.S. bank loan to the Haitian government was negotiated, but the funds thereby obtained were primarily used to pay the interest on the national debt.

President Herbert Hoover, who disliked the U.S. occupation of Haiti, appointed a special commission to investigate the prospects for withdrawing U.S. troops. This commission reported that there had been enough improvement toward stability in order to conduct a general election. In 1930 Haitians voted on a new legislature, and Sténio Vincent, an ardent nationalist, was elected president. U.S. troops were gradually withdrawn from the country. The military occupation finally ended on August 21, 1934. In spite of Franklin D. Roosevelt's Good Neighbor Policy of that era, the United States continued to control Haiti's finances until 1947.

"Second Independence." After the U.S. occupation, Haiti continued to suffer from its long-term problems of grinding poverty, class conflicts, and political instability. In 1935 Haiti's President Vincent had the constitution changed so he could serve a second five-year term. In 1941 he personally chose Élie Lescot, another mulatto, as his successor. Five years later, a military junta dissolved the legislature, put into effect a new constitution, and ordered elections for a new legislature, which was empowered to choose the president.

In 1946 Dumarsias Estimé became the first black president since the U.S. occupation of 1915. He launched the so-called "Black Revolution," in which the government began showing preference to blacks rather than mulattos. Estimé promoted

social security and labor legislation. For a few years he allowed greater freedom for newspapers and opposition political parties. In 1950, however, after he tried to run for a second term, he was sent into exile by a military coup.

Haiti's new military leaders wrote yet another constitution. It provided for the direct election of a one-term president; however, the military leaders kept control over nominations and the counting of votes. That same year, General Paul Magloire, a popular black leader, was elected to a six-year term. Under Magloire, there were some signs of growing stability, and the demands of the Korean War (1950-1953) stimulated economic growth. Although promising to safeguard constitutional rights, Magloire increasingly ruled in a dictatorial fashion. When he tried to get around the constitution to remain in office, a resistance movement forced him into exile on December 12, 1956. This was followed by nine months of general anarchy.

"Papa Doc" Duvalier, 1957-1971. Into this climate of disorder and uncertainty, Dr. François Duvalier emerged as a popular leader of the black masses. The military had him elected president on September 22, 1957. A physician who practiced Voodoo, Duvalier (often called "Papa Doc") had held cabinet posts in the Estimé government. He recognized that the key to keeping power was to maintain firm control of the army and police forces. For this reason he created a personal security force of 10,000 Tontons Macoutes ("machete uncles" or "bogey men").

Even more than earlier governments, Duvalier's regime inspired fear by its widespread use of torture, imprisonment without trial, paid police informants, and censorship of the media. His potential opponents were either quietly executed or sent into exile.

In addition to fear and oppression, Duvalier also ruled by awarding government appointments and favors to his friends and supporters. As a proponent of noirism—a movement promoting black culture and unity—Duvalier expelled most elitist mulattos from the government. This policy clearly had great appeal among the impoverished majority. In his speeches and writings, moreover, Duvalier managed to convince many uneducated Haitians that he himself possessed mystical powers as a Voodoo priest. In 1961 Duvalier suspended the constitution so he could continue as president for a second term. In mid-1964 he used his growing power to make himself "president for life" under a new constitution.

With the general corruption and inefficiency of Duvalier's dictatorship, there was a clear decline in Haitian living standards. Haiti's reputation as a police state kept out both tourists and foreign investments. In 1963 the U.S. government discontinued most of its military and economic assistance to Haiti. A few years later, Duvalier began to make limited reforms to try to promote economic growth, and the United States resumed limited economic assistance.

"Baby Doc" Duvalier, 1971-1986. As Duvalier became seriously ill in the late 1960's, he again revised the constitution so that his young son, Jean-Claude Duvalier, would inherit his position. When he died on April 21, 1971, his son (called "Baby Doc") was named president for life. The younger Duvalier exercised less personal power than his father, and he authorized several liberal reforms. He allowed some freedom of the press and released many political prisoners.

The Tontons Macoutes continued to suppress the opposition, but with less use of torture and executions. For a while, foreign investors began to build a few more factories in the country, and the U.S. government resumed most of its military assistance. By the 1980's, however, a decline in the price of bauxite severely hurt Haiti's economy. Reports of the country's AIDS epidemic persuaded many tourists to avoid Haiti. Thousands of desperate "boat people" tried to flee to Florida. In 1984 food rioting broke out for the first time since the anarchy of 1956-1957.

Haitian president François ("Papa Doc") Duvalier poses with his son, Jean-Claude ("Baby Doc") Duvalier, in late February, 1971. When Duvalier died two months later, his son succeeded him as president. (AP/Wide World Photos)

In 1985 Jean-Claude Duvalier's regime agreed to constitutional changes, including legalization of opposition parties and the appointment of a prime minister. Early in 1986, however, the popular insurrection became so violent that Duvalier decided to leave with his family for France. There his property and investments were reported to total more than a billion dollars.

Post-Duvalier Dictatorship. Following the Duvalier period, Haiti's government was almost bankrupt. About half of the nation's working population was unemployed, and real wages were down. There was some hope for a political settlement when a provisional government under General Henri Namphy sponsored a more liberal constitution, which was approved in a referendum. The scheduled elections of 1987, however, were postponed when paramilitary forces attacked voters and opposition leaders. After the military utilized a special commission to control the elections in January, 1988, the results of the elections were considered fraudulent. That same year, General Namphy seized power in a coup. A few months later General Prosper Avril took over in another coup. Avril was an especially repressive leader who revived the Tontons Macoutes.

Following mass demonstrations and a general strike, General Avril agreed to turn over power to an interim president, Madame Ethra Pascal-Trouillot. Her government supervised the elections of December, 1990, which are considered the first genuinely free elections in Haitian history. The candidate of the left-wing Lavalas (Flood) Party, Jean-Bertrand Aristide, won two-thirds of the vote.

Aristide was a popular Roman Catholic priest whose ambitious agenda included land redistribution, a literacy campaign, price controls on food, an increase in the minimum wage, and some degree of socialism. Aristide's Lavalas Party, failing to gain control of a plurality of the legislature, was unable to further its program through legal means. Aristide appealed to the masses to engage in direct political action, and in one speech he defended "necklacing" (the burning of a tire around an opponent's neck).

Haiti's economic elite and conservative military

Future Haitian president Jean-Bertrand Aristide in 1988, when he was gaining a reputation as a Roman Catholic priest unafraid to speak out against the government without the support of his church. (AP/Wide World Photos)

leaders strongly opposed Aristide's program, and they were alarmed at the possibility of civil war. In January, 1991, a failed military coup resulted in seventy-four deaths. In September, General Raoul Cédras assumed power in a bloody coup, forcing Aristide into exile. Cédras and his military junta instituted a reign of terror, resulting in hundreds of deaths. Thousands of Haitians attempted to flee to the United States, often in makeshift and overcrowded boats.

Second U.S. Intervention. Although President George Bush condemned the Haitian coup, he strongly disagreed with much of Aristide's left-wing program. U.S. economic sanctions against Haiti were weak and poorly enforced. U.S. agencies circulated reports that cast doubts on Aristide's men-

Haiti

1492	Christopher Columbus discovers Hispaniola.
1697	France acquires western part of island of Hispaniola through Treaty of Ryswick.
1791	Haitian insurgency begins under Pierre Toussaint-L'Ouverture.
1804	Jean-Jacques Dessalines proclaims Haiti's independence.
1859	Haiti becomes a republic.
1915	United States occupies Haiti.
1934	(Aug.) U.S. occupation ends.
1941	Haiti declares war on Axis powers during World War II and allows United States to build airfields on island.
1946	Dumarsais Estimé begins Haiti's "Black Revolution."
1950	General Paul Magloire becomes president of Haiti after rigged election.
1956	(Dec. 12) Magloire's fall begins nine months of anarchy.
1957	(Sept. 22) François "Papa Doc" is elected president.
1964	(June 14) Duvalier makes himself president for life.
1971	(Apr. 21) François Duvalier dies; his son, Jean-Claude "Baby Doc" Duvalier, inherits his presidency for life.
1986	Jean-Claude Duvalier goes into exile.
1988	General Henri Namphy heads military junta.
1990	(Dec.) Jean-Bertrand Aristide is elected president in Haiti's first free national elections.
1991	(Sept.) Aristide is overthrown after nine months in office.
1993	(July 3) Military junta agrees to Aristide's return.
1994	(Oct. 15) Aristide returns to Haiti with help of U.S. troops.
1995	(Dec. 17) René Preval is elected president.
1997	(Mar.) U.S. occupation forces begin to leave Haiti.
1997	(Dec.) Chamber of Deputies rejects Herve Denis's nomination as premier.
1998	(Feb. 7) Haiti reopens its embassy in Havana, more than thirty years after breaking diplomatic ties with Cuba.
1998	(Mar. 2) Haiti asks United States, Panama, and Honduras to extradite leaders of 1991 coup that ousted Aristide.
1998	(Apr. 16) Haiti's second rejection of Herve Denis's nomination as premier continues ten-month impasse without a functioning government.
1998	(Sept.) Hurricane Georges kills nearly one hundred Haitians and devastates all of Hispaniola.
1999	(Jan. 11) Haitian president Rene Preval announces his intention to rule by decree in attempt to break stalemate with parliament.

1999	(Feb.) General Charles E. Wilhelm, commander of U.S. Army's Southern Command, recommends remaining five hundred U.S. troops in Haiti be withdrawn because of rising political violence.

tal stability and commitment to democracy. Fearing a large influx of Haitian refugees into the United States, the Bush administration intercepted "boat people" on the high sea and returned them to the island without any asylum hearings.

During the U.S. presidential election of 1992, Democratic candidate Bill Clinton condemned the forced repatriations as "immoral and illegal." However, after becoming president in 1993, he basically continued the same policy, whose legality was upheld by the U.S. Supreme Court.

Clinton put great pressure on both Aristide and Cédras to compromise their differences. On July 3, 1993, the two men signed the Governor's Island Accord, stipulating that Cédras would resign in exchange for amnesty, and that Aristide would return as president.

United Nations (U.N.) peacekeepers were to supervise the change in government, and the United States promised an aid package of $1 billion. In October, however, the arrangement fell apart when the first foreign troops prepared to enter the country. A paramilitary group, the Front for the Advancement and Progress of Haiti (FRAPH), threatened violence to prevent Aristide's return, and the U.N. forces, fearing a bloody confrontation, quickly withdrew from the area. Cédras and his junta appeared to be acting in cooperation with the feared FRAPH.

The Clinton administration responded with a new "tough" policy which strengthened the economic embargo, further eroding the living standards of the Haitian people. Just as Clinton appeared ready to order an armed invasion, a U.S. delegation led by ex-president Jimmy Carter worked out a new agreement with Cédras on the evening of September 18, 1994.

Cédras and his major associates promised to take "an early and honorable retirement" once parliament voted on an armistice, and Aristide would then serve as president until his term ended in less than two years. The accord provided for an initial U.S. occupation force of about 20,000 troops, with the dual purposes of maintaining order and training a new Haitian army and police force. Once order was restored, U.S. troops were to be replaced by a U.N. peace-keeping mission. Despite many reservations, Aristide agreed to the terms within a few days.

Most Haitians were enthusiastic about Aristide's return to the island on October 15, 1994. After confronting FRAPH, U.S. troops took control of the country, and Aristide was coerced into making many compromises with his program and his political appointments. He was not allowed to supervise the training of the new army and police, and he had to grant more authority to the conservative parliament.

With U.S. pressure, the Haitian government approved an economic plan which included free market principles, the elimination of half of the civil service jobs, a limit on state regulations, and a greater encouragement of foreign investments. An arrangement with the World Bank and the International Monetary Fund (IMF) provided Haiti with US$700 million in aid, which was to be used primarily to pay the foreign debt and stimulate development.

Another Beginning. The U.S. intervention appeared to be partially successful from a political perspective. By March, 1995, U.S. forces were beginning to leave as 1,200 U.N. peacekeepers assumed the responsibility for security. On December 17, 1995, Haiti held a free election in which a moderate Lavalas candidate, René Preval, was chosen as president. For the first time in the country's history, one elected president peacefully transferred power to another.

By the end of 1997, only some three hundred U.N. police advisers remained. Haiti's new civilian police, although small and imperfectly trained, was a great improvement over the past. However, stories of police violence and corruption continued to be reported.

Following Preval's election, the Lavalas movement split into left-wing and right-wing factions.

A U.S. marine strolls through Cap Haitien during the brief U.S. occupation of Haiti in 1994. (AP/Wide World Photos)

Believing that the government was moving too far in accepting free-market principles, Aristide and his leftist followers organized the Lafanmi (family) section of the movement. In the capital, Lafanmi and the larger Lavalas organization competed for jobs and political influence, and it was believed that radical elements within Lafanmi were responsible for several riots. Aristide continued to enjoy great popularity, and he was expected to run for the presidency in the year 2000.

Despite the accomplishments of the U.S. intervention, Haitians for the most part did not see much improvement in their standard of living. With a per capita income of US$270 a year, Haiti remained the poorest country in the Western Hemisphere. Little had really been done to deal with the continuing problems of overpopulation, soil erosion, unemployment, and illiteracy. Fearing

insurrection or seizure of property, foreign investors remained hesitant about doing businesses in Haiti. Unless economic conditions could somehow be improved, it appeared unlikely that the country would develop into a true constitutional democracy with free elections and a respect for human rights.

Thomas T. Lewis

For Further Study

Of the many books that survey the history and culture of Haiti, two of the best are Robert Heinl and Nancy Heinl, *Written in Blood: The Story of the Haitian People* (1996) and Selden Rodman, *Haiti: The Black Republic* (1984). An excellent overview of the larger region is in Franklin Knight, *The Caribbean: The Genesis of a Fragmented Nationalism* (1990). For Toussaint-L'Ouverture and the establishment of Haiti as an independent country, see Thomas Ott, *The Haitian Revolution, 1789-1804* (1973). The best study of the first U.S. intervention is Hans Schmidt, *The United States Occupation of Haiti* (1971). For a scholarly and interesting account of the Duvalier dictatorship, see Elizabeth Abbott, *Haiti: The Duvaliers and Their Legacy* (1988). Bernard Diederich and Al Burt provide a detailed journalistic account in *Papa Doc: The Truth About Haiti Today* (1969).

Jean-Bertrand Aristide explains his ideology and vision for reform in *Aristide: An Autobiography* (1993).

From a U.S. viewpoint, a short and skeptical account of the two military interventions is in Gaddis Smith, "Haiti: From Intervention to Intervention," in *Current History* (February, 1995). One of Aristide's advisers, Irvin Stotzky, presents a favorable, but perhaps excessively optimistic view of the second U.S. intervention, in *Silencing the Guns in Haiti: The Promise of Deliberative Democracy* (1997). A left-wing critique of the intervention and its results is in Tony Maingot, *Haiti in the New World Order: The Limits of Democratic Revolution* (1977).

Jamaica

One of the most volatile nations in the Caribbean, Jamaica suffered through a three-century period of colonial rule during which it experienced problems with racism, slavery, and social unrest. After gaining its independence in 1962 Jamaica enjoyed a decade of steady economic growth. Despite this success, problems with unemployment and the unequal distribution of wealth led to social and political turmoil. A faltering economy in the late 1970's accentuated these difficulties and led to increases in poverty, unemployment, crime, and election-related violence. The government was forced to borrow money from international lending agencies to maintain operating costs. Subsequently, this heavy foreign debt became a major constraint on Jamaica's economic prospects. Nevertheless, Jamaica has been one of the most successful black democracies in the world. It has not experienced coups or dictatorships and has a free press and independent judiciary.

The largest of the three islands in the Greater Antilles, an arc of islands in the western Caribbean Sea, Jamaica is also the third-largest of the Caribbean Islands. It lies 90 miles south of Cuba, 700 miles south of Miami, and 550 miles north of the Panama Canal. With an area of 4,243 square miles, it is approximately the size of Connecticut. Kingston is Jamaica's capital, largest city, and principal port.

Jamaica's green, mountainous landscape, sand beaches, and tropical climate lure thousands of tourists every year. Its main sources of income, other than tourism, are bauxite, sugar, citrus fruits, bananas, spices, and coffee. Much of the earth in Jamaica is reddish in color because of the large amount of bauxite and other minerals in the soil.

Jamaica has a diverse population of approximately 2.6 million people. About three-quarters of Jamaicans are black African, and about 15 percent are of mixed African and European descent. In the traditional Jamaican social system, people ranked one another according to skin color. The system grew out of slavery and colonialism. A small group of light-skinned Europeans and Middle Easterners made up the elite class, while blacks made up the lower class. Brown-skinned individuals of

Profile of Jamaica

Official name: Jamaica
Independent since: 1962
Former colonial ruler: Great Britain
Location: south of Cuba
Area: 4,243 square miles
Capital: Kingston
Population: 2,615,600 (1997 est.)
Official language: English
Major religions: Protestantism; Roman Catholicism
Gross domestic product: US$8.4 billion (1996 est.)
Major exports: crude materials (metal ores and scrap metals); food; beverages and tobacco, machinery and transport equipment
Military budget: US$30 million (1995-1996)
Military personnel: 3,320 (1997)

Note: Monetary figures rendered as "US$" are U.S. equivalents of values in local currencies.

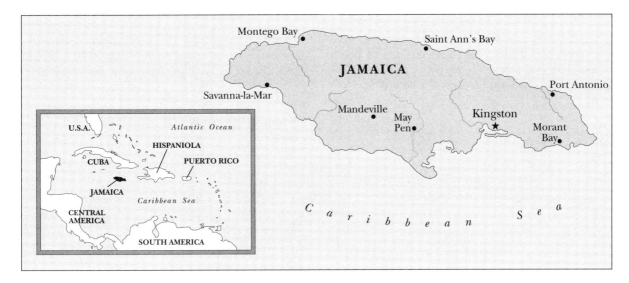

mixed European and African ancestries were generally in the middle.

The ancestors of most black Jamaicans were slaves brought to the island to help its English colonists grow sugarcane. Approximately two million Africans were brought to Jamaica as slaves. While English is the country's official language, nearly all Jamaicans speak a patois that is a mixture of English and African words with a few words from other languages.

Most Jamaicans are Christian, with the Anglican Church being the largest established church. There are also communities of Jews, Hindus, and Muslims. A relatively small number of Jamaicans are Rastafarians, who belong to an indigenous messianic movement that uses the Old Testament and celebrates blackness. Also known as Rastas, they are best known for their dreadlocks and reggae music. Rastafarians believe they are direct spiritual descendants of King Solomon's liaison with the queen of Sheba as told in the Old Testament. They also believe the true god is embodied in Ethiopian emperor Haile Selassie.

Colonization. Jamaica was settled during the Stone Age, about 6000 B.C.E. Its original inhabitants were displaced between 600 and 900 C.E. by Arawaks, an Indian people from the coastal region of Venezuela and Guyana in northern South America. An Arawak-speaking group of people known as the Taino settled in Jamaica.

In 1494 Spanish explorer Christopher Columbus landed on the island and claimed it for the Spanish monarchy. The Spaniards conquered, enslaved, and virtually wiped out the Taino. Many Taino committed suicide or escaped into the mountains and forests rather than become slaves. Columbus was stranded in Jamaica in 1503 and 1504 while he repaired his armada's ships. Spanish settlers from Santo Domingo, a Spanish colony on the nearby island of Hispaniola, established two colonies on Jamaica in 1509. Sugarcane cultivation began in 1520. Spanish plantation owners turned to Africa to replace the dwindling Taino slave population. The first African slaves reached Jamaica in 1513.

In 1655 a British armada conquered Jamaica after a one-day battle. Spanish troops later made an unsuccessful effort to recapture Jamaica. Jamaica officially came under British rule in 1670. The major British colonization of Jamaica began in the early 1660's. Bands of British privateers who plundered the ships and settlements of nations hostile to England found a home and protection in Jamaica. At one point the famous privateer Henry Morgan was the lieutenant governor of the island.

The British crushed a slave rebellion in 1690. Sugar production in Jamaica increased as England's demand for sugar to sweeten tea imported from Asia grew. In 1694 a French fleet invaded the north shore of British Jamaica in an effort to divert British forces from Europe, where the British and French were at war.

The British waged a continuing battle with the escaped slaves who had fled into the mountains and forests. In their struggle for freedom, many escaped slaves, called Maroons, built heavily fortified strongholds from which they could attack the plantations and plantation owners. The First Maroon War against British rule began in 1690.

In 1737 the Maroons and the British signed a peace agreement. The Maroons were given tax-free land and the right to govern themselves. They also agreed to capture runaway slaves and return them to their British owners and to help the British suppress future slave rebellions. Slave rebellions occurred in 1746, 1760, and 1793.

Freedom from Slavery. In 1800 the population of Jamaica consisted of approximately 300,000 blacks and 20,000 whites. The wealth of the island derived from its sugar and coffee crops. Following increasing popular sentiment in Britain, the slave trade was outlawed by the Act for the Abolition of the Slave Trade of 1808. The sugar industry suffered because many former slaves refused to per-

Born in Jamaica, Marcus Garvey came to the United States after World War I and founded the country's first black mass movement, the Universal Negro Improvement Association. In his self-styled capacity as "provisional president" of Africa, he occasionally wore a flamboyant uniform during UNIA conventions in Harlem. (AP/Wide World Photos)

form the difficult work of harvesting sugarcane for low wages. However, it would take thirty more years for black Jamaicans to achieve full emancipation from slavery.

The Western Liberation Uprising of 1831-1832, led by a slave, Sam Sharpe, marked a decisive turning point in the African Jamaican's struggle against slavery. The uprising set African Jamaicans on the path to freedom. The slaves originally intended to withhold their labor until they won emancipation, and plantation owners agreed to pay a fair wage for their services. While many of the slaves who participated in the revolt were executed, the revolt crippled the institution of plantation slavery and showed British and Jamaican authorities that it was perilous to postpone emancipation much longer.

In 1834 Britain passed the Act of Emancipation to free all slaves within its empire. When slaves in Jamaica were fully freed four years later, however, they were not granted the rights of full citizenship. In return for the loss of their slaves, the British government compensated plantation owners but not the slaves who did their work.

An 1865 uprising known as the Morant Bay Rebellion was quelled with great severity by the white minority in power. The outcry that followed forced the recall of the British governor and the disbanding of the House of Assembly. In the aftermath Jamaica became a British colony. Achieving the status as a colony meant that power shifted from the white minority to the crown. In 1866 British troops defeated rioting Jamaican laborers.

Toward Independence. During the 1920's and 1930's Marcus Garvey was perhaps the most feared and ridiculed black leader of his generation. From his base in New York City's Harlem, he challenged African Jamaicans to assert their rights and to be proud of their African heritage. He urged black Jamaicans to liberate themselves from the bonds of colonialism, build national self-esteem, and have pride in their racial heritage. Many white Jamaicans felt uncomfortable with Garvey's revolutionary message that black people should coexist with other Jamaicans and peoples of the world as equals. Garvey, who founded the People's Political Party, the Universal Negro Improvement Association (UNIA), and a back-to-Africa movement, struggled to

Jamaican prime minister Michael Manley (left) with Cuban president Fidel Castro during the latter's state visit to Jamaica in September, 1977. (AP/Wide World Photos)

make Jamaica a black nation governed by black leaders.

Jamaica moved from colonialism to full independence and statehood between 1938 and 1962. In 1938 a strike at the West Indies Sugar Company turned deadly and led to strikes, protests, and looting all over the island. That same year, Alexander Bustamante organized Jamaica's first officially recognized labor union, the Bustamante Industrial Trade Union (BITU). The BITU was the first trade union in the Caribbean. Bustamante was one of the founders of modern Jamaica.

In the same year lawyer Norman Washington Manley, father of future prime minister Michael Manley and Bustamante's cousin, formed the first political party in Jamaica, the People's National Party (PNP). Subsequent Jamaican political parties began either as trade-union-based populist movements or as national movements based on the demand for self-government.

Bustamante and Manley fought for improved working conditions and political reform. Manley led the campaign for universal suffrage and freedom from colonial administration. In 1943 Bustamante established his own political party, the Jamaica Labour Party (JLP). From their very beginnings, the PNP and the JLP fought each other for political power. The JLP developed into a party with a liberal and capitalist ideology, while the PNP leaned toward democratic socialism. The JLP oriented itself toward the West, especially the United States, and advocated a liberal economic policy. The PNP advocated greater governmental control and social reforms.

On November 20, 1944, Jamaica was given a new constitution that provided for universal suffrage. It was the first step toward Jamaican independence. In 1957 Britain gave Jamaica the right to govern its own internal affairs. Jamaica became a popular tourist site in the late 1950's, in part because of the advent of the intercontinental jet airplane.

Independence. Jamaica became an independent country within the British Commonwealth on August 6, 1962. By virtue of the Jamaican

Jamaica

1494	Christopher Columbus discovers Jamaica.
1509	Spain establishes first colony on Jamaica.
1513	First African slaves arrive.
1520	Sugarcane cultivation is introduced.
1655	Great Britain seizes Jamaica from Spain.
1690-1737	First Maroon War
1834	British Parliament legislates abolition of slavery throughout British Empire.
1838	Slavery ends in Jamaica.
1865	Morant Bay Rebellion erupts.
1866	Jamaica becomes a British Crown Colony.
1914	Marcus Garvey organizes Universal Negro Improvement Association in Jamaica.
1919	Garvey shifts headquarters of his movement to New York.
1938	Alexander Bustamante organizes Jamaica's first recognized labor union, Bustamante Industrial Trade Union (BITU).
1938	Workers' strike at West Indies Sugar Company turns deadly, leading to further strikes, protests, and looting throughout Jamaica.
1938	Norman Washington Manley launches Jamaica's first political party, People's National Party (PNP).
1943	Bauxite mining begins.
1944	(Nov. 20) Universal suffrage is inaugurated, as Britain signals its willingness to relinquish control over Jamaica.
1961	Jamaica and Trinidad and Tobago withdraw from Federation of West Indies.
1962	(Aug. 6) Jamaica becomes independent.
1968	Rodney riots leave three people dead and millions of dollars in property damage.
1972	Michael Manley becomes prime minister.
1976	National elections are marred by violence.
1979	Rioting disrupts Kingston.
1980	Violence mars national elections.
1997	P. J. Patterson wins unprecedented third consecutive term as prime minister.
1998	(July 29) Cuban president Fidel Castro pays state visit to Jamaica.

Independence Act, Jamaica formally assumed independent status as a dominion partner within the Commonwealth of Nations. This event ended one of the longest, unbroken periods of colonial rule in modern history—307 years.

The 1962 constitution established a parliamentary system based on the United Kingdom's model. A prime minister, assisted by a cabinet of fellow ministers, heads the government of Jamaica. The monarch of Great Britain is the formal head of state. A governor general, whose duties are purely formal and ceremonial, represents the queen. Jamaica was the first nation to have a provision guaranteeing a leader of the opposition written into its constitution. This provision ensures a two-party system. Bustamante, head of the JLP, became the first prime minister. The departure of British troops in 1962 marked the ending of colonial rule that began in 1655.

Between 1962 to 1972, Jamaica's economy steadily grew because of investments in bauxite, alumina, and tourism. Bauxite, the raw material for making aluminum, was mined for the first time in Jamaica in 1943.

Social and Economic Problems. In 1968 social and political disturbances highlighted the failure of the Jamaican political system to address the pressing issues of unemployment and the unequal distribution of wealth. Three people were killed and millions of dollars worth of property were destroyed in the Rodney riots of that year.

In 1972 Michael Manley, a trade unionist who headed the left-wing PNP, was elected prime minister. Manley helped forge stronger ties with communist Cuba. Between 1976 to 1980 Jamaica's economy declined, and unemployment rose. The Manley government resorted to foreign loans to keep operating. Manley turned to the international lender of last resort, the International Monetary Fund (IMF), which imposed strict borrowing conditions. Violence marred the 1976 elections, and the Manley government imposed martial law. Despite the violence and economic difficulties, Manley won reelection.

In 1980, amid violent elections that left numerous people dead, Edward Seaga became prime minister. Seaga was a member of the moderate, free-enterprise JLP. Under his leadership, the JLP was fiercely anticommunist and prodemocracy. Seaga accused Manley of wanting Jamaica to become another Cuba. In 1980 the most violent episode since the Morant Bay Rebellion of 1865 occurred. Street fighting

left hundreds of people dead, including 167 elderly women who lost their lives in an arson attack on a poorhouse. Seaga won the election in a landslide, and his mandate expanded in the 1983 elections.

Manley returned to power in 1989 for his third term in office. Thanks to an accord between Manley and Seaga, violence was limited during the 1989 election campaign. However, thirteen people lost their lives in minor disturbances. Ill health forced Manley to resign in 1992. He was replaced by Percival J. Patterson of the PNP. Twelve people were killed and dozens injured in gunfights during the 1993 election campaign, which was won by Patterson.

In the early 1990's Jamaica was troubled by depreciation of the Jamaican dollar, high inflation, labor unrest, unemployment, and crime. By the late 1990's Jamaica was the foremost producer of marijuana in the Caribbean region and an increasingly significant cocaine trans-shipment country for illegal drugs destined for the United States.

The major constraint on Jamaica's economic prospects is its heavy foreign debt. In addition, much of the wealth produced from tourism, manufacturing, and bauxite mining flows to foreign investors. Poverty aggravates the tensions of daily life. Historically, emigration by Jamaicans in search of better economic opportunities was heavy. Since the United Kingdom restricted immigration in 1967, the major flow of people has been

Jamaica's Gray Economy

During the 1990's Jamaica had one of the greatest disparities in personal income levels among its citizens of any country in the world. The majority of Jamaica's citizens gain little from the income generated by the nation's tourism, bauxite mining, and manufacturing industries, as much of that income goes to foreign investors. According to some estimates, approximately 85 percent of all Jamaicans can be considered as living in poverty. They are either unemployed or work at menial and seasonal jobs, as hotel maids, banana packers, sugarcane cutters, or sweatshop seamstresses. The nation's poverty imperils national stability. To earn subsistence living, many Jamaicans work in the "gray" or underground market. Some work as "higglers," middle-level merchants who buy wholesale and sell retail. Others raise goats and garden vegetables. Still others work as day laborers. Jamaica's underground economy springs from a tradition dating back to the slavery era.

to the United States and Canada.

Jamaica is a country with potential for growth and modernization. In 1995 a new party, the National Democratic Movement headed by Bruce Golding, was formed with the goal of restoring Jamaica to economic and moral health. In 1997 Patterson won an unprecedented third consecutive term in Jamaica's elections.

Fred Buchstein

For Further Study

A valuable guide to the history of the Jamaican people is *The Story of the Jamaican People* (1998), by Philip Sherlock and Hazel Bennett. The authors tell the story of the Jamaican people from an African Jamaican perspective. *Jamaica: A Guide to the People, Politics and Culture* (1993), by Marcel Bayer, provides readers with an introduction to the Jamaica. To gain an understanding of Jamaica's political culture, read *Distant Neighbors in the Caribbean: The Dominican Republic and Jamaica in Comparative Perspective* (1992), by Richard S. Hillman and Thomas J. D'Agostino. To better understand the history of conflict in Jamaican history, read *Ideology and Class Conflict in Jamaica: The Politics of Rebellion* (1990), by Abigail B. Bakan.

For a richer perspective on the role of slavery in Jamaican history, read *The Economics of Emancipation: Jamaica & Barbados, 1823-1843* (1995), by Kathleen Mary Butler, and *The Problem of Freedom: Race, Labor, and Politics in Jamaica and Britain, 1832-1938* (1992), by Thomas C. Holt. Clinton G. Hewan's *Jamaica and the United States Caribbean Basin Initiative: Showpiece or Failure?* (1994) provides an in-depth analysis of U.S. foreign policy initiatives on Jamaica. To learn more about Jamaica's economy, read Steven B. Webb's *Prospects and Challenges for the Caribbean* (1997). An analysis of the people of Jamaica may be found in Elisa Janine Sobo's *One Blood: The Jamaican Body* (1993).

To learn more about the conflicts in Jamaica and in the Caribbean, consult *A Short History of the West Indies* (1987), by J. H. Parry, P. M. Sherlock, and A. P. Maingot; *A Brief History of the Caribbean: From the Arawak and the Carib to the Present* (1992), by Jan Rogozinski; and *The Haunting Past: Politics, Economics and Race in Caribbean Life* (1997), by Alvin O. Thompson.

Internet information on Jamaica is limited and often targeted at tourists. Perhaps the best all-around site is http://www.jamaica-info.com.

Puerto Rico

The major political problem facing modern Puerto Rico is its status as part of the United States. Puerto Rico faces three choices, each of which has a potential for violence. At issue is whether Puerto Rico should become a U.S. state, achieve independence as a separate nation, or continue as a nonvoting member of a United States commonwealth. While many Puerto Ricans are satisfied with their present status, nationalistic pride has surfaced among those disillusioned with U.S. administration of the island and among fervent patriots.

Puerto Rico became part of the United States after the Treaty of Paris, which ended the Spanish-American War, was signed on December 10, 1898. Accordingly, Article IX of the Treaty of Paris provided that the civil rights and political status of the native people of the territories ceded by Spain would be determined by Congress.

The Foraker Act enacted by Congress in 1900 provided for the installment of a civil government in Puerto Rico and other ceded territories. In 1904 the U.S. Supreme Court ruled in *Gonzales v. William* that Puerto Ricans were not "aliens" under U.S. immigration law and were entitled to the protection of the United States at home and abroad. This ruling assured that persons born in Puerto Rico were classified as citizens of Puerto Rico until a further order of the U.S. Congress.

Unincorporated Territory. In 1917 Congress passed the Jones Act, which granted U.S. citizenship to Puerto Rican residents but gave them fewer rights. At the same time, the Jones Act reorganized the local civilian government of Puerto Rico. However, this act did not resolve the ultimate status or fate of Puerto Rico, which has retained the status of an unincorporated territory. In other words, the people of Puerto Rico are statutory citizens rather than constitutional ones. Puerto Rico is governed by Congress based on the Jones Act and the U.S. Supreme Court decision in *Balzac v. People of Puerto Rico* (1922). This decision stated that the basic requirements for the protection of individual rights must be at the forefront of any decision made by the federal government regarding the people of Puerto Rico.

In 1957 the U.S. Supreme Court reiterated in *Reid v. Covert* that Congress and the federal government controlled Puerto Rico in a temporary manner only. This decision stated that "locality" determines the application of the constitution. Hence,

Profile of Puerto Rico

Official name: Commonwealth of Puerto Rico
Status: dependency of United States
Former colonial ruler: Spain
Location: east of island of Hispaniola
Area: 3,515 square miles
Capital: San Juan
Population: 3,828,500 (1997 est.)
Official languages: Spanish; English
Major religions: Roman Catholicism; Protestantism
Gross domestic product: $31.6 billion (1996 est.)
Major exports: chemicals and chemical products; food; machinery

unlike the states, U.S. unincorporated territories were not "localities" to which the constitution had been extended, so that citizens of Puerto Rico could not enjoy permanent U.S. citizenship or nationality until such time as Congress extended to them the provisions of the Constitution.

The status of Puerto Rico has broad and significant implications for U.S. citizens and Puerto Ricans alike. Even though the rights and status of U.S. citizens are protected by the Fourteenth Amendment to the Constitution, if citizens becomes residents of Puerto Rico or any other unincorporated U.S. territory, they will lose their rights as constitutional citizens of the United States.

Police Violence. Self-determination in one form or another has been at the forefront of politics and daily life in Puerto Rico since the Jones Act of 1917. It was not until 1948 that Puerto Rico was able to elect its own governor. Until that time, Washington appointed the governor. This change effectively stoked the fires of the status debate for Puerto Rico. In 1950 Public Law 81-600, known as the Puerto Rico Federal Relations Act, was enacted by Congress. This law authorized the process for democratically instituting a local constitutional government in Puerto Rico and, in effect, allowed for the creation of a local government with the consent of the people and the approval of Congress.

In 1936 violence rose to the surface as the result of the murder of insular police chief E. Francis Riggs. Two nationalist youths, Elias Beauchamp and Hiran Rosado, were implicated. In the aftermath of the Riggs shooting, these two suspects were taken to police headquarters. Although the ensuing events are still open to question, the police said that the two young men reached for guns and were killed in a barrage of police gunfire. The violence

by members of the nationalist group was denounced, but it was widely believed that the killing of Beauchamp and Rosado by the police was unwarranted.

The following year, as the Nationalists were holding a peaceful march through the streets of Ponce, the police made matters worse by perpetrating what became known as the Ponce Massacre. The Nationalists had gone ahead with their march even though their permit had been withdrawn shortly before the march began. The police encircled the marchers in fear that trouble was brewing. A shot was heard, and in the ensuing barrage of bullets nineteen innocent participants and bystanders were killed. As a result of these events, political unrest involving the status of Puerto Rico and the imposition of a "foreign" government and culture on the Puerto Ricans came to the forefront of Puerto Rican politics.

Debate over Commonwealth or Independence. At the heart of the matter is whether a plebiscite should be held to determine the status of Puerto Rico. In the 1993 plebiscite, 48 percent voted for commonwealth status, 46 percent for statehood, and 4 percent for independence. Clearly the battle lines were drawn between statehood proponents and those who wish to remain members of the United States commonwealth. However, nationalistic pride has often been the catalyst for violence even in the halls of government.

The advocates of the status quo—commonwealth status—have argued that Puerto Ricans have the best of both worlds. They earn salaries in U.S. dollars but pay no income taxes. They may vote in U.S. presidential primaries but not in general elections. They have their own Olympics teams but get billions of dollars in aid from the U.S.

government. At the same time, opponents point to the fact that Puerto Ricans can be drafted into the U.S. military without enjoying full citizenship.

In the late 1990's Puerto Rican Governor Pedro Roselló led the forces of statehood. They wanted to use the centennial of the end of the Spanish-American War to make Puerto Rico the fifty-first state of the United States. The New Progressive Party, of which Governor Roselló was a member, wanted to mark the anniversary in an appropriate way. After the statehood forces submitted a bill to spend $98,000 to create a commission to study how best to mark the occasion, opponents of statehood were upset that the bill did not use the word "invasion," since it is their belief that the American landing in 1898 was an invasion and not an act of liberation.

Statehood advocates point to the fact that Puerto Rico enjoys a standard of living that is the envy of Latin America. At the same time, they point to Puerto Rico's per capita income of $8,000 as one of the reasons why statehood should be welcomed. Under statehood, Puerto Rico would get $3 billion to $4 billion in additional benefits, according to a 1990 study by the Congressional Budget Office. The amount of aid Puerto Rico receives from certain federal programs is capped. After statehood, Puerto Rico would get an additional $1.2 billion in Medicaid, $900 million in Supplemental Security Income (a program that was not available to Puerto Ricans in the late 1990's), and many more millions in benefits that were not available to Puerto Ricans in the late twentieth century.

U.S. congressional opponents of statehood or of

When U.S. president Dwight D. Eisenhower (left) visited Puerto Rico in 1960, he was hosted by Governor Luis Muñoz Marín, a life-long proponent of Puerto Rican independence who did much to increase the island's autonomy under American rule. (Library of Congress)

Puerto Rico

1492	Christopher Columbus reaches the Caribbean.
1508	Juan Ponce de Leon explores Puerto Rico and begins Spanish settlement.
1898	United States defeats Spain in Spanish-American War.
1898	(Dec. 10) Treaty of Paris cedes Puerto Rico to United States.
1900	U.S. Congress passes Foraker Act, establishing civil government in Puerto Rico.
1904	U.S. Supreme Court rules that Puerto Ricans are not "aliens" and are entitled to same protections at home and abroad as U.S. citizens.
1917	Congress passes Jones Act, making Puerto Ricans U.S. citizens.
1936	Violence erupts after arrest of two nationalists for the murder of a police chief.
1948	Puerto Ricans vote for their own governor for first time.
1950	Congress passes Puerto Rico Federal Relations Act, authorizing creation of locally elected constitutional government.
1952	Puerto Rico becomes self-governing commonwealth of United States.
1967	One-third of registered voters heed pro-independence factions' call for boycott of referendum on Puerto Rico's status.
1992	Pro-statehood New Progressive Party is elected to power.
1993	Voters favoring continuation of Puerto Rico's status as freely associated state win 48 percent plurality in referendum.
1997	Congress introduces U.S.-Puerto Rico Political Status Act, designed to grant Puerto Rico full self-government.
1997	In new referendum 51 percent of voters prefer continuation of Puerto Rico's commonwealth status.
1998	(Dec.) Puerto Ricans again vote to maintain the status quo in a referendum.
1998	(Dec. 13) Bare majority of Puerto Rican voters select "none of above" over statehood, independence, free association, and commonwealth in nonbinding referendum on future of the island's relationship with United States.

allowing a plebiscite have pointed out that the revenue collected by the Internal Revenue Service (IRS) under statehood would fall drastically short of the federal outlay in benefits to the island. In fact, many have argued that Puerto Rico was becoming a welfare state. Others have pointed out that the imbalance between federal revenues and outlays was exaggerated in the 1990 congressional study, because the study did not include billions of dollars that corporations doing business on the island would have to pay.

In fact, since the election of the pro-statehood government in 1992, federal tax exemptions have been eliminated. This alone has provided an additional $3 billion to $4 billion to the IRS. However, opponents of statehood have argued that the residents of the island would shoulder the biggest burden, because it would be necessary to impose a sales tax to make up the difference in lost revenue.

The purpose of House of Representatives bill 856, introduced in 1997, was to provide a mechanism leading to full self-government for Puerto Rico. Congress did not pass the bill. A subsequent plebiscite showed that 51 percent of Puerto Ricans that voted wanted to preserve the commonwealth status. The pro-statehood forces countered by saying that the voters were misinformed and that another plebiscite would bring different results. The potential for conflict remains. Puerto Rico, although it has the highest standard of living in Latin America, ranks below any U.S. state or territorial possession. Much disaffection exists among the poor, many of whom do not speak or wish to speak English. A repeat of the violence of 1936 and other years could reoccur at any time, as the issue will not go away.

In December, 1998, Puerto Ricans were again invited to vote on the territory's political status. Voters were asked to choose between Puerto Rico's current commonwealth status, statehood, full independence, and a "free association" form of independence, with ties to the United States. With 71 percent of Puerto Rico's 2.2 million registered voters participating, the referendum once again resulted in an endorsement of the status quo. Just over half of the voters selected "none of the above"—the position favored by those who wanted Puerto Rico to remain a commonwealth, while opposing the wording of the commonwealth option on the referendum ballot.

Supporters of Puerto Rican statehood jam the street outside the headquarters of the New Progressive Party before the December 13, 1998, referendum on the island's future status. Advocates of the status quo won by a narrow margin in the nonbinding vote. (AP/Wide World Photos)

Pro-statehood governor Pedro Rosello claimed a moral victory for his position. He did not recognize the "none of the above" option as valid, and the statehood option he favored garnered 46.5 percent of the vote. Nevertheless, by 1999 it appeared that Puerto Rico would remain a commonwealth with local autonomy for at least a few more years.

Peter E. Carr

For Further Study

A valuable overview of Puerto Rican politics and it history may be found in Arturo Morales Carrion's *Puerto Rico: A Political and Cultural History* (1983). Of specific interest to the status question is Surendra Bhana's *The United States and the Development of the Puerto Rican Status Question, 1936-1968* (1975). For an overview of U.S. Caribbean relations see Ransford W. Palmer's *U.S.-Caribbean Relations: Their Impact on Peoples and Culture* (1998). One very informative pro-statehood Web site is found at: http://www.puertorico.51.org. Also, see "Puerto Ricans Remain Undecided on Political Status," *The Miami Herald* (April 21, 1997) and "Puerto Rico Plebiscite Bill Slanted Opponents Charge," *The Miami Herald* (August 17, 1997).

Trinidad and Tobago

The island nation of Trinidad and Tobago has a long and unique history that sets it apart from its Caribbean neighbors. It is closer to South America than the rest of the Caribbean, and geologically speaking, not part of the Antilles islands arc. Whereas the peoples of most Caribbean islands are primarily African in heritage, the population of Trinidad and Tobago is almost equally divided between Africans and East Indians. Moreover, the discovery of oil in the early part of the twentieth century gave the islanders an economic bargaining tool their neighbors lacked, and strong labor unions provided a ready springboard for self-government. Despite a long history of European exploitation, the transition from British Crown Colony to independent nation was characterized, not by violence, but by strong partisanship and a fierce sense of nationalism often missing from other former dependencies. However, independence only created another set of problems. The political battle lines were racial during the early 1970's and economic and religious during the late 1980's.

The islands of Trinidad and Tobago are located in the Caribbean Sea just off the northeast coast of Venezuela, near the Orinoco River Delta. The two islands total 1,981 square miles in area and constitute the southernmost portion of the Lesser Antilles island chain. Trinidad, the larger of the two islands, is believed to have broken off from South America, while Tobago, twenty miles to the northeast, is part of a sunken mountain chain. Though topographically quite different, both islands feature a warm, humid climate with abundant rainfall.

Aside from a low mountain range, Trinidad's topography consists mainly of flatlands and low, rolling hills that made it well suited for colonial sugar plantations. Mountainous Tobago is densely forested with hardwoods.

Early History. Two indigenous ethnic groups, the Caribs and the Arawaks, originally populated the islands of Trinidad and Tobago. They are believed to have emigrated from South America. Christopher Columbus landed on Trinidad in 1498. The first Spanish colony was established in 1510. The mines and sugar plantations required more labor than could be provided by European servants. The first African slaves were brought over in 1517 but only made up 11 percent of the population—a ratio that would change drastically throughout the next two centuries.

To increase revenue, Spain opened the island of Trinidad to immigration in 1776. Many Roman Catholic planters from the neighboring islands established sugar plantations. They were eager to escape the religious and political persecution of the British and take advantage of Spanish promises of land grants and tax concessions. To further encourage immigration, Trinidad linked land ownership to the ownership of slaves—more slaves equaled more land. Free nonwhite immigrants also received land grants and were offered citizenship after five years.

British Rule. Great Britain conquered Trinidad in 1797 during the unrest in the Caribbean that followed the French Revolution. Spain ceded formal ownership in 1802. The British established Trinidad as a Crown Colony. This meant that the island was ruled by an executive council that included an appointed governor and a few top officials. It was augmented by local advisors. A somewhat larger body, the legislative council, advised the governor and passed local laws.

The number of colonists and plantations continued to rise under British rule. More than 20,000 of the 28,000 residents were slaves, and the native population was reduced to a few hundred scattered throughout the rural areas. By the early nineteenth century Trinidad's economy was based on sugar cane, cacao, coffee, and other export crops. The average plantation was approximately six hundred acres in size, larger than on any other island.

Great Britain ended the slave trade in 1807 but did not follow with complete emancipation in its possessions until 1938. In 1814 Britain took control of Tobago. Starting in 1844 the British allowed colonists to bring in indentured laborers from India to replace the captive workforce. While the other English-speaking islands suffered, Trinidad's sugar production quadrupled from 1828 to 1895, mostly because of the imported labor force. As of 1871 there were nearly 28,000 East Indians, totaling 22 percent of the population. Small numbers of other ethnic groups, such as Chinese and Portuguese, also immigrated during this time.

The British government united the two islands in 1889 in an attempt to economize on government expenses. Sugar was being produced more cheaply elsewhere, and Trinidad and Tobago ceased to be profitable. Tobago became a ward of Trinidad in 1898, losing its local government.

Labor Movement. Many Trinidadians fought beside the British during World War I. Among them was Captain Andrew Arthur Cipriani, who had served as commander of the West India Regiment. Known as "the champion of the barefoot man," Cipriani resented the fact that his forces were relegated to labor battalions in Egypt.

Profile of Trinidad and Tobago

Official name: Republic of Trinidad and Tobago
Independent since: 1962
Former colonial ruler: Great Britain
Location: Off northeast coast of Venezuela
Area: 1,981 square miles
Capital: Port of Spain
Population: 1,130,300 (1997 est.)
Official language: English
Major religions: Roman Catholicism; Protestantism; Hinduism
Gross domestic product: US$17.1 billion (1996 est.)
Major exports: refined and Crude petroleum; anhydrous ammonia; iron and steel
Military budget: USs$83 million (1994)
Military personnel: 2,100 (1996)

Note: Monetary figures rendered as "US$" are U.S. equivalents of values in local currencies.

Upon Cipriani's return to Trinidad, he worked to instill in the islanders a sense of national pride. Under his leadership, the Trinidad Workingman's Association became the Trinidad Labour Party (TLP) in 1935. Within two years it had 125,000 members. Cipriani was elected to the legislative council in 1925 and remained a member until his death in 1945. He was also elected mayor of Port of Spain, the capital city, eight times.

During the Great Depression of the 1930's, plantation workers were faced with fewer jobs, poor health conditions, low wages, and growing resentment of wealthy, foreign ownership in the oil and sugar industries. Unemployment was high, and wages were low. An unskilled laborer on a sugar plantation carned the equivalent of thirty-five U.S. cents per day.

Through it all, the plantations and refineries continued to show a profit and pay dividends to their stockholders. The difference between workers' wages and stockholder dividends led to riots on sugar plantations and in the oil fields in 1937. Tubal Uriah Butler emerged as the leader of the black oil workers, organizing strikes and calling for racial unity among black workers. His party became known as the Butler Party.

In response, the British deployed soldiers and established two separate commissions to investigate the conditions in their Caribbean colonies.

The commissions determined that the riots were caused by poor working conditions and low wages. They recommended improved housing, diversified agricultural, and an increased local role in government with the end goal of self-rule.

In the years following the 1937 riots, Butler succeeded Cipriani as the leader of the Trinidadian labor movement. Several more unions were formed, including the Oilfield Workers Trade Union (OWTU), All Trinidad Sugar Estates and Factory Workers Trade Union (ATSE/FWTU), and Federated Workers Trade Union (FWTU), which covered railroad and construction workers.

Global Influence and Elections. World War II brought global influence to the islands of Trinidad and Tobago. In 1941 Great Britain and the United States adopted the Lend-Lease Agreement, known

A distinguished scholar educated in the United States and Great Britain, Eric Williams founded the People's Nationalist Movement and led Trinidad and Tobago to independence in 1962. (Popperfoto)

also as the "bases-for-destroyers" agreement. This included ninety-nine-year leases of the harbor in the Chaguaramas district of northwest Trinidad to the United States Navy and of Waller Field in central Trinidad to the United States Army.

Work on the new bases brought U.S. and Canadian workers in close contact with the islanders and introduced a higher standard of living. This led to increased urban migration, a shortage of workers on the plantations, and unrealistic economic expectations as a result of exposure to American culture and consumption habits.

The 1946 elections were the first open to all adults. However, fewer than one-half of the registered voters actually cast ballots. Butler ran for the legislative council but lost to trade unionist Albert Gomes. The unions failed to present a united front and fragmented along racial lines. This problem would plague the islands for the remainder of the twentieth century.

The 1956 election was a turning point for Trinidad and Tobago. The People's National Movement (PNM) defeated Gomes and took the majority of seats in the government, an advantage they held until 1981. PNM founder Eric Williams, an islander, had spent nearly twenty years in the United States and Great Britain. A series of scholarships led to an Oxford University degree. He also worked for the Anglo-American Caribbean Commission in Washington, D.C., from 1948 to 1955 and helped coordinate nonmilitary policy toward the island region. Despite his academic accomplishments and high-profile position, Williams still felt the sting of racial discrimination, something that profoundly affected the rest of his personal and professional life.

Williams returned to Trinidad in 1948 as the deputy chairman of the commission's Caribbean Research Council. He entered politics in 1956 as the chairman of the PNM, made up mainly of middle-class blacks, with some support from the white and East Indian communities. Williams was everything the British wanted: a strong, charismatic leader with education and international experience.

Road to Independence. In 1958 Great Britain created the West Indies Federation, a modified attempt at self-government for its island territories. For the British, the benefits were primarily financial and administrative, while the islanders saw it as the first step toward total independence. The federation ultimately included ten island nations: Jamaica, Trinidad and Tobago, Barbados, Grenada, St. Kitts-Nevis-Anguilla, Antigua and Barbuda, St. Lucia, St. Vincent and the Grenadines, Dominica, and Montserrat.

The two largest nations, Trinidad and Tobago and Jamaica, spent the next four years at odds. Leading politicians from both nations refused to participate in federation elections. Trinidad and Tobago favored a strong federal government, while Jamaica favored a weak one. Trinidad and Tobago had higher revenues and therefore wanted representation based on economic contribution, while Jamaica preferred representation based on population. Jamaica's withdrawal from the federation in 1961 led Trinidad and Tobago to do the same, so that they would not become financially responsible for the remaining eight islands. The federation was dissolved in 1962.

Even with William's appeal and the support of Great Britain, the PNM still had to fight to maintain their base of power. In yet another racially polarized election in 1958, several groups opposed the PNM, including the Democratic Labour Party (DLP), composed mainly of East Indians fearing a loss of cultural identity under Williams's Afrocentric rule.

Great Britain continued to increase the amount of self-rule. In 1959 the executive council became the cabinet, and the chief minister was renamed "premier." This greatly benefited the PNM, who chose the U.S. withdrawal from the Chaguaramas naval base as their campaign issue for the next elections. Throughout 1959 and 1960 Williams repeatedly vowed that he would not trade British colonialism for U.S. colonialism and declared the 1941 Lend-Lease Agreement void.

In 1960 British prime minister Harold Macmillan promised to open negotiations with the United States with regard to Chaguaramas, with Trinidad and Tobago as an independent participant.

Satisfied at being regarded as an equal with the two international powers, Williams ceased his anti-imperialistic speeches. In December of that same year, the three nations reached a settlement that allowed the United States to remain until 1977 in exchange for US$30 million in assistance. However, the naval base at Chaguaramas was closed in 1967.

Led by Williams and the PNM, Trinidad and Tobago gained independence from Great Britain in 1962, one of the first states of the Commonwealth Caribbean to do so. Unlike many of the nations, the transition from commonwealth to independence was without bloodshed and upheaval. The PNM remained in power for the next thirty years.

Black Power. The Black Power movement took root in Trinidad and Tobago in 1970, led by the National Joint Action Committee (NJAC). The NJAC blamed foreign and local white capitalists for the country's 14 percent unemployment rate. A 1970 survey supported that claim—86 percent of business leaders were white. Williams had not held a press conference in over five years, and the poorest segment of the population had become disenfranchised.

On February 26, 1970, the NJAC joined the Students Guild in Port of Spain for a march protesting the trial of a group of Trinidadian students in Canada accused of occupying a computer center. Nine marchers were arrested, spawning a series of solidarity marches over the next few months. Williams attempted to placate the Black Power movement with his support and paid the fines of the Trinidadian students in Canada.

The marches continued, attracting additional supporters, until 30 percent of Tobago's population participated in solidarity marches during the first part of April, 1970. The deputy prime minister, A. N. R. Robinson, resigned from the cabinet.

A. N. R. Robinson waves to his supporters after learning that his National Alliance for Reconstruction has won an overwhelming victory in the December, 1986, elections. (Reuters/Bob Strong/Archive Photos)

Williams declared a state of emergency on April 21, hoping to prevent a march on the capital as well as a general strike. In response, some members of the Trinidad and Tobago Defense Force seized control of an army barracks, forcing Williams to purchase additional weapons from the United States and Venezuela. The remainder of the 2,500-member defense force stayed loyal to Williams. The crisis passed after trade unions called off their scheduled strikes.

Following the 1970 uprising, a disillusioned Williams introduced several measures to limit individual freedoms, broaden police search powers, and require licenses for firearms. A bill proposing state control over public meetings and freedom of speech was defeated. Concern about these measures led to the drafting and adoption of a new constitution in 1976. Williams died in 1981, and the PNM remained in power until it was replaced by the National Alliance for Reconstruction (NAR), a coalition party led by Robinson.

Oil Boom and Bust. The discovery of oil in 1907 supplemented the islands' economies and further differentiated them from the rest of the Caribbean. Exports did not begin until 1909. During World War I Trinidad and Tobago became the major source of oil for the British Royal Navy. Output rose from 125,000 barrels per year in 1910 to more than two million barrels by 1920. Foreign oil companies began competing for control. Eventually, oil replaced sugar as the islands' primary export.

The oil industry provided Trinidad and Tobago with something virtually unheard of in any other developing country—a strong middle class. Demands for jobs, improved working conditions, and better housing increased. As the economy deteriorated, unemployment rose to 15 percent by the late 1960's. This fueled the growing resentment of foreign ownership of essential industries—oil, sugar, and banking—which were all held by multinational corporations.

The mid-1970's oil boom saved Trinidad and Tobago from the recession affecting the rest of the world. Oil prices quadrupled, spurring rapid economic growth. Unemployment dropped to 8 percent. Prime Minister Williams invested the government's share of the oil money in minority and majority interests in over fifty corporations

Trinidad and Tobago

1498	Christopher Columbus reaches Trinidad during voyage of discovery for Spain.
1510	Spain establishes its first colony on Trinidad.
1517	First African slaves arrive in Trinidad.
1776	Spain opens Trinidad to immigration.
1797	Great Britain seizes Trinidad from Spain.
1802	Spain formally cedes island of Trinidad to Britain.
1807	Britain outlaws slave trade.
1814	Britain takes control of Tobago.
1838	Britain ends slavery throughout its empire.
1844	Britain allows colonists to import indentured laborers from India.
1889	Britain unites Trinidad and Tobago as one Crown Colony.
1898	Tobago becomes administrative ward of Trinidad, thereby losing its own local government.
1907	Oil is discovered off coast of Trinidad.
1925	Trinidad and Tobago take first steps toward independence with limited local elections.
1935	Trinidad Labour Party is founded by Captain Andrew Arthur Cipriani.
1937	Oil field and sugar plantation workers riot to protest low wages and poor working conditions.
1941	Lend-Lease Agreement between United States and Britain provides for establishment of U.S. airbase on Trinidad.
1945	Cipriani dies.
1946	First election open to all adults is held.
1956	People's National Movement (PNM), led by Eric Williams, assumes power.
1958	Britain creates West Indies Federation.
1959	Britain establishes cabinet government in Trinidad and Tobago.
1960	(Dec.) U.S.-British Lend-Lease Agreement is renegotiated.
1961	Jamaica withdraws from West Indies Federation, followed closely by Trinidad and Tobago.
1962	(Aug. 31) Trinidad and Tobago gain independence from Britain.
1967	U.S. Naval base in Chaguaramas harbor closes.
1970	(Feb.-April) Black Power movement holds solidarity marches.
1970	(Apr. 21) Williams responds to marches by declaring state of emergency.
1976	Constitution is redrafted to make Trinidad and Tobago a republic.
1980	Tobago's local assembly is reinstated.
1981	Eric Williams dies.
1986	(Dec. 17) A. N. R. Robinson becomes prime minister after National Alliance for Reconstruction (NAR) wins national election by large majority.

(continued)

1990	(July 27) Attempted coup by Muslim extremist movement, Jamaat-al-Muslimeen.
1992	PNC returns to power as Robinson loses reelection bid to Patrick Manning.
1995	National elections split legislative power between PNC and UNC.

doing business on the islands. Some were nationalized with compensation, while others were purchased outright, both by the government and private citizens. By the end of the decade, the government had become the largest employer in the country.

Everything changed when the bottom fell out of the oil industry in the early 1980's. Decreased oil production lowered government revenues. Fiscal deficits prompted the government to decrease subsidies, increase taxes and utility rates, and cut capital expenditures. In an attempt to stabilize the trade deficit, the government instituted a new import licensing system and a dual exchange rate, increasing tensions with the other Caribbean nations. By 1987 unemployment had soared to 17 percent. Some farmers began growing coca, the primary source of the drug cocaine, instead of the less profitable traditional crops.

Robinson was sworn in as prime minister on December 17, 1986. A former member of the PNM, he had served as finance minister from 1961 to 1967 and as minister of external affairs from 1967 to 1970, when he resigned from the party during the Black Power movement. Robinson promised to conduct a more open government. He attempted to stimulate economic growth with a number of new construction projects. A less popular cost-cutting measure was his elimination of the cost-of-living allowance in the public sector, which brought about a rash of union protests.

Coup d'État. Muslims make up 6 percent of the population of Trinidad and Tobago. However, few had ties with the extremist Jamaat al-Muslimeen (Group of Muslims), who advocated a radical mixture of left-wing politics and religious fundamentalism. Their leader was a former policeman who went to school in Canada as Lennox Phillip and returned as Imam Yasin Abu Bakr, an ardent Islamic radical.

Bakr's stated goal was to rid Trinidad of corruption, drugs, and poverty. Though most members

were Trinidadians of African descent, they denounced black nationalism in favor of Islam. Bakr, along with most of his three hundred followers, lived on a commune near Port of Spain. The group illegally appropriated eight acres of government land to build schools, shops, and a mosque and refused all official requests to relinquish the land.

On the evening of July 27, 1990, just as a car bomb destroyed Port of Spain's downtown police headquarters, Bakr and seventy of his followers seized control of the Trinidad and Tobago television studios. At the same time, a second group of gunmen attacked the parliament building, taking Robinson and over fifty other people hostage, including seven cabinet ministers. When the dust settled, Bakr addressed the nation on the state-owned television channel, stating that he and his followers had overthrown the government. He demanded that Robinson resign, new elections be held, and all who supported him be granted amnesty.

As looters nearly destroyed the main shopping district in Port of Spain, government troops surrounded Bakr and his followers. After five days without food, Bakr agreed to release Robinson, who had been shot in the leg. The following day, the rest of the hostages were released and the rebels surrendered, thinking they had been granted amnesty. According to government sources, Robinson had agreed to Bakr's terms but did so under duress. Therefore, his promises were nonbinding. Subsequently, 114 Jamaat al-Muslimeen members were charged on twenty-two counts, the most serious of which were murder and treason.

More troubling than the attempted coup was the outbreak of looting, which nearly destroyed Port of Spain's main shopping district. In a violent symptom of the growing discontent, capital residents emptied many stores and burned down others. The collapse of the oil industry had led to 20 percent unemployment and the worst violence since the Black Power riots of the early 1970's.

UNC Gains Power. The August, 1990, Iraqi invasion of Kuwait, which occurred just as Trinidad and Tobago's coup attempt ended, drove up oil prices. This greatly benefited all the other oil-producing nations, including Trinidad and Tobago. However, Robinson's troubles did not end with the increased oil production and higher revenues. Despite the restoration of many government programs, many black voters (most notably the urban poor) returned to the PNC.

At the same time, many of the NAR's East Indian supporters left to form their own party: the United National Congress (UNC) under former NAR deputy Basdeo Panday. This fragmentation allowed PNC leader Patrick Manning to defeat Robinson's 1992 bid for reelection. The NAR retained only two seats in its traditional stronghold of Tobago. The newly formed UNC managed to capture 29 percent of the vote, better than any Indian party had done before.

Heartened by their strong showing, the UNC set out to broaden its membership by courting mixed-race Trinidadians, Chinese, and non-Hindu Indians. After gaining the support of the Spiritual Baptists, a church that mixes Christianity with African traditions, the UNC increased its share of the vote from 29 to 45 percent in 1995, capturing a share in the government equal to that of the PNC.

P. S. Ramsey

For Further Study

Historical Dictionary of Trinidad and Tobago (1997), by Michael Anthony, provides a broad summary of the islands' history. Younger readers should seek out *Trinidad and Tobago* (1990), by Patricia Urosevich, for a similar overview. A third book, *David Frost Introduces Trinidad and Tobago* (1975), edited by Michael Anthony and Andrew Carr, provides a broad historical and cultural reference.

To learn more about the effects of the slave trade on Trinidad and Tobago, see *Africa in America: Slave Acculturation and Resistance in the American South and the British Caribbean, 1736-1831* (1993), by Michael Mullin.

Two books, *Under the Eagle: U.S. Intervention in Central American and the Caribbean* (1982), by Jenny Pearce, and *The Caribbean: Issues in U.S. Relations* (1984), by Raymond Carroll, provide a detailed look at the U.S. involvement in the Caribbean region. For a detailed study of the islands' political evolution since gaining independence, see *Class Alliances and the Liberal Authoritarian State: The Roots of Post-Colonial Democracy in Jamaica, Trinidad and Tobago, and Surinam* (1998), by F. S. J. Ledgister. For an in-depth account of the 1992 attempted coup, see *Against the Trinity: An Insurgent Imam Tells His Story: Religion, Politics and Rebellion in Trinidad and Tobago* (1997), by Maximilian Christian Forte.

A good overview of the region as a whole can be found in *A Brief History of Caribbean* (1994), by Jan Rogozinski. Other regional references include *Continent of Islands: Searching for Caribbean Destiny* (1992), by Mark Kurlansky, and *The Caribbean in the Wider World, 1492-1992: A Regional Geography* (1992), by Bonham C. Richardson.

Central America

Most violent conflicts in Central America have resulted from economic issues. These include a long history of unequal land ownership and use, unfair exploitation of workers, and abuses of political power. Political power has derived from combinations of land ownership and control over its use and its workers. The powerful presence of aggressive, profit-seeking foreign companies has also contributed to aggravating local economic problems. Fears of countries such as the United States about the spread of communism caused those nations to support unpopular governments. Opposing groups within Central America have fought civil wars over land reform and resource control, civil rights violations, and political control. Long-term economic disadvantages and hardships, inequality, and the negative effect of wars on the social order have contributed to growing incidents of violent crime

Articles in This Section

While most of Mexico is considered to be part of North America, southernmost Mexico and its Yucatan Peninsula are considered physically part of Central America, along with Guatemala, Belize (British Honduras until independence in 1981), El Salvador, Honduras, Nicaragua, Costa Rica, and Panama. Since the European Conquest began five centuries ago, Central America has never been totally isolated from foreign influence. However, its tropical jungles and mountains make travel difficult or impossible in many areas. The lengthwise chain of mountains includes active volcanoes whose past eruptions gave the area rich land. They still erupt from time to time.

Central America's coasts have long been the region's centers of commerce because of the importance and reliability of ocean transport. The fifty-mile-long Panama Canal, which crosses that country with a system of locks for ships, links the Atlantic and Pacific Oceans. The United States built the canal in the early twentieth century in order to avoid the long and expensive ocean trip around the southern tip of South America. As promised in the treaty made during construction nearly a century ago, Panama has regained most control of the canal, but only after some violent incidents. The Pan-American Highway, also largely constructed with U.S. money, runs the length of Central America, but with many parts in disrepair.

Modern Cultures. Central America's peoples are descended from numerous Amerind (Native American) groups, as well as European, Afro-Caribbean (Africans by way of the Caribbean islands), and Asian roots. A majority of the people in most of the region's countries are called mestizos—persons of mixed ancestry. The populations of southern Mexico, Guatemala, and Honduras are heavily Amerind. Costa Rica's population, by contrast, is mostly European by descent, with many Afro-Caribbeans and Asians living on the country's east coast. Belize, a former British colony, has large numbers of people of British descent.

Many Central Americans deny that discrimination is ethnic or racial. They say that it is economic: the few rich discriminate against the many poor. However, due to historical oppression, disproportionate numbers of poor are of either Amerind and Afro-Caribbean descent.

Languages. Before the explorer Christopher Columbus arrived in the New World in 1492, there were dozens of language families in the Americas. Modern Central America has six families of languages, each with numerous related languages. The largest language family spoken mainly within Central America itself is the Maya family. It has eleven main branches containing at least eighty separate languages.

Although many Central Americans speak more than one language, government and business are usually conducted in Spanish in all countries but Belize. Within the cities, many educated people study foreign languages such as English, in addition to Spanish. Due to the large numbers of retired U.S. citizens in Costa Rica and the many U.S. citizens working in the Panama Canal Zone, both

Spanish and English are frequently spoken in those places. However, many Central Americans speak only Spanish, and many Amerinds speak only their own native languages.

Pre-Columbian History. The first highly developed culture in Central America, the Olmec civilization arose around three thousand years ago (c. 1200 B.C.E.). It flourished until about 100 C.E. The Olmecs are best known for the huge stone heads they left near Veracruz, Mexico, as well as for their use of higher mathematics. Their societies had agricultural and professional classes, ruled by hereditary priests. Olmec society and the civilization that followed were founded on military conquest and colonization of other Amerind groups. Violence in Central America thus predates the European conquest.

The later Maya Empire covered parts of southern Mexico, all of Guatemala, Belize, and parts of

Panamanian students burn a U.S. flag in late 1995 to protest the continued presence of U.S. military bases in their country and to express their objections to the possibility of Panama's renegotiating its 1977 treaty with the United States guaranteeing the departure of all U.S. troops by the end of 1999. (AP/Wide World Photos)

Central America

Honduras until about 900 c.e. Like the Olmec, the Maya used a system of higher mathematics based on the zero (which the Romans did not have). They also used astronomy to predict solar eclipses and build an advanced calendar system. The Maya constructed monumental stone cities and were the only pre-Columbian people to develop a written language. However, the Maya had neither the wheel nor draft animals, and they used only stone tools. The Maya used slave labor to build their monuments.

The Classic Maya period ended suddenly about a thousand years ago. Theories suggesting large-scale agricultural failures or violent rebellions against the ruling class have been advanced as possible causes.

European Conquest. Christopher Columbus claimed Central America for Spain in 1502. Be-

cause many Spanish conquerors (also known as conquistadors) were motivated by greed for gold and by religious zeal, they killed many Amerinds to take their land and possessions or because the Indians refused to convert to Christianity. Roman Catholic Church authorities at the time of the Spanish Conquest discussed whether the Amerinds were human in the same sense as Europeans. The Spanish often mistreated Indians, justifying their exploitation as if they were beasts of burden. However, not all Spaniards mistreated the Amerinds, and more Amerinds died from European diseases, to which they had no natural resistance, than because of Spanish mistreatment.

Economic problems based on land ownership and use have been a root cause of violent conflicts in Central America since the sixteenth century. Immediately before the Spanish arrived members of many Central American societies shared their land and lived simple rural lives. To encourage aggressive exploration and colonization, the Spanish crown granted explorers both huge tracts of land and the right to use forced Indian labor.

Most Amerinds eventually converted to Roman Catholicism, while often retaining elements of their ancestral religious beliefs. Though European and Indian religious traditions blended over the centuries, the socioeconomic practices and the legal system did not foster mixture of the peoples. Central Americans of European descent were clearly favored. Though the Spanish explorers never found as much gold in Central America as they had hoped to discover, the Spanish prospered. They became landowners of huge estates worked by forced Indian labor (and later imported African labor). In general, Central Americans of European descent became wealthy, while those of Amerind descent remained poor. Racial distinctions were officially fostered by the colonial government.

Independence. The process of winning independence in Central America began in the early nineteenth century and ended when British Honduras gained its complete independence, as Belize, from Great Britain in 1981. The other Central American countries won their independence from Spain more than a century earlier, when virtually all of Latin America rebelled against colonial rule.

Immediately after winning their independence from Spain in 1823-1824, the nations now known as Guatemala, El Salvador, Honduras, Nicaragua, and Costa Rica rejected Mexican rule and attempted to form a union of their own, with a constitution similar to that of the United States. Due to violent uprisings, it failed. Each of the countries then became independent on its own. Since the early nineteenth century, each of them has typically been ruled by a series of dictators.

Economic Issues. Resentment about foreign exploitation of Central American resources and people has led to much violence, both in protest of the exploitation and in attempts to maintain control. Central America's rich land—which is especially good for plantation agriculture—began attracting foreign companies soon after the countries became independent.

Foreign-owned businesses have played an important role in influencing both Central America's

governments and U.S. policy toward these countries. In return for monetary gain and political support from the foreign companies and the U.S. government, many local dictators have granted favors to the companies and the United States. The dependence of Central American countries on foreign companies contributed to their being sarcastically dubbed "banana republics."

Ecological Issues. Ecological destruction threatens much of Central America. A major problem is deforestation, which has caused the land to lose its nutrients and produce fewer crops. Deforestation has been a byproduct of excessive logging—mostly by foreign companies—and the indigenous system of slash-and-burn agriculture, which Central American farmers have long used to clear and fertilize crop land. Honduras and El Salvador face the additional problem of rapidly growing populations and a consequent need for more farm land.

Guatemala. Guatemala is called the Land of Eternal Spring because of its usually pleasant climate. In contrast, the country has suffered a long history of a violent political climate. In 1998 the Roman Catholic bishop Juan Gerardi published a report cataloging human rights abuses by all sides during the country's thirty-six-year-old civil war. Drawing on more than 6,500 interviews, the report blamed the Guatemala military for nearly 80 percent of 150,000 deaths and 50,000 disappearances of persons during the war. Most victims were unarmed civilians, and three out of four were Maya.

In the late 1970's Gerardi was bishop of Quiche province, where most of 422 massacres occurred. After being the target of an assassination attempt, he fled to Costa Rica. He returned in 1984 and founded the Guatemala Archdiocese's Human Rights Office in 1989. He was murdered two days after publishing his report in 1998.

The centuries-old land practices and historical oppression of the Amerind majority of the population is behind much of the Guatemalan violence. The U.S.-owned United Fruit Company was the largest landowner in the country by the 1950's. Numerous violent incidents have resulted from clashes between the Amerind demands for rights and the landowners' attempts to maintain the status quo. These clashes escalated into a civil war between the Guatemalan military and rebels. After General Romeo Lucas García became Guatemala's president in 1978, death squads swept the country to eliminate opposition. By 1984 nearly 200,000 Guatemalan Amerinds had sought exile in Mexico.

Some Guatemalans have tried to resolve the country's conflict by using the political system and by writing in protest. Nobel Peace Prize-winning writer Rigoberta Menchu is a Quiche-speaking Amerind from Guatemala. In 1978, at the age of nineteen, she realized that learning Spanish and participating in political and legal processes was a key to helping her suffering people because the discriminatory government and business were conducted in that language. She dictated her experiences and the story of her people to a Venezuelan writer and they were published as the book *I, Rigoberta Menchú* (1984). An earlier Guatemalan writer, Miguel Angel Asturias, also won the Nobel Prize for Literature in 1967. His works include the novel *El Señor Presidente* (1946), which describes a fictional dictator.

Belize. The smallest country in Central America, Belize has an early history marked by violence. The first European settlement in Belize was established by English pirates at the mouth of the Belize River in 1638. Pirates used the region as a refuge because a barrier reef made landing difficult for enemies. Other Englishmen came later to log the forests and start plantations with slave labor. During the eighteenth century, the Spanish attacked repeatedly but the English won in the end. In the mid-nineteenth century, both Mexico and Guatemala tried to claim the area. A potential source of future violence lies in Guatemala's continuing claims to Belize. A popular Guatemalan bumper sticker says *Belice es nuestro* (Belize belongs to us).

While the English-speaking faction in Belize has remained economically and politically strong, the Spanish-speaking component of the population is growing. This is another source of mostly minor violence, but it holds the potential for future problems.

El Salvador. The struggle for political power in El Salvador began even before the country gained its independence. Moreover, other Central American countries, especially Guatemala, have interfered in its politics. El Salvador came to be ruled by a series of military regimes in the mid-twentieth century. Fraudulent elections, death squads, coups, and general violence were commonplace. For example, in 1932 the government of Maxi-

miliano Hernández Martínez had an estimated thirty thousand civilians killed in mass assassinations known as the Massacre.

When General Carlos Humberto Romero won a fraudulent election in 1977, death squads overran the country. In 1980 a revolutionary junta, the Revolutionary Democratic Front (FDR), claiming to be more moderate, seized power. That same year, the popular Salvadoran archbishop Oscar Romero was murdered during mass. He was known for speaking out against violence.

In protest, the Farabundo Martí Front for National Liberation (FMLN)—named for a communist leader from the early 1930's—unified guerrilla forces. The Sandinista Party of Nicaragua, which shared the FMLN's Marxist philosophy, sent military and logistic support while the FMLN remained in power. The violent struggle officially continued until the late 1990's, when peace was officially declared. However, the peace has not always been honored.

According to some newspaper investigations in the United States, El Salvador was a planning base for a series of bombings in Cuba in the last few years of the twentieth century. Reportedly, Cuban exiles work with Salvadoran criminals to create violent unrest in Cuba with hopes of a revolution against Fidel's Castro regime.

Honduras. The Spanish made the area of modern Honduras part of the military regime of the kingdom of Guatemala. Through the colonial era, they extracted huge amounts of gold until the mines ran out. After Honduras became independent, its location between Central America's two biggest powers—Guatemala and Nicaragua—gave the country continuing problems.

Nicaragua. The chief source of violence in Nicaragua in the second half of the twentieth century has been a conflict between rival political factions with differing economic philosophies. The unpopular dictator Anastasio Somoza surrendered to the Sandinista National Liberation Front (FSLN) in 1979. The Sandinistas favored economic and social reform and focused on the nation's continuing fears of invasion by the United States to maintain popular support.

U.S. intervention in Nicaraguan affairs began in 1855 when William Walker, a U.S. citizen, conquered Nicaragua with a personal army and declared himself president. He also reinstated slavery,

On his arrival in Managua in early 1995, Pope John Paul II is greeted by Nicaraguan president Violeta Chamorro, the first female head of a Central American government. (AP/Wide World Photos)

which had been abolished in most of Latin America but not in the United States. Although Walker's government was immediately recognized by the United States, both the United States and Great Britain helped depose him a year later.

U.S. Marines landed in Nicaragua in 1909 to support a Conservative rebellion against a Liberal president, which triggered a civil war. This was quashed by the Marines in 1912, as was another civil war in 1926. However, in 1933 the army of Nicaraguan General Augusto César Sandino (for whom the Sandinistas were later named) drove the Marines out. He was assassinated in 1934 by the Nicaraguan National Guard, which had been reorganized by the United States under the command of Anastasio Somoza García. Somoza began a forty-five-year family dynasty that was generally supported by the U.S. government.

After Anastasio Somoza Debayle surrendered to the Marxist FLSN in 1979, the U.S. government feared that Nicaragua might align with the Communist bloc. Under Ronald Reagan's administra-

tion during the 1980's, the United States supported a rival faction in Nicaragua known as the Contras with money and military advisors. The Contras originated in elements of the defeated personal army of the deposed Somoza who had escaped to Honduras to plan a counter-revolution (*contrarrevolución*), from which they took their name. At least 50,000 Nicaraguans died in the fighting.

The Nicaraguan people tired of the efforts of the Sandinista government to maintain power. In 1984 they elected one of the few women to serve as president of a Latin American country, Violeta Chamorra, a non-Sandinista newspaper publisher.

Costa Rica. Taking its name from the Spanish for "rich coast," Costa Rica has been called the Switzerland of Central America because it, like Switzerland, has had a successful democracy. Within Central America, Costa Rica is unique in several ways. Its territory was comparatively ignored during the Spanish Conquest because it offered little wealth that could be shipped back to Spain. As a result, it was settled mostly by individu-

Nicaraguans celebrate the seventeenth anniversary of the Sandinista revolution by forming a human pyramid in Managua's Plaza of the Revolution in July, 1979. Many hold flags of the Sandinista National Liberation Front (FSLN). (AP/Wide World Photos)

als who worked their own land, instead of rich plantation owners who used slave labor.

Costa Rica is the only Central American country with a population made up primarily of people of European-descent. It has never had an army, navy, or air force. Although it experienced a brief period of political disorder in 1948, Costa Rica has maintained its democratic institutions and political neutrality. During the 1980's Costa Rica's President Oscar Arias Sánchez closed down the Contra bases in his country as one of his first official acts. He then organized a summit meeting among the Central American countries torn by war, especially Nicaragua. Arias Sánchez won the Nobel Peace Prize in 1987 for his efforts to broker peace in the region.

During the 1990's Costa Rica lost some of its innocence. The National Congress in the capital city of San José was attacked by Nicaraguan extremists seeking international attention. Terrorists also kidnapped American tourists from a resort on the west coast. Both armed and unarmed people have been assassinated.

Panama. Much of the violence in Panama has been related to economics stemming from the U.S. role in financing the Panama Canal and Pan-American Highway. By 1998 the Pan-American Highway still ended about two hundred miles from Panama's border with Colombia. One reason given by the U.S. government for not paving the gap is that a totally complete highway would make access directly into the United States easier for illegal drug trafficking by the Colombian drug cartels. The fears of drug trafficking via Panama are underlined by the conviction of former Panamanian president Manuel Antonio Noriega in U.S. courts for that offense.

U.S. president George Bush ordered American troops to invade Panama and arrest Noriega in 1989. Despite this foreign intrusion, no significant violent protests ensued in Panama. The reason apparently lay in the fact that 80 percent of Panamanians approved Noriega's overthrow.

The United States has promised to turn over full control of the Panama Canal and the U.S. military bases surrounding it by 1999. However, the U.S. and Panamanian governments have discussed maintaining a U.S. troop presence in the Canal Zone because of the drug threat posed by the Pan-American Highway and Panama's border with Colombia.

Debra D. Andrist

For Further Study

There is a comparatively large literature in English on Central America. For an overview of the region, a good starting point is *Middle America and the Caribbean* (1995), edited by David Levinson, in Yale University's *The Encyclopedia of World Cultures*. Another good source is Dario Moreno's *The Struggle for Peace in Central America* (1994).

Much has been published about Central America's pre-Colombian cultures. *The Legacy of Mesoamerica: History and Culture of a Native Civilization* (1995), edited by Robert M. Carmack and others,

Central America

1502	Christopher Columbus claims Central America for Spain.
1763	British sign Treaty of Paris recognizing Spanish rule in Central America.
1821	(Sept. 15) Central American Declaration of Independence is issued.
1823-1824	Central American nations reject Mexican rule and attempt to form United Provinces of Central America.
1825-1829	Civil War divides Central America.
1837-1840	Second Central American civil war is fought.
1842	All Central American nations except Costa Rica form defense pact that recognizes individual nations' independence.
1850-1855	U.S. business interests build trans-Panama railroad.
1855	American adventurer William Walker takes control of Nicaraguan government.
1857	U.S. and British governments help depose Walker in Nicaragua.
1898	After Spanish-American War, United States begins to increase its presence in Central America.
1903	Panama secedes from Colombia.
1903	United States and newly independent Panama sign treaty authorizing construction of Panama Canal.
1909	Landing of U.S. Marines in Nicaragua triggers civil war.
1912	U.S. Marines quash Nicaraguan civil war.
1926	U.S. Marines stop renewed civil war in Nicaragua.
1933	Augusto César Sandino leads effort to drive U.S. Marines out of Nicaragua.
1934	Sandino is assassinated; Farabundo Martí Liberation Front unifies Nicaraguan guerrillas.
1948	Civil uprising in Costa Rica.
1948	(Apr. 30) Organization of American States is formed.
1949	Costa Rican army is abolished.
1954	Guatemala president Jacabo Arbenz is overthrown by CIA-backed invasion launched from Honduras.
1955	U.S. government mines harbor in Managua, Nicaragua.
1960	Treaty of Managua creates Central American Common Market.
1964	Great Britain grants self-rule to British Honduras, which becomes Belize.
1978	Guatemalan Bishop Juan Gerardi flees to Costa Rica after assassination attempt.
1979	President Anastasio Somoza Debayle surrenders to Sandinista National Liberation Front in Nicaragua.
1980	Revolutionary Democratic Front (FDR) seizes power in El Salvador.
1980's	President Arias Sánchez closes contra bases in Costa Rica and organizes Central American summit.

(continued)

1980	Salvadoran archbishop Oscar Romero is assassinated.
1981-1988	U.S. government supports Nicaraguan Contras.
1981	Farabundo Martí Liberation Front mounts offensive against Salvadoran government.
1981	(Sept. 21) Belize gains full independence.
1984	Bishop Gerardi returns to Guatemala.
1987	Costa Rican president Arias Sánchez wins Nobel Peace Prize.
1989	Bishop Gerardi founds Guatemala Archdiocese's Human Rights Office.
1989	United States invades Panama to arrest Panamanian president Noriega.
1990's	Tzotzil farmers in Chiapas, Mexico organize as Zapatista rebels.
1992	Nicaraguan extremists attack Costa Rican National Congress.
1992	Guatemalan Rigoberta Menchú wins Nobel Peace Prize.
1997	Terrorists kidnap U.S. tourists in Costa Rica.
1997	(Apr.) Declarations of peace in El Salvador; Salvadoran criminals provoke incidents in Cuba and other Latin American countries.
1998	Guatemalan Bishop Gerardi publishes *Never Again*; he is assassinated two days later.
1998	U.S. students are robbed and assaulted in Guatemala.
1998	(Nov.) Hurricane Mitch rips through Central America.
1999	Date for total Panamanian control of Canal according to treaty.
1999	(Jan.-Feb.) Number of undocumented migrants passing through Mexico from Central America surges because of devastation caused by Hurricane Mitch.
1999	(Mar.) U.S. president Bill Clinton visits El Salvador, Nicaragua, Honduras, Guatemala, and Panama; while apologizing for U.S. support of repressive Guatemalan regimes of the past, he pledges U.S. support for reconciliation efforts throughout Central America.

is useful for relating the remote past to the present. *Central America Since Independence* (1991), edited by Leslie Bethell, is a collection of essays on Central America's political history. Another useful collection is *Central America: Historical Perspectives on the Contemporary Crises* (1988), edited by Ralph L. Woodward, Jr.

U.S. relations with Central American nations is the subject of numerous books. Though a bit dated, Jenny Pearce's *Under the Eagle: U.S. Intervention in Central America and the Caribbean* (1982) remains useful. More recent analyses include Ronald W. Cox, *Power and Profits: U.S. Policy Toward Central America* (1994), and Donald E. Schulz and

Deborah Sundloff Schulz's *The United States, Honduras, and the Crisis in Central America* (1994).

The many books on Central America written for young readers include *Central America: Opposing Viewpoints* (1990), edited by Carol Wekesser, and others; Faren Bachelis, *The Central Americans* (1990), in Chelsea House's Peoples of North America Series; and Graham Hovey and Gene Brown, *Central America and the Caribbean* (1980), in Ayers's Great Contemporary Issues Series. Several books on the region by Marion Morrison include *Central America* (1995), in Watts's Places and Peoples Series.

El Salvador and Honduras

The border between Honduras and El Salvador in Central America has been the site of violent conflict for more than two hundred years. Three factors have contributed to this unrest. First, the border has been ill defined since the beginning of the Spanish colonial era. As a result, certain areas along the border have been claimed by both El Salvador and Honduras. The second cause of friction along the border is rooted in the social and economic disparity between the two countries. This inequality can be traced back to the colonial period and is directly influenced by differences in topography, the availability of natural resources, and population distribution between El Salvador and Honduras. The general political climate of Central America is the third factor in the El Salvador-Honduras border dispute. In addition to the conflicts experienced among all the Central American states throughout the years since Spain exited the region, El Salvador and Honduras have both suffered intense internal strife, often leading to civil war. These internal power struggles have spread across the border, further aggravating the territorial dispute.

Honduras and El Salvador are situated in Central America between Guatemala to the west and Nicaragua to the east. Honduras is bordered on the north by the Caribbean Sea, while the Pacific Ocean runs along El Salvador's southern coast. Honduras possesses a small Pacific coastline along its southern border on the Gulf of Fonseca. The conflict between El Salvador and Honduras has centered on the border connecting northern El Salvador and southern Honduras, as well as the Gulf of Fonseca.

The topography of each country has had a significant influence on the separate development of their social and economic systems. Although Honduras is the second-largest country in Central America, the availability of land for cultivation is limited. With the exception of the coastal plain, rugged mountains dominate the landscape. Because the topography limits the amount of flat, arable land and the use of other natural resources, the population density of Honduras is less than that of El Salvador and other Central American countries.

In contrast, the topography of El Salvador is marked by volcanoes, some of which are still active. Volcanic ash, lava, and sediment have made the soil very fertile, especially along the Pacific coast. Even though El Salvador is smaller in geographical area than Honduras, the lush growing conditions have made the land favorable for cultivation. Therefore, El Salvador has been able to support large populations for thousands of years.

Colonial Rule. The Spanish Conquest and subsequent rule has also shaped the economic and social structure of both nations. During the early sixteenth century, Spanish conquistadors arrived in Central America searching for precious metals. Pedro de Alvarado and his army invaded the territory now known as El Salvador, while expeditions led by Gonzáles Dávila and Cristóbal de Olid explored Honduras. They encountered the Pipil Indians in El Salvador and the descendants of the

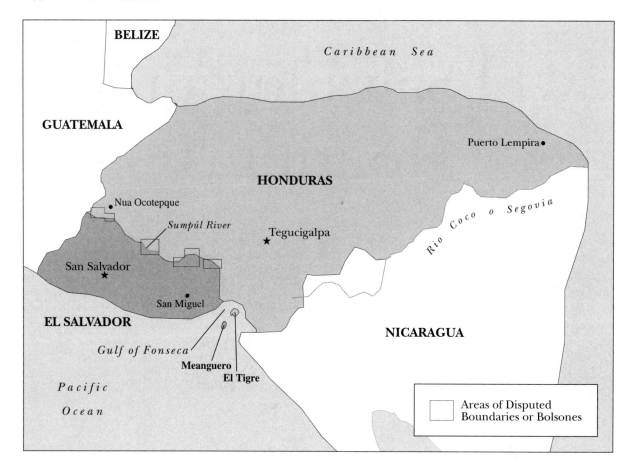

Maya in Honduras. The Spanish subsequently forced the native population to work the land, as well as the gold and silver mines. Intermarriage between the Spanish settlers and native peoples produced a large population of mestizos, or people of mixed Spanish-indigenous heritage.

When mining declined in the provinces in the mid-sixteenth century, the only exploitable resource became the land. In each province, the Spanish devised the *encomienda* system, in which large tracts of land were granted by the Spanish crown. Grantees were given the right to collect tribute from the native peoples within their designated areas. This resulted in widespread oppression of the Indians as well as land grabbing by the Spanish overlords.

In El Salvador, which was rich in agricultural resources, a rigid social structure evolved in which most of the productive land was owned by an elite few. In contrast, the ruling class of Honduras was much poorer than their Salvadoran counterparts.

The Honduran peasants lived in widely scattered villages isolated from one another by mountain ranges. Consequently, the Honduran landowners found it impossible to organize the lower class into cohesive units in order to control them. Because of their relative independence, Honduran peasants were better off than the underprivileged people in El Salvador and actually fared better than the Honduran upper class. Moreover, as the Honduran peasants engaged in the exporting of livestock, precious metals, lumber, indigo, sarsaparilla, rum, and tobacco, their incomes rose, while the coffers of the elite grew little.

The contrast between the El Salvadoran oligarchy's control over the poor and the Honduran upper class's relatively weak power over the peasants influenced the social and economic conditions of both countries. It led to a more oppressive class structure in El Salvador, which in turn led to a wide gap between rich and poor. Honduras evolved into a more egalitarian society. The overcrowded conditions and the gulf between the upper and lower classes in El Salvador motivated more people to seek a better future across the border in Honduras. As people began to flock to Honduras, especially in the seventeenth and eighteenth centuries, border disagreements began to emerge.

Independence. By the early nineteenth century, Spanish influence had declined considerably. On September 15, 1821, all the Central American provinces declared their independence from Spain. On July 1, 1823, the five states of El Salvador, Guatemala, Honduras, Nicaragua, and Costa Rica established the United Provinces of Central America. Because of persistent antagonism between Conservative and Liberal factions in the various states, the federation was short-lived.

On November 15, 1838, after two Central American civil wars, Honduras became a nation in its own right. In January of 1841, El Salvador followed suit. The formation of independent nations did not bring the desired stability to the region. Honduras, El Salvador, Guatemala, and Nicaragua all had borders in common and constantly fought for predominance in the region. The situation was further aggravated by continued squabbling between Liberals and Conservatives in different nations. For the remainder of the nineteenth century and well into the twentieth century, Honduras, El Salvador, and their neighbors routinely interfered with one another's internal politics.

The early twentieth century was a period of continued unrest for Honduras and El Salvador, both internally and externally. Both countries were ruled by a succession of dictators, and coups and coup attempts were commonplace. For example, from 1920 to 1923, there were seventeen coups or uprisings in Honduras alone.

U.S. Intervention. As the economic and political instability of the region continued to deteriorate, the United States began to make headway into the region. Its presence increased after the Spanish-American War ended in 1898. The decision to build a canal in nearby Panama that would link the Atlantic and Pacific Oceans opened the door to expanded commercial activities for U.S. companies and a more active role for the U.S. government. The United States began pouring money into the economies of El Salvador, Honduras, and their neighbors. The United States also became a major influence in fighting left-wing political factions, promoting democracy, and arbitrating disputes between nations.

By the late 1950's and early 1960's, U.S. power was firmly established in Central America. Foreign businesses invested freely without any thought to economic balance between countries. Because El Salvador was more industrialized than Honduras, it received the largest portion of capital, further contributing to imbalance. Between 1965 and 1968 El Salvador exported more than five times the amount of goods to Honduras than it had in the past, while Honduran exports to El Salvador declined.

Honduran manufacturers could not compete with the glut of Salvadoran products. The Honduran economy was nearing a crisis. Unemployment, trade deficits, and scandals within the regime of López Arellano contributed to the mounting social and political unrest. The government cracked down on any opposition. The situation was espe-

Profile of El Salvador

Official name: Republic of El Salvador
Independent since: 1821
Former colonial ruler: Spain
Location: south of Honduras
Area: 8,124 square miles
Capital: San Salvador
Population: 5,661,800 (1997 est.)
Official language: Spanish
Major religions: Roman Catholicism; Protestantism
Gross domestic product: US$12.2 billion (1996 est.)
Major exports: coffee; paper products; clothing; pharmaceutical; raw sugar
Military budget: US$101 million (1996)
Military personnel: 28,400 (1996)

Note: Monetary figures rendered as "US$" are U.S. equivalents of values in local currencies.

cially serious in the Honduran countryside. As the population grew, the numbers of landless and unemployed people grew as well.

At this point, 300,000 undocumented Salvadoran immigrants, most of them living along the border between El Salvador and Honduras, became the scapegoats for the López regime's problems. To divert further criticism, the government, along with the landowners, began to exploit anti-Salvadoran feelings. In 1966 the powerful Federación Nacional de Agricultores y Ganaderos de Honduras (FENAGH) was formed by the large farmers and cattle ranchers in Honduras to protect their own interests against the growing pressure from the peasants for agrarian reform. FENAGH accused the Salvadorans of illegal land invasions.

In January of 1969 FENAGH urged the Honduran government not to renew the 1967 Bilateral Treaty on Immigration with El Salvador. This agreement had been designed to regulate immigrant flow across their common border. In April the Honduran government began to expel the Salvadoran squatters from their lands. The military took charge and enforced the edict with violence. In late May Salvadorans began to cross the border back to an overpopulated El Salvador. By June five hundred Salvadoran families had been dispossessed and had lost everything. The Salvadoran press fueled the controversy by engaging in anti-Honduran tirades.

Soccer War. As a result of the immigrant problem, tensions between El Salvador and Honduras were running high in June of 1969. The breaking point came when the two nations faced each other in a three-game elimination match in the regional World Cup soccer competition. Trouble among fans of both countries erupted during the first game in Tegucigalpa, the capital of Honduras.

The situation deteriorated further when the second game was played in the capital of El Salvador, San Salvador. Honduran fans were attacked, the Honduran flag was desecrated, and the Honduran national anthem was ridiculed. Salvadorans living in Honduras became targets of violence. Many were killed, and thousands more were ousted from the country. El Salvador filed a grievance with the Inter-American Commission on Human Rights, charging Honduras with genocide. Diplomatic ties were broken on June 27, 1969.

On July 14 Salvadoran warplanes attacked targets inside Honduras. The Salvadoran army launched major offensives along principal roads connecting the two countries and invaded the Honduran islands in the Gulf of Fonseca. They then attacked and captured the provincial capital of Nueva Ocotepeque. With a population of five thousand people, it was the largest city over which the Salvadorans gained control. The offensive then stalled because of Honduran reprisals. Honduran air strikes caused extensive damage to Salvadoran oil reserves, contributing to El Salvador's growing fuel shortage.

The day after the war began, the Organization of American States (OAS) called for an immediate cease-fire and withdrawal of El Salvador's forces from Honduras. For several days, El Salvador refused to give in to OAS demands. Finally, a cease-fire was arranged on July 18, 1969, and took effect on July 20. El Salvador continued to resist pressure to withdraw its troops from Honduras but finally agreed to do so by the first days of August.

The war proved devastating to both sides, and there was no winner. Between 60,000 and

Profile of Honduras

Official name: Republic of Honduras
Independent since: 1821
Former colonial ruler: Spain
Location: north of El Salvador and Nicaragua
Area: 43,278 square miles
Capital: Tegucigalpa
Population: 5,751,400 (1997 est.)
Official language: Spanish
Major religions: Roman Catholicism; Protestantism
Gross domestic product: US$11.5 billion (1996)
Major exports: coffee; bananas; shrimp and lobsters; zinc
Military budget: US$42.5 million (1997)
Military personnel: 18,800 (1996)

Note: Monetary figures rendered as "US$" are U.S. equivalents of values in local currencies.

Members of a Salvadoran family flee their home after renewed fighting around San Salvador in late 1989. (Reuters/Corinne Dufka/Archive Photos)

130,000 Salvadorans had been ejected from Honduras. Up to two thousand people had been killed, the majority of them Hondurans. Thousands of other Hondurans were made homeless, and airline service between the two nations was disrupted for over ten years. Although the actual war lasted only a few days, it took more than a decade for Honduras and El Salvador to negotiate a peace settlement.

General Peace Treaty of 1980. During the 1970's, the border dispute between El Salvador and Honduras continued to fester. El Salvador was headed for civil war. By early 1980 two Salvadoran guerrilla organizations, the Popular Liberation Forces and the Revolutionary Army of the People, had established bases in six *bolsones*, or demilitarized pockets of land that had been set up along the Salvadoran-Honduran border after the 1969 war. These bases were used by the rebel forces to smuggle arms, troops, and ammunition into El Salvador.

As the Salvadoran army tried to rout the guerrilla forces, thousands of Salvadoran peasants escaped into Honduras. At the instigation of the United States, the Honduran and Salvadoran armies collaborated in order to suppress rebel activity and stop the influx of Salvadorans into Honduras. According to some claims, a massacre on the Sumpúl River took place on May 14, 1980. At that time, the Salvadoran and Honduran armies were participating in a joint counterinsurgency operation. When hundreds of peasants attempted to cross the Sumpúl River, Honduran troops forced them back into El Salvador, where Salvadoran troops gunned them down. Reports of the massacre were denied by both countries. Amid conflicting accounts, El Salvador and Honduras gradually conceded that something had happened but said nothing more.

The United States, interested in supporting the government of El Salvador against the leftist Salvadoran rebels, was by this time deeply entangled in Central American affairs. One way for the United States to accomplish its objective of foiling the leftist revolt was to bolster the military alliance between Honduras and El Salvador. For this reason, the United States became a moving force in bringing about a formal conclusion to the 1969 Soccer War by getting the two nations to sign a peace treaty.

The general peace treaty of 1980, signed by El Salvador and Honduras in Lima, Peru, on October 31, was the first genuine breakthrough in resolving the border dispute. However, border demarcation and indemnification issues remained unresolved. The treaty stated that if both parties could not reach an agreement in five years concerning the boundary dispute, they were to present their suit to the International Court of Justice (ICJ) in The Hague in the Netherlands. By 1985 the two nations had not resolved their differences. In 1986 the case was submitted to the ICJ.

International Court of Justice Ruling. The ICJ ruled on the border dispute on September 11, 1992. Of the 170 square miles in question, almost two-thirds were awarded to Honduras. Of the six *bolsones*, Honduras was given complete control of one and 80 percent of another. The remaining four were split with El Salvador. El Salvador was awarded the islands of Meanguera and Meanguerita, and Honduras was awarded the island of El Tigre. The ICJ ruled that Honduras should have free passage to the Pacific Ocean. Because the two nations possessed a shared history as provinces of Spain and subsequent membership in the United Provinces of Central America, the court ruled that the Gulf of Fonseca does not represent international waters and that it should be shared by El Salvador, Nicaragua, and Honduras.

The verdict pleased the Hondurans but disappointed the Salvadorans. Many of the residents in the territories awarded to Honduras considered themselves Salvadorans and were afraid that they would be harassed by the Honduran government. One of the more troubling issues was that the Honduran government did not permit foreigners to own land within twenty-five miles of the border. This caused grave concern among the Salvadorans who had lived near the border for generations.

The decision also added to the internal strife in El Salvador. Many of the inhabitants of the disputed territories were sympathizers or members of the Frente Farabundo Martí para la Liberacíon Nacional (FMLN), a former guerrilla organization that had become a legal political party. The leaders of the front had been counting on the people in the disputed territories to form part of their political base in the upcoming elections. Now that the territories were part of Honduras, the clout of the FMLN was weakened.

In succeeding months, the residents petitioned both governments to allow the *bolsones* to remain demilitarized. The also asked that land ownership be respected and that the owners be granted property titles, that dual nationality be granted, that residents be able to form their own municipalities, and that state powers not be imposed until the Honduran-Salvadoran bilateral commission reached an agreement on these situations. The Honduran government rejected

World Court Decision on Honduras-El Salvador Border Dispute

Jose Sette-Camara of Brazil, presiding judge of the five-member World Court panel, said that the case concerning the border dispute between El Salvador and Honduras was the most complicated in the court's history. After studying over twelve thousand pages of documentation, including land records from the Spanish colonial period, it took the panel fifty judicial sessions to sort out conflicting claims and come to a verdict. Honduran president Rafael Leonardo Callejas and Salvadoran president Alfredo Cristiani praised the court ruling, holding it up to the international community as an example of cooperation and respect for peace.

After the court's 1992 decision, life changed overnight for Hondurans and Salvadorans living along the border. Residents of El Zanduco, Honduras, for example, went to sleep in El Salvador and awoke in Honduras. "We were born here and have always lived here and we've always been Salvadoran," lamented María Pío Hernandez. "How can they say this is Honduras? I don't have any Honduran documents." Her reaction to the World Court decision was typical of the confusion many Salvadorans felt as they struggled to adjust to a new national identity.

Honduran labor union members celebrate May Day in 1998 by marching to demonstrate against a rise in their government's sales tax and by burning a U.S. flag to protest U.S. restrictions on immigration. (AP/Wide World Photos)

the petition, unequivocally stating that the territories were Honduran and that they would send Honduran officials to oversee them. Because the Salvadoran inhabitants were not happy with the Honduran government's stance, tensions ran high. Violence occasionally erupted.

Life After the ICJ Decision. Even though boundaries were established in 1993, the unresolved issues of citizenship, free transit, human rights, property, and land tenure continue to cause conflict between Salvadorans and Hondurans living along the border. For example, in March of 1997 illegal timber harvesting triggered a confrontation between Salvadoran loggers and Honduran authorities. For many years the Salvadorans have harvested wood from the forests of Nahauterique, which became Honduran territory after the ICJ decision. However, this activity violates Honduran conservation laws. Consequently, the Salvadorans

who harvest timber have been arrested by Honduran police. In February, 1997, the situation came to a head when Honduran army troops detained sixteen Salvadoran logging trucks for ten days. The crisis ended with the release of the trucks.

This is only one example of continuing strife along the Salvadoran-Honduran border. Hondurans living in El Salvador are the frequent victims of Salvadoran bandits, who the Hondurans claim are former soldiers and rebels from El Salvador's civil war. In April of 1997 the Hondurans who live on the Salvadoran side of the border met with Honduran president Carlos Roberto Reina. They asked the Salvadoran authorities to give them better protection, indicating that the Salvadoran Civilian National Police would be preferable to the army, which they claimed was repressive.

On April 25, 1997, after four days of talks, special working groups from both countries signed an

El Salvador and Honduras

1522	Spanish conquest of Honduras region begins.
1524	Pedro de Alvarado invades El Salvador.
1821	(Sept. 15) Central American Declaration of Independence is issued.
1823	(July 1) United Provinces of Central America is established.
1825-1829	Civil war divides Central America.
1837-1840	Second Central American civil war is fought.
1838	(Oct. 26) Honduras declares itself independent of Central American Federation.
1841	(Jan.) El Salvador declares its independence from federation.
1862	(May 8) Republic of Honduras is proclaimed.
1892-1894	Civil war splits Honduras.
1898	Spanish-American War begins to increase U.S. presence in Central America.
1903	Civil war is fought in Honduras.
1913	American-owned United Fruit Company acquires Tela Railroad concession in Honduras.
1918	Honduran currency is pegged to U.S. dollar.
1941-1945	Honduras and El Salvador participate in World War II.
1963	Lopez Arellano takes power in Honduras.
1966	FENAGH is formed by Honduran farmers and cattle ranchers; it accuses Salvadorans of illegal land invasions.
1967	Bilateral Treaty on Immigration signed by El Salvador and Honduras is designed to regulate flow of people across their mutual border.
1969	(June 27) El Salvador and Honduras sever diplomatic ties.
1969	(July 14) El Salvador bombs targets in Honduras, beginning "Soccer War."
1974	(Feb.) Antigovernment guerrilla activity begins in El Salvador.
1976	Agrarian reform in Honduras provides land for 13,000 families; dispute over border between El Salvador and Honduras is renewed.
1980	(May 14) Alleged Sumpúl River massacre takes place.
1980	(Oct. 31) Treaty between El Salvador and Honduras formally ends Soccer War of 1969.
1981	Leftist guerrilla movement Farabundo Marti National Liberation Front (FMLN) begins offensive in El Salvador, staring new civil war.
1986	El Salvador and Honduras submit their border dispute to World Court.
1992	(Jan. 31) FMLN insurgent war in El Salvador ends.
1992	(Sept. 11) World Court awards most of disputed territory to Honduras.
1997	Illegal timber harvesting triggers showdown between Salvadoran loggers and Honduran officials.
1997	(Nov.) Carlos Flores Facusse is elected president of Honduras.

1998	(June 24) Three of five El Salvadoran national guardsmen convicted of killing U.S. nuns in 1980 are paroled.
1998	(Nov.) Hurricane Mitch devastates Honduras.
1999	(Mar.) U.S. president Bill Clinton visits El Salvador and Honduras.

agreement that would give inhabitants of the re-drawn border areas two years to chose their nationality, with property rights guaranteed whether they chose Honduran or Salvadoran citizenship. This was a significant step toward ending persistent border problems and could signal the resolution of the conflict.

Pegge Bochynski

For Further Study

Comprehensive treatments of the history, economics, sociology, and governmental structure of El Salvador and Honduras can be found in *El Salvador: A Country Study* (1990), edited by Richard A. Haggerty, and *Honduras: A Country Study* (1995), edited by Tim L. Merrill. Each book is part of the area Handbook Series prepared by the Federal Research Division of the Library of Congress. An excellent presentation of recent Honduran history and the role that the United States has played in Honduran politics, including its relationship with El Salvador, is Donald E. Schulz and Deborah Sundloff Schulz's *The United States, Honduras, and the Crisis in Central America* (1994). *The War of the Dispossessed: Honduras and El Salvador, 1969* (1981), by

Thomas P. Anderson, explores the problems of overpopulation, poverty, and dependence on undiversified agriculture in both countries that culminated in the Soccer War in 1969.

Mark Danner's *The Massacre at El Mozote* (1994) recounts a mass killing in a small village at the border. A useful book for young readers is *El Salvador* (1995), by Erin Foley. Jose Angel Moroni Bracamonte and David E. Spencer, *Strategy and Tactics of the Salvadoran FMLN Guerrillas: Last Battle of the Cold War, Blueprint for Future Conflicts* (1995), explores the civil war in El Salvador and its influence on the border dispute between El Salvador and Honduras.

For a discussion on the General Peace Treaty of 1980, see "Honduras: El Salvador Ties Restored," in *Facts on File World News Digest* (November 14, 1980). "Honduras, El Salvador Settle Border Dispute: World Court Decides Contested Areas," in *Facts on File World News Digest* (September 24, 1992), gives the details of the ICJ decision. For a good overview of the political and social conditions in Honduras after the General Peace Treaty of 1980, see Mike Edwards, "Honduras: Eye of the Storm," in *National Geographic* (November, 1983).

Guatemala

Since early 1997 Guatemala has enjoyed formal peace. It is a change that contrasts with thirty-six years of guerrilla war and harsh official repression, during which more than 100,000 persons were killed. By the late 1990's all forms of political violence had sharply declined, though nonpolitical crime remained widespread. Three major problems cloud the horizon, each of which might contribute to a resumption of political violence. The country's indigenous Maya peoples have not fully been drawn into Guatemala's emerging democratic system. Second, poverty affects most Guatemalan families and contributes to widespread frustration over the slow pace of economic improvement since peace was achieved. Finally, the state's electoral, legal, and military institutions must complete reforms they have promised if the hopes of average Guatemalans are to be met peaceably.

Guatemala is both the northernmost and the most heavily populated country in Central America, with a population estimated at 11,685,700 in 1997. Its area of 42,042 square miles makes it about the same size as Ohio. However, it possesses great natural and cultural diversity.

The prospects for a lasting peace in Guatemala are shaped by somewhat different forces than are present elsewhere in Central America. Poverty, landlessness among rural people, and violent political traditions are problems shared by other Central American nations. However, Guatemala differs from its neighbors. It is the only Central American country in which most people are Native Americans, those of indigenous ethnicity.

Nearly 30 percent of Guatemalans do not speak Spanish as their first language. In this regard, Guatemala resembles the southern Mexican state of Chiapas—a region in open rebellion since 1994—more closely than other parts of Central America. Twenty-two separate indigenous dialects are spoken in Guatemala, chiefly in the country's Western Highlands. The indigenous people are the poorest group in a nation in which poverty is the norm: About 80 percent of all Guatemalans live in poverty.

Ethnic Disunity. As is the case among many other ethnically divided states around the world, national unity long has eluded Guatemalans. The country's indigenous people have never effectively joined together as a single united political force. The barriers to their unity have been, and continue to be, many. The country's natural mountainous terrain imposes physical distance between indigenous groups. The colorful clothes that members of each group wear set them apart from members of other indigenous when they meet. The lack of a common indigenous language further inhibits communication among members of different groups. Moreover, the widespread custom of marrying members of one's own group reinforce the separation of indigenous communities from one another.

Spanish-speaking Guatemalans who wear Western clothes and identify with Hispanic culture are known as ladinos. Like Native Guatemalans, most ladinos are poor. However, they do not have the same disadvantage of having to overcome discriminatory attitudes, which have weakened the potential of the native peoples to form an effective political party or movement. Disunited for more than four hundred years, Guatemala's Maya peoples have been relatively easily dominated by a Guatemalan political and economic system run by and for the richest elements in the Hispanic community.

Struggle for Democracy. Efforts to create a truly democratic political system in Guatemala began in 1944. That year university students and reform-oriented military officers led a revolution that toppled the dictatorship of Jorge Ubico. The two elected presidents who governed the country over the following decade initiated broad reforms. These reforms were designed to institutionalize democratic processes by establishing political parties, social security laws, and labor codes.

The result of these reforms, however, was increased social polarization. The land reform programs begun by President Jacobo Arbenz Guzman during the early 1950's were popular among the landless poor. However, these programs threatened to confiscate untitled lands owned by wealthy Guatemalans and by the powerful U.S.-owned United Fruit Company.

The United Fruit Company responded to the reform program by leading a public relations campaign focusing on the dangerous influence of the communist Guatemalan Workers Party (PGT), which President Arbenz had legalized. When Arbenz defied a U.S. arms embargo by importing weapons from Czechoslovakia, then a Soviet ally, U.S. president Dwight D. Eisenhower authorized the Central Intelligence Agency (CIA) to intervene in Guatemala to remove Arbenz from power.

A National Liberation Movement (MLN) already had formed among conservative Guatemalans. With CIA support, its leader, former Colonel Carlos Castillo Armas, mounted a small invasion into the country from neighboring Honduras. Arbenz's government failed to enlist effective support, from either the Organization of American States (OAS) or the United Nations (U.N.). As a result, Arbenz was overthrown by a military uprising in mid-1954. Castillo Armas was then proclaimed president.

Castillo Armas's government banned the communist PGT and overturned all the reform laws of the previous decade before Castillo Armas himself was assassinated in 1957. After Castillo Armas, Gua-

Profile of Guatemala

Official name: Republic of Guatemala
Independent since: 1821
Former colonial ruler: Spain
Location: at southeastern end of Mexico
Area: 42,042 square miles
Capital: Guatemala City
Population: 11,685,700 (1997 est.)
Official language: Spanish
Major religions: Roman Catholicism; Protestantism
Gross domestic product: US$39 billion (1996)
Major exports: coffee; sugar; bananas; vegetable seeds
Military budget: US$128.3 million (1996)
Military personnel: 44,200 (1996)

Note: Monetary figures rendered as "US$" are U.S. equivalents of values in local currencies.

temalan politics remained unstable. Further military coups followed in 1963, 1982, and 1983. These coups reflected a political system in which conflict resolution had not been institutionalized.

Rising Political Violence. The overturning of government reforms during the 1950's propelled Guatemalan politics toward violence. Key conservative political forces, such as the MLN, and business groups embraced the idea of preventing radicals from participating in government. Irregular paramilitary forces arose to enforce their will. Many people who advocated social reforms that would benefit the poor were jailed or killed during the decades following Arbenz's downfall.

By the early 1960's many Guatemalans who had hoped democratic politics would produce social reform had abandoned electoral politics in favor of armed opposition. By 1969 the first round of fighting appeared decisively to have been won by the U.S.-trained Guatemalan army and its paramilitary allies, known as "death squads." Remnants of the PGT and of other radical groups survived, however. They provided leadership to a new generation of Guatemalans after a blooming rural cooperative movement and labor union movement were spoiled by violence during the late 1970's.

During the 1970's and 1980's, several other Central American nations also suffered from internal wars. Nicaragua, Guatemala, and El Salvador all endured separate, long, bitter conflicts among

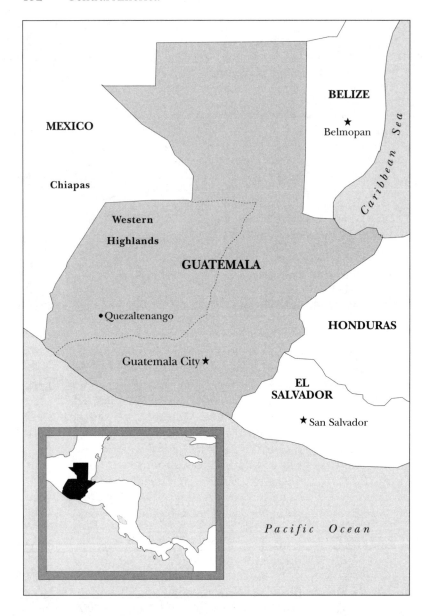

be understood as a war between ethnic groups. The war pitted the official armed forces of Guatemala against loosely allied guerrilla bands. After 1980 these bands called themselves the Guatemalan National Revolutionary Unity, or URNG. Although most top URNG leaders were ladinos, most URNG fighters, especially during the final two decades of the war, were indigenous peoples. The leaders of the Guatemalan army that opposed them were all ladinos. Moreover, much of the political violence centered in the Western Highlands and other predominantly indigenous areas. In those areas, the great majority of victims were members of indigenous ethnic groups. During the early 1980's, at the peak of the fighting, more than four hundred villages were destroyed.

Guerrilla warfare itself and the government measures to suppress it during the 1980's helped to break down some of the barriers that long divided Guatemala. Civic organizations composed of both ladinos and Native, Guatemalans, such as the Mutual Support Group (GAM), emerged during the early 1980's to campaign for the restoration of missing persons abducted by the government. Although ladinos, such as Nineth Montenegro, were the most articulate leaders of these human rights advocacy groups, much of GAM's support came from Native Guatemalans.,

Other more predominantly indigenous civic rights and human rights groups cut across ethnic lines. These groups, such as the Runujel Junam Council of Ethnic Communities (CERJ), encouraged Native Guatemalans to speak out about their shared problems under government repression.

their peoples. However, the 1990's saw a new era of peace being to unfold. Guatemala's conflict was the last one to end, on December 29, 1996. Although steps toward real peace have been taken, more remains to be done.

Ethnicity and War. Guatemala has been different from its Central American neighbors in the late twentieth century in having the longest-lasting internal war. Between 1960 and 1996 more than 100,000 Guatemalans perished, and more than 40,000 other people became missing.

Major aspects of Guatemala's conflict may best

Turning Away from Violence. In still other indigenous communities, such as in Santiago Atitlan during the early 1990's, the violence stimulated local interest in finding nonviolent direct action strategies. Indians and ladinos joined together to keep both the army and the guerrillas out of their picturesque market town beside Lake Atitlan. Other indigenous activists, such as Rigoberta Menchu, learned to speak Spanish so they could work more effectively with sympathetic ladinos to solve what the Committee for Peasant Unity (CUC) regarded as common problems of all poor Guatemalan communities. Menchu's human rights work in behalf of her fellow, Native Guatemalans was recognized by the Nobel Peace Prize in 1992.

Two of the major guerrilla fighting forces in the Guatemalan National Revolutionary Unity movement, the Revolutionary Organization of People in Arms (ORPA) and Guerrilla Army of the Poor (EGP), found most of their support among Native Guatemalans. All major URNG leaders, however, were ladinos—just as almost all Guatemalan presidents and generals have been since the Spanish Conquest.

Since military rule was replaced by civilian government in 1986, the increasing democratization of Guatemalan politics has helped integrate Native Guatemalans into political life. By the late 1990's, however, only eight members of the eighty-member Guatemalan National Congress were Native Guatemalans.

Guatemala's indigenous leaders have made more progress in winning local elections. Forty of the approximately three hundred Guatemalan municipal mayors were Native Guatemalans by the late 1990's. They included the mayor of Guatemala's second largest city, Quetzaltenango. However, although Native Guatemalans increasingly supported ladino-run national political parties during the 1980's and 1990's, they remained largely excluded from real power in national government. Although political violence greatly declined after 1996, some violence has continued. For example, leftist politician and CERJ founder Amilcar Mendez fled the country when he was faced with renewed death threats in 1997.

Violence and Social Leadership. The conflict that concluded in 1996 was not simply an ethnic war. A large percentage of the conscripted soldiers of the Guatemalan army were indigenous people themselves. Rural civil defense patrols (PACs) organized by the government army during the 1980's thus pitted Native Guatemalan army allies against primarily indigenous guerrilla bands. For this reason, guerrilla forces found only limited support within some areas of the Western Highlands, such as Totonicapan.

Ladinos also fought on both sides of the conflict. Throughout the war, leaders working for the poor

Rigoberta Menchu

Few modern figures have known as much personal pain, or have risen as far in overcoming it, as 1992 Nobel Peace Prize winner Rigoberta Menchu. Born in 1959 the daughter of poor farm laborers in the village of Chimel, Rigoberta entered life near the bottom of Guatemala's rigid social system. A migratory laborer as a child and a maid for wealthy *ladinos* in Guatemala City as a teen, Rigoberta knew firsthand the exploitation of the indigenous people of Guatemala. Her father became a leader of the Committee for Peasant Unity (CUC) in the 1970's, but both parents and a brother were tortured and killed by the army. Rigoberta and many other activists became involved with the Guatemalan National Revolutionary Unity (URNG) guerrillas, but she found that insensitivity toward indigenous culture was common there also. Rigoberta fled into exile from 1981 to 1994, where her saga, and the plight of her indigenous Maya people, became known worldwide.

After being awarded the Nobel Peace Prize in December, 1992, Rigoberta established the Rigoberta Menchu Tum Foundation to advocate the rights of the indigenous. In 1994 she returned to Guatemala. Her foundation chose not to affiliate with any political party in the 1995-1996 elections but conducted educational programs designed to encourage participation in the electoral process, especially by women and indigenous people. This nonpartisan stance angered some of her former allies. Since the conclusion of the guerrilla war, Menchu has been among the Guatemalans who have demanded only a narrow application of the amnesty law enacted prior to the peace agreement. In October, 1997, Guatemalan courts ruled in support of this position.

Nobel Prize-winner Rigoberta Menchu speaking at a March, 1998, press conference in Mexico City, where she was working to help bring peace to the Mexican state of Chiapas. (AP/Wide World Photos)

were assassinated and abducted. (Abductees were known as "disappearances.") Publicly advocating open and nonviolent protest was dangerous. Guatemalan army soldiers and allied irregulars known as "death squads" menaced priests, journalists, human rights advocates, college professors, union officials, university students, and many others.

While many of these victimized social leaders were ladinos, most who were targeted also sympathized with the plight of the indigenous or related causes (such as the trade union movement). The real danger of violence and abduction naturally inhibited the development of leadership in the kinds of voluntary organizations needed to support the growth of a healthy civil society.

Economic and Social Inequality. Guatemala has long been an economically divided nation, with one of the biggest gaps between rich and poor in the world. Within Latin America, only Brazil has a larger gap. Because Guatemala's governments have long been indifferent to this inequality, effec-

tive problem solving by private civic organizations remains vitally important.

As late as 1989 the poorest 80 percent of Guatemalans received only 37 percent of national income. Moreover, the poorest 40 percent of the people received only 7.9 percent of national income. Malnutrition, hunger, and diseases such as dysentery that are related to inadequate diets are thus endemic problems.

Guatemala's upper class—the top 10 percent of families—for centuries has enjoyed a lifestyle similar to that of Europeans and North Americans. In 1989 the richest 20 percent of Guatemalans received 63 percent of national income. The gap between rich and poor is also accentuated by the insensitivity of the rich toward the poor. Rigoberta Menchu, herself a poor Maya woman, described the mistreatment she suffered while working as a maid in a ladino home. She recalled that even the family dog was treated better than her.

Abandoned Reforms. During the early 1950's former army colonel Jacobo Arbenz tried to narrow these social and economic gaps while he was president. He tried to transfer unused farmlands to the landless, to enforce labor laws, to permit farmworkers to organize, and to provide social insurance to poor workers. His measures angered upper-class ladino plantation owners and foreign landowners, especially the United Fruit Company.

Arbenz's support from the communist Guatemalan Workers Party gave the U.S. government an excuse to help overthrow his government in 1954. Over the next thirty-one years no Guatemalan government, military or civilian, was free from direct military control. Even as late as the early 1990's, persons who advocated social reforms benefitting the poor were charged with being communists. Persons so charged often disappeared and were tortured. One such person was the American Roman Catholic nun Dianna Ortiz. Ortiz survived her experience in 1989. However, others, such as the Guatemalan anthropologist Myrna Mack, who was killed in 1990, and thousands of other Guatemalans were less fortunate.

U.S. Pressure on Guatemala's Military Rulers. The first steps toward creating a Guatemalan government that would address social injustices came during the last decades of the war. In response to U.S. president Jimmy Carter's human rights policy,

Guatemala's ruling generals refused further U.S. military aid after 1977.

During the 1980's the U.S. Congress and President Ronald Reagan sharply disagreed over many aspects of American policies in Central America. Despite Reagan's inclination to help Guatemala's ruling generals, little U.S. aid was officially given to the Guatemalan government. Forced to find alternative sources of aid on their own, the Guatemalan army established many businesses and their own bank. This strategy helped the army conduct its war; however, it put the army into direct business competition with groups among Guatemala's rich.

Years of war also contributed to corruption within the army. Large ranches found their way into the hands of generals, for example, and bribery became a widely accepted aspect of doing business. Some officers were later shown to have been involved in international drug production and smuggling. These abuses of power continued to strain relations with the Guatemalan government's key ally, the United States.

As Central America's self-destructive wars continued during the 1980's, political leaders in Washington, D.C., came to agree on one narrow point: The U.S. anticommunist cause in Central America should promote elected governments as alternatives to communism. The U.S. government cut back on aid to Guatemala's last military rulers, General Efrain Rios Montt and General Oscar Humberto Mejia Victores, who ruled the country from 1982 through 1986. To regain U.S. aid for their war effort, Guatemala's leaders had to make the transition to elected government.

In 1986 Guatemala held a fair election in which no generals or guerrilla groups competed. Afterward, a civilian administration led by Christian Democrat Vinicio Cerezo took office.

Transition to Democracy. The first phase of democratization under the Christian Democrats did not go well. Many of its best leaders had already died at the hands of death squads. Although some corrupt military and police officials were removed, Cerezo could not control corruption among others in his party. Although he was president, he exercised only a fraction of the real power associated with his office. Twice during his term, army factions nearly toppled his government. In this tense atmosphere, few campaign promises of social reform were heard after 1986. Cerezo's most significant achievement was to preside over a peaceful transition to another elected president, Jorge Serrano, in 1991.

A Protestant ladino without deep ties to any well-established political party, Serrano was not the strongest candidate on the evangelical right. Former dictator General Rios Montt led in the polls; however, he was barred from running for office because of his involvement in an unconstitutional coup in 1982. Thus, Cerezo succeeded in peacefully passing on the presidential office to an elected civilian, the first such transfer between elected civilian presidents in modern Guatemalan history.

Crisis of 1993. Without an effective base of support in the Guatemalan congress, President Serrano opened peace talks with leaders of the URNG. However, he was frustrated in other policy areas. In the spring of 1993 he attempted to use Guatemala's traditional power of presidential decrees to suspend the constitution and press free-

Guatemalan president Jorge Serrano at a press conference in May, 1993—a week after he dissolved parliament and put all power in his own hands. (AP/Wide World Photos)

Guatemala

1523-1524 Spanish under Pedro de Alvarado conquer Guatemala region.

1821 Guatemala becomes first Central American nation to declare its independence from Spain.

1824-1838 Guatemala is part of Central American Federation.

1944 University student demonstrations set off revolution leading to elected government by Juan Jose Arevalo.

1950 Reformist president Jacobo Arbenz is elected.

1953-1954 Arbenz enacts land reform measures.

1954 Guatemalan army, aided by U.S. Central Intelligence Agency, and exiled Colonel Castillo Armas, overthrow Arbenz.

1960 Central America Common Market is created by Treaty of Managua.

1960 First guerrilla uprising begins.

1963 Army retakes power to prevent election of leftist ex-president Arevalo.

1976 Earthquake devastates western Guatemala.

1978 Army massacres Indian protest marchers at Panzos, Alta Verapaz.

1978-1979 Death squads murder prominent reformist politicians, labor leaders, priests, and professors.

1978-1983 Widespread army violence ravages Western Highlands.

1980 Guatemalan National Revolutionary Unity (URNG) is formed from three guerrilla groups and Communist Party.

1982 General E. Rios Montt seizes power and increases antiguerrilla war efforts.

1983 General O. H. Mejia Victores overthrows Rios Montt.

1986 Civilian president Vinicio Cerezo is elected.

1992 Rigoberta Menchu receives the Nobel Peace Prize.

1993 Jorge Serrano is elected president; he opens peace talks with URNG.

1993 Serrano fails to create dictatorship in face of public protests and army and U.S. opposition.

1993-1996 Ramiro de Leon Carpio leads return to democracy; United Nations mediates peace talks.

1996 Alvaro Arzu is elected president; peace negotiations accelerate.

1996 National Reconciliation Law extends amnesty to members of army and guerrilla groups for misdeeds during war.

1996 (Dec. 29) Comprehensive Peace Accord is signed; URNG ends thirty-six-year-long war.

1997 URNG demobilizes and becomes legal political group.

1998 (Jan. 27) Guatemala announces restoration of diplomatic relations with Cuba.

1998 (Apr.) Roman Catholic bishop Juan Gerardi Condera is beaten to death shortly after releasing report criticizing government for human rights abuses; who is responsible for his death remains controversial issue through rest of year.

1999	(Feb. 25) Report of independent Historical Clarification Commission presents evidence of U.S. support of Guatemalan military, when it committed acts of "genocide" against Mayans during country's long civil war.
1999	(Mar. 10) During official visit to Guatemala, U.S. president Bill Clinton apologizes for past U.S. support of repressive Guatemalan regimes and pledges U.S. support for future reconciliation efforts throughout Central America.
1999	(Mar. 12) Former Guatemalan leftist guerrilla leader Jorge Ismael Soto formally apologizes to nation for abuses his faction committed during civil war.

dom. He tried to fire his enemies in congress and on the supreme court. He even tried to get rid of Ramiro de Leon Carpio, the honest conciliator he had appointed to investigate past government human rights violations.

Serrano's challenge to the evolving democratic system backfired. After several tense weeks of crisis, he was forced to resign. His resignation proved to be a critical turning point in the move toward a true democratic system. First, Guatemalans mobilized to oppose Serrano's efforts to seize dictatorial powers. In response to appeals from elected members of congress, Guatemalans took to the streets to demonstrate against Serrano. An important established business group, the CACIF, joined others in a broad civilian movement, the Instancia or National Petition of Consensus, to oppose Serrano's power grab.

A second factor in reversing a slide away from democracy in 1993 was heavy international pressure. Many influential Guatemalans realized that their nation would become more isolated if Serrano's unconstitutional power grab succeeded. U.S. president Bill Clinton's administration suspended aid programs to Guatemala. The European Community and Japan followed with similar steps. The Organization of American States also formally condemned Serrano's coup.

Faced with the threat of complete isolation for their nation, Guatemalan army commanders forced Serrano to resign. In contrast to the military uprisings of the 1980's, however, army leaders quickly agreed to turn over power to a transitional government led by the one civilian official who enjoyed the confidence of congress and the people, human rights prosecutor Ramiro de Leon Carpio, whom Serrano had fired.

Over the next three years de Leon's administration established its reform credentials. It forced two defense ministers into retirement; it ended the conscription of young men into the army; and it abolished the feared "military commissioners," who had often used their powers over conscription to elicit bribes. De Leon then oversaw two changes of great importance: the restoration of elected government in 1996 and the acceleration of peace negotiations to end the war.

With the assistance of U.N. negotiators, the Guatemalan government reached five separate agreements with the URNG in 1994 and 1995. The most important of these was a March, 1994, agreement on human rights that permitted deployment of a U.N. mission to verify Guatemala's human rights progress. Another agreement in 1994 established a Truth Commission to investigate and to publicize—but not to prosecute—political crimes committed during the war.

Shortly after his election as president in 1996, Alvaro Arzu, a prosperous ladino civilian, reached an understanding with the country's leading business interests and the army on reforms, including the reduction of the size and power of the army.

International Pressures. While credit for the peace agreement signed on December 29, 1996, must ultimately go to de Leon's elected successor, President Arzu, forces outside Guatemala helped push the nation toward change. The end of the global Cold War in 1991 enabled the United Nations to become more active as a facilitator of transitions to peace throughout the world.

U.N. peace efforts began in Guatemala in 1991, when U.N. negotiators got the URNG to accept that Guatemala's constitution had to be the legal framework for further peace discussions. This sub-

Students confront riot police in Guatemala City in February, 1997, when they joined with other discontented Guatemalans to protest government economic policies. (AP/Wide World Photos)

stantial concession by the URNG reassured army factions of the neutrality of U.N. efforts. U.N. mediation efforts would have been suspended if Serrano's coup had succeeded in early 1993. By then, however, the momentum toward negotiated settlements to Central American conflicts had gathered strength. An election had finalized a peaceful end to Nicaragua's civil war in 1990, and U.N. mediation had produced a peace agreement in El Salvador in 1992.

External pressures to settle Central American conflicts through democratic processes were felt not just by official armies and governments. The demise of Sandinista rule in Nicaragua in 1990 and the breakup of the Soviet Union in late 1991 ended any hopes that URNG guerrillas might have had for continued external assistance. After de Leon's caretaker administration replaced Serrano, Nor-

way (one of the URNG's major backers), Colombia, Venezuela, Spain, Mexico, and the United States set up a "Group of Friends" that strongly urged both sides in the Guatemala conflict to resume negotiations.

In this context, U.N. mediation efforts brought Guatemalans to consider reform of society as part of the peace discussions. In the end, fundamental changes were accepted by important elements of most significant Guatemalan political forces. Among the more significant changes agreed to in nine separate accords were: constitutional and electoral reforms, protection of human rights, safe return of refugees and guerrillas to civilian life, land and economic reforms, protection of the rights of Native Guatemalans, and a 33-percent reduction in the size of the armed forces.

The war formally was concluded at a Guatemala

City ceremony on December 29, 1996. Demobilization of the 3,500 URNG guerrilla fighters still in the field took place during the following spring, with U.N. peacekeepers supervising their final disarming. A new civilian police force was organized, and most military units stopped performing their long-feared policing roles.

Implementation of the promises made in these agreements remains problematic. The significant foreign support needed to finance reforms has been slow to reach Guatemala. Frustration over a wave of common crimes led to a rise in vigilante actions and more than a dozen lynchings in 1997 and 1998. Kidnappings, death squad threats to reformers, and assassinations continued to undermine public confidence in the country's fragile democratic system.

Gordon L. Bowen

For Further Study

The cultural backdrop against which Guatemalan politics unfolds is movingly recorded in the introductory chapters of Rigoberta Menchu's book, *I, Rigoberta Menchu: An Indian Woman of Guatemala* (1984). The stunning violence at the heart of the army's antiguerrilla campaign is conveyed through Menchu's later chapters, as well as in Jesuit priest Ricardo Falla's *Massacres in the Jungle: Ixcan, Guatemala, 1975-1982* (1994). Both books sear the reader. Insights into the guerrilla resistance can be found in Jennifer Harbury's *Bridge of Courage: Life Stories of Guatemalan Companeros* (1994). Major steps in Guatemalan democratization are evaluated skeptically in Robert Trudeau's *Guatemalan Politics: The Popular Struggle for Democracy* (1993). A more sympathetic portrait of Guatemala's emerging democratic culture can be found in articles by Rachel M. McCleary: "Guatemala's Postwar Prospects," *Journal of Democracy* 8, no. 2 (1997), and "Guatemala: Expectations for Peace," *Current History* (February, 1996).

Guatemalan coverage on the Internet is abundant, but of uneven quality. The most comprehensive list of links can be found at the University of Texas's comprehensive Latin American site (http://128.83.142.37/la/ca/guatemala/). Current events reported from Guatemala City appear on http://www.sigloxxi.com/snews. Also of interest is the site of Rigoberta Menchu's Foundation (http://ourworld.compuserve.com/homepages/rmtpaz/mensajes.htm).

Nicaragua

Political conflict in the Central American nation of Nicaragua has long been aggravated by the local habit of seeking international support in order to dominate political opponents. This tactic has been used by rivals in Nicaragua since the early 1900's and made political violence and civil war there more intense throughout the 1980's. With the end of the Cold War, organized violence among Nicaraguans decreased. During the 1990's political disputes were settled through elections rather than revolution. Two successive peaceful elections occurred in 1990 and 1996, and all forms of political violence sharply declined. Nevertheless, frustrations with the slow pace of improvement in the quality of life remained widespread. This stemmed, in part, from unresolved disputes over land ownership. These issues have undermined social support for each successive elected government. Thus, the democratic system in Nicaragua remains fragile, and resumption of armed conflict among Nicaraguans remains a possibility.

In the center of Central America, Nicaragua is bordered to the north by Honduras, to the south by Costa Rica, to the east by the Caribbean Sea, and to the west by the Pacific Ocean. Covering an area of 49,998 square miles, Nicaragua had a population of 4,386,400 people in 1997. The capital city is Managua.

Profile of Nicaragua

Official name: Republic of Nicaragua
Independent since: 1821
Former colonial ruler: Spain
Location: between Honduras and Costa Rica
Area: 49,998 square miles
Capital: Managua
Population: 4,386,400 (1997 est.)
Official language: Spanish
Major religions: Roman Catholicism; Protestantism
Gross domestic product: US$7.7 billion (1996 est.)
Major exports: industrial products; coffee; crustaceans; beef
Military budget: US$27.48 million (1996)
Military personnel: 17,000 (1996)

Note: Monetary figures rendered as "US$" are U.S. equivalents of values in local currencies.

Historical Background. Nicaragua was a key battleground in the final decades of the fifty-year Cold War that pitted the United States and its allies against the Soviet Union and its supporters. Indeed, the defeat of the pro-Soviet Sandinista government of Nicaragua in a free election in 1990 symbolized the outcome of the Cold War. It also symbolized the ascendance of democratic means of resolving disputes worldwide. However, the delicate fabric of Nicaraguan national unity had been torn by international interventions that had occurred before the Cold War. The Cold War era ended in a civil war in Nicaragua that destroyed the land, divided its people, and reinforced the habit of looking abroad for support. During the 1990's Nicaragua found itself without political leaders experienced in the arts of compromise needed to make democracy effective in a divided society.

International intervention began to divide Nicaraguans

shortly after they gained their independence from Spain in 1821 and from the other Central American states in 1838. Rivals in the Conservative Party looked to the United States for support, while Liberal Party factions favored a more nationalistic and anti-U.S. stance. After 1853, U.S. Marines landed repeatedly to keep favored Conservatives in charge.

Nicaraguan society changed under the influence of powerful international forces. During the latter half of the nineteenth century, coffee production for export to Europe and the United States transformed Nica- ragua. Land holdings became concentrated as coffee producers struggled to maximize profits. Vagrancy laws forced formerly self-sufficient Indians and peasants to become peons, or landless laborers, who worked the coffee plantations.

Lands once titled to the Roman Catholic Church were reduced to facilitate growth in

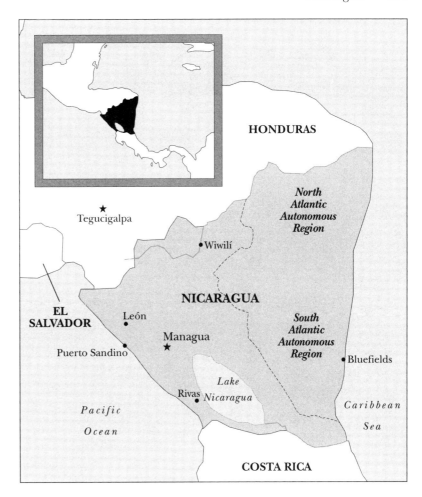

coffee acreage, and *ejidos* (communal Indian lands) were made into plantations. Great Britain financed the expansion of the coffee economy, and the Nicaraguan government guaranteed repayment. Thus, Nicaragua's entry into the international system of capitalism indebted not only plantation owners but also the Nicaraguan state.

U.S. Intervention. Prominent Nicaraguans who failed to benefit from these trends gathered under the banner of the Liberal Party. Its charismatic leader, José Santos Zelaya, seized power in 1893. U.S. Marines invaded Nicaragua to protect American investments four times during his reign. The United States also conveyed displeasure at Nicaraguan negotiations with Britain and Japan concerning a hypothetical canal across the isthmus of Central America that might rival the U.S. project in Panama.

Zelaya held on to the presidency until dislodged

by a U.S.-backed revolt of Conservatives in 1909. U.S. Marines remained the effective power behind Nicaraguan authorities until 1933.

Like much of the world outside Europe, the Nicaraguan state of the nineteenth and early twentieth centuries had proven vulnerable to changes imposed upon it by outsiders. Foreigners exercised influence over which Nicaraguans would rule. They also shaped key decisions in domestic affairs, including the use of valuable land and the allocation of tax revenues. These revenues were primarily used to pay debts to foreign banks. Though Nicaragua was independent, in practical terms Nicaraguan rulers retained power only as long as they held the foreigners' concerns to be central priorities.

In time, leading elements of both the Conservative and the Liberal Parties accommodated themselves to this reality, but only after a bitter civil war (1927-1933) in which the U.S. Marines again

Cheering Nicaraguans crowd the streets of Managua as Sandinista leaders advance on the national palace after driving President Anastasio Somoza out of the country in 1979. (AP/Wide World Photos)

proved to be the final arbiter in Nicaraguan life. Elections in 1928 and 1932 were won by pro-U.S. Liberals. Under budgetary pressure at home, U.S. president Herbert Hoover arranged a final U.S. withdrawal.

Sandino. An armed faction of the Liberal Party was led by a poor peasant named Augusto César Sandino. He refused to accept any form of continued U.S. influence, which he viewed as a limit on Nicaraguan sovereignty. When the last U.S. Marines left Nicaragua in 1933, Sandino negotiated a cease-fire with the civilian authorities. The agreement to stop fighting fell far short of the complete military victory Sandino's peasant supporters had sought. He succeeded, nonetheless, in imposing an end of hostilities on them.

Sandino failed to recognize that the real power had transferred from the U.S. Marines to the U.S.-trained National Guard rather than the Liberal Party government with whom he had signed a truce. The National Guard supposedly was a nonpolitical Nicaraguan army. However, in February, 1934, its leader, Anastasio Somoza García, betrayed the peace promised to Sandino. After a meeting with President Juan Batista Sacasa and others in Managua, Sandino was detained by the National Guard and murdered. Later that evening over three hundred of his followers were massacred by the National Guard at their cooperative farm at Wiwilí.

Sandino's martyrdom transformed this leader of a minor rebellion into a folk hero. His advocacy of peasant rights and his militant anti-Americanism became part of the mainstream of Nicaraguan nationalism. His spirit would live on among Nicaraguans such as 1980's Interior Minister Tomas Borge, who, as a young schoolboy during the 1940's, refused to shake Somoza's hand out of respect for Sandino.

Somoza Dynasty. Ties to international forces shaped Nicaraguan politics during the twentieth century. The commander of the National Guard, General Anastasio Somoza García, was well equipped to maintain these ties. He was fluent in English, and during the 1920's he had served as the translator for U.S. president Hoover's emissary to Nicaragua, Henry Stimson. After seizing complete power in 1936, President Somoza shrewdly renamed a major boulevard in the capital after U.S. president Franklin D. Roosevelt.

Virtually alone among the smaller Latin American states, Somoza's Nicaragua readily declared war on U.S. enemies during World War II. Nicaragua also gave unwavering support to U.S. Cold War plans in the Americas. It consistently supported the United States at the United Nations (U.N.) and in the Organization of American States (OAS).

Moreover, in 1952 Somoza urged U.S. president Harry S Truman to take measures to stop the growth of communism in nearby Guatemala. When President Dwight D. Eisenhower's administration undertook a successful Central Intelligence Agency (CIA) campaign to remove Guatemalan president Jacobo Arbenz in 1954, Somoza assisted the operation. He was awarded increased U.S. military aid.

Somoza, however, was no Rooseveltian social democrat. Labor unions and leftist, noncommunist political groups were repressed throughout his rule. Elections were rigged, and officials who displeased Somoza were swiftly removed from office. Widespread corruption and graft enriched the Somoza family and the National Guard, while nearly all other Nicaraguans lived in grinding poverty. An assassin killed Somoza in 1956. He died in a U.S. hospital in Panama.

The sons of the fallen dictator then assumed power: Luis Somoza Debayle became president. His younger brother, Anastasio Somoza Debayle, a graduate of the U.S. Military Academy in New York, became head of the National Guard. They rounded up and tortured dozens of innocents they alleged had ties to the assassination, including opposition newspaper editor Pedro Joaquín Chamorro Cardenal.

The 1959 Cuban Revolution reintroduced hope among some Nicaraguans for an end to American influence and an end to the Somoza dynasty. Under President Luis Somoza, state repression relaxed considerably. This provided an opening in which dissent quickly surfaced. University students and other radicals formed the revolutionary Sandinista Front for National Liberation (FSLN) in 1961.

Throughout the 1960's Sandinista militants Tomas Borge, Daniel Ortega Saavedra, and many others traveled to Cuba for military and political training. The anti-American attitudes shared by Nicaraguan radicals and their Cuban benefactors were eventually reinforced by finances and arms. Other support for the Sandinistas came from the Panamanian strongman Omar Torrijos and Social Democrats in Venezuela and Costa Rica.

United States and the Somoza Dynasty. U.S. Cold War foreign policy in Latin America during the early 1960's was dubbed the Alliance for Progress. Its strategy aimed at preventing the emergence of more Soviet allies such as Cuba by focusing on reform of the genuine grievances communists exploited in order to win support: corruption, poverty, and land distribution. Luis Somoza embraced aspects of the alliance, but true power remained in the unreformed hands of the commander of the National Guard, Anastasio So-

moza Debayle. Substantial U.S. military aid continued throughout the 1960's and 1970's.

The Somozas also continued to support the Unites States' regional anticommunist policy. They aided the CIA's ill-fated 1961 Bay of Pigs invasion of Cuba in many ways, not least by permitting it to be launched from Nicaraguan ports. The Somozas also sent troops to join in the U.S. occupation of the Dominican Republic in 1965, which dislodged another anti-American government.

In 1972 Somoza Debayle joined with Guatemalan generals to help conservative officers in El Salvador stop an attempted coup by Christian Democrats and reformists. This action, carried out principally by Salvadoran officers, blocked the presidential election of José Napoleon Duarte, who later became the key leader in a U.S.-backed reform government in El Salvador during the 1980's. Duarte served as the pro-U.S. president of El Salvador from 1984 to 1989.

Although the Somozas maintained strong ties with Central American and U.S. leaders, their regime had weak support outside the National Guard within Nicaragua. Corruption had created enemies among their natural allies in business circles. Since the beginning of Anastasio Somoza García's reign, the Somozas had acquired over 20 percent of the arable farmland of the nation. Through export monopolies and corrupt use of the customs offices, the Somozas reaped great personal wealth by controlling the international trade of the nation. Bribery was endemic throughout the state bureaucracy, with payoffs finding their way to the top.

Under President Anastasio Somoza Debayle, most major exporters, businessmen, and public officials were forced to pay fees and kickbacks to Somoza-run fronts. Corruption in the state budget and its spending accounts was widespread, with thousands of "phantom" employees' checks working their way into the ruling family's hands. From one small farm in the early 1930's, the Somozas had amassed a fortune of at least US$500 million by 1979.

Corruption Ignites Unrest. Somoza Debayle's personal style greatly offended many religious Nicaraguans, notably Archbishop Obando y Bravo of Managua. Corruption reached its height in the wake of a tremendous earthquake in 1972. Ten thousand people died, and 75 percent of Managua's housing was destroyed. An economic crisis of major proportions emerged as 90 percent of the commercial plants in the capital had been made inoperative. As is traditional in such emergencies, international relief aid poured in, but much of it was either channeled into the reconstruction of Somoza's businesses or siphoned off into the family's bank accounts.

Businessmen became livid at this abuse of the tragedy. The corruption of Managua's reconstruction involved the abandonment of the center of the destroyed city. The sprawl created by new construction on the periphery nearly doubled the land area of the city, but thousands of Nicaraguans still failed to find opportunities for housing or employment. This tragedy turned existing social strain into a seedbed of revolution. Even before the earthquake, only 28 percent of Managua had sewers. Conditions were far worse in the countryside: Less than 4 percent of homes had safe drinking water.

During the 1970's pressure for change mounted. Business groups demanded an end to corruption. Roman Catholic priests, influenced by reformist doctrines then ascendant in the Church, documented and denounced the growing number of violations of human rights by the National Guard. After 1977 U.S. president Jimmy Carter declared that the United States would send further aid to Nicaragua only if human rights were improved. Despite the growing security threat posed by armed guerrillas of the FSLN, Somoza attempted to cling to power.

In Managua Pedro Joaquín Chamorro, the Conservative anti-Somoza publisher of an influential daily newspaper called *La Prensa*, became recognized as the conscience of the nation. His murder in 1978—widely attributed to Somoza's allies—ignited a firestorm of anger. Spontaneous popular uprisings further undermined the authority of the regime. However, it was the military prowess of the FSLN, backed by substantial Cuban military aid to the Sandinistas, that most decisively led to Somoza's exit into exile. He first went to Miami and later to Paraguay, where he was killed by a terrorist bomb in September, 1980. On July 19, 1979, the FSLN entered the capital, to a huge popular welcome.

Sandinistas Take Power. In July, 1979, a transitional ruling committee representing a broad variety of political forces took charge of the task of restoring order. Included in the new government were business representatives, three graduates of U.S. universities, two ordained Roman Catholic priests, several Sandinistas, and Violeta Barrios de Chamorro, the widow of the martyred Pedro Joaquín Chamorro.

An uneasy balance existed between the authority of the moderate successor administration and the practical reality of FSLN power in the streets. Men with guns continued to hold the upper hand in Nicaraguan politics. Between seven thousand and nine thousand members of the National Guard were jailed. About one hundred were executed in the first days after the fall of Managua.

Within months the FSLN secured practical control over the government. They made their party's army, the Popular Sandinista Army (EPS) the official national army. Meanwhile, all non-Sandinistas were withdrawn from the government. Sandinista Party first secretary Daniel Ortega Saavedra became the nation's chief executive. Cuban leader Fidel Castro was keynote speaker at the first anniversary celebrations of the revolution in July, 1980.

Relations with the United States Deteriorate. The United States and the Sandinista government immediately clashed. Despite polite approaches by the Carter administration, Sandinista leaders were little disposed to listen to U.S. concerns. They were committed to their ideology of Nicaraguan nationalism. Because of their alliance with Cuba, they were skeptical of those who warned of the dangers of communism. Furthermore, the Sandinistas bore personal animosities toward the United States because U.S. military aid to the Somozas had only been suspended in the final moments of that forty-three-year dynasty.

The Sandinista government quickly moved to challenge U.S. interests. In 1981 Ronald Reagan, a firm anticommunist, became president of the United States. These factors combined to produce a recipe for conflict that further fractured Nicaragua. Sandinista military aid to guerrillas in neighboring El Salvador began only months after the 1979 revolution. Cuban advisors assisted in a variety of projects ranging from military training to the highly successful project of teaching reading to illiterates throughout Nicaragua. An anti-United States bias was clear from the start: Primary level reading texts depicted Americans as enemies. In addition, lyrics in the new national anthem referred to Americans as "enemies of humanity."

Nicaragua

1821	Nicaragua declares its independence from Spain.
1855	American adventurer William Walker takes control of Nicaraguan government.
1857	U.S. and British governments help depose Walker.
1893	Liberal Party leader José Santos Zelaya seizes power.
1896	(Mar.) American and British marines land in Nicaragua to protect their nationals.
1909	Landing of U.S. Marines triggers civil war.
1912	U.S. Marines quash civil war.
1927-1933	U.S. Marines and Nicaraguan allies fight rebels led by Augusto César Sandino.
1934	Sandino is assassinated; Farabundo Martí Liberation Front unifies Nicaraguan guerrillas.
1936	National Guard commander Anastasio Somoza García seizes power; his family rules until 1979.
1955	U.S. government mines harbor in Managua.
1956	Somaza García is assassinated; power falls to his sons.
1972	(Dec. 25) Earthquake levels Managua.
1979	President Somoza Debayle surrenders to Sandinista National Liberation Front in Nicaragua.
1979	(July 20) FSLN takes control of Managua.
1980	Daniel Ortega becomes chief executive of Nicaragua.
1981-1990	U.S.-supported Contras wage war against Sandinista Nicaragua.
1984	Daniel Ortega of FSLN is elected president.
1990	(Feb. 25) Violeta Barrios de Chamorro, backed by UNO coalition, is elected president.
1990	(May 25) Chamorro takes office.
1992-1993	Demobilization of armies produces uprisings.
1996	Arnoldo Aleman of Liberal Alliance Party is elected president.
1996	(Feb.) Pope John Paul II visits Nicaragua.
1997-1998	Aleman signs treaties with disarmed rebel forces.
1998	(Jan. 30) FSLN temporarily shuts down its newspaper, *Barricada*, for lack of funds.
1998	(Mar. 3) Former president Ortega is accused by his stepdaughter of having sexually abused her; FSLN leaders denounce her accusation as politically motivated.
1998	(May 23) Daniel Ortega is reelected secretary general of Sandinista National Liberation Front.
1999	(Feb. 26) President Aleman goes on television to deny Comptroller Agustin Jarquin's charges that he has used his office to enrich himself.

Committees for the Defense of Sandinism (CDS) were set up. These neighborhood-level organizations of social control were designed to dispense revolutionary guidance. They also provided a conduit for supporters to report disloyal neighbors to the Sandinista authorities. They were a straight copy of similar committees employed in Cuba. Ration cards for scarce goods were given out by the CDS and became a potent means of rewarding friends and punishing foes.

The CDS were only part of a real explosion in the creation of new political structures. For example, People's Anti-Somocista Tribunals, staffed with nonlawyers, were set up to handle charges against disloyal Nicaraguans. Up to one-half of the adult population became active in one or more grassroots sociopolitical organizations by 1984. All these facts were of great concern to the Reagan administration.

However, nothing was more worrisome than the substantial involvement by communist states. The Sandinistas received financial aid in the form of loans and grants from the European communist states allied with the Soviet Union. Aid from Western Europe and Canada initially was greater than that from the communist states, but only until 1984. No U.S. aid was granted after 1980. The United States used its influence to stop other loans to Nicaragua from the World Bank and the Inter-American Development Bank.

Military aid from the Soviet Union to the Sandinistas began early in the regime and continued at high levels, especially from 1984 to 1988. Top Sandinista officials traveled regularly to the Soviet Union's capital, Moscow. Sandinista delegations consistently voted with the Soviet Union at the United Nations, even when it meant publicly supporting the brutal Soviet military occupation of Afghanistan.

Contra Rebels. In the fall of 1981 in Guatemala City, Guatemala, a group of Nicaraguan exiles met with officials of the CIA. They formed the anti-Sandinista political movement later known as the Contras ("against" in Spanish). Contra military

Sandinista leader Daniel Ortega (right) watches as Violeta Chamorro succeeds him as Nicaragua's president after her party defeated the Sandinistas in free elections in early 1990. (AP/Wide World Photos)

Contra trainees crawl through mud under barbwire. The woman in the foreground was the only female member of her fifty-person unit.
(Reuters/Nancy McGirr/Archive Photos)

commander Enrique Bermudez and others were veterans of the Somoza-era National Guard, but the Contras were a diverse group. They came to include disgruntled FSLN heroes and businessmen from the Somoza era who had, at first, backed the FSLN revolution. More than 80 percent of the Contras' foot soldiers during the 1980's were poor, a majority were illiterate, and only one in four had ever owned land.

Throughout the 1980's the Honduras-based Contra movement evolved to become a persistent annoyance to the Nicaraguan authorities. The Contra army of U.S.-trained Nicaraguan exiles never directly defeated major forces of the Sandinista army. However, the Sandinistas were unable to break the substantial public support the Contras' political allies in the United Nicaraguan Opposition (UNO) coalition came to enjoy inside Nicaragua.

Attempts by the Sandinistas to widen support included a major land reform that reassigned for-

merly Somoza-owned lands and other large estates. The FSLN also attempted to show the world a democratic face. Party leader Daniel Ortega was elected president in a competitive election without Contra participation in 1984.

A new constitution was promulgated in 1987, and autonomy was granted to the Atlantic Coast region, a major area of rebellion by non-Hispanic minorities. However, the FSLN used the effect of a U.S. economic boycott of Nicaragua and the military threat posed by the Contras to justify harsh measures against Nicaraguan citizens. By October, 1985, the Sandinistas had suspended most civil liberties and rights. This action revealed key weaknesses in the Sandinista regime. Repression caused discontent with the government to increase. Furthermore, protection of rights of the free press had been an important element in garnering continued support from Western European governments and opponents of Reagan inside the United States.

After 1986 the Sandinistas turned more and more toward a Soviet Union that was beginning to question the costs associated with a far-flung empire of pro-Soviet states. Mikhail Gorbachev withdrew defeated Soviet troops from Afghanistan in February of 1989. He removed Soviet troops from Eastern Europe later the same year. This further pulled the rug of international communist support from under President Ortega and the Sandinistas.

As foreign support eroded, the FSLN government simply printed money to pay its bills. Inflation in 1988 roared to over 33,000 percent and remained above 1,600 percent in 1989. In this atmosphere the Sandinistas negotiated a cease-fire with the Contras and planned an election in 1990. They sought public reaffirmation of their revolutionary rule.

Exit the Sandinistas. Ortega entered the 1990 campaign confident of victory. From his perspective things looked good. His army had fought off a U.S.-backed group of former National Guardsmen who had killed over thirty thousand Nicaraguans. His election opponent was Violeta Barrios de Chamorro, and no woman had ever been elected to any high Nicaraguan office.

While the FSLN had a large grassroots base of support, Ortega's opponent's presidential campaign was poorly linked to the separate UNO Party's campaign to grab back the legislature. Finally, the opposition was set back further when Chamorro broke her knee. This forced her to travel to the United States for treatment and limited her public campaign appearances in Nicaragua.

However, Chamorro was the widow of Pedro Joaquín Chamorro, the martyr of the revolution. Her moderate views were widely known, as she had remained publisher of a leading opposition newspaper. Ortega and the FSLN underestimated her appeal. After war, revolution, and a decade of revolutionary rhetoric amid civil war, the average Nicaraguan voter was weary of conflict. Chamorro, able to criticize both the Contras and the FSLN, offered a window that opened toward a lost normalcy. Chamorro won the February 25, 1990, election 55 to 41 percent.

Chamorro took major steps to turn Nicaraguan politics away from civil war and toward peaceful means of competition. The FSLN remained the best organized political party and held command of the armed forces. However, Chamorro had won

the votes of most Contra supporters. Therefore, early gestures of conciliation were important. A disarmament agreement with the Contras in May, 1990, was paired with Chamorro's promise to retain FSLN military leader Humberto Ortega as army commander. These steps helped win broad support for the important decision to reduce the role of the EPS and to cut its size from nearly 100,000 to 15,000 troops by 1993. The reformed army proved an effective tool in keeping lawful order. They disarmed Contras and rebellious ex-Sandinistas alike during tense uprisings in 1992-1993.

Organized violence continued to decline. By the mid-1990's new political parties had split from the FSLN and UNO to present voters with wider alternatives. Major constitutional reforms in 1995 strengthened the legislative branch and weakened the executive branch by barring Chamorro's re-election or her replacement by close relatives. Both the FSLN and Chamorro opposed these constitutional reforms, indicating that Nicaraguan politics had moved beyond the conflict of the 1980's and the older tradition of strong executive government.

The peaceful election of a second non-Sandinista president, Arnoldo Alemán, Managua's anti-FSLN mayor, in 1996 suggested the limited appeal of Sandinism. Ortega captured less than 38 percent of the vote to Alemán's 51 percent. However, Alemán's supporters in the Liberal Alliance Party were not able to win a majority in the legislature.

Persistent Flash Points. Nicaraguan society remains highly divided. Few pressing social problems, such as access by the poor to adequate land, have been addressed by government reforms. During the 1980's significant land reforms had granted peasants access to some farms. Many large estates had been seized, and about 20 percent of farm acreage had been made into state farms or cooperatives. As the Sandinistas exited office in 1990, they took control of many estates and large homes. The Sandinistas' gifts to themselves angered many Nicaraguans, who viewed this as a return to Somoza-era corruption.

During the 1990's the legality of all these land-ownership changes were challenged by former owners, even as the Chamorro team tried to buy social peace by handing over another 66,000 properties to former Contras, former military men of the EPS, and others. Courts, which were filled with political appointees, proved poorly equipped to build public support for the law as they sorted out competing claims of ownership. More than two dozen judges were charged with corruption.

The Chamorro and Alemán administrations attempted to manage this situation by making further agreements with both the FSLN and the former Contras. However, the situation did not fully stabilize, especially in regions with large numbers of former EPS and Contra soldiers. Some of these ex-soldiers formed bands resembling criminal gangs. Amnesty offers and government programs to buy weapons from former fighters reduced but did not eliminate problems with rebels.

An economic recession throughout the 1990's forced many small farmers to sell the lands that various reforms had granted to them. Landless rural laborers, who earned less than US$30 per month in 1998, had seen little overall benefit after decades of soaring rhetoric. In urban areas high rates of unemployment and similarly low wages aggravated poverty. Chamorro's decision to end low subsidized prices of basic foodstuffs, a position unaltered by the Alemán government, made these matters worse.

Alemán's Liberals continued to win at the polls. However, secession-minded parties in the Atlantic Coast Autonomous Region, a regional hub of rebellion during the 1980's, did well in 1998 regional elections. In the populated western regions, the FSLN tried to foment uprisings several times in 1997 and 1998. Grievances about powerlessness and poverty again ripened in the late 1990's. Nicaraguan officials confirmed that at least nine separate armed groups continued to menace public order in 1998.

Gordon L. Bowen

Notes for Further Study

The historic roots of the 1979 Nicaraguan revolution are explored in John Booth, *The End and the Beginning: The Nicaraguan Revolution* (1982), and Thomas Walker, *Nicaragua: The Land of Sandino* (1991). Walker's many works concerning the conflict of the 1980's include the edited volumes *Reagan Versus the Sandinistas* (1987) and *Revolution and Counterrevolution in Nicaragua* (1991). Most informative concerning the 1990's is Walker, editor, *Nicaragua Without Illusions* (1997). For detailed contemporary news coverage, consult two newsletters from London, *Latin America Weekly Report* and *Caribbean and Central America Report.* Readable analyses of Nicaraguan trends appear regularly in *Current History.* On the Internet, the Library of Congress study of Nicaragua is found at http://lcweb2.loc.gov/frd/cs/nitoc.html Excellent university surveys of Nicaragua can be found at http://lanic.utexas.edu/la/ca/nicaragua and http://www.ohiou.edu/~latstudy/misc.htm.

Panama

Many of the problems that most threaten violent conflict in Panama are related to its location on a narrow isthmus on the southernmost portion of Central America. Since its independence in 1903, Panama has experienced a troubled relationship with the United States. The United States established a protectorate over Panama to safeguard the security of the American-built Panama Canal, but Panamanian leaders came to resent the U.S. military presence. Panama gradually assumed control of the Panama Canal and all American military bases on Panamanian soil, a process that was to be completed by the end of 1999. A second major concern has been Panama's struggle to establish a democratic government following a period of military rule. The United States invaded Panama in 1989 to overthrow Manuel Antonio Noriega and install a civilian government, but Noriega's old political party returned to power in 1994. Therefore, Panama's democracy remains unstable. Finally, Panama's location has made it an important staging area for the shipment of cocaine by Colombian drug cartels to markets in the United States and elsewhere. The illegal drug trade has contributed to rising crime rates and the corruption of public officials, further undermining Panamanian democracy and jeopardizing Panama's relationship with the United States.

Panama's history, economy, and society have been dominated by its strategic geographical position. A country of 30,193 square miles, or slightly smaller in size than the state of South Carolina, Panama sits astride the southernmost and narrowest part of the isthmus connecting North America and South America. It is bordered by Costa Rica to the west, Colombia to the east, the Pacific Ocean to the south, and the Caribbean Sea to the north. For centuries it has served as an important trade route linking the two continents and the Pacific and Atlantic Oceans.

Background to the Panama Canal. Attempts to ease passage across the isthmus go back to the early sixteenth century. The region's Spanish colonizers constructed the Camino Real, or royal road, to transport shipments of gold and silver bullion from mines in Peru to treasure ships on the Caribbean coast. During the California gold rush of the mid-nineteenth century, U.S. investors seeking a speedier passage between the East and West Coasts of the United States built a trans-isthmian railroad. During the 1870's Frenchman Ferdinand de Lesseps, famed builder of the Suez Canal in Egypt, at-

tempted a similar canal across Panama. After running into technical and financial problems, he abandoned the scheme in 1889. The United States eventually took up the canal project in 1903, and the Panama Canal opened for business in 1914.

The Panama Canal became the single most important factor affecting Panama's society, economy, and politics. Panama's role as a transit zone has contributed to the ethnic diversity of its society. Like that of many former Spanish colonies, Panama's population of almost 2.7 million is largely Spanish-speaking and Roman Catholic. Mestizos, or people of mixed European and American Indian ancestry, constitute about 70 percent of the population, while about 6 percent are American Indian. Approximately 14 percent are English-speaking, Protestant, West Indian blacks, many of whom are descendants of the original workers brought in to construct the canal. There are also significant numbers of Chinese, Jewish, Arab, Greek, South Asian, European, and North American residents who moved to Panama to take advantage of the commercial opportunities offered by the canal.

Canal's Influence on the Economy and Politics. The Panama Canal has shaped Panama's economic development. The canal itself has been a major source of wealth for the nation as a result of revenue created by canal traffic, the influx of workers to build and maintain it, and the large U.S. military and civilian presence to operate and defend it. The canal reinforced the service-oriented nature of Panama's economy. By 1995 the canal, banking, and other services accounted for 74 percent of Panama's gross domestic product (GDP), the total value of all goods and services produced within Panama. By contrast, industry accounted for only 16 percent and agriculture, principally bananas, 10 percent of GDP. Traditionally, Panama's leaders have neglected efforts to develop industry and agriculture.

The canal has similarly dominated Panama's politics and foreign relations. Panama declared its independence from Spain in 1821 and became part of Colombia the following year. In the early twentieth century, however, Panamanian separatists demanded independence from Colombia. In 1903 the United States failed to obtain Colombian approval to take over the Panama Canal project from the failed French enterprise.

U.S. president Theodore Roosevelt responded by using U.S. naval forces to secure Panama's independence. Within days of Panama's successful revolution, the United States signed a treaty with the new nation, securing the right to build a canal. Thus, it was the prospect of a canal that spurred the creation of an independent Panama, established a special relationship between Panama and the United States, and set the precedent for future U.S. intervention in Panamanian affairs.

Canal Treaties. The 1903 treaty between U.S. secretary of state John Hay and Philippe Bunau-Varilla, the former chief engineer of the French Panama Canal Company who represented Panamanian interests in Washington, D.C., caused resentment in Panama. The treaty gave the United States the exclusive right to build, operate, and fortify a canal. It also granted the United States a ten-mile-wide strip of Panamanian territory, known as the Canal Zone. Although Panama would receive a US$10 million payment and an annuity of US$250,000, Panamanian nationalists objected to the loss of sovereignty over their own soil.

Over the years, the canal became a central theme in Panamanian politics. The Canal Zone effectively became a U.S. colony in which American residents enjoyed immunity from Panamanian laws and a privileged existence. On several occasions, U.S. troops directly intervened in Panamanian politics to supervise elections and establish order. Increasingly, Panamanian political leaders channeled widespread resentment against the United States into nationalist protests and demands for a more equitable treaty. By focusing resentment on the United States, moreover, the handful of wealthy families that dominated Panamanian politics until the 1950's steered popular anger away from themselves.

In 1977, after years of discussions and several minor revisions to the 1903 treaty, Brigadier General Omar Torrijos Herrera, who had seized power in a 1968 military coup, achieved many of the nationalists' objectives. Torrijos and U.S. president Jimmy Carter signed two treaties. The Panama

Profile of Panama

Official name: Republic of Panama
Independent since: 1903
Formerly part of: Colombia
Location: between Nicaragua and Colombia
Area: 30,193 square miles
Capital: Panama City
Population: 2,693,400 (1997 est.)
Official language: Spanish
Major religions: Roman Catholicism; Protestantism
Gross domestic product: US$14 billion (1996 est.)
Major exports: bananas; shrimps; coffee; clothing
Military budget: US$78 million (1995)
Military personnel: military abolished in 1991, replaced by 11,000 national police force

Note: Monetary figures rendered as "US$" are U.S. equivalents of values in local currencies.

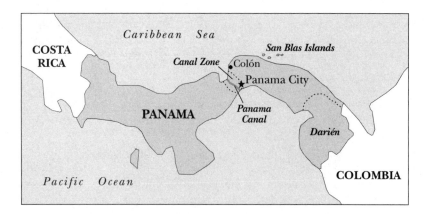

Canal Treaty, which replaced the Hay-Bunau-Varilla Treaty, established Panama's control over the disputed Canal Zone and set up the Panama Canal Commission to operate the canal and prepare for its transition to Panamanian control at the end of 1999.

A second agreement, the Neutrality Treaty, provided for joint Panamanian and U.S. responsibility for protecting the canal. Over the strong objections of the Panamanians, however, the U.S. Senate added an amendment to the treaty stipulating that the United States could use its own military forces in Panama to reopen the canal in the event of an emergency. The Carter-Torrijos treaties eliminated some of the friction in U.S.-Panamanian relations, but many Americans harbored reservations about Panama's ability to operate, maintain, and defend the canal effectively. Likewise, many Panamanians feared future U.S. military intervention.

Torrijismo. In addition to lingering problems concerning the canal, U.S.-Panamanian relations also remained strained because of Panama's failure to establish a democratic civilian government. Until 1968 Panama was a constitutional democracy, but it had always lacked strong political parties. Its government was usually dominated by a small ruling elite of wealthy families. Beginning during the 1950's, National Guard officers began to challenge the elite's monopoly of power. In 1968 the military deposed President Arnulfo Arias Madrid, who had twice before been ousted from office in favor of candidates preferred by the military. This time, however, National Guard commander Omar Torrijos established a military government and abolished all political parties.

Unlike the elite, who had ruled in the interest of a handful of white, aristocratic families, Torrijos built a popular base of support. He especially appealed to lower- and middle-class blacks and mestizos, who made up the ranks of the National Guard. Under a program that became known as Torrijismo, Torrijos combined modest social welfare reforms, such as extending public health services in the countryside and safeguarding the rights of workers, with a nationalistic foreign policy. Torrijos liked to refer to his rule as "dictatorship with a heart." In 1972 the military imposed a new constitution that gave Torrijos extensive powers as chief of government.

In 1978 Torrijos began a process of democratization. This was partly the result of pressure from the United States, which insisted on a return to civilian rule as a condition for approving the new canal treaties. It also reflected growing opposition to Torrijos from Panamanians who had only been willing to support him while he was negotiating for control of the canal. Even though Torrijos stepped down as head of state, he seemed determined to continue to exercise power behind the scenes. He remained commander of the National Guard, and his hand-picked national assembly selected the new civilian president, Aristides Royo.

When the government again legalized political parties, Torrijos's Democratic Revolutionary Party (PRD) was among the first to be organized. The PRD attracted support from a coalition of rural workers, labor groups, and lower- and middle-class mestizos and blacks who wanted to continue Torrijismo. It seemed that Torrijos was preparing to run as the PRD's candidate in the 1984 presidential election, but he died in an airplane crash in July, 1981.

Growing Tensions and U.S. Intervention. Manuel Antonio Noriega, Torrijos's head of military intelligence, quickly won the power struggle that followed Torrijos's unexpected death. The democratization process apparently continued with a series of constitutional reforms that provided for the direct election of the president and the legislature and prohibited members of the National Guard from participating in elections. In reality, however, Noriega exercised real power. He oversaw the modernization and expansion of the National Guard into the Panama Defense Forces, made himself commander, and assumed responsibility for all internal and external security affairs. In effect, the civilian president of Panama served at the pleasure of Noriega and the military, a fact plainly revealed in July, 1982, when President Royo announced his resignation on grounds of ill health.

The 1984 presidential election demonstrated the fragility of civilian rule and the extent of Noriega's power. With the backing of the military, the PRD and five smaller political parties selected an economist, Nicolás Ardito Barletta Vallarina, as their presidential candidate. He was opposed by Arnulfo Arias Madrid, a longtime enemy of the military. On election day, the PRD and its military supporters engaged in widespread voter fraud to ensure Ardito Barletta's victory.

Nevertheless, Ardito Barletta soon fell out of favor with Noriega. In order to reduce Panama's massive debt of over US$4 billion, one of the largest per capita foreign debts in the world, the new president began to cut government expenditures. This antagonized the military, which, since Torrijos's day, had used such spending to build popular support. More seriously, Hugo Spadafora, an outspoken critic of the military, claimed to have evidence linking Noriega to drug trafficking and ille-

U.S. Drug Enforcement Agency officers escort deposed Panamanian president Manuel Noriega onto an Air Force transport plane that took him to the United States in January, 1990. (U.S. Air Force)

Panama

1501	Spanish explorer Rodrigo de Bastidas becomes first European to reach Isthmus of Panama.
1513	Vasco Nuñez de Balboa crosses isthmus and claims Pacific Ocean for Spain.
1519	Spanish colonial capital is established at Panama City.
1821	Panama declares its independence from Spain.
1822	Panama joins Gran Colombia (dominated by modern-day Colombia, Venezuela, and Ecuador).
1855	U.S. investors complete construction of trans-isthmian Panama railroad.
1878-1889	French Panama Canal Company goes bankrupt trying to build trans-isthmian waterway.
1903	(Aug.) Colombian senate refuses to ratify treaty granting United States right to build Panama Canal.
1903	(Nov.) Panama secedes from Colombia and signs Hay-Bunau-Varilla Treaty granting United States right to build and operate trans-isthmian canal.
1914	(Aug. 14) Panama Canal officially opens.
1964	Panamanians in Canal Zone demonstrate against U.S. presence.
1968	National Guard commander Omar Torrijos seizes power and abolishes political parties.
1972	Military imposes new constitution giving Torrijos extensive powers as chief of government.
1977	Treaty establishes Panamanian sovereignty over U.S.-administered Canal Zone and provides for transition of canal and U.S. military bases to Panamanian control by end of 1999.
1978	Torrijos initiates democratization process; progovernment Democratic Revolutionary Party (PRD) is established.
1981	(July) Torrijos dies in air crash.
1982	(July) President Aristides Royo resigns under National Guard pressure.
1983	Manuel Antonio Noriega becomes commander of new Panama Defense Forces.
1984	Nicolás Ardito Barletta wins controversial presidential election with military support.
1985	Hugo Spadafora denounces Noriega for drug trafficking and illegal arms dealing and is found murdered; Noriega forces President Ardito Barletta to resign.
1987	(June) Street demonstrations calling for Noriega's resignation are brutally put down.
1987	(July) United States suspends all aid to Panama.
1988	(Feb.) Two U.S. grand juries indict Noriega on charges of racketeering, drug trafficking, and money laundering; President Delvalle attempts to fire Noriega but is forced to resign.
1988	(Mar.) United States imposes economic sanctions on Panama.
1989	(May) Noriega nullifies presidential election victory of opposition candidate Guillermo Endara.
1989	(Oct.) Army officers coup attempt against Noriega fails.
1989	(Dec.) U.S. military invasion of Panama captures Noriega and installs Endara as president.
1990	Endara government abolishes Panama Defense Forces; agreement among four former opposition parties to cooperate in national assembly breaks down.

1992	Miami, Florida, court convicts Noriega on eight charges and sentences him to forty years in U.S. prison.
1994	PRD candidate Ernesto Pérez Balladares narrowly wins presidential election.
1995	Free market labor reforms spark strikes and riots.
1996	Pérez Balladares admits to receiving campaign contributions from Colombian Cali drug cartel.
1997	Panama joins World Trade Organization.
1997	(Dec.) United States and Panama announce agreement in principle to establish multilateral counternarcotics center at former U.S. military bases.
1998	Legislative assembly passes constitutional amendment allowing Balladares to run for reelection in 1999, but voters reject it.
1998	United States and Panama announce abandonment of counternarcotics center proposal.
1999	(Mar. 11) United States gives Panama first of five military bases to be handed over before transferring full ownership of Panama Canal at end of year.

gal arms deals. In September, 1985, Spadafora was found murdered. Ardito Barletta promised a full investigation, but Noriega forced him to resign in favor of vice president Eric Arturo Delvalle Henríquez.

Until the mid-1980's, despite strong evidence that Noriega was allowing Colombian drug dealers to use Panama as a base of operations, the U.S. government tolerated him. He assisted U.S. efforts to overthrow the Sandinista government in Nicaragua and reportedly supplied intelligence information on Fidel Castro's Cuba. As evidence of Noriega's list of crimes mounted and Panamanians increasingly protested his strong-arm tactics, however, the U.S. government pressured him to resign.

In July, 1987, the United States suspended all economic and military aid to Panama. The following February, two U.S. grand juries indicted Noriega on various counts of drug trafficking and money laundering. When President Delvalle tried to fire Noriega, the military overthrew Delvalle and forced him into hiding. In March, 1988, the United States imposed economic sanctions on Panama.

Despite pressure from the United States and mounting opposition at home, Noriega tenaciously held on to power. He survived two attempted coups by fellow officers, ruthlessly put down street demonstrations, and annulled the 1989 presidential election that opposition candidate Guillermo Endara seemed to have won. In December, 1989, after armed clashes between Panamanian and U.S. forces in the Canal Zone, U.S. president George Bush dispatched twenty thousand troops to overthrow Noriega.

In a one-sided struggle, the U.S. invasion force quickly subdued the Panama Defense Forces, captured Noriega, and took him to Miami, Florida, to stand trial. In 1992 a court in Miami convicted Noriega on eight drug trafficking, money laundering, and racketeering charges. He was sentenced to eight years in prison.

Struggle to Restore Democracy. The Torrijos and Noriega years left a difficult legacy that Panama is still striving to overcome. Although the United States installed Guillermo Endara, the apparent winner of the 1989 election, as president, the transition to civilian rule proved difficult. The new government tried to prevent a return to military control by abolishing the Panama Defense Forces, firing many of the senior officers, and establishing the civilian Public Force to carry out police duties.

The government also divided police responsibilities among seven different agencies in order to prevent one individual from monopolizing power. These reforms, however, seriously weakened law enforcement efficiency. Urban crime dramatically increased during the first years of civilian rule, and Panama continued to serve as a shipment point for narcotics traffickers. Indeed, critics claimed that the overlapping jurisdictions among the law enforcement agencies merely created new opportunities for corrupt public officials. Some former military officers also refused to surrender power readily. They staged several unsuccessful coup attempts against Endara, one of which required another intervention by U.S. troops to keep order.

Endara's troubled presidency highlighted the fragmented nature of Panamanian party politics. Endara headed a four-party coalition that had opposed Noriega and the PRD, but it proved to be an ineffective government. Almost immediately, the coalition partners fell out over the allocation of government positions and patronage. Party leaders resorted to the sort of backroom deal-making over the division of spoils that had characterized Panamanian politics before Torrijos. Even Endara's own

party, the Arnulfistas—named for the recently deceased Arnulfo Arias—expressed dissatisfaction by replacing him as party leader with Arias's widow, Mireya Moscoso de Gruber.

Popular support for Endara's government also quickly eroded because of Panama's serious economic problems. The combination of U.S. sanctions before the 1989 invasion and economic mismanagement during the years of military rule saddled Panama with a huge external debt and an unemployment rate of almost 25 percent. The invasion itself caused an estimated US$2 billion in damages, not to mention several hundred civilian deaths.

Endara, under pressure from international lending agencies such as the International Monetary Fund (IMF), moved to cut spending by laying

After the United States swept Noriega out of power, a Panamanian expressed his gratitude to U.S. president George Bush in this graffiti outside Panama City. (Reuters/Santiago Lyon/Archive Photos)

off government workers, reducing salaries, and selling off numerous government-run industries to the private sector. These actions helped to reassure foreign investors and spur overall economic growth, but they also provoked widespread labor unrest. The economic benefits, moreover, failed to reach most Panamanians, over 50 percent of whom were living below the poverty line by 1994. Although the unemployment rate fell, it continued to hover around 15 percent. By the end of Endara's term, the brief period of euphoria that had followed the U.S. invasion had been replaced by a sense of disillusionment and frustration.

Return of the PRD. The 1994 elections fully revealed the extent of popular discontent. In what was probably Panama's fairest election, approximately 70 percent of the electorate turned out to vote for sixteen political parties and seven presidential candidates. To the surprise of many, PRD candidate Ernesto Pérez Balladares narrowly won the presidency over three major rivals with only 33 percent of the vote. The PRD also emerged as the single largest party in the legislative assembly, capturing thirty-two of its seventy-two seats. The party most closely associated with the preinvasion military regime had returned to power.

The PRD's revival owed much to Pérez Balladares's ability to distance himself and his party from past ties to Noriega and the military. Although Pérez Balladares had worked as campaign manager for Noriega's hand-picked presidential candidate in 1989, he emphasized his commitment to the progressive principles of Torrijismo. In order to allay U.S. fears, he also noted his American university education and stressed his willingness to cooperate with the United States to resolve outstanding problems. He signaled his conciliatory attitude by appointing Gabriel Lewis Galindo, a former ambassador to the United States and a prominent businessman unconnected with the PRD, to head the foreign ministry.

Despite Pérez Balladares's efforts to conciliate the United States and reassure Panamanians that his Democratic Revolutionary Party is genuinely committed to democracy, there were signs that the

In 1995 the United States turned over Fort Davis, seen below the Panama Canal in this picture, and Fort Gulick to the Panamanian government under the terms of the two countries' 1977 treaty. (AP/Wide World Photos)

transformation was not yet complete. Panama continued to operate under a constitution that was imposed by the military in 1972.

In 1998, moreover, Pérez Balladares's supporters in the legislative assembly passed a controversial constitutional amendment allowing the president to run for a second consecutive term in 1999. Panamanian voters overwhelmingly rejected the amendment in a popular referendum. Opposition parties have also expressed alarm at other proposed constitutional changes that would restrict freedom of speech. They note with concern that many former Noriega supporters have returned to positions of prominence.

The opposition's concerns about Pérez Balladares's long-term political intentions have been heightened by their own inability to present a united front. Although two-thirds of Panamanians did not vote for Pérez Balladares in 1994, and the PRD won less than half of the seats in the legislative assembly, the president has skillfully exploited divisions among the other parties to maintain a governing coalition. The continuing factionalism among the opposition became apparent in June, 1998, when three parties agreed to support Mireya Moscoso of the Arnulfista Party in the 1999 presidential election.

No sooner had the announcement been made, however, than Alberto Vallarina, Moscoso's rival for leadership of the Arnulfista party, threatened to ally himself with three other parties and run as a third candidate. As was the case in 1994, it seemed as though a fragmented opposition might open the door to another PRD electoral victory in 1999.

Further Uncertainties. Pérez Balladares's handling of the economy generated mixed reviews. He committed himself to improving Panama's competitive position in the world economy by following the development model of the so-called Asian tigers: Taiwan, Singapore, Hong Kong, and South Korea. To the surprise of many of his own PRD supporters, he continued the privatization of the economy begun under Endara and reduced tariffs to encourage greater efficiency by Panamanian producers.

In 1995, amid a storm of protest, Pérez Balladares repealed many of the benefits that workers had enjoyed since the days of Torrijos. The following year, the government reached agreement with Panama's creditors to restructure its US$6 billion foreign debt. In 1997 Pérez Balladares achieved one of his major objectives when Panama joined the World Trade Organization. While such reforms pleased international investors and encouraged steady economic growth, neither the unemployment rate nor the poverty rate improved significantly.

Uncertainties also remained concerning the transition of the Panama Canal to complete Panamanian control and the elimination of the last U.S. military bases. Shippers expressed confidence in Panama's ability to manage and operate the canal, but doubts remained about its capacity to perform expensive routine maintenance work estimated at US$500 million per year and its ability to preserve the surrounding rain forest watershed that provides the necessary water for the operation of the canal's locks. Another worry was the loss of some US$500 million previously pumped into the Panamanian economy each year by U.S. service personnel and their dependents.

The Panamanian government devised a series of plans for the former U.S. military bases, ranging from tourism to manufacturing facilities, but a majority of Panamanians wanted some continued U.S. military presence for economic reasons. In December, 1997, the United States and Panama announced an agreement in principle to transform Howard Air Force Base into a multilateral counternarcotics center. Student groups, peace activists, nationalist organizations, and several opposition politicians immediately began campaigning against the proposed center. In September, 1998, Panama and the United States announced that negotiations to establish the counternarcotics center had failed.

Looming over all these developments is the continuing shadow cast by the international drug trade. Panama's geographic location close to the major cocaine-refining facilities and drug-trafficking routes of the Colombian drug cartels continues to cause problems. Drugs destined for the United States and Europe still arrive by air and sea, either at the major ports of entry or at the dozens of small landing strips on the San Blas Islands and in the eastern province of Darién. Drug lords commonly "launder" their money in Panama by purchasing real estate and businesses.

In 1996 journalists discovered that President Pérez Balladares had received an illegal US$50,000 donation, unknowingly he claimed, during his 1994 election campaign from José Castrillon Henao, a leader of the Cali drug cartel. As late as the late 1990's, rising crime rates and the pervasive influence of drug money still posed serious problems for Panama's fledgling democracy.

Richard V. Damms

For Further Study

A good source of basic information on Panama's history, economy, and society is Sandra W. Mereditz and Dennis M. Hanratty, editors, *Panama: A Country Study* (1989). David McCullough's long but highly readable *The Path Between the Seas: The*

Creation of the Panama Canal, 1870-1914 (1977) describes in detail the early history of the canal, while Walter LaFeber's *The Panama Canal: The Crisis in Historical Perspective* (1978) traces the events leading up to the revision of the canal treaties in 1977. The developing crisis in relations between the United States and Panama under General Manuel Antonio Noriega is detailed in books by John Dinges—*Our Man in Panama* (1990)—and Frederick Kempe—*Divorcing the Dictator* (1990). The impact of the 1989 U.S. invasion of Panama and the difficulties of building a stable democracy are discussed in two articles by Steve C. Ropp, "Things Fall Apart: Panama after Noriega," *Current History* 92 (March, 1993) and "Panama: Tailoring a New Image," *Current History* 96 (February, 1997). Noriega's own account can be found in Manuel Antonio Noriega and Peter Eisner, *America's Prisoner: The Memoirs of Manuel Noriega* (1997).

Two good sources of information on current events in Panama can be found on the Internet. "Panama SUN," an online weekly newsletter compiled from Panamanian newspapers, is particularly informative on Panamanian politics and can be found at http://www.panamasun.com. More in-depth articles are available from "Panamá Update," published quarterly by the Fellowship of Reconciliation Task Force on Latin America and the Caribbean, an interfaith peace group, and available at http://www.nonviolence.org/for/panama. For current statistical information, see the Panama page of the "CIA Factbook" (http://www.odci.gov/cia/publications/factbook/pm.html).

South America

South American countries have occasionally fought wars among themselves, and Argentina waged a short war with Great Britain in 1982. However, most of the continent's violent conflicts have taken place within the individual countries. Such conflicts have recurred throughout modern history because of rebellions, organized crime, social unrest, and military coups. Conditions vary among the many countries, but several themes underlie most of these struggles. Small groups of wealthy families have dominated political and economic power in each country, while the majority populations have remained poor and relatively powerless. Attempts to change these imbalances have sometimes led to large-scale conflicts. Moreover, racial discrimination has long separated whites, Native Americans (Amerinds), African Americans, and people of mixed heritage; racial repression has also often led to violence. Finally, national militaries have often disobeyed civilian political leaders, taken over governments, and operated money-making enterprises on their own. Although political, economic, and social conditions generally improved during the 1990's, South America remains one of the most troubled continents.

Articles in This Section

South America is the world's fourth largest continent in area and the fifth largest in population. Its 330 million people live in twelve independent nations and one French-ruled colony. Brazil dominates the continent in land area, size of gross national product (GNP), and population. The remaining nations, in descending order of population size, are Colombia, Argentina, Peru, Venezuela, Chile, Ecuador, Bolivia, Paraguay, Uruguay, Guyana, and Suriname. French Guiana, the last European colony on the continent, has the smallest population.

Cultural Diversity. Independent Guyana (formerly British Guiana), independent Suriname (formerly Dutch Guiana), and French Guiana retain strong cultural characteristics of their colonial rulers. Brazil, settled by the Portuguese, and the remaining nine countries—all former colonies of Spain—are considered part of Latin America. Nevertheless, the appearance of common culture and language indicated by the term Latin America is misleading. The continent is home to hundreds of indigenous Amerind nations, whose people speak more than 180 languages. Indeed, many Amerinds speak little or no Spanish or Portuguese.

Most native American languages have few remaining speakers. However, Quechua, common in the central Andes Mountains of Ecuador and Peru, has 6.2 million speakers. It is the largest surviving Native American language. Additionally, large numbers of Africans were brought to South America as slaves in the eighteenth and nineteenth centuries. Moreover, some immigrants and their descendants from European nations other than Spain and Portugal, as well as India, Japan, China, and Indonesia, continue to speak the languages of their homelands as their first tongues.

South America's great cultural diversity is complex and causes much political injustice and some-

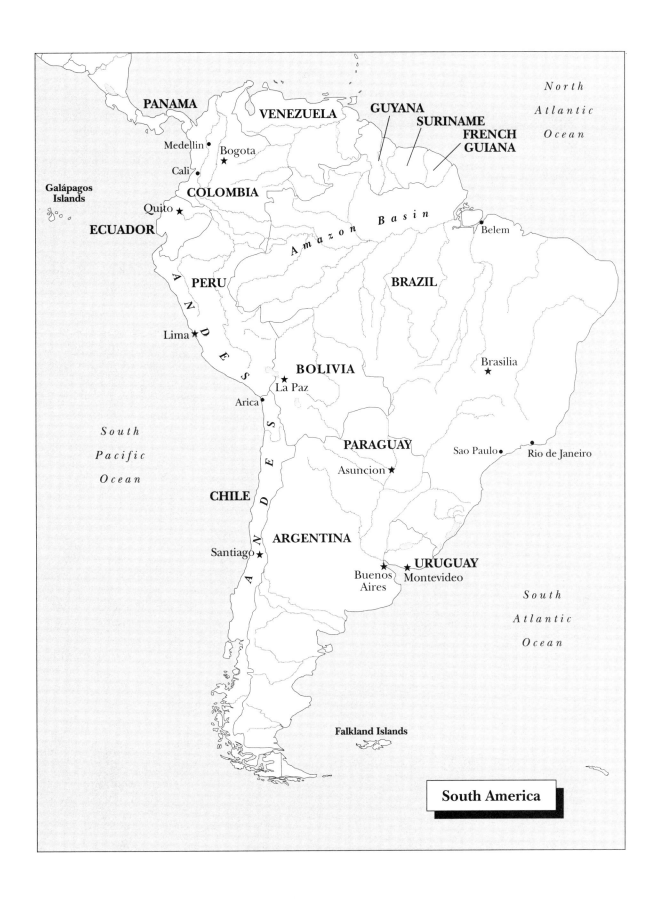

PANAMA

VENEZUELA

GUYANA

SURINAME

FRENCH
GUIANA

*North
Atlantic
Ocean*

Medellin • • Bogota
Cali •

**Galápagos
Islands**

COLOMBIA

Quito ★

ECUADOR

A m a z o n   B a s i n

Belem

PERU

BRAZIL

Lima ★

*A
N
D
E
S*

BOLIVIA

La Paz ★

Brasilia ★

Arica •

*South
Pacific
Ocean*

PARAGUAY

Sao Paulo •   • Rio de Janeiro

Asuncion ★

CHILE

*A
N
D
E
S*

ARGENTINA

Santiago ★

Buenos
Aires ★   ★ URUGUAY
Montevideo

*South
Atlantic
Ocean*

Falkland Islands

South America

times violence. Throughout the continent's history distinctions in race and culture have determined a person's prestige and access to political power, land, military rank, and business resources.

After founding their first colonies in the sixteenth century, the Spanish and Portuguese soon controlled most of the wealth and had nearly all the political power. Their descendants still consider themselves the ruling elite. Later immigrants, especially European Christians, have been next in status, followed by mestizos, people of mixed white-Amerind parentage. Generally lowest on the socio-economic scale are people of pure African descent, people of mixed African-white heritage called mulattos, mixed African-Amerind people called zambos, and Amerinds.

Although a measure of cultural unity was established when missionaries converted Amerinds to Roman Catholicism, the Church long encouraged them to think of whites as their superiors. There was little intermarriage among the races; however, many children were born out of wedlock and could not inherit property, a source of jealousy and bitter rivalry.

Early History. About twelve thousand years ago nomads began filtering into South America from North America, passing through the Isthmus of Panama. They slowly spread throughout the continent and adapted to the great variety of climates: the hot, humid equatorial rain forest, the cool high valleys of the Andes, the dry plains of Argentina, and the frigid, windy headlands of Tierra del Fuego in the far south.

The peoples of the central west coast and the Andes developed advanced cultures as early as 1500 B.C.E. The state systems of those early cultures used warfare to extend their territory and demanded tribute from conquered peoples. The most successful empire builders were the Incas. Theirs was also the last strong indigenous empire on the continent before the arrival of the Spanish at the end of the fifteenth century. Fierce and well organized, the Incas conquered the mountain and coastal regions, from the modern Ecuador-Colombian border region to what is now central Chile.

At its height the Inca Empire ruled twenty million subjects and had great riches in gold, silver, food stores, textiles, and cultivated land. It was administered from the capital at Cuzco (now in Peru). There were also hundreds of smaller Amerind nations throughout the continent. Many of them were fiercely independent.

After Francisco Pizarro led 180 Spanish soldiers into the Andes in 1532, the Inca Empire fell swiftly to the invaders. In part, the Spanish victory was due to Old World diseases they brought with them, against which native South Americans had no natural resistance. Pizarro also happened to arrive at a time the Incas were weakened by civil war. The Spanish Conquest was also a product of the cunning and ruthlessness they used to goad the Incas into fighting each other. Within five years of his arrival, Pizarro ruled the Incas. In 1542 Peru became an official territory of Spain, ruled by a viceroy, the personal representative of the Spanish king.

By the end of the seventeenth century Spain ruled nearly all of South America except Brazil, which was a territory of Portugal. While the Spanish and Portuguese occupied the political offices and

Revolutionary Leaders in South American History

Simón Bolívar (1783-1828): Known as the Great Liberator, Bolívar was born in Venezuela and died in Colombia. He fought Spain to win independence for Chile, Peru, Ecuador, Colombia, and Venezuela.

Che Guevara (1929-1966): Argentina-born guerrilla leader who participated in revolutions in Caribbean and South American countries. He was killed by Bolivian army troops.

Abimael Guzmán (1934-   ): Peruvian philosophy professor who founded and led the Shining Path. He was captured by police in 1992 and jailed.

Juan Perón (1895-1974): Argentine army officer who staged a coup, winning wide popularity with his sweeping reforms to help workers and the poor and his strong nationalism. He died during a second term as president of Argentina following a long exile.

Camilo Torres (1929-1966): Colombian priest and sociologist who fought as a guerrilla to end repression of the poor. He was killed in an army ambush.

After being venerated for centuries for beginning the Spanish conquest of South America, Francisco Pizarro has come to be seen as a symbol of oppression. In February, 1998, the city council of Lima, Peru, voted, to remove this old statue of Pizarro. (AP/Wide World Photos)

officer ranks in the military, it was left to missionaries of the Roman Catholic Church to turn peaceful Amerinds into loyal subjects of the king by converting them to Christianity and educating them. In return the Spanish crown granted the Church extensive tracts of land and economic privileges.

To both Spain and Portugal the new continent meant great opportunities for enrichment. It held a rich diversity of new foods, large tracts of arable land, and vast lodes of valuable minerals. These resources—gold and silver in particular—went back to Spain and Portugal to provide revenue for the royal governments and to enrich merchants. The two Iberian countries came to depend on their colonies economically. Many of their own people came to South America to win their fortunes, hoping to return to Europe wealthy. They employed, or enslaved, Amerinds to work their mines and plantations. When too many Native Americans died from European diseases, the European land owners imported black slaves from Africa.

Revolutions. By the mid-eighteenth century there existed a large number of South American-born whites, known as Creoles. European officials and military officers often denied Creoles the same status and political power as European-born whites. This discrimination caused jealousy and led to revolts in which the Creoles allied themselves with mestizos and mulattos in their common hatred of native Europeans.

Spain and Portugal successfully repressed the revolts until the early nineteenth century. Then, led by brilliant Creole military leaders, such as Simón Bolívar and José de San Martín, the Spanish colonies gained independence. By 1825 the political map of the continent was divided into essentially the same countries that exist today, although the borders were somewhat different. Brazil became technically independent of Portugal in 1822 but remained close to the parent country and had its own Portuguese-based monarchy until 1889.

During the new nations' early years, their leaders tried to imitate the democracy of the United States or modified parliamentary systems, like that of Great Britain. In fact Bolívar dreamed of uniting South America under one large federal government, a United States of South America. It was not to be, however, and democracy never took a firm hold.

Regional rivalries over land and resources among wealthy Creoles prevented continental union. Led by economic and military strongmen, called caudillos, the elites ruled their territories like private clubs; nonwhites had few rights. Revolutions occurred, but until the late twentieth century they usually only replaced one group of elite white rulers with another. Small communities of Amerinds in remote areas, such as the high Andes valleys and the Amazon rain forest, were free to follow their traditional ways of life. Most, however, lived as peasants on large estates or in segregated villages.

Intra-American Wars. South American countries have fought several wars over disputed territory.

South Americans have often made the United States the focus of their discontent; here Venezuelan students burn a U.S. flag in 1997 to protest policies of the International Monetary Fund. (Reuters/Nicola Rocco/Archive Photos)

Tiny Paraguay lost the War of the Triple Alliance (1865-1870) to the combined forces of Argentina, Brazil, and Uruguay. The War of the Pacific (1879-1884) pitted Chile, the eventual victor, against Peru and Bolivia. It resulted in Chile's extending its coastal territory northward, cutting off Bolivia's land connection to the Pacific Ocean.

Bolivia and Paraguay fought each other to what was essentially a bloody draw in the Chaco War (1932-1935), in which each sought to gain control of a valuable oil field that had not been correctly mapped. A long quarrel between Peru and Ecuador over their eastern border erupted into a brief war in 1941. Ecuador lost about a quarter of its eastern territory as part of the treaty ending the conflict.

Ecuador repudiated its border treaty with Peru in 1960. Another war between them broke out in 1981, which Ecuador also lost. In 1995 the two countries skirmished for possession of less than fifty miles of the Condor mountain range along the southeastern border of Ecuador. Other nations arranged a cease-fire, but the dispute remained unsettled. The Ecuadorians wanted the area so it could gain access to tributaries of the Amazon River; however, each country insisted that the land had historically belonged only to it.

Tensions between Peru and Ecuador subsided in 1998 when El Niño-spawned storms devastated both countries. Peruvian president Alberto Fujimori and Ecuadorian president Fabian Alarcon pledged mutual aid to help each other recover from the storm damage. Nevertheless, possession of the disputed land has long been a matter of patriotic pride in both countries, an attitude which could spark further fighting.

No other such South American discord led to open warfare during the same period, even though Guyana had long-standing border disputes with Venezuela and Suriname, and Bolivians still resent losing their land link to the Pacific coast to Chile. However, Venezuela and Colombia threatened each other in 1997. At issue was the behavior of guerrilla units of Colombia's National Liberation Army, which for several years had been infiltrating Venezuela from Colombian bases to rob villagers and ranchers.

In 1995 Colombian guerrillas killed eight Venezuelan marines, increasing tensions between the two countries. Venezuela wanted Colombia to patrol the border and stop its guerrillas. Although both countries sent army troops to the region, the danger of their actually fighting each other—as well as the guerrillas—was small because the economies of both nations would suffer from the loss of trade.

Brazil and Argentina, long major commercial rivals, have sometimes issued warnings to each other over international trade policies. In 1997, when they quarreled over what should be the export price of sugar—a vital export for both countries—political tensions between them escalated. However, a 1996 military pact between them almost guaranteed there would be no battles. Moreover, negotiations in 1994 and 1998 for a trade treaty covering the entire Western Hemisphere, the Free Trade Area of the Americas, reduced the chance of military conflict because of trade disagreements throughout the region, even though the treaty was not scheduled to take effect until 2005. Also, membership in the Organization of American States (OAS) and in regional trading pacts has encouraged member countries to negotiate their disagreements rather than go to war.

Falklands Dispute. One lingering territorial dispute involves Argentina and a country from another continent—Great Britain. At stake are the Falkland Islands, which lie about three hundred miles east of southern Argentina in the Atlantic Ocean. The Falklands' two large islands and dozens of islets have belonged to Great Britain since 1833, when a British naval force overwhelmed a small Argentine military base post there. Argentina had maintained a token presence there since 1820 and called the archipelago Las Islas Malvinas.

After the British takeover, Argentina still considered the islands Argentine territory, insisting that the British presence there constituted an act of war. In 1965 the two countries began trying to negotiate a settlement, but nothing came of it. On April 2, 1982, Argentina invaded the islands. They quickly defeated the small British garrison and proclaimed Las Islas Malvinas part of Argentina once again. British prime minister Margaret Thatcher responded by sending a substantial naval task force. After several sea, air, and land battles, Great Britain retook the islands in mid-June. They were the Falkland Islands again—at the cost of nearly a thousand British and Argentine lives.

Although the 2,100 permanent residents of the Falkland Islands voted to remain British, Argentina still claimed the islands. In case the Argentine military should try again to enforce that claim, the British strengthened the island defenses and proclaimed a 150-mile-wide "exclusive economic zone," which overlapped Argentine territorial waters. Further conflict could occur over fishing rights in these waters or over possession of the islands themselves.

Rebels and Insurgent States. Until the mid-twentieth century, it was nearly impossible for outsiders to win their way into the ruling elites who controlled the economies and politics of South American countries. Indians, African Americans, and poor people of all ethnic groups had especially hard times. They were the disfranchised peoples with no meaningful roles in political decision making. One way for the disfranchised to gain some control over their own destinies was to rebel against established governments.

South America has a long history of rebellions, most of them unsuccessful. It has been typical for left-wing intellectuals to gain support of the disfranchised by promising them more social services and greater participation in government. Leftists have formed guerrilla armies, manned largely by the poor, and battled the conservative right-wing elements in the government. The latter have usually controlled the national armies and wanted to keep the traditional power structure. When leftist guerrillas have won and taken over governments, right-wing forces have often formed guerrilla groups of their own, starting new cycles of rebellion.

Between 1956 and 1998 twenty-eight major revolutionary organizations conspired to overthrow one or more of the South American governments. Nearly all of these organizations were left-wing and wanted to create socialist or communist states. Most relied upon support from the underprivileged and disfranchised. During the 1990's, almost all South American guerrilla activity occurred in Venezuela, Colombia, Bolivia, and Peru.

Peru's Shining Path. The most famous and feared revolutionary organization during the 1980's and 1990's was Peru's Shining Path (*Sendero Luminoso* in Spanish), a radical offshoot of a communist political party. Led by a former philosophy professor, Abimael Guzmán, Shining Path consisted mostly of Quechua-speaking peasants in the Andes. Many of them looked back with pride to their fierce Incan ancestors. Through propaganda, assassination of government officials, skirmishes with the Peruvian army, and bombings, Shining Path gradually gained control of large areas in the southern Andes. More than thirty thousand people are believed to have died in the struggle, and hundreds of thousands fled the violence and settled around Lima.

Shining Path's "state within a state," called an insurgent state, was financed by bank robberies, extortion, and taxes imposed on the growing of coca or the manufacture of cocaine. By 1992 Shining Path was so successful that there was concern that Peru's government might collapse. That year Peruvian president Alberto Fujimori dissolved the national legislature and suspended the courts, both thought to be corrupt or indecisive, in order to battle Shining Path and other rebel groups more efficiently. Later the same year, a special police unit captured Guzmán. In prison Guzmán renounced violence and told his followers to stop fighting. These startling developments crippled Shining Path. However, a splinter group, Red Sendero, denounced Guzmán as a traitor and continued the violence. In July, 1995, for example, sixteen soldiers and twenty rebels died in a battle in the Huallaga valley, a Shining Path stronghold.

Another Peruvian rebel group, the Tupac Amaru Revolutionary Movement, grabbed world headlines in 1997 by occupying the Japanese embassy in Lima and holding seventy-two hostages. Taking its name from an early Inca prince who had fought the Spanish, Tupac Amaru demanded release of its members from prison. However, its long-range goal was to rid Peru of all North American, European, and Spanish influences, including the current government. After a four-month standoff, Peruvian special forces stormed the embassy, killed all the guerrillas, and rescued all but one hostage.

Other countries have not done as well as Peru in combating rebel movements. Also financed by profits from shipping illegal drugs to the United States, Colombia's largest guerrilla group, the Revolutionary Armed Forces of Colombia, has established an insurgent state in rural areas. The rebels have clashed both with the Colombian army and with private armies, called paramilitary groups, employed by wealthy landowners and caudillos. In 1998 the guerrillas dealt the military its worst defeat in thirty years, killing eighty-three soldiers and wounding thirty in a day-long battle. Rebel groups have also bombed pipelines in Colombia and Venezuela and taken tourists hostage. They have also tried to disrupt Colombian elections by kidnapping officials and blowing up power lines.

Drug Trafficking. Colombia also had the largest organized crime problem of South America during the 1980's and 1990's. In its western cities of Medellín and Cali especially, large organizations, called cartels, of growers, drug manufacturers, and distributors controlled cocaine and heroine sales to North America and Europe. The illicit industry collected an estimated US$500 billion in profits every year during the mid-1990's. The cartels enforced their control of the drug trade by assassinating judges, government officials, journalists, and politicians who opposed them; hundreds of people died. They also exploded bombs in Colombia's capital, Bogotá, to terrorize opponents and bribed others into helping them.

U.S. presidents Ronald Reagan, George Bush, and Bill Clinton pressured the Colombia government to destroy the cartels, offering U.S. military advisors and money to help in the effort. In December, 1993, a major breakthrough occurred when Colombian government agents killed the leader of the Medellín cartel, Pablo Escobar. Leaders of the Cali cartel were later captured.

Peru, Venezuela, and Bolivia also hunted "narcotraffickers," sometimes with direct help of U.S. government agents. For example, in April, 1998, hundreds of Bolivian police and army troops occupied a cocaine-producing region after skirmishes with gunmen that left four dead. Bolivian president Hugo Banzer vowed to rid his country of all drug trafficking.

Cocaine and heroine have continued to flow out of South America, however. New cartels formed to replace those destroyed by police, and, according to some observers, guerrilla organizations, such as Shining Path in Peru and the Revolutionary Armed Forces of Colombia, took over some drug production and distribution operations.

In cooperation with U.S. State Department narcotics and law enforcement officials, Colombian police officials burn a cocaine laboratory near Curillo in 1998. (AP/Wide World Photos)

Social Unrest and Ethic Conflict. According to sociologists, social conflict is nearly inevitable in a class-divided society. Moreover, when a society's largest class is impoverished, as is the case throughout South America, the chances for conflict are still greater. Even in prosperous times, such as the 1990's, the income of more than half of South Americans remains below the poverty line. Many South Americans are desperately poor, and 130 million were homeless or lived in unfit housing in 1994.

Large numbers of rural poor have migrated to South American cities in the hope of finding jobs. Rings of slums have grown up around industrial cities, especially Lima in Peru and São Paulo and Rio de Janeiro in Brazil. Because of high unemployment rates and low incomes among the working poor, poor South Americans often turn to crime, such as theft and drug dealing, to support themselves. Police forces in major South American cities are hard pressed to control it. As a result police have grown repressive, even murderous, in some countries.

The slums of Brazilian cities, known as *favelas*, have contained the most notorious examples of brutal crime and law enforcement. According to one study, São Paulo police killed 6,053 people between 1983 and 1992, while 351 police died in action. Another study found that police in Rio de Janeiro killed almost 600 street children in 1995 alone. Human rights organizations doubt that police representatives have told the truth when claiming to have killed only in self-defense. Merchants in Rio de Janeiro reportedly paid police to murder street children, who regularly steal from sidewalk stalls and shops. Until jobs and wages increase and the number of poor people declines, the crime rate among slum dwellers is likely to remain high and violent conflict with police and paramilitary groups to continue.

During the 1970's and 1980's the Brazilian government tried to relieve the crowding in cities and improve the life of many poor people by encouraging them to colonize unoccupied land in Amazon forests. Land is a greatly prized possession among South Americans, the main means to self-sufficiency and status. Because of it many poor people accepted the government's National Integration Plan. The program was much like the Homestead Act of 1862 in the United States, which opened the western part of the country to farmers.

Like the U.S. Homestead Act, however, the National Integration Plan caused conflict when colonists began settling in large numbers. Cattle ranchers objected because the new farms blocked access to grazing ranges, and developers tried to bully the peasants from their land in order to acquire large tracts. In some states, such as Pará in north-central Brazil, the resulting violence left thousands of people dead.

Confrontations also took place between colonists and local Amerind communities, to whom the allegedly empty land was their traditional homeland. However, most violent conflicts involving Amerinds were with workers invited by the government to extract natural resources. After gold was discovered in Pará in 1980, for example, clashes occurred between the miners and members of the Kayapó nation. Amerinds fought with bows and arrows, blowguns, and spears, while mineworkers used guns and machetes. It finally required the intervention of government troops to remove the miners and assure peace.

In 1993 Brazilian gold miners who had illegally entered Venezuela massacred sixteen Yanomamis. The Yanomamis later took two miners hostage to prevent further slaughter, and the affair attracted world attention. The miners were released and the confrontations ended when the Venezuelan government expelled the miners. Similar conflicts have occurred among Amerinds and colonists and oil workers in Ecuador and Peru, mainly because the colonists and oil workers bring diseases and the oil extraction pollutes the land and water.

While world demand for oil remains high and South American countries depend upon the petroleum industry for jobs and investments, the exploitation of traditional Amerind territory will probably continue, even though human rights groups and environmentalist organizations try to help the Amerinds. Likewise, as long as there is free land for the poor to colonize, and governments help them to do so, colonization will continue despite Amerind objections.

Further social conflict has involved quarrels among ethnic groups and, less often, hatred for religious groups. Anti-Semitism surfaced in Argentina in 1992, for example, when a bomb killed twenty-nine people at the Israeli embassy in Buenos Aires. Another bombing killed eighty-six persons at a Jewish welfare office in 1994. Although foreign agents were suspected, local police were accused of helping them. Jewish cemeteries were also vandalized on two occasions.

Military Coups. *Coups d'état* are attempts to force change in governments suddenly and without general public approval. Because of ambition, frustration with existing politics, or fear of some threat to the state, leaders of coups, usually high-ranking military officers, use national troops and armaments to capture civilian leaders and scare opponents into silence. Sometimes fighting during coups costs dozens of lives. If fighting started by a coup spreads, it can turn into a civil war. However, the threat of violence is usually enough to put the military in charge—a "bloodless coup." Only a small fraction of coups succeed.

South American nations have had hundreds of coups in their history, many by right-wing leaders and some by left-wing leaders. Paraguay, an especially unstable country, has had more than 250 coups, but not a single peaceful and constitutional change of government in 185 years. Between 1950 and 1990 coups put military officers in power at least once in almost every South American country. In fact, the only South American countries not yet ruled by military juntas were Guyana and French Guiana. The latter remains a European-administered colony. Guyana has gained its independence but has not had powerful domestic military organizations.

At issue in most coups has been the question of how to develop national economies and who should control them: whether to have free-market systems, as in the United States and Western Europe, or to have centralized economic control under a socialist or communist system.

During the period of military dictatorships, juntas suppressed political opponents, often arresting and jailing them without trial. While Chile was ruled by General Augusto Pinochet and Argentina was under a succession of generals, government suppression was so brutal that the governments of both countries were said to have waged "dirty wars" against citizens suspected of antigovernment activity. Police and military squads secretly arrested people and confined them in military prisons, where they often were tortured and killed. These prisoners were called the "disappeared."

Former Chilean strongman Augusto Pinochet enters the senate in early 1998 to assume the seat guaranteed to him by the constitution as a former president. (AP/Wide World Photos)

South America

1498	Christopher Columbus explores Venezuelan coast, not realizing he has found new continent.
1532	Francisco Pizarro begins Spanish conquest of South America.
1809	Ecuador declares its independence from Spain.
1810	Venezuela-Colombia declares its independence.
1811	Paraguay declares its independence.
1816	Argentina declares its independence.
1818	Chile declares its independence.
1821	Peru declares its independence.
1822	Brazil becomes an empire independent of Portugal.
1825	Bolivia declares its independence.
1832	Great Britain occupies Falkland Islands.
1865-1870	Paraguay is defeated by Uruguay, Argentina, and Brazil in War of Triple Alliance.
1879-1884	Chile defeats Bolivia and Peru in War of the Pacific.
1889	Brazil abolishes monarchy and becomes a republic.
1930	Revolutions in Argentina and Brazil.
1932-1935	Paraguay and Bolivia fight the Chaco War over border territory.
1948	(Apr. 30) Organization of American States is formed.
1960	Ecuador repudiates border treaty with Peru.
1964-1989	Era of military dictatorships in Brazil (1964-1984), Argentina (1966-1970, 1976-1984), Chile (1973-1989), Peru (1968-1979), Uruguay (1976-1985), Suriname (1980-1988), and Paraguay (1954-1989).
1965	Great Britain and Argentina's attempt to negotiate Falklands settlement fails.
1966	Guyana wins its independence from Great Britain.
1966	Brazil begins programs to open Amazon region to exploitation and colonization by poor.
1970-1973	Chilean president Salvador Allende moves toward a socialist state but is assassinated.
1974	"Dirty War" by Argentina's military against guerrillas and dissidents.
1975	Suriname receives its independence from the Netherlands.
1977	Argentine Mothers and Grandmothers of Plaza de Mayo begin weekly vigils seeking information from government about "disappeared" children.
1980	Gold is discovered in Brazil's Pará province; violence between miners and local Indians begins.
1981	Ecuador and Peru fight over mutual border.
1982	Great Britain defeats Argentina in three-month war over ownership of Falkland Islands.
1989	Juan Carlos Wasmosy becomes first elected civilian president of Paraguay.
1990	Most South American countries return to democratic governments and free economies.

1991	Brazil and Argentina sign military pact.
1992-1995	Peruvian president Alberto Fujimori suspends congress and rules by decree.
1992	Peru's capture of Abimael Guzmán and other leaders of Shining Path cripples revolutionary movement.
1993	Sixteen Yanomamis are massacred in Venezuela by Brazilian gold miners.
1994	Thirty-four South American, North American, and Caribbean nations begin negotiations to establish Free Trade Area of the Americas in 2005.
1995	Peru and Ecuador skirmish over disputed border.
1997	Tupac Amaru Revolutionary Movement seizes Japanese embassy in Peru.
1998	Colombian guerrillas increase activity, bombing oil pipelines and defeating national army in major battle.
1998	Ravaged by El Niño-caused flooding, Peru and Ecuador conclude mutual aid pact.
1998	(Oct. 16) Acting on order of Spanish judge, British police arrest former Chilean dictator Augusto Pinochet in London on charges of ordering murder of Spanish citizens while he was in power; arrest begins protracted diplomatic crisis among Britain, Chile, and Spain.
1998	(Oct. 26) Ravaged by El Niño weather conditions, Ecuador and Peru sign treaty resolving their long-standing border dispute.
1998	(Nov.) Representatives of more than 160 nations meet in Buenos Aires to work out plans for implementing international accord to reduce global warming.
1998	(Dec. 6) Former coup leader Hugo Chavez Frias is elected president of Venezuela.
1999	(July 25) Chavez's leftist coalition wins large majority of seats in election to constitutional assembly expected to realign Venezuela's balance of power.

In Argentina an estimated nine thousand to thirty thousand citizens disappeared between 1976 and 1983. In Chile about three thousand people disappeared between 1973 and 1990. The national and international outcries against the dirty wars helped cause the fall of the juntas and the restoration of free elections in both countries. However, the deep anger of citizens, and especially family members of the disappeared, did not subside during the 1990's. These people remained angry because few military officers were ever brought to trial for the executions they had ordered.

When Chile's General Pinochet tried to become a senator in 1998, other senators bitterly fought to keep him out, even though Chile's 1980 constitution required his admission. Lingering resentment over the dirty wars kept tensions high among the military, politicians, and citizens; some commanders suspected of ordering torture and killings vowed to fight rather than submit to trial, further increasing the possibility of attempted coups.

Political Instability During the 1990's. Further coups were attempted, or threatened, during the 1990's in Argentina, Paraguay, Ecuador, Venezuela, and Peru. Only that in Peru succeeded, and it was led by the country's incumbent president Fujimori, who was helped by the Peruvian military. Fujimori suspended Peru's constitution and closed the national congress and courts. In 1997, however, rumors circulated that the military might stage a coup against President Fujimori if he sought reelection.

Coups have been most likely to occur in countries whose economies are small, crippled by inflation, or threatened by strikes. South American countries all suffered high rates of inflation during the 1980's, but most brought the problem under control during the 1990's and raised the standard of living. Political analysts thereby expected there would be less chance of successful coups after 1990. Nevertheless, a large portion of South American society stayed poor, and if economies should worsen and social and political turmoil should occur, military coups remain possible.

A complicating factor is that the militaries in some countries operate their own factories and businesses. They can also grant foreign corporations, such as oil companies, access to resources and share the profits. Money acquired from such enterprises gives the military both power and considerable independence from civilian government control.

Defeated South American political parties routinely claim that the elections they have lost are dishonest and refuse to accept their outcomes. Such was the case in Venezuela, Colombia, Guyana, Suriname, and Paraguay during the 1990's. Another source of potential political conflict comes from unions and political action organizations. Despite the material prosperity of many countries, and of Chile in particular, during the 1990's, industrial workers and some professionals believed they did not receive the wage increases due to them. Strikes by public school teachers in Bolivia led to violent confrontation by police and paralyzed the capital, La Paz, in 1998. Strikes or riots over political corruption have also occurred in Colombia, Argentina, Peru, and Brazil.

According to political analysts, democracy based upon free elections is unsteady throughout South America. The key to its survival lies in continued economic growth and a rising standard of living for all citizens. Political leaders hope that the Free Trade Area of the Americas treaty will solve economic problems, but many South Americans resent the influence of the United States and fear being dominated. There is significant opposition to the treaty. Unless national leaders can allay the citizens' concerns, the treaty could become another source of political strife.

Environmental Conflict. The governments with territory in the Amazon River basin were under great international pressure to end destruction of the rain forest during the 1980's and 1990's. Brazil, Peru, and Ecuador had difficulty in complying: Each had based much of its economic growth on exploitation of Amazon resources, such as gold, oil, and timber; and each had encouraged colonists,

who cut down to clear farmland. Government attempts to satisfy the international criticism were denounced as insufficient by environmental groups in the United States and Europe.

Attempts to restrict field burning, logging, and hunting were either ignored or met with harsh opposition by Amazon residents. For example, as much as 80 percent of the logging in the Brazilian Amazon violates laws, according to the government. Furthermore, South American citizens and foreigners have invaded Amerind territories to capture rare animals and harvest plants with medicinal properties. If Amerinds fail in trying to enlist government support to keep out these "eco-pirates," the indigenous peoples may resort to violence.

Roger Smith

For Further Study

The Penguin History of Latin America (1992), by Edwin Williamson, and *The Epic of Latin America* (4th ed. 1992), by John A. Crow, explain the economics, politics, and culture of South America throughout its history. Based on a Public Broadcasting Service series, *Americas: The Changing Face of Latin America and the Caribbean* (1992), by Peter Winn, describes the changes in South America since 1970 in a simple, vivid style and with many photographs. Arthur Morris supplies basic facts about land, climate, and natural resources in *South America* (1987). Information-rich summaries of the history, politics, and economies of South American countries are in *Geography* (7th ed. 1994), edited by H. J. de Blij and Peter O. Muller.

Roger D. Stone's *Dreams of Amazonia* (1985) and *Contested Frontiers in Amazonia* (1992), by Marianne Schmink and Charles H. Wood, tell how the Amazon basin was settled by Europeans and describes their conflicts with the Amerind peoples already there. Joe Kane's *Savages* (1995) is the moving story of the efforts of an Amerind nation of Ecuador, the Huaorani, to prevent oil companies from ruining their ancestral land.

Jerome R. Adams's *Latin American Heroes* (1991) presents short biographies of influential men and women during South American history. Alma Guillermoprieto describes the lives of South Americans in the early 1990's in *The Heart That Bleeds: Latin America Now* (1994). *Out of the Shadows* (1993), by Jo Fisher, describes the violence suffered by women looking for husbands and children kidnapped by the military governments of some South American countries. Timothy P. Wickham-Crowley describes revolutionary groups operating after 1956 and their reasons for fighting in *Guerrillas and Revolutions in Latin America* (1992).

Web sites on the Internet cover many aspects of South American culture and business and provide links to the news media. Many have text in Spanish only; however, most South American countries maintain informative Web sites for English-speaking tourists and business people. Examples include Argentina (http://www.sectur.gov.ar/; Bolivia (http://www.ine.gov.bo/); Brazil (http://www.brasil.gov.br/); Chile (http://www.camara.cl/); Colombia (http://www.presidencia.gov.co). Others can be found through Web text searching.

The U.S. State Department also provides information on South American countries at http://www.state.gov/www/regions/ara/index.html. Another site provides warnings about crime, security, and rebel movements (http://travel.state.gov/travel_warnings.html). The Library of Congress offers detailed, well-structured information about the geography, government, and history of most countries at http://lcweb2.loc.gov/frd/cs/cshome.html.

Argentina

Argentina's major conflicts have been the result of the military dictatorship that ruled the country between 1976 and 1982. That period temporarily ended constitutional rule and led to what has been called "the Dirty War." In those years the military attacked leftists as thousands of Argentines either fled the country or were kidnapped, tortured, and killed by the military regime. The 1982 war with Great Britain over the Falkland (Malvinas) Islands brought defeat to Argentina's military and led to its withdrawal from power. Since then, elected presidents have had to deal with the legacy of military crimes against the people of Argentina and serious economic problems. A time limit for bringing accusations against the military was supposed to bring a conclusion to this issue. However, those who search for justice have felt betrayed by this process and demand accountability. Argentina has again become a stable democracy with an improved economy, but at the end of the twentieth century it faced economic problems that left many without jobs and threatened the role of organized labor as the government sold off state-owned companies to private firms.

Argentina is the second-largest country, in area, in South America after Brazil. Covering 1,068,296 square miles, it is about one-third the size of the United States. From its north, where it is hot, to the colder southern regions, Argentina spans many different climates. Most of the nearly 36 million Argentines live in the central part of the country. Nearly one-third of them live in and around the capital city of Buenos Aires, making it by far the country's largest city. Located on the Rio de la Plata, Buenos Aires is also Argentina's largest port. Meat and wheat are two of Argentina's most important exports.

Argentina is bordered by Uruguay on the east; Paraguay, Brazil, and Bolivia on the north; and Chile on the west. The long border between Chile and Argentina created several border disputes in the past. The two countries have not gone to war over these disputes, but they have mobilized their armies and threatened each other with war. The Andes Mountains have historically separated Argentina from Chile to the west. When both of these regions were part of the Spanish Empire between the sixteenth and nineteenth centuries, there was no need to make a precise determination of the boundary. However, after the two countries became independent during the early nineteenth century, confusion over the border brought conflict.

An 1881 treaty between Argentina and Chile was imprecise and started an arms race between them that nearly caused a war in 1898. That year negotiations began. In 1902, the issue was put before King Edward VII of Great Britain, leading to a General Arbitration Treaty. In 1904 the two nations celebrated the peaceful resolution of this issue by erecting the Christ the Redeemer statue in the Andes on the border west of the city of Mendoza, Argentina. However, a new border conflict arose in the twentieth century and again nearly brought war between the two countries.

Three small islands at the mouth of the Beagle Channel south of the island of Tierra del Fuego were claimed by both countries. Argentina, with its city of Ushuaia nearby, claimed that these islands were in the Atlantic and subject to its control. Chile, which owns the small island south of Ushuaia, claimed that these islands were south of the Beagle Channel, which formed the boundary between the two countries.

In 1971 Queen Elizabeth II of Great Britain was asked to decide the issue. Her 1977 report awarded the islands to Chile. The Argentine military government refused to honor the decision, and both countries' militaries were put on a war footing. Pope John Paul II offered to arbitrate the dispute in 1978, but his decision was not complete by 1982 when the Argentine military government fell. The subsequent civilian government accepted the pope's decision to give the islands to Chile. In May, 1985, both countries signed a treaty that settled the issue.

Era of Military Rule. The greatest conflict experienced in Argentina during the latter part of the twentieth century was the military government that ruled between 1976 and 1982. The 1976 coup against President Isabel Perón was expected by most Argentines. She had inherited the government from her late husband, the popular but aged Juan Perón, who died in July, 1974.

As the elected vice president, Isabel Perón became president of Argentina in her own right. However, she had few political skills and relied on a variety of advisors who were unable to stop the mounting problems. Inflation continued to cripple the economy. Young rebels attacked army bases and kidnapped foreign businesspeople. Politicians from many parties hoped the military would remove Isabel from power and permit new elections.

The military faction that took over after the coup had no intention of returning the government to civilian rule. Its leaders believed that Argentina was threatened by international forces and could only be saved through a kind of "holy war" that would destroy the country's enemies. To this end the military announced that all political parties were banned and began a dictatorship that was more violent than any in Argentina's past.

Death squads associated with the government broke into the homes of professors, students, and others suspected of being rebels or of being sympathetic to the rebels. Many were tortured, thousands were killed, and a few, such as the well-known journalist Jacobo Timerman, were re-leased. Many simply disappeared without a trace, and their families never knew what had happened to them.

Many Argentines were frightened into a state of shock at the violence. Some fled the country. Others remained but submitted in silence. A few thought that the crimes the government was accused of were exaggerated or were lies circulated by opponents. Slowly, however, they learned from friends that there were too many missing people to ignore. These disappearances angered many relatives, and a small group of mothers began to demand that the military government explain what had happened. They put pictures of their children on posters and went to the main plaza of Buenos Aires, the Plaza de Mayo, located in front of the presidential office building. Those responsible for the disappearances could see the mothers marching.

The military officers who condoned the violence as a necessary measure against the enemies of the nation were shocked that they would be accused in such a public way. However, they could not send the police to attack the women. The marches continued, and the women became known as the Mothers of the Plaza de Mayo. They were among the first to publicly oppose the military regime and gave others confidence. Increasing

Profile of Argentina

Official name: Argentina Republic
Independent since: 1816
Former colonial ruler: Spain
Location: southern Atlantic coast of South America
Area: 1,068,296 square miles
Capital: Buenos Aires
Population: 35,798,000 (1997 est.)
Official language: Spanish
Major religion: Roman Catholicism
Gross domestic product: US$296.9 billion (1996 est.)
Major exports: food products and live animals; manufactured products; machinery and transport equipment; petroleum products
Military budget: US$4.6 billion (1996)
Military personnel: 73,000 (1997)

Note: Monetary figures rendered as "US$" are U.S. equivalents of values in local currencies.

numbers of Argentines, including the labor movement, began to demand an accounting from the military government and opposed their policies more openly.

Falkland Islands War. Argentina and Great Britain disagreed over control of a small island group off the southern coast of Argentina. Great Britain called these islands the Falkland Islands and had administered them since 1833. Most of the inhabitants of the islands, called "kelpers," were British citizens and wished to remain so. They opposed Argentina's attempts to gain control of the islands. The two countries had argued for many years about the sovereignty of these islands.

Argentina claimed that the Malvinas Islands, as they called them, belonged to Argentina and that Great Britain had invaded in 1833, removing Argentine settlers and authorities. By 1982 Argentina had negotiated with the British government for many years and had also brought the issue before the United Nations. Little had been accomplished, although the two countries had continued to discuss the matter.

In early 1982 the military government in Argentina began to fear that opposition within Argentina was mounting. Its leaders looked for an issue that would unite all Argentines behind their government. The leaders of the armed forces thought that a surprise invasion of the Falkland Islands would bring all Argentines to support their government. They also thought that such an unexpected invasion would be successful and, once achieved, would be difficult for the British government to oppose. Argentina's military leaders planned the invasion in secrecy.

On April 2, 1982, the Argentine army landed a force on the Falkland Islands that surprised the small British force. The Argentines quickly took control of the islands and claimed victory. Crowds that had marched in opposition to the military government voiced their support for the attack. Argentina had won a great victory, and its people were thrilled at the military's bold move. They expected the government of Great Britain to acknowledge Argentina's control of the islands and negotiate a transfer of sovereignty.

The government of Prime Minister Margaret Thatcher in Great Britain was shocked and angered by the Argentine invasion. Thatcher called on the Argentines to withdraw immediately or face a British assault. The president of the United States, Ronald Reagan, sent his secretary of state, Alexander Haig, to both London and Buenos Aires to seek a negotiated settlement to the conflict. Neither government was willing to make concessions, however, and so the war began.

The Argentine military occupying the Falkland Islands was not well supplied or well trained. Their hope was that the islands were too far from Britain for the British to mount a successful operation. With the assistance of the United States, however, Great Britain was able to send a small fleet and air force to the area with commandos who prepared to storm the island. Argentine and British forces clashed for more than one month in the South Atlantic. Argentine air force planes sank British ships with missiles. The British fleet declared an exclusion zone around the islands and attacked enemy ships within the zone. They even sank one

Juan Perón (left) campaigning for the presidency in 1946; his wife, Eva Perón (in white hat) stands behind him. (National Archives)

Members of the Mothers of the Plaza de Mayo, a human rights group formed when Argentina was under military rule, picket the headquarters of an army regiment in March, 1996, to denounce officers responsible for the crimes of the earlier "Dirty War." (Reuters/Enrique Marcarian/Archive Photos)

Argentine cruiser, the *Belgrano*, that was reportedly outside the zone. Finally, in June, 1982, the British forces attacked the islands and defeated the larger Argentine force, ending the war.

The defeat shocked the people of Argentina. It appeared to them that their military government had failed not only to run the country effectively but also to win a war that had appeared to be certain victory. Massive opposition to the government made it impossible for the military leaders to continue in power, and they began negotiating an end to their regime.

The outgoing military feared that they would be arrested by the new civilian government. The price they exacted from the civilian politicians was to limit any investigations or accusations regarding their actions during the Dirty War. With those assurances, they turned over power and permitted elections. Raul Alfonsín, candidate of the moder-

ate Radical Civic Union Party (UCR), was elected with 52 percent of the vote to a six-year term as president and took office in 1983.

Legacy of Military Dictatorship Era. Alfonsín was confronted by several serious problems at the beginning of his term. The most immediate was the need to punish those members of the military who had committed crimes against the people of Argentina. Alfonsín appointed a commission to investigate the disappearance of almost nine thousand Argentines. Nine military commanders were eventually tried, but subordinate officers and enlisted men were exempted after a 1987 revolt by the military. They argued that they had only followed orders.

The entire process of civilian judgment of its military was unusual. Military leaders claimed that they were in a state of war with leftist elements and that they could not be judged by civilian courts.

Argentina

1536	Buenos Aires, future capital of Argentina, is founded.
1776	Spain creates Viceroyalty of Rio de la Plata.
1810	Buenos Aires declares self-rule.
1816	Argentina declares its independence from Spain.
1829	Juan Manuel de Rosas is named governor of Buenos Aires.
1852	Rosas is overthrown.
1853	Argentine constitution is written.
1890	Radical party leaders rebel against government.
1912	Major electoral reforms are undertaken.
1930	Military coup ends Radical party government.
1943	Military coup brings Juan Perón to prominence.
1945	Perón is elected president.
1955	Perón is overthrown by military.
1973	Perón returns to Argentina after long exile and is elected president.
1974	(July) Perón dies; his wife, Isabel Perón, becomes president.
1976	Military coup overthrows Isabel Perón.
1982	(Apr.) Argentina begins war with Great Britain over ownership of Falkland Islands, which it calls Islas Malvinas.
1982	(Apr. 2) Argentina occupies British bases in Falkland Islands.
1982	(June 14) Britain completes its recapture of Falklands.
1983	Raul Alfonsín's election as president ends military dictatorship.
1985	(May) Argentina and Chile sign border treaty.
1989	Carlos Menem is elected president.
1990	Argentina and Great Britain resume normal diplomatic relations.
1992	Terrorist bomb rips Israeli embassy in Buenos Aires.
1994	Terrorist bomb destroys Jewish cultural center in Buenos Aires.
1995	Menem is reelected president.
1997	(Mar.) French president Jacques Chirac visits Argentina and criticizes government's investigation of its former military regime.
1998	(Jan. 15) Government arrests former navy captain Alfred Astiz after he boasts about his participation in death squad under old military regime.
1998	(Mar.) Argentine congress repeals its earlier amnesty laws.
1998	(May) Government charges Iran with responsibility for anti-Jewish bomb attacks in Buenos Aires in 1992 and 1994.

(continued)

1998	(May 17) Denying complicity in Buenos Aires bombings, Iran expels Argentine commercial attaché from Teheran and threatens trade sanctions.
1998	(Oct.) President Menem visits Great Britain.
1998	(July 14) Former president Rafael Videla is indicted on child-abduction charges stemming from so-called "dirty war."
1999	(Mar.) Argentine Chamber of Deputies votes to uphold constitutional provision that bars Menem from seeking third-straight term as president.
1999	(Mar. 9) Great Britain's Prince Charles begins state visit to Argentina, where he pays homage to Argentine troops who died in Falkland Islands war.

Argentine citizens, including the Mothers of the Plaza de Mayo, demanded that all those guilty of crimes be punished. The conflict made it difficult for Alfonsín to unite the people of Argentina and weakened the newly established democratic regime.

Families of those who had disappeared turned to international commissions for human rights and to medical experts who could help them discover what had happened to their loved ones. With the assistance of the Blood Center of New York and the American Association for the Advancement of Science in Washington, D.C., deoxyribonucleic acid (DNA) studies were conducted to determine the identities of children and even grandchildren who had been missing. Eventually a National Genetic Data Bank was established in 1989 to keep records. In this way families separated by disappearance or death can ultimately be reunited or learn the fate of their relatives.

The military regime in Argentina is also accused of murdering foreigners during their period of rule. On March 18, 1997, French president Jacques Chirac ended an official visit to Argentina with an angry statement about the deaths of thirteen French citizens during the military regime. He repeated a French request that Argentine navy captain Alfredo Astiz be extradited to France. In 1990 a French court sentenced Captain Astiz to life imprisonment for his role in the deaths of two French nuns during the 1970's.

International Grievances Against Argentina. A Spanish court also demanded that Argentina turn over General Leopoldo Galtieri, head of the military government from 1981 to 1982, for trial in Spain. General Galtieri had been arrested in 1984 and sentenced to twelve years in prison for "negligence" in his invasion of the Falkland Islands that led to war with Great Britain in 1982. He was found not guilty of the disappearance of seven hundred people during the time he was head of the Second Army Command in Rosario, Argentina's second-largest city. In 1990, after six years in jail, he was pardoned by President Carlos Menem and released. He was later accused in Spain of genocide, terrorism, kidnapping, and the murder of four members of a Spanish family living in Argentina.

The government of Argentina has rejected the claims of European governments, citing its sovereignty over crimes committed within its territory. The government of Argentina claimed that it alone can determine whom to try and on what evidence, and rejected the French and Spanish courts' legitimacy in such cases. However, since Argentina had ceased trying members of the military, some Argentines believed that foreign courts were their only hope for punishing the military. In March, 1998, Argentina's congress responded to ongoing criticism by repealing earlier amnesty laws for human rights abuses committed during the 1976-1982 dictatorship.

In another case related to human rights abuses, Argentine courts instituted proceedings against British soldiers for murdering Argentine soldiers after their surrender in the Falkland Islands at the end of the 1982 war. In 1996 a British veteran, Ken Lukowiac, traveled to Buenos Aires to promote his book *Soldier's Song*, in which he confessed to killing an Argentine soldier after his surrender at Tumbledown on the Falkland Islands. By the time an arrest order was issued in Argentina, Lukowiac had left the country. Later, new evidence by authors Adrian Weale and Christian Jennings in their book *Green-Eyed Boys* detailed the murder of an Argentine conscript after the battle of Mount Longdon by retired British army corporal Gary Sturge.

By the end of the 1990's Argentina's political system had gone through three peaceful elections and two transitions of power. The Radical Party (UCR) and the Peronist Party are the two most important groups. While these political parties contest openly for power with free elections, in 1997 the UCR made charges of fraud and irregularities against the government of Carlos Menem.

In calling for an investigation into these charges, the UCR

Argentine president Carlos Menem speaking at a Latin American economic conference in Miami, Florida, in early 1998. (AP/Wide World Photos)

claimed that corruption had occurred in the procurement of uniforms for the Federal Police, that there were irregularities in the privatization of the state-owned petroleum company YPF, and that electoral fraud had occurred in the city of Avellaneda and the province of Santiago del Estero. These political conflicts may stem partly from the desire to embarrass the government, but they may also indicate an ongoing problem of graft that has plagued many administrations in Argentina.

Economic Conflict. When Alfonsín took over as president of Argentina in 1983, he was faced with a US$50 billion foreign debt that the country could not pay. In order to take out additional loans from the International Monetary Fund (IMF), he had to implement a strict austerity plan that drastically cut government spending. Even so, inflation soared to 700 percent in 1985, and a new currency, the austral, was introduced to replace the nearly worthless peso. This was accompanied by a wage and price freeze that reduced inflation to 100 percent but caused severe recession and a fall in real wages.

The terrible economy brought political opposition not only from the rival Peronist Party but also from labor unions and many middle-class Argen-

tines. The popularity of Alfonsín plummeted when his economic plan started to fall apart in 1987 and inflation surged. Elections in 1989 brought defeat to Alfonsín's Radical Party, and a Peronist, Carlos Menem, was elected. There was such bitter resentment against Alfonsín's failure that the government permitted Menem to take office early, throwing out Alfonsín in disgrace.

President Menem had better luck with the economy, which helped him politically even though he violated many of the principles of the Peronist Party. Named for Juan D. Perón, president of Argentina from 1946 to 1955, the Peronist Party favored participation by the state in the economy. Perón had created or fostered state monopolies for airlines, telephones, railroads, petroleum, steel, and other industries and services. This was part of Perón's plan to nationalize Argentina's economy and to keep foreign companies from controlling critical elements of the economy. Perón called it economic nationalism, and his party cherished those principles even after its leader's death in 1974.

In 1990 Menem began a process of privatizing or selling off state-owned firms to private companies, both foreign and domestic, that was contrary to the legacy of Peronism. He believed that Argentina needed to overcome its economic problems within the world markets of the 1990's and that this required privatization of industry and services. Aerolinas Argentinas, the national airlines, was sold to Iberia, a Spanish firm, in 1990. That year also saw the auctioning off of the state-owned telephone company, Entel. These measures caused a split among Peronists in Menem's party, and part of the labor movement broke away in opposition. Nevertheless, the privatization continued. Many of the nation's highways were privatized and turned into toll roads. By 1995 the combined value of all privatized companies amounted to US$27 billion.

There have been many economic advances. Inflation was reduced from a 17 percent annual rate in 1992 to under 1 percent in 1997. The gross domestic product (GDP), the total value of all goods and services produced within Argentina, increased by 8 percent in 1997 over the previous year. The Southern Cone common market, known as MERCOSUR, has helped Argentina's economy while also reducing some conflicts with neighboring countries. Established in March, 1991, MERCOSUR is a free-trade common market uniting Brazil, Argentina, Uruguay, and Paraguay. MERCOSUR brings together 190 million people in these four countries with a combined 1993 GDP of US$715 billion. Argentina, with approximately 36 million people, had a GDP of US$270 billion in 1994. The per capita income was US$7,700.

Despite economic advances, the impact of these economic policies has been different for various groups. Foreign-owned firms have moved to Argentina and brought new capital. The Buenos Aires stock exchange, the Bolsa, has increased its value. The economic activity has led to construction of buildings and roads and brought new services, such as cellular telephones and new technology. However, many firms have fired employees. State-owned firms were not required to be profitable and maintained high payrolls, sometimes for political reasons. Private companies must pay off loans and show a profit, so they have reduced labor costs. This has led to increasing unemployment in Argentina and a relative decline in wages, making the working class unhappy.

Anti-Semitism. The economic and social pressures felt by various groups in Argentina have brought out latent resentment against the well-established Jewish community in the country. Beginning in the late nineteenth century, Jewish immigrants traveled to Argentina from several European countries. During the 1930's Jews fleeing Nazi Germany were allowed to settle in Argentina.

After World War II, Jews from Europe continued to be welcomed. Buenos Aires boasts of Jewish schools, synagogues, and a Jewish population of 180,000. However, bombings of the Israeli embassy in 1992 and of a Jewish cultural center in Buenos Aires in 1994 shattered the belief that anti-Semitism had disappeared in Argentina. The inability of the government to find those responsible led some critics to suggest that the government is not as concerned with its Jewish citizens.

At the end of the twentieth century, Argentina showed signs that it had recovered from the disruption of military dictatorship and death squads. However, economic and social tensions still divided Argentines. Many people fondly remember the beginning of the century, when Argentina was considered one of the more economically advanced countries, on par with Canada and Australia. However, Argentina did not advance equally with these other countries. With the resolution of some of its twentieth century conflicts, Argentina and its people have become more optimistic about the future.

James A. Baer

For Further Study

One of the most complete overviews of Argentina is David Rock's *Argentina, 1516-1982: From Spanish Colonization to the Falkland Islands War* (1985). Robert Potash wrote about the army in Argentine politics in *The Army and Politics in Argentina, 1962-1973: From Frondizi's Fall to the Peronist Restoration* (1996). For a good biography of Juan Perón, see Joseph A. Page's *Perón: A Biography* (1983). Daniel James's *Resistance and Integration: Peronism and the Argentine Working Class, 1946-1976* (1988) relates the story of Perón and his influence on the working class up to the time of his death. Peter Ranis's book on *Class, Democracy, and Labor in Contemporary Argentina* (1995) focuses on workers' class consciousness, and *Labor Movements and Dictatorships: The Southern Cone in Comparative Perspective*, by Paul Drake (1996), analyzes the relationship between labor and military dictatorships.

Newspapers in the United States with the most information on Argentina include the *Washington Post, The New York Times, Christian Science Monitor,* and *Miami Herald.* All these newspapers maintain Web sites on the Internet. Other English-language sources of information on Argentina on the Internet include the *Buenos Aires Herald* (http:// www.buenosairesherald.com).

On the Falkland Islands war, see Peter Calvert, *The Falklands Crisis: The Rights and Wrongs* (1982); Jack Child, "War in the South Atlantic," in *United States Policy in Latin America: A Quarter Century of Crisis and Challenge, 1961-1986,* edited by John D. Martz (1988); and Max Hastings and Simon Jenkins, *The Battle for the Falklands* (1983).

Brazil

Whereas the giant South American nation of Brazil was relegated to minor roles on the world stage during the Cold War, it has found itself under the spotlight reserved for world-class actors in the post-Cold War era. Brazil's current relevance does not stem from any sudden increase in its national power. Rather, it results from a shift in international priorities from political, ideological, and military concerns toward economic and environmental concerns. Brazil's economic output, population, size, and bounty of natural resources all rank in the top ten among nations in the world. As a frontier society that aggressively expanded across a territory seen as infinite, Brazilian culture developed a sense of large-scale wastefulness. In particular, the belief that "bigger always means better" has caused problems for Brazil. This attitude continues to plague Brazil as global critics point to wasteful economic and environmental practices tied to crash programs intended to solve problems quickly via massive spending on huge public projects.

Brazil occupies nearly one-half of the area of South America and borders on nine of the continent's eleven nations. At 3,286,470 square miles, Brazil is slightly larger in area than the forty-eight states of the continental United States. Its climate is mostly tropical or semitropical, with a temperate zone in the south. Vast stretches of dense forest dominate the northern region, a semiarid plain can be found along the northeastern coast, while mountains and hills typify the southwest.

Brazilians are a heterogeneous people. Of the four major groups of Brazilians, the most numerous are the descendants of Portuguese colonists who first arrived in South America during the sixteenth century. Second numerically to the Portuguese are the Afro-Brazilians. The first slave ship arrived in Brazil in 1538, supplying cheap labor for Brazil's profitable sugar industry. Thousands more ships followed in its wake, as 3.5 million slaves—six times the number brought to the United States—were imported.

Brazil's abolition of slavery in 1888 created a labor shortage on its booming coffee plantations. This problem was resolved by a massive influx of European and Asian immigrants—most notably from Japan, Germany, and Italy—who constitute

the third group of Brazilians. Finally, while indigenous peoples continue to exert a cultural influence in Brazil, their numbers have dwindled to less than 1 percent of Brazil's 164.5 million inhabitants. The nation's aggressive exploitation of its rain forests has devastated indigenous peoples relying on these ecosystems for their existence.

One aspect of Brazilian society that may prove instructive for the future of the United States is Brazil's widespread miscegenation over the last five hundred years. One-third of all Brazilians are racially mixed, which exceeds the rate of racial blending in North America.

Despite its social heterogeneity, Brazil possesses a coherent national culture shared by most of its citizens. Racial miscegenation is one factor contributing to a widely accepted social tolerance. While examples of racial and ethnic discrimination can be cited in Brazilian history, they are less virulent, overt, and institutionalized than those experienced by minorities in the United States. Another factor binding Brazilian culture is the pervasive role of the Roman Catholic Church, to which 80 percent of the population belongs.

History. Brazil was claimed by the Portuguese navigator Pedro Álvares Cabral in 1500. Colonial Brazil was ruled from the Portuguese capital of

Lisbon until 1808. In that year, the Portuguese royal family fled from French emperor Napoleon Bonaparte's invading army and established its seat of government in Rio de Janeiro, on Brazil's Atlantic coast.

Brazil became a kingdom under Dom João VI, who returned to Lisbon in 1821 to exercise power from Portugal. Dom João left his son, prince Dom Pedro I, to rule as regent in Brazil. Brazil's independence was declared by the prince on September 7, 1822. He then became emperor, taking the title of Dom Pedro I. His son, Dom Pedro II, ruled from 1831 until 1889, when a federal republic was created following a coup. Slavery had been abolished in 1888, one year before the creation of the republic.

From 1889 to 1930 Brazil operated as a constitutional democracy. A military coup occurred in 1930 that put Getúlio Vargas in power as dictator until 1945. From 1945 until 1964, elections resulted in the presidencies of Eurico Dutra, Vargas, Juscelino Kubitschek, Jânio Quadros, and João Goulart. Economic difficulties and radical political activism in the early 1960's motivated the armed forces to once again stage a military coup on March 31, 1964.

No elections were held in Brazil until the generals relinquished power to Tancredo Neves, who was chosen as president by an electoral college in 1985. Brazil completed its transition to a popularly elected government in 1989 when Fernando Collor de Mello won a brief stay in the presidential palace. However, he was impeached for corruption and resigned in 1992. With the nation beset by economic problems such as high inflation and massive external debt, Brazilians elected Fernando Henrique Cardoso to the presidency in 1994. His economic program, known as the Real Plan, appeared to be the best way to reform the underlying policies causing Brazil's dysfunctional economy.

Desenvolvimento. One aspect of Brazilian culture that has frequently placed the nation in trouble is its tendency toward grandiosity, known in Portuguese as *desenvolvimento* when the term is applied to economic development projects. Scholars cite various historical factors to explain why the maxim that "bigger is always better" goes unchallenged in the Brazilian mind-set. Such a reality takes on added importance in the post-Cold War era when the Northern and Southern Hemispheres often clash over both economic and environmental issues. In this milieu, Brazil faces international pressures that challenge its long-held values, which favor creating public works megaprojects in search of quick and bold solutions to its most pressing problems.

Many of these projects have risked huge investments on poorly planned ventures, often resulting in massive financial losses. The motivation has been to find a shortcut to the promised land of economic development that has continued to elude Brazil. For much of the twentieth century, Brazil's vast natural resources led observers to predict that this sleeping giant would awaken to realize its latent potential. A succession of failed expensive gambles, each based on borrowed foreign money, has proven costly to the nation. These failures cannot merely be blamed on the military regimes common in Brazil during the twentieth century, since they have been undertaken by democrats as well as dictators.

In fact, possibly the greatest proponent of *desenvolvimento* was President Juscelino Kubitschek, who

Profile of Brazil

Official name: Federative Republic of Brazil
Independent since: 1822
Former colonial ruler: Portugal
Location: eastern South America
Area: 3,286,470 square miles
Capital: Brasília
Population: 164,511,400 (1997 est.)
Official language: Portuguese
Major religions: Roman Catholicism; Protestantism
Gross domestic product: US$1.022 trillion (1996 est.)
Major exports: iron and steel; machinery; minerals; vehicles; wood pulp and paper products; coffee; sugar
Military budget: US$6.736 billion (1994)
Military personnel: 314,700 (1997)

Note: Monetary figures rendered as "US$" are U.S. equivalents of values in local currencies.

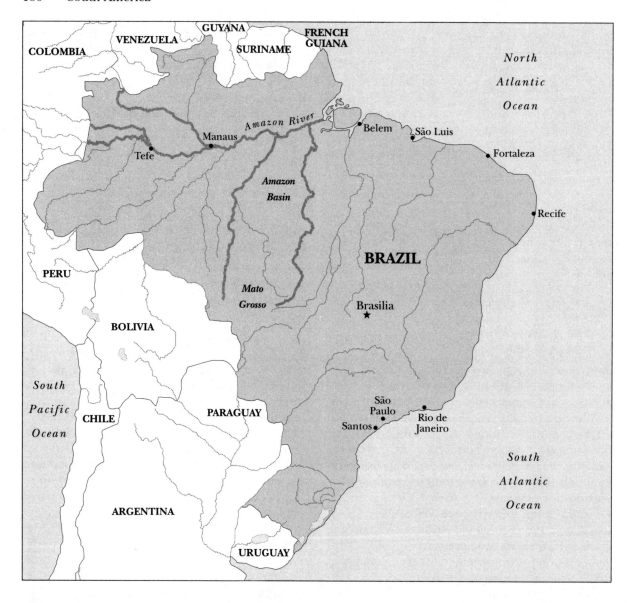

oversaw a period of rapid industrialization in Brazil during the 1950's and 1960's. The popular leader is still revered as a national hero and is immortalized in a massive mausoleum fit for a king in the heart of Brasília, Brazil's capital city.

Born of a Czech father, who died soon after his birth, and a schoolteacher mother, the young Kubitschek worked his way through medical school, taking internships in three European cities in the process. After serving as governor of his native state of Minas Gerais, Kubitschek was elected to a five-year term as president of Brazil in 1955. Shortly before assuming office, he visited the United States in search of investment money to exploit Brazil's vast natural resources.

In a *Time* magazine interview on February 20, 1956, he promised, "No matter how busy I may be, any foreign investor who comes to Brazil will find my door open." Later that year, U.S. vice president Richard Nixon visited Brazil and announced that the U.S. Export-Import Bank had approved a US$35 million loan to expand Brazil's steel industry. Domestic steel was needed by Kubitschek as the foundation on which to build his most cherished form of industrial expansion: a large automobile industry centered around the city of São Paolo.

Industrialization. Kubitschek's rapid industrialization also sped the process of urbanization. Concentrations of poor people lived outside Rio de Janeiro and São Paolo in giant slums known as *favelas*. Most residents of *favelas* were squatters for whom local governments could not supply basic services such as sewage collection, clean water, and electricity. Kubitschek sought to relieve some of the pressure from urban areas by building paved roads into hitherto inaccessible areas of the Amazonian rain forest.

Kubitschek's largest gamble, however, was his plan to end the country's traditional concentration in the Atlantic coastal region by moving the capital city from Rio de Janeiro to a central location carved out of the high desert region. Amazingly, this ambitious megaproject went from concept to completion during his first five-year term in office. Named Brasília, this planned city remains impressive in its scope and futuristic vision. Its completion gave Brazilians a newfound sense of pride and elevated their president to hero status. The long-term economic consequences, however, were equally monumental and burdened Kubitschek's successors for decades.

The fact that the military dictators who ruled from 1964 to 1985 were forced to cope with fiscal woes unleashed by Kubitschek's spending spree did not prevent them from succumbing to the temptations of *desenvolvimento*. In all, they initiated thirty-three expensive megaprojects of their own. Under the slogan "Land without people for people without land," they expanded his wilderness highways into a US$1 billion trans-Amazonian system that linked Recife on the Atlantic coast with the Peruvian border to the west. The dictators expanded Kubitschek's promotion of migration to the Amazon by offering free 100-acre plots to urbanites willing to become Amazonian farmers.

The generals underwrote not only individuals but also corporations, in abortive Amazonian development projects such as the one known as Grand Carajas. This huge mining project, begun in 1967 in the southeastern Amazon basin, was intended to produce iron ore, gold, and manganese. It has become better known for producing red ink and causing ecological damage. In the same year, the military regime extended large tax incentives to lure U.S. billionaire Daniel Ludwig to purchase an area larger than Austria along the Jari River, a

tributary of the Amazon, for US$3 billion. Ludwig hoped to harvest lumber taken from rapidly growing trees imported from Asia, but this grand scheme also foundered when the Asian transplants died in the thin Amazonian soil.

The generals' plan to industrialize the Amazon basin required electricity, and many dams were constructed for that purpose. The Tucurui Dam on the Tocantin River, the largest ever built in a tropical forest, cost nearly US$10 billion and flooded 1,000 square miles of virgin woodland. To harvest the trees, the government subsidized the operation of a company with no experience clearing trees. The company went bankrupt, and only a fraction of the wood was recovered.

Inflation Problems. The increased cost of goods and services in an economy, known as inflation, causes problems that lead most governments to undertake measures intended to keep the annual rate of inflation below 5 percent. During the 1980's Brazil became one of the few countries during the late twentieth century forced to deal with yearly inflation greater than 100 percent. One of the main causes of inflation is the deficit in current accounts resulting from governments spending more money than they collect in taxes.

Overspending on dubious megaprojects by successive Brazilian administrations was not followed by responsible fiscal strategies, such as raising taxes or cutting spending. Instead, subsequent leaders chose the short-term, easy way out, which produced deeper, long-term problems. During the 1970's Brazil's military regime borrowed large amounts of money to fund its megaprojects. Few of the projects succeeded, however, and Brazil exited the 1970's owing more than US$120 billion to financial institutions. This massive debt created by risky, grandiose projects exacerbated the already troublesome inflation rate eroding the nation's economy. Brazil's government also printed new money whose value was doomed to devaluation, which further contributed to inflationary pressures.

One of the most insidious effects of inflation is that it hurts poor people more than anyone else, since life's basic necessities make up a higher percentage of their expenses. By borrowing heavily to fund megaprojects and printing new money to service the debt, successive Brazilian governments condemned the majority of its citizens—the impoverished—to become even more impoverished. The rich became richer and the poor became poorer during the 1970's and 1980's. Some critics referred to this as "Hood-Robin economics": robbing from the poor and giving to the rich. By 1990 Brazil was identified by the World Bank as the country with the most unequal distribution of wealth, as the richest 1 percent enjoyed the same income as the poorest 50 percent of its society.

Economic Nationalism. Another pervasive aspect of *desenvolvimento* has been official corruption enabling governmental officials, and their friends, to enrich themselves at the public's expense. The self-interest of Brazil's elite class has motivated five decades of public economic policies crafted largely to maximize the private interests of these powerful and wealthy individuals. Since these same elites are the owners of big business in Brazil, governments have followed the general policy of economic nationalism, which tries to shield domestic producers from foreign competition.

Economic nationalism helps domestic companies through tax breaks, taxes on imported goods (tariffs), quotas on amounts of foreign goods importable, assistance in researching and developing new products, and propaganda campaigns to persuade citizens to buy domestic products. The protectionism afforded by economic nationalism directly helps those who work for domestic manufacturers as well as those who own these companies.

However, economic nationalism hurts everyone else in the society by taking foreign producers out of the economic game, thus artificially reducing competition. This increases the cost of goods and services and encourages inefficiency in the operation of domestic companies otherwise unable to compete successfully. Modern economists agree that economic nationalism has hurt Brazil badly. The failures of *desenvolvimento* spurred Brazil's leaders to retreat further into a protectionist shell, when a commitment to free and open trade would have served the nation much better.

All of these economic difficulties—high inflation, huge foreign debt, and economic nationalism—discouraged foreign investors from risking their money in a country not considered to be following sound economic policies. Wealthy Brazilians similarly sought more promising venues for their investments. Creditor organizations such as the World Bank and the International Monetary Fund (IMF), as well as creditor nations such as the United States, Japan, and Germany, urged serious economic stabilization measures as a necessary condition for extending further aid to Brazil. However, it took a long time for external pressure to produce results in Brazil.

It was not until the election of Henrique Cardoso in 1994 that such politically difficult, but fiscally responsible, policy choices were made. Cardoso's Real Plan sought to lower inflation, privatize many state-run companies, reduce protectionist barriers to free trade, and expand the economy at a reasonable rate. Cardoso's reforms forced many citizens to reduce their spending but were based on sound economics and met most of the Real Plan's objectives.

Environmental Problems. The negative economic consequences of Brazilian culture's penchant for grandiosity are matched by its outsized degradation of its environ-

Brazilians opposed to the government's plan to privatize a giant mining company confront riot police at Rio de Janeiro's stock exchange, where the company was scheduled to be auctioned in April, 1997. (AP/Wide World Photos)

Brazilian president Fernando Henrique Cardoso greets Venezuelans in late 1998, while inaugurating a Venezuelan new link of a highway system cut through the Amazon rain forest. (AP/Wide World Photos)

ment. Based on the myth of an "infinite country," Brazil's extensive natural resources have always been misinterpreted as not merely extensive, but as limitless. The string of developmental shortcuts financed by Brazilian leaders has been characterized by environmental wastefulness.

Brazil's rain forests came to symbolize its environmental problems. Two of Brazil's five ecosystems are forests. Fully 93 percent of its Atlantic forest had already been destroyed before the 1990's. More remained of its Amazonian forest, but a combination of logging, mining, cultivation, and intentional burning were annually reducing it by an area of more than 11 million acres, the size of Washington State, in the late 1990's. Logging operations by wood-starved Pacific nations, such as Japan, Taiwan, and South Korea, were facilitated by

the Brazilian government's routine approval of massive removals of trees.

The world's growing population and increased burning of fossil fuels serve to highlight the critical role of rain forests in converting carbon dioxide into oxygen. However, with the loss of rain forests also comes loss of biodiversity. Approximately one million Amazonian species exist. Since most new medical drugs used to treat diseases derive from species unknown even one generation ago, every case of species extinction represents a potential pharmacological and medical loss to humans.

The majority of Brazil's megaprojects involved efforts to colonize the Amazon wilderness in the country's north via mining operations, fish farms, highway construction, electrical projects, and timbering activities. A population explosion resulted from these endeavors. In the state of Amazonas, the population went from 2 million in 1960 to 20 million by 1998, an increase with which local governments were ill-prepared to cope. Each of these environmentally costly migrations also damaged the cultural integrity of the few remaining indigenous peoples.

Although people in the Northern Hemisphere tend to focus on the rain forests, even worse environmental degradation accompanied the rapid industrialization process begun during the 1960's. No other city symbolizes urban industrial blight in Brazil as poignantly as Cubatão, which became known during the 1970's as "the valley of death." The road leading east from São Paolo crosses a beautiful mountain range on its way to the most scenic coastline in Brazil. However, it must also run through Cubatão—a denuded, brown, and barren valley of endless smokestacks.

Originally a large swamp, Cubatão was eventually drained and covered with landfill. Cubatão's

Brazilian police forcibly evict residents of a slum built on the outskirts of São Paolo in 1998. (AP/Wide World Photos)

strategic location near both São Paolo's ten million people and South America's largest port at Santos inspired President Juscelino Kubitschek to install oil refineries, steel mills, fertilizer manufacturers, cement factories, and petrochemical plants. In 1980 the World Health Organization described this as the most polluted spot on Earth. Alarming levels of birth defects, infant mortality, and serious lung disease were routinely chronicled.

Brazilian Economic Policy. Brazil is a big, bold country. Precisely these qualities pervade both the nation's physical attributes and its culture. In contributing to the belief that "bigger is always better," bigness and boldness have caused serious economic and environmental problems for Brazil. In an era when the rich Northern and poor Southern Hemispheres find much to disagree about, Brazil presents a large target for northerners to criticize. This is especially true concerning the economic and environmental issues that have highlighted the global agenda in the post-Cold War era. Such criticism has come from wealthy nations such as the United States; international financial institutions such as the World Bank, the Inter-American Bank for Reconstruction and Development, and the IMF; and nongovernmental organizations (NGOs) such as the Sierra Club and the World Wildlife Fund (WWF).

Since high-risk economic policies based on *desenvolvimento* worsened socioeconomic inequality, human rights NGOs such as Amnesty International, Human Rights Watch, and Human Rights Internet all decried the injustices associated with gross inequality as ethically repugnant. During the 1980's U.S. presidents Ronald Reagan and George Bush, both highly committed to free trade policies, led a group of nations condemning Brazil for protectionist trade policies that closed its domestic market to foreign products.

The IMF, whose policies tilt toward the views of rich northern countries that make the largest contributions, routinely pressured Brazil to introduce austerity measures that would reduce high-level governmental spending, privatize state-run enterprises, and allow free market forces freedom to operate. In most instances, the IMF would not grant loans needed to pay off foreign debt without these steps toward a free market economy.

Pressures to abandon *desenvolvimento* also came from some domestic quarters. Although Brazilians

Brazil

1500	Navigator Pedro Álvares Cabral claims part of Brazil for Portugal.
1501	Navigator Amerigo Vespucci returns to Portugal with cargo of brazilwood, from which Brazil takes its name.
1530	Portuguese king John III begins systematic colonization of Brazil.
1532	Sugar cane is introduced at São Vicente.
1538	First slave ship arrives in Brazil.
1549	Thome de Souza arrives as first governor-general, making Bahia his capital.
1693	Gold is discovered in central Minas Gerais region.
1720	Coffee is introduced from French Guyane.
1729	Diamonds are found north of gold mines in Minas Gerais.
1763	Portuguese premier Marques de Pombal expels Jesuits from Brazil.
1808	Portuguese royal family flees from Lisbon to Rio de Janciro.
1822	(Sept. 7) Brazil declares itself independent, with King João's son, Dom Pedro I, as its emperor.
1831-1889	Emperor Pedro II advances Brazil's prestige through his statesmanship.
1850	Wave of immigrants begins to arrive to work in coffee plantations.
1853	Importation of African slaves is outlawed.
1888	Brazil is last country in Western Hemisphere to abolish slavery.
1889	Brazil abolishes monarchy and declares itself a republic.
1898	Jose de Moraes Barros becomes first civilian chief executive.
1912	Rubber boom collapses.
1941	Brazil sides with Allies in World War II and receives U.S. aid for industrial expansion.
1955	(Oct.) Juscelino Kubitschek is elected president.
1956	(Jan.) Kubitschek announces ambitious five-year development plan.
1960	Kubitschek makes good on pledge to create new capital city at Brasília.
1964	(Mar. 31) Military coup initiates two decades of military regimes.
1965	New legislation severely restricts civil liberties of citizens.
1970's	Megaprojects are financed by heavy foreign borrowing.
1982	Government reschedules loan repayments to buy time.
1985	Tancredo Neves is first civilian president elected in twenty-one years.
1987	Government declares moratorium on interest payments to preserve foreign exchange reserves and stop transfer of resources to creditors.
1988	New constitution provides for direct popular election of presidents.
1988	Activist Francisco Mendes Filho is assassinated.
1992	U.N. Earth Summit held in Rio de Janeiro produces Agenda 21 as blueprint.

(continued)

1992	President Fernando Collor de Mello is impeached for corruption.
1994	Fernando Henrique Cardoso is elected president.
1995	Cardoso initiates "Real Plan" of fiscal responsibility.
1998	(Jan. 26) Government releases report showing that 1994-1995 deforestation was worst in Amazonian history.
1998	(Apr.) Sudden deaths of government leaders Roberto Viera da Motta and Lujis Eduardo Magalhaes are threats to Cardoso's economic reforms.
1998	(June 20) Federal Indian Bureau announces discovery of previously unknown tribe living in Amazon rain forest near Peruvian border.
1998	(July 29) Riot police battle demonstrators protesting government sale of national telephone company to foreign companies.
1998	(Oct. 4) Cardoso becomes first Brazilian president elected to second term.
1998	(Oct. 28) Cardoso announces austerity plan that will raise taxes and cut government spending.
1998	(Nov. 13) United States and International Monetary Fund announce $42 billion aid package to Brazil to prevent it economic collapse.
1999	(Jan. 1) Cardoso is inaugurated for second term in austere ceremony.
1999	(Jan. 15) Brazil's removal of exchange controls on its currency causes South American and world markets to fluctuate.

generally exhibit a high degree of tolerance for suffering and political apathy, the runaway inflation of the 1980's did produce a public-opinion backlash on the part of normally docile citizens. All in all, the range of pressures arrayed against policies based on *desenvolvimento* was formidable.

The 1994 economic reform package of President Cardoso helped reduce some of the criticism that Brazil had become accustomed to receiving from the world community. Yet despite his efforts to ground the economy in a market-oriented foundation, many structural economic problems were difficult to correct in a short time period. Cardoso's first term in office witnessed the taming of inflation, some privatization, a reduction in trade barriers, and reduced governmental spending. Still remaining, however, were large foreign debts, sizable trade deficits, stubborn pockets of governmental corruption, and the ever-widening gap between the few rich and the many poor. Voters decided in 1998 to give Cardoso the opportunity to continue his economic policies by reelecting him to a second term as president.

Brazilian Environmental Policy. The Cardoso administration succeeded in significantly reducing international criticism aimed at Brazilian economic policy. More intractable, however, was the international condemnation of Brazilian environmental policy. The first Cardoso administration managed to pass a broad range of environmental laws. This fact impressed many U.S. citizens who believed, from North American experience, that changes in the law routinely produce changes in behavior. However, in Brazilian culture, the role of legislation has generally been limited by either the will or the ability of the governmental bureaucracy to enforce it.

In 1992, only two years before Cardoso was elected president, Rio de Janeiro had been selected by the United Nations as the site for the United Nations Conference for Environment and Development (UNCED), better known as the Earth Summit. Most of the world's countries, thousands of journalists, and numerous NGOs participated in a meeting featuring some of the world's best minds.

The daunting task of the summit was to identify a blueprint for the future that balanced the conflicting priorities of the rich Northern and poor Southern Hemispheres. The essence of the northern view favored environmental integrity in the service of improved quality of life for current and future generations. In sharp contrast, the south saw environmentalism as secondary to the inalienable right of poor peoples to pursue economic development that would result in a higher standard of living for the world's disadvantaged.

These two divergent goals had traditionally been seen as unreconcilable, but the approach taken at Rio was different. The Earth Summit defined environmentalism and development as potentially complementary. Around this idea was forged a rare global consensus pointing toward a new goal: sustainable development.

This concept of environmentally conscious development as the common goal for humankind's future was formalized in a document called Agenda 21. Reaching an agreement on Agenda 21 represented a considerable achievement, but its acceptance as a political symbol could not answer whether sustainable development was possible. It soon became apparent that while both the Northern and Southern Hemispheres saw enough of what they wanted in Agenda 21 to accept its goal of sustainable development, the north focused on the sustainability component, while the south prioritized economic development for poor countries.

The Cardoso administration was challenged during its second term not only to enforce obsolete environmental laws already on the books but also to catch up with a variety of Central American countries that have engaged in creative programs absent in Brazil. One such program called the debt-for-nature swap was pioneered by Thomas Lovejoy, director of the WWF, in Guatemala in 1987.

In debt-for-nature swaps, a northern NGO such as the Sierra Club repays some of the debt owed by a poor country to an international financial institution. In turn, the poor country guarantees it will protect an environmental asset in its territory. In effect, all parties involved benefit. The environmental NGO protects an environmental asset, the debtor nation enjoys debt reduction, and the financial institution receives some overdue payment. Such a program could address Brazil's foreign debt problem and repair its negative environmental image.

Another creative response advocated for use in Brazil is the extraction reserve. When Brazilian trade union leader and preservation activist Francisco Mendes Filho was assassinated in 1988, he was advocating this concept, which is attuned to both sustainability and profitability. Only 10 percent of resources such as gas, timber, fish, or coal may be harvested in an extraction reserve, as a compromise between hands-off nature reserves and unfettered commercial enterprises.

Another idea is for Brazil to promote ecotourism. In 1998 tiny Costa Rica hosted more than six million ecotourists, while fewer than two million ecotourists brought foreign currency into giant Brazil. Brazil's failure to incorporate these and other new ideas that would promote sustainable development contributed to continued criticism of the country at the end of the twentieth century.

Michael Strada

For Further Study

A useful general introduction to Brazilian culture is provided by Joseph A. Page's *The Brazilians* (1995). The cultural concept of *desenvolvimento* is chronicled in *Desenvolvimento: Politics and Economy in Brazil* (1997), by Wilber A. Chaffee. Brazilian political culture is afforded more detailed coverage in Ronald M. Schneider's *Brazil: Culture and Politics in a New Industrial Powerhouse* (1996) and in Ted G. Goertzel's *Fernando Henrique Cardoso: Reinventing Democracy in Brazil* (1999). A good general history of Brazil can be found in E. Bradford Burns, *A History of Brazil* (1993).

An examination of Brazil's economic dilemmas can begin with an article by Peter Flynn entitled "Brazil: The Politics of the 'Plano Real,'" in *Third World Quarterly* (1996), and one by Matt Moffett called "Deep in the Amazon, an Industrial Enclave Fights for Its Survival," in *The Wall Street Journal* (July 9, 1998). Other useful sources on the subject include *The Brazilian Economy: Structure and Performance in Recent Decades* (1997), edited by Maria Willumsen and Eduardo Giannetti, and *Political Constraints on Brazil's Economic Development* (1993), edited by Siegfried Marks. The World Bank Group's Web page on Brazil's economy can be found at www.worldbank.org/html/extdr/offrep/lac/brazil.html.

For information on Brazilian environmental and global sustainable development issues, see Warren Dean, *With Broadax and Firebrand: The Destruction of the Brazilian Atlantic Forest* (1994); A. Revkin, *The Burning Season: The Murder of Chico Mendes and the Fight for the Amazon Rainforest* (1990); United States and Brazil, "Joint Statement on the U.S.-Brazil Common Agenda for the Environment," (August 19, 1997); Virginia Morell, "On the Origin of Amazonian Species," *Discover* (April, 1997); Howard LaFranchi, "Spare the Ax, Spoil the Amazon," *The Christian Science Monitor* (May 14, 1997); Barry Ames and Margaret Peck, "The Politics of Sustainable Development: Environmental Policy Making in Four Brazilian States," *Journal of Interamerican Studies and World Affairs* (1997-1998); Richard Leakey, *The Sixth Extinction* (1996); John Vandermeer and Ivette Perfecto, *Breakfast of Biodiversity: The Truth About Rainforest Destruction* (1995); Gareth Porter and Janet Welsh Brown, *Global Environmental Politics* (1996); Alan Gilpin, *Dictionary of Environment and Sustainable Development* (1997); Colin Kirkpatrick and Norman Lee, *Sustainable Development in a Developing World* (1997); and Ian Moffatt, *Sustainable Development: Principles, Analysis, and Policies* (1996).

Colombia

The most difficult problem facing Colombia when it became independent in the early nineteenth century was its natural geography. Mountain chains kept it divided into regions isolated from one another until the advent of modern transportation. It had little sense of political unity, and its economic development had been retarded. Modern development began with the construction of railroads and roads beginning at the end of the nineteenth century. However, the rise of party politics during the 1840's generated hostility and civil wars that lasted through the 1950's. Even afterward, old party loyalties remained hereditary in families. Meanwhile, drug trafficking and political violence became major problems during the 1970's that continued into the 1990's. During the 1980's with the help of the army and police, right-wing paramilitary groups emerged and fought rebel guerrillas. Later undesirables were targets also. All attempts to achieve a cease-fire have been only partially successful and temporary.

Located at the northwestern corner of South America, the Republic of Colombia is bounded on the north by the Caribbean Sea and Venezuela, on the east by Venezuela and Brazil, on the south by Brazil, Peru, and Ecuador, and on the west by Panama and the Pacific Ocean. The Andes Mountains are the country's most prominent natural feature, as well as the most important physical influence upon its history. On the Ecuadorian-Colombian border the Andes form a single range. However, they divide into three ranges in southern Colombia: the Cordillera Occidental between the Pacific and the Cauca River, the Cordillera Central between the Cauca and Magdalena Rivers; and the broad Cordillera Oriental running northeast into Venezuela.

The Cordillera Occidental runs roughly parallel to the Pacific Ocean and terminates in three low, wooded spurs that merge into the coastal plains of the Caribbean coast. The Cordillera Central, the highest range, is separated from the other two ranges by the Magdalena River on the east and on the west by the Cauca River, the principal tributary of the Magdalena. The Cordillera Oriental, the longest range, has the densest population and contains several plateaus and elevated valleys that lie within the vertical temperate zone.

The mild climate and fertile soil of the Sabana de Bogotá, the largest of the plateaus, make the area desirable and profitable, especially among Colombians of European descent. The lightly populated plains of the eastern part of the country are covered with tropical grasses in the northeast and Amazon forest in the southeast and separated from the more populous areas by mountains.

The division of the country into three parts by the mountains severely limited transportation and communication until the twentieth century. Even with the construction of railroads and roads, transportation remained difficult and expensive. Air service has shortened travel times among major cities, but it is too expensive to transport inexpensive or bulky items.

Colonial Period. Through Colombia's long colonial era and into the nineteenth century, contact among the regions was limited. Each of the three major regions tended to be politically and economically self-sufficient. Even the independence movement did not create a nation or a concept of Colombian nationhood.

Toward the end of the colonial period major uprisings occurred in New Granada, as Colombia was then called. When Spain imposed new tax laws in 1810, protests known as the Revolt of the Comuneros quickly broke out. These uprisings were easily suppressed, but a new viceroy repealed many unpopular taxes and regulations. The battle was lost, but the war was won.

The Revolt of the Comuneros became a part of national patriotic folklore. However, exactly how it affected the nineteenth century independence movement is unclear. It had the effect of making Spanish officials more cautious. However, even during the revolt there appeared to be little cooperation among the regions of the viceroyalty, and no single leader was recognized by all rebels.

Independence. Colombia's independence movement did not have the same causes as the movement had in Venezuela, where the revolt against Spanish rule started. Within Colombia the rivalry between Creoles—whites born in the colony—and European-born Spaniards was more important than Spanish restrictions on trade and industry. Local loyalties were more important to Creoles than their attachment to the mother country. Although few Creoles initially advocated independence, growing numbers of them wanted some measure of autonomy within the framework of the Spanish Empire.

South American independence movements were triggered by events in Europe. A crisis in the Spanish monarchy in 1808 provided the stimulus for independence. France's Napoleon Bonaparte

invaded Spain in 1808 and placed his brother on the Spanish throne as King José I. Spanish protests developed into a popular resistance movement headed by a central junta in Seville. The junta claimed that it controlled the Spanish Empire. In Spanish America most royal officials and people recognized the junta's claim. However, a minority of South Americans refused to recognize any ruler but Ferdinand VII—the king ousted by Napoleon—and claimed the right to establish juntas themselves. Forced to choose between two competing juntas, Spanish Americans had a unique opportunity to work for their own political aims, either autonomy or independence.

Between 1809 and 1819 both South American patriots and Spanish authorities won military victories and were in control for periods of time. The division and lack of cooperation among South Americans were overcome by the Venezuelan Simón Bolívar. His army's decisive victory at Boyacá in 1819 assured the independence of Colombia. After this victory a Venezuelan congress declared the union of the Spanish provinces of New Granada, Ecuador, Peru, and Venezuela in an independent republic. (This republic has been called Gran Colombia to distinguish it from the modern nation of Colombia.)

Despite some initial acceptance of the union, problems imposed by geography and regionalism doomed it to failure. Venezuelans resented inclusion in a union centered in Bogotá. Ecuador also resisted the Bogotá government, and Peru never entered the union. The dissolution of Gran Colombia occurred in 1829.

Nineteenth Century Politics. New Granada established a liberal constitution following the breakup of Gran Colombia. However, the difficulties of traveling among the provinces prevented true economic and political integration. Most regions remained largely self-sufficient. Custom duties were the easiest taxes for the government to collect, but limited trade meant limited government revenue.

After 1840 political divisions within Colombia began to stabilize

Profile of Colombia

Official name: Republic of Colombia
Independent since: 1810
Former colonial ruler: Spain
Location: northwestern South America
Area: 439,733 square miles
Capital: Bogota
Population: 37,418,300 (1997 est.)
Official language: Spanish
Major religion: Roman Catholicism
Gross domestic product: US$201.4 billion (1996 est.)
Major exports: petroleum products; coffee; chemicals; forestry and fisheries
Military budget: US$2 billion (1995)
Military personnel: 146,300 (1997)

Note: Monetary figures rendered as "US$" are U.S. equivalents of values in local currencies.

in two distinct political parties: the Liberals and Conservatives. The Conservatives formally adopted their name in 1849; the Liberals emerged a little later. Membership in the parties was not determined by social and economic status. Both parties included commercial and professional interests, as well as large and small landowners. Members of the clergy were overwhelmingly Conservative because of the anticlerical program of the Liberals.

Both parties were national; however, the Liberals were stronger in the outlying areas, and the Conservatives were strongest in and around Bogotá. The programs and policies of the two parties were not radically different. The Conservatives were proclerical (that is, pro-church) and favored strong central government. The Liberals were anticlerical and favored a federal system over a strong central system of government.

In the early years, Colombian party loyalty tended to be based upon allegiance to individual political leaders. Gradually, family and regional loyalties to specific parties became rigid. Although it was often easier for diverse factions within a party to cooperate with their counterparts in the opposite party than with other members of their own party, party loyalties remained fierce. Not until the late 1950's and the rise of the National Front government did animosity between the two original national parties abate.

Growing Political Stability. Both the Liberal and Conservative Parties controlled the national government for extended periods of time: the Liberals from 1849 to 1885, and the Conservatives from 1885 to 1904. Under both parties Colombia, as the nation was officially renamed in 1863, began to develop economically with the construction of internal improvements and increased trade with the

outside world. Coffee, grown mainly on small holdings, became the largest export product.

However, Colombia still lacked the concept of nationhood. Growing federalism and fanatical party allegiance weakened the national government. The liberal constitution adopted in 1863 granted sweeping powers to the country's state governments, leaving national presidents with little control over the states. Anticlerical measures and the final abolition of slavery antagonized factions of the Conservative Party. Civil wars were frequent, both within individual states and between states and the federal government.

A Liberal uprising in 1899 started a civil conflict known as the Thousand Day's War that lasted three years. By 1900 the Liberals, unable to field an army, had turned to guerrilla warfare. The exhaustion of all the combatants, the loss of perhaps as many as 100,000 lives, and the devastating economic cost of the war prepared the way for peace in 1902.

While the Thousand Day's War was being fought, the United States and Colombia were negotiating for a concession that would give the United States the right to dig a canal across the Isthmus of Panama that would join the Pacific and Atlantic Oceans. At that time, what is now the Republic of Panama was an integral part of Colombia. A canal treaty was drafted; however, the Colombian senate voted it down in August, 1902. Three months later anti-Colombian revolution erupted in Panama, whose rebels were supported by the U.S. government. It led to the independence of Panama, which immediately signed a treaty with the United States to build what became the Panama Canal. Colombians were outraged.

The Thousand Day's War and the loss of Panama forced the Colombians to reexamine their political system. General Rafael Reyes, elected president in 1904 as a Conservative, believed that Colombians needed to rise above debilitating partisan struggles and concentrate on economic development. Using dictatorial powers, he introduced the principle of guaranteed minority representation, carried out reforms placing the army under civilian control, and promoted the modernization of the nation and the growth of the economy.

Twentieth Century Politics. The system of minority representation was maintained until 1930. The old issues that divided the parties in the nineteenth century, the Church question and liberal reforms, were giving way to the issue of controlling the national government and patronage. Expansion of Colombia's coffee trade and growth in its production of textiles, oil, and bananas promoted economic nationalism. While coffee farms and textile factories were locally owned, oil production and banana cultivation were financed by U.S. capital. There were strikes in both industries, and labor unrest led to the organization of leftist labor unions.

The worldwide Great Depression that began in 1929 after the Conservatives had long held power contributed to their loss of support. In the national election of 1930 Conservative support was split, making possible the election of the Liberals, who continued in power until 1946. The transfer of power in Bogotá occurred without any problems.

Sporadic violence that erupted in the provinces was quickly suppressed.

Liberal president Alfonso López Pumarjó (1934-1938) felt that reform from the top would prevent a revolution from the bottom. He proclaimed the "Revolution on the March," a program to give to the masses greater economic and political participation in national life. Under his administration, the national constitution was amended to give the federal government greater power and to give the vote to more Colombians. However, there was no noticeable improvement for the masses.

The Conservatives grew more and more unhappy with the liberal reforms. The close cooperation between the United States and Colombia during World War II aroused a nationalistic reaction. Increased Conservative opposition and a split in the Liberal Party, which led to the nomination of two Liberal candidates, gave the 1946 election to the Conservatives. Jorge Eleícer Gaitán, a charismatic Liberal leader and one of the defeated Liberal presidential candidates, became the focus of a reorganized Liberal Party.

The Violence. During the Inter-American Conference hosted by Colombia in 1948, Gaitán was assassinated. For three days the country was torn by rioting in which several hundred people lost their lives. Liberals widely believed that the Conservative administration was behind the assassination, and Conservatives believed that an international leftist conspiracy threatened the nation.

Political strife became so violent that the period which followed became known as *La Violencia* (The Violence). It lasted until 1957. Confined mainly to the rural areas, political violence grew worse during presidential election campaigns. Between 100,000 and 200,000 people died, often in brutal ways. In addition to politically motivated killings, there were charges of government persecution of Protestants. Despite the violence, however, Colombia's economy experienced near record growth. The gross domestic product sustained steady increases, industrial production rose even faster, and urban areas grew by more than 50 percent in size.

In 1953 President Laureano Gómez was overthrown by the military in Colombia's first coup since 1900. Popularly believed to be a fascist, Gómez had espoused conservative constitutional reforms that even members of his own party opposed. When he attempted to remove army chief of staff Gustavo Rojas Pinilla, the general removed him instead.

New president Rojas Pinilla faced the opposition of traditional party politicians. His often arbitrary actions, attempts to gain the support of labor, and increasing violence throughout the country led to the signing of a pact by Liberal and Conservative Party leaders to remove Rojas Pinilla and share power themselves. A general strike supported by the business and professional establishment led the military high command to persuade Rojas Pinilla to leave the country voluntarily.

With civilians back in power, a new era of peace and reconciliation began. Rules devised by the two political parties and approved by a public referendum provided for sharing power and government positions. In this arrangement, known as the National Front, all elective and appointive positions had to be shared equally by the two parties, with the presidency alternating between them. Other parties were excluded from power altogether. The new agreement, which lasted until the 1970's, favored social and economic development for the country.

Antigovernment Resistance Groups. As early as the late 1960's the exclusion of parties other than the Liberals and Conservatives from power promoted armed resistance by leftist groups, who waged sporadic guerrilla warfare against the government. Dissatisfied factory workers and landless peasants supported dissident groups advocating political change through violence.

The three major leftist groups—all of which were anti-United States—were the Revolutionary Armed Forces of Colombia (FARC), the Army of National Liberation (ELN), and the Movement 19 April (M-19).

The communist FARC was strongest in the upper Magdalena Valley. The ELN, inspired by Fidel Castro's Cuban Revolution, was centered in the middle Magdalena. M-19, named for the 1970 election that General Rojas Pinilla narrowly lost, operated mainly in the cities. M-19 charged that because the government stole the people's political victory, only revolutionary violence could bring changes to Colombia.

Because the three revolutionary groups could not unite or even coordinate their activities, they did not pose a serious threat to the government. They did, however, control a few portions of the

countryside, where they extorted money from large landowners. Government efforts to suppress their activities became a serious drain on government revenues, and no administration was willing to assume the fiscal and political cost of an all-out effort to eliminate the guerrillas.

In 1980 M-19 gained worldwide attention by seizing the Palace of Justice and taking over the Dominican Republic's embassy in Bogotá during a reception. When government troops recaptured the justice building, half the members of the country's supreme court and all the guerrillas were killed. In the process M-19 lost most of its top leaders, as well as whatever public sympathy it had enjoyed.

After Belisario Betancur Cuartas was elected president in 1982, he began peace negotiations with antigovernment guerrillas, despite the opposition of influential political party and army leaders. The guerrillas accepted a truce but soon violated it. As a result, all the guerrilla groups except the ELN not only lost their chance to become legitimate participants in the political system, they lost their public support. Members of the ELN, by contrast, laid down their arms and achieved more at the polls than they had earlier achieved through violence.

Drug Trafficking and Political Violence. The problems of maintaining public order in Colombia became more complicated during the 1980's. During that period politically motivated guerrilla violence became entangled with violence generated by the growing trade in illegal drugs. At the same time, right-wing paramilitary groups formed to counter the older leftist groups. Leaders of the drug trade, known as the Medellín cartel after the name of a city, used bribery, assassination, and kidnapping to intimidate persons in the justice system.

The Medellín cartel and the Cali cartel that arose later also attacked each other and innocent bystanders lost their lives. The leftist guerrillas and the drug lords came into conflict when the drug lords bought rural estates and refused to pay protection money to leftist guerrillas, as other landlords had. They also supported right-wing paramilitary armies. In cooperation with other landowners, the army, and regional police, the drug lords created rural self-defense forces that kept guerrillas away from their estates.

In the late 1980's the assassinations of Minister of Justice Rodrigo Lara Bonilla and presidential hopeful Luis Carlos Galán led to a government crackdown on the drug trade that achieved some success. However, it was not until the election of President César Augusto Gaviria in 1990 that a new approach to combatting drug violence brought more lasting success.

President Gaviria began negotiations with the drug traffickers and the leftist guerrillas. He promised that any trafficker who surrendered and pled guilty to one or more charges would be tried and sentenced in Colombia, not extradited to the United States, where they were likely to face more severe punishments. Men associated with the Medellín cartel began surrendering. With the surrender of the leader of the cartel, Pablo Escobar, the drug war was for all practical purposes over. The drug trade, however, was not.

In January, 1991, members of the Revolutionary Workers Party threw their weapons into the ocean and turned to political activity to achieve their objectives. Two months later members of the Popular Liberation Army also accepted the amnesty offered by the government. The policy of negotiation seemed to be working.

Renewed Violence. In September of 1992 Pablo Escobar escaped from jail, and the violence escalated. Kidnapping and killings became a means of making money that was not necessarily related to leftist guerrilla activity. Attacks upon the oil fields in the eastern foothills of the Andes resulted in large payments by foreign oil companies who were willing to buy off attackers.

Pablo Escobar himself was killed while resisting arrest in December, 1993. With the deaths of Escobar and other leaders of the Medellín cartel, the cartel again declined, and the Cali cartel took over.

Colombians calling for President Ernesto Samper's resignation demonstrate in Bogota in early 1996. (AP/Wide World Photos)

Colombia

1525	City of Santa Marta is founded.
1538	Bogotá is founded.
1718-1740	Viceroyalty of New Granada is established.
1811-1824	Colombians fight for independence from Spain.
1831	Newly formed republic of New Granada includes what later will become Colombia and Panama.
1840's	Conservative and Liberal Parties emerge in Colombia.
1849-1885	Liberals control government.
1863	New Granada is renamed Colombia.
1885-1904	Conservatives control government in era known as the "Regeneration."
1899-1902	Thousand Days War is fought.
1902	(Aug.) Colombia rejects canal treaty with United States.
1903	Panama becomes independent of Colombia.
1904-1930	Conservatives rule Colombia during era of "Peace and Coffee."
1934-1938	Era of "Revolution on the March."
1948	Jorge Eleícer Gaitán is assassinated; period known as "The Violence" begins.
1953	President Laureano Gómez is overthrown by military led by General Gustavo Rojas Pinilla.
1958-1978	National Front coalition controls government.
1980's	As drug trade rises, Medellín Cartel emerges.
1980	M-19 guerrillas seize Palace of Justice and Dominican embassy.
1981	Violence increases, and kidnapping for ransom begins.
1982	President Belisario Betencur Cuartas begins negotiations with guerrillas.
1984	Minister of Justice Rodrigo Lara Bonilla is assassinated.
1984	Government tries to crack down on drug trade.
1984	One year truce with Popular Liberation Army and M-19.
1984	(May) Cease-fire begins.
1985	(Dec.) Truce with guerrillas ends.
1986	Liberal Bario Virgilio Vargas is elected president.
1987	President Vargas asks for end to power-sharing agreement.
1988	Drug lords buy country estates.
1988	(May) No candidate receives majority in presidential election.
1989	Luis Carlos Galán, probable Liberal presidential nominee, is assassinated.
1989	President Virgilio Barca begins largest-scale drug war to date.
1990	President César Augusto Gaviria begins negotiations with drug traffickers.

(continued)

1991	Pablo Escobar surrenders as drug war winds down, but paramilitary violence and banditry increase.
1992	(Sept.) Escobar escapes from jail, and guerrilla war intensifies.
1993	Guerrillas begin attacks on oil fields.
1993	(Dec.) Escobar is killed while resisting arrest.
1994	(Feb.) Peace talks begin.
1994	(June) Ernesto Samper is elected president.
1994	(Aug.) Social cleansing by paramilitary armies begins.
1995	(Aug.) Samper is accused of taking drug money but is later absolved by congress.
1998	Guerrillas bomb oil pipelines and defeat army troops in major battle but agree to peace talks with President-elect Andrés Pastrana.
1998	(Feb. 26) U.S. president Bill Clinton's administration issues report "decertifying" Colombia's efforts to combat drug traffic but gives Colombia waiver allowing it to receive U.S. aid.
1998	(Feb. 27) Leftist Revolutionary Armed Forces of Colombia call for boycott of national elections.
1998	(Mar. 8) Liberals retain majority in national elections.
1998	(Apr. 10) *Washington Post* reports that U.S. Defense Intelligence Agency paper predicts Colombian government will lose control to leftist rebels within five years.
1998	(May 31) Liberal candidate Horacio Serpa Uribe and Conservative candidate Andrés Pastrana each win 34.3 percent of vote in national election, forcing runoff.
1998	(June 21) Pastrana wins runoff election.
1998	(Aug. 7) Pastrana is inaugurated as president in midst of renewed fighting between government and leftist forces.
1998	(Oct. 7) An estimated 650,000 public-sector workers go on strike to protest government's proposed austerity plan.
1998	(Oct. 14) President Pastrana orders government troops to begin withdrawing from southeastern townships claimed by FARC in effort to promote peace talks with rebels.
1999	(Jan. 7) FARC leaders began peace talks with government.

The two cartels were actually quite different. Whereas Escobar had been undisputed leader of the Medellín cartel, the Cali cartel was a loose organization of autonomous drug rings. Unlike the Medellín cartel, it did not use violence against the judicial system, the economic and political elite, or civilians.

The Cali cartel did not make its rival's mistake of becoming too visible. It did not attempt to win political office or to gain popular support by financing public projects such as housing or recreational facilities in poor areas of cities. The Cali cartel did, however, use bribery of officials and cooperation with the elite.

The decline of the Medellín cartel did not reduce the violence. Right-wing paramilitary armies, leftist guerrillas who had not accepted the government amnesty, and bandits with no agenda except making money continued their violent activities.

The moderate candidate Ernesto Samper won the presidential runoff election in June, 1994. He organized a three-prong attack against the violence that included military intelligence, counterinsurgency units, and a generous rehabilitation program to help guerrillas and bandits return to ordinary civilian life. The program showed no initial success, however, and violence actually increased. Paramilitary armies, organized by members of the police and army, the elite, and the landowners and financed by drug money, began to use assassination to eliminate kidnappers, leftist guerrillas, politicians, and those elements of society they regarded as "undesirables," such as prostitutes, drug runners, street children, petty criminals, and the poor.

Within a year of his inauguration, President Samper was accused of accepting almost US$6 million from the drug lords for his campaign. Samper charged the U.S. government with complicity in a kidnapping attempt and with trying to force him out of office. The crisis continued through the end of the year. Some cabinet members and the 1994 campaign manager were convicted of accepting drug money and bribery and sent to prison, but the Colombian congress refused to impeach Samper and dropped all charges.

Some cabinet members and 1994 campaign committee members said that Samper knew about the drug money and had negotiated with the drug lords for favorable treatment if they were caught. Samper denied all charges and refused to resign. He continued in office, but his effectiveness was impaired by the scandal. Using favoritism and bribery he was able to maintain his congressional support.

By 1997 competition from other drug-producing nations, a decline in drug prices, and a massive government crackdown in Cali had led to the decline of the Cali cartel. However, activities of paramilitary armies and bandits actually increased. The government was no longer able to control all areas of the nation. In June it agreed to cede temporary control of rural areas to guerrillas to stop the violence.

Tired of violence, many Colombians no longer supported antidrug programs. They had no confidence in President Samper and backed the politi-

During a public employees' strike in Cali in October, 1998, student demonstrators turn on the police, precipitating a riot. (AP/Wide World Photos)

cal opposition that was becoming more and more vocal against Samper.

None of the three candidates in the May, 1998, presidential election received a majority. The two leading candidates, Conservative Andrés Pastrana, who had lost to Samper in 1994, and Liberal Horacio Serpa, the handpicked candidate of Samper, entered a runoff election on June 21. Voting was accompanied by violence, and a lack of confidence in the electoral process was evident. Pastrana won with the largest majority since the National Front governments. He pledged to incorporate dissident elements into the government and to negotiate with leaders of the guerrillas and paramilitary armies personally. Once again Colombians hoped that their problems would be solved.

Robert D. Talbott

For Further Study

Colombia has received less scholarly attention than most other nations in Latin America. Even Colombian historians wrote few professional studies before the 1960's. A useful reference source for general information on the country is Robert H. Davis's *Historical Dictionary of Colombia* (2d ed. 1993) in Scarecrow Press's Latin American Historical Dictionary series. A good, highly readable, and interesting general history is David Bushnell's *The Making of Modern Colombia: A Nation in Spite of Itself* (1993). This work gives a balanced coverage to all periods. Robert H. Dix's *The Politics of Colombia* (1987) concentrates on political developments with an emphasis upon the twentieth century.

The leftist movements arising during the 1960's are handled well. Harvey F. Kline's *Colombia: Portrait of Unity and Diversity* (1983) contains a brief discussion of the nation before the decade of the 1920's but a more detailed coverage of economic and political developments beginning in 1939. For labor developments in Colombia see Charles Bergquist's *Labor in Latin America: Comparative Essays on Chile, Argentina, Venezuela, and Colombia* (1986). For relations between the United States and Colombia see Stephan J. Randall's *Colombia and the United States: Hegemony and Interdependence* (1992). Randall concentrates on the period after 1920. Good current information on Colombia can be found in *The New York Times* and *Washington Post*.

Ecuador

Two problems, never solved for long, have troubled Ecuador's history. First, most of its many governments have been short-lived and ineffective. This instability derives from an intense and long-term rivalry between the nation's coastal and mountain regions and from the domination of the middle class and poor by a small group of wealthy white landowners. Second, Ecuador and Peru fought a long series of skirmishes and small wars over their border. Since the late 1960's a third problem has arisen: how to develop the country's oil-rich eastern region without destroying its rain forest and the cultures of Native Americans who have lived there for thousands of years. A small country with limited resources, Ecuador faces challenges in building a healthy economy and avoiding further military conflict and political strife.

Named after the equator, which runs through it, Ecuador is located on the western shoulder of South America. It is bordered to the north by Colombia and to the south and east by Peru. Ecuador is the fourth-smallest country on the continent, with an area of 109,483 square miles. It is, however, the most densely populated country on the continent, with about twelve million people.

Ecuador's population is spread unevenly among three regions: the Costa (coast); the Sierra (Andes Mountains); and the Oriente—the region east of the Andes in which rain forest flourishes around the headwaters of the Amazon River. Located high in the Andes, the capital city, Quito, has always been the country's seat of political power, even though most of the country's wealth—which is concentrated in agriculture and fishing—has belonged to the coastal regions. Ecuador's largest city is also its principal port, on the south coast, Guayaquil, which has more than 1.8 million people.

After the late 1960's crude oil from fields in the Oriente began accounting for a steadily increasing share of Ecuador's national economy. Until the 1970's, Amerind tribes populated the Oriente almost exclusively, many living as hunter-gatherers in inaccessible areas of the rain forest. At that time farmers and oil company employees began moving in; however, the area still accounted for less

Profile of Ecuador

Official name: Republic of Ecuador
Independent since: 1822
Former colonial ruler: Spain
Location: western South America
Area: 109,483 square miles
Capital: Quito
Population: 12,105,100 (1997 est.)
Official language: Spanish
Major religion: Roman Catholicism
Gross domestic product: US$47 billion (1996 est.)
Major exports: food and live animals; mineral fuels; basic manufactures
Military budget: US$390.2 million (1996)
Military personnel: 57,100 (1996)

Note: Monetary figures rendered as "US$" are U.S. equivalents of values in local currencies.

than 5 percent of the country's total population.

Although only about 7 percent of Ecuadorians are estimated to be pure-blood descendants of Spanish settlers, they have always dominated the other social groups politically and economically. Mestizos, or persons of mixed blood, account for 65 percent of the population; Amerinds, 35 percent; and African Americans, 3 percent. About 45 percent of the population lives in the country, farming and ranching. The wealthiest 20 percent own 83 percent of the land. Many of the rest, mostly poor, have been employed on large estates, where they lived almost as slaves until well into the twentieth century. More than half of Ecuadorians still subsist below the poverty level.

Agriculture earns Ecuador foreign money, especially U.S. dollars, from exports. Coffee, cocoa, and bananas have been the most important crops. In fact, the country depended almost entirely on cocoa exports in the early twentieth century and bananas in the mid-twentieth century to expand the economy and finance government projects. When those exports declined, the national economy shrank too, sometimes disastrously. This boom-and-bust pattern again repeated itself after 1970, as Ecuador relied more on exporting crude oil, whose international prices rose and fell.

Early History. Ecuador had diverse, thriving civilizations in the Costa and Sierra regions when the Incas from Peru invaded the region around 1490. After the Incan conquest, Quito became a second capital of the empire, the favored residence of Inca emperor Huayna Capac. Around the year 1528, Huayna Capac's son Atahualpa, who was half Quitan, rebelled against his half brother, Huáscar, who had become emperor and lived in Peru. Atahualpa won the civil war, which is still a source of pride to Ecuadorians.

Atahualpa was on his way to Cuzco, Peru, to be crowned in 1532, when he encountered the Spanish conquistador Francisco Pizarro, who was in command of 180 Spanish soldiers. Through trickery, Pizarro captured Atahualpa and later had him murdered. Soon afterward, Pizarro and other Spanish adventurers gained control of the Inca empire.

In 1540 a Spanish viceroy, the personal representative of the king of Spain, began ruling northwestern South America from Lima, Peru. Ecuador, then called the Audencia of Quito, was one of the main provinces of the Viceroyalty of Peru. In 1720 the Spanish crown transferred the Audencia of Quito to the new Viceroyalty of Granada and granted it limited self-government.

The Spanish colonists divided up the region's land among themselves and used the diverse indigenous population to enrich themselves. They put Amerinds to work tending crops and livestock or digging gold and silver from mines. Spanish laws required many Indians to live on the property of white landowners and pay for their food and quarters through work. Other Amerinds were grouped into special villages near mines or textile factories. Any Amerinds who remained free had to pay taxes by working on Spanish projects. However, the Amerinds were not really free. The growing population of mestizos had greater privileges but could not own land or enter politics. Even whites born in Ecuador, called Creoles, were second-class citizens.

The first Africans arrived from a slave ship wrecked on the north coast in 1570. They stayed away from the Spanish, intermarrying with local Amerinds. A small number of slaves were later imported from Africa to work on coastal sugar plantations. This economic and social structure created resentment.

Ecuador's relations with Spain and its officials increased the resentment. Much of the wealth in gold and silver and from taxes went to support the Spanish government. Ecuador, like the other Spanish colonies, was not even allowed to trade its goods within South America. Everything had to be sent first to Spain. For the most part, Creoles were excluded from high government and military ranks. Mestizos had few economic opportunities, and Amerinds had almost no rights.

The resentment reached the point of rebellion before the nineteenth century. French emperor Napoleon Bonaparte's invasion of Spain in 1808 preoccupied Spanish rulers, making it easier for rebellions to develop in South America. In 1811 revolutionaries expelled Spanish forces from Quito and declared it independent. The Spanish quickly crushed this rebellion, but rebel troops that were part of Simón Bolívar's wider revolution finally defeated Spanish loyalists in the Battle of Pichincha in 1822.

Republic of Ecuador. Although free of Spanish control in 1822, Ecuador was not yet fully independent. It became part of Gran Colombia, created and ruled by Bolívar, the Great Liberator of South America. Its capital in Bogotá included the old Audencia of Quito, Colombia, and Venezuela. After the new nation fought a brief war with Peru over their mutual border in 1829, a treaty officially fixed the boundary at the same line that had divided the Audencia of Quito from the Viceroyalty of Peru during the colonial period.

Gran Colombia was politically unstable. Ecuador withdrew from it in 1830, and a constitution was written for the Republic of Ecuador. One of Bolívar's generals, Juan José Flores, became Ecuador's first president. The Spanish who had revolted and the Ecuadorian Creoles held all the political power. Independence brought few changes for most of the rest of the population. As

members of this white elite fought among themselves for control of the country, Ecuadorian history unfolded in a series of coups and civil wars.

Himself a member of the Quitan elite, General Flores ruled as if he were a dictator, suppressing opposition and, apparently, having rival politicians murdered. He also sought to expand Ecuador's territory. In 1832 Ecuadorian forces occupied the uninhabited Galápagos Islands. However, later that year the army tried to take Cauca Province from Colombia but failed. Flores's harsh rule and military expenditures made many enemies. In 1834, a rebellion by José Vicente Rocafuerte, a member of the Guayaquil elite, sent Flores into exile. However, Flores later returned to the presidency.

This power struggle between caudillos (a widely used Spanish term for strongmen) from Guayaquil and Quito for political and economic control lasted throughout the nineteenth century. It involved a difference in political philosophy. Those from Guayaquil were usually Liberals, who wanted to end the vast power of the Roman Catholic Church in the country and to reform land ownership laws to improve living conditions for nonwhites. Conservatives from Quito wanted to preserve the traditional elite hold on power and the official status of the Church.

Political struggles and government corruption sapped Ecuador's strength and increased its debts

Ecuador's Shrinking Territory

Date	Area Remaining	Remarks
1740-1811	400,282 sq. mi.	Ecuador's colonial period
1832	272,516 sq. mi.	Ecuador breaks from Gran Colombia
1904	245,882 sq. mi.	Ecuador signs Treaty of Tobar-Rio Branco with Brazil
1916	182,423 sq. mi.	Ecuador signs Treaty of Muñoz Vernaza-Suárez with Colombia
1942	109,483 sq. mi.	Ecuador signs Rio Protocol with Peru

as the government borrowed money from foreign banks. The situation grew so turbulent that by 1859—which is remembered as the Terrible Year—Ecuador was in danger of falling apart. Several caudillos ruled provinces as if they were independent domains. The Peruvian army captured a large part of southern Ecuador. The caudillo in that region agreed to a treaty with Peru that gave the latter Ecuador's southern provinces. Shocked, the rest of Ecuador united in renouncing the treaty and pushing the Peruvians out of Ecuador.

Modern Political Conflict. The Conservatives ruled from 1860 to 1895, despite power struggles within the party and attempted coups by the Liberals. Much the same occurred after the Liberals came to power in 1895, following a bloody civil war. The party had to survive another civil war in 1911. However, by then the country was gradually becoming more prosperous from exports of cocoa. When disease destroyed much of the cocoa crop during the 1920's, the decaying economy and political corruption weakened the Liberals' hold on power.

In 1925 a military group called the League of Young Officers took power in a bloodless coup. The group hoped to start a new era in which meaningful economic reforms and honesty in government were more important than loyalty to a party. Well intended, the effort was soon crippled by economic collapse during the Great Depression. More trouble soon followed: election fraud, labor strikes, quarreling between Ecuador's congress and presidency, and a four-day civil war in 1932.

After World War II, during which Ecuador was a member of the Allies, greater political stability reigned. Unlike its neighbors, Colombia and Peru, Ecuador seldom has been troubled by guerrilla fighters. However, some rebels began operating on the coast in the early 1960's, and there were terrorist incidents. Fearing a communist revolution similar to Cuba's, and upset with a weak Liberal government, the military again seized power. A junta ruled until 1966. It permitted elected presidents to hold power between 1966 and 1972, when again the junta took direct control of the government until 1979.

In 1979 a new constitution was enacted, the seventeenth in Ecuador's history, and a presidential election brought a civilian politician into office once more. Legal changes of power continued thereafter, although not without trouble. Power struggles between the congress and presidents caused confusion and prevented passage of important reform laws.

Ecuador's economy came close to collapse during the 1980's because the government could not repay its massive debts to other countries and international banks. Politicians routinely charged each other with corruption and election fraud. The bickering became especially intense in 1997. President Abdala Bucaram was forced from office on charges of official misconduct. He was replaced by the leader of the congress, Fabian Alarcón.

Because of Ecuador's tradition of discord among parties and between the executive and legislative branches of government, political analysts believe democracy in Ecuador is fragile. Further internal conflict may endanger it.

Territorial Wars. After Ecuador seceded from Gran Colombia in the early nineteenth century, its territory extended past Iquitos on the Amazon River, and the country bordered Brazil. The boundaries were based upon Spanish colonial records from the Audencia of Quito. However, Spanish records for the Amazon border region—a wilderness next to impossible to map at the time—were vague and open to differing interpretations. As a result, neighboring countries lay claims to parts of Ecuador.

In 1904 Ecuador gave more than 26,000 square miles of its eastern territory to Brazil. In 1916 it transferred another 63,000 square miles to Colombia—a territory shift that removed Ecuador's border with Brazil. (Colombia later ceded some of this land to Peru.) Ecuador thus found itself enclosed by Peru to the south and east and by Colombia to the north, both much larger, wealthier countries.

Peru wanted still more of Ecuador's land. Their armies battled over the border for a short time in 1932. In 1941 Peru invaded Ecuador. Outnumbered and facing superior weapons, the Ecuadorian forces fought poorly during a ten-day war— partly because the president withheld the best army units to protect Quito. The United States, Brazil, and Argentina mediated a treaty at a meeting in Rio de Janeiro on January 29, 1942. Often called the Rio Protocol, the official title was the Protocol of Peace, Friendship, and Boundaries. Two-thirds of Ecuador's Oriente went to Peru, which thereby grew to nearly four times the size of Ecuador.

Ecuador

1532	Inca empire, which includes Quito as a major center, falls to Spanish forces under Francisco Pizarro.
1533	Port city of Guayaquil is founded.
1544	Ecuador becomes part of Viceroyalty of Peru, whose capital is Lima.
1720	Ecuador becomes province of Viceroyalty of New Granada, whose capital is Bogotá.
1809-1811	Series of rebellions ends with creation of independent Ecuador state centered in Quito.
1812	Spanish forces recapture Quito and end independence.
1820	Independence is again declared in Guayaquil, part of a larger rebellion led by Simón Bolívar and José de San Martín.
1822	Battle of Pichincha ends Spanish influence; Ecuador becomes part of Gran Colombia.
1829	Gran Colombia briefly fights Peru over their border, which is defined by treaty.
1830	Ecuador withdraws from Gran Colombia and drafts its own constitution.
1832	Ecuador takes possession of Galápagos Islands.
1859	Ecuador's "Terrible Year."
1859	Peru invades Ecuador; Treaty of Mapasingue, which gives southern provinces to Peru, is later repudiated and Peruvian army is forced out.
1908	Guayaquil-Quito railroad is completed.
1911	Brief civil war fails to overthrow Ecuador's government.
1925	League of Young Officers stages coup to install reformist government.
1929	Great Depression in United States causes Ecuador's exports to plummet, and its economy is devastated.
1932	Bloody four-day civil war is fought.
1941	Ecuador loses brief war with Peru over disputed border.
1942	(Jan. 29) Ecuador signs Rio Protocol with Peru, an agreement sponsored by United States, Brazil, and Argentina.
1960	President José María Velasco renounces Rio Protocol.
1963	Coup places military junta in power for three years.
1964	Agrarian Land Reform Law goes into effect but does little to help the poor.
1967	Large oil deposits are discovered in Oriente region.
1972	Coup places military junta in power for seven years.
1973	Ecuador joins Organization of Petroleum Exporting Countries (OPEC).
1979	Democratic government is restored with election of Jaime Roldós as president.
1981	Ecuador fights another brief border war with Peru.
1982	Weather changes caused by severe El Niño condition bring destructive storms and drought.
1995	Ecuador battles Peru to stalemate in month-long border war.

(continued)

1996	Abdala Bucaram is elected president.
1997	Bucaram is forced out of office by congress and replaced by Fabian Alarcón.
1998	(Mar.) Flooding caused by El Niño weather and subsequent damage leads to mutual-help agreement with fellow-suffering Peru.
1998	(July 12) Quito mayor Jamil Mahuad Wit is elected president; leading opponent Alvaro Noboa charges electoral fraud.
1998	(Aug. 10) Mahuad is inaugurated as president and sets recovery from damage done by El Niño storms and improving relations with Peru as government priorities.
1998	(Oct. 26) Ecuador and Peru sign a peace treaty defining their common border and allowing Ecuador access to Amazon River.
1999	(Mar. 9) Government declares sixty-day state of emergency in response to general labor strike.
1999	(Mar. 11) Mahuad announces sweeping austerity program to combat country's worst economic crisis since Depression.

Afterward, Ecuadorians bitterly resented the treaty. They believe that Ecuador was pressured to agree to it quickly because the United States wanted to devote its attention to World War II, which it had entered in December, 1941. Because of the treaty, Ecuador lost its access to the Amazon River and, thus, a direct trade route to Europe via the Atlantic Ocean. Other regions of Ecuador suffered wide destruction during the war, which further hurt the nation's economy.

Resentment against the treaty remained high among Ecuadorians, who considered it patriotic to call for the return of lost Oriente territory. The primary objective of later foreign policy of all governments was to defend the country from further territorial losses. In 1960 President José María Velasco tried to make himself more popular by renouncing the Rio Protocol. He had an economic motive, too: The lost territory was suspected to be rich in oil and gold deposits.

Animosity between Peru and Ecuador increased after 1960 and stayed strong. Small skirmishes between their armies occurred often. In 1981 they fought a four-day war in the eastern foothills of the Cordillera del Condor (Range of the Condor). A fifty-mile section of the border there lay at the heart of the dispute. Ecuador wanted the area because it held the headwaters of the Cenepa River, which flowed into the Marañon River, a major tributary of the Amazon.

Small-scale fighting occurred yearly thereafter around the January 29 anniversary of the Rio Protocol. On January 27, 1995, the skirmishes escalated into a war that spread outside the Cordillera del Condor area. It started when Ecuador captured Peruvian border posts. Peru tried to retake the posts with troops backed by helicopter attacks and mortar barrages. Ecuador mined roads connecting the countries and expelled thousands of Peruvians living in border towns. Peruvian and Ecuadorian jets bombed each other's strongholds along the border, while about ten thousand troops moved into the battle areas. Each side accused the other of starting the war in order to increase the popularity of its president or to justify spending money on its armed forces.

To stop the war from spreading further, diplomats from the United States, Brazil, Chile, and Argentina met to negotiate a cease-fire with Ecuadorian and Peruvian officials in Rio de Janeiro on February 2. On February 14, both sides signed a cease-fire agreement. However, eight days later the truce was broken by the heaviest fighting of the war. A second cease-fire agreement, signed on March 1, succeeded in stopping the conflict. Military observers from the mediating nations went to the battle zones to make sure the truce held. Together Peru and Ecuador had seventy-eight dead and more than two hundred wounded. Peru lost five helicopters and three jet aircraft, but Ecuador suf-

A Native Ecuadorian Speaks Out

We live with the spirit of the jaguar. We do not want to be civilized by your missionaries or killed by your oil companies. Must the jaguar die so that you can have more contamination and television?

Moi, a Huaorani leader in the Ecuadorian Amazon, 1993

fered the most economically. Its war expenses, more than US$250 million, used up its money reserves.

In January, 1996, the two armies again exchanged gunfire after the sale of Israeli-built fighter-bomber jets to Ecuador angered Peru. There were no casualties, however, and tensions eased afterward. In early 1998 Ecuador and Peru pledged mutual aid to recover from destructive storms caused by severe El Niño weather conditions. Later the same year they concluded a peace treaty defining their border and allowing Ecuador to use a river passage to the Amazon.

Indigenous Societies in the Oriente. During the colonial era, Spanish leaders made Ecuador's Amerind peoples of the Sierra and Costa regions the lowest class of workers. The Amerinds of the Oriente, however, stayed free. The swampy rain forest they inhabited was too difficult for the Spanish to colonize. Moreover, several Amerind societies were strong enough to drive away Spanish, and later Ecuadorian, soldiers. Considered to be "ferocious," the tribes were greatly feared—some because they were reputed to be head hunters. Well into the twentieth century, these tribes continued to live apart from the rest of Ecuador's people, rarely participating in trade or government.

In 1967 large deposits of oil were discovered in the Oriente. The Ecuadorian government encouraged foreign oil companies, such as Conoco and Texaco, to drill

for the oil. By 1971 a pipeline was carrying oil to the coast for export. The money earned from it greatly boosted the national economy, and the government sponsored further oil exploration. The local Amerinds saw their lands occupied by oil companies. Roads plowed through their forests, drill sites were cleared, and crude oil spilled into the streams. The Amerinds had no power to stop the oil companies. Moreover, people from the Costa and Sierra came to clear land for farming along the new roads. With these groups came diseases to which the Amerinds had no resistance. Many consequently became sick and died.

Ecuador's government invited foreign missionaries to start schools and medical care for some tribes, and oil companies often employed Amerinds. Nonetheless, conflicts were frequent. Amerinds were often punished for stealing, because many did not share Western concepts of private property. To protect their traditional ways of life, other Amerinds wrecked drill sites and kidnapped and killed oil workers and missionaries. The conflicts were small and sporadic; nevertheless, the

Despite El Niño-caused flooding, outdoor markets remained open in Guayaquil in early 1998. (AP/Wide World Photos)

Peruvian president Alberto Fujimori (right), Brazilian president Fernando Henrique Cardoso (center), and recently elected Ecuadorian president Jamil Mahuad (left) meet in Brasilia in September, 1998, to settle Peru and Ecuador's long-standing border dispute. (AP/Wide World Photos)

Ecuadorian army was mobilized to guard oil company facilities and suppress two small guerrilla organizations thought to be associated with the Amerinds: Puka Inti (Red Sun) and Alfaro Vive, Carajo (Alfaro Lives, Damn It). The combination of the army, settlers, and new foods and consumer goods given to the Amerinds destroyed the traditional cultures of some communities by the 1980's.

Violence continued into the 1990's, but many Ecuadorian Amerind societies adopted a new strategy to protect themselves—political influence. They joined the nationwide Confederation of Indigenous Nationalities of Ecuador (CONAEI), or regional organizations. These groups used strikes and public demonstrations to pressure the government into granting Amerinds more control of their lands. Foreign environmental and human rights organizations also pressured the government. Individual tribes sometimes succeeded in winning new rights. For example, the government hired the Cofan people to patrol their traditional hunting grounds as park rangers, empowering them to keep out other hunters and to check for oil pollution.

CONAEI wanted more than such local arrangements, however. In the late 1990's its primary goal was a new constitution for Ecuador, creating a "plurinational state." This state would respect the cultural diversity of Amerind nations, distribute the country's income evenly, decentralize the government, and give Amerind communities control of their economy and natural resources. Because Ecuador's politicians and military commanders are unlikely to support such broad changes, violent and nonviolent conflict may further disturb the Oriente.

Roger Smith

For Further Study

There is no up-to-date English-language history of Ecuador, but *The Penguin History of Latin America* (1992), by Edwin Williamson, sketches its history and culture, as well as those of the other countries in South America. More detailed historical overviews can be found in *Ecuador: A Country Study* (1991), edited by Dennis M. Hanratty, based upon Library of Congress research in 1989, and in *Ecuador: An Andean Enigma* (1987), by David W. Schodt. Frank MacDonald Spindler's *Nineteenth Century Ecuador: A Historical Introduction* (1987) reviews Ecuador's turbulent birth and formative years. In *The Process of Political Domination in Ecuador* (1982), Agustín Cueva, an Ecuadorian political scientist, explains how leaders gained power, especially under military governments, and *Unsettled Statescraft: Democracy and Neoliberalism in the Central Andes* (1994), by Catherine M. Conaghan and James M. Malloy, discusses the effect of economic crisis on the Ecuadorian military and civilian rulers during the 1980's. Anita Isaacs's "Ecuador: Democracy Standing the Test of Time?" in *Constructing Democratic Governance* (1996), edited by Jorge I. Domínguez and Abraham F. Lowenthal, reviews the politics of Ecuador during the early 1990's, concluding that the country may be succeeding, slowly, in establishing a solid democracy. In *Savages* (1995) Joe Kane tells a thrilling adventure story about his life among the Huaorani Indians in the Oriente; the book also describes how oil companies and colonists are destroying the Huaorani homeland.

The World Wide Web contains several sites to browse for information. At http://lcweb2.loc.gov/frd/cs/cshome.html can be found an on-line version of *Ecuador: A Country Study*. General information can also be obtained at http://www.theordoralcom/wfb/ecuador_geographyl.html and http://www.viaecuador.com/ecuador.html (intended primarily for tourists). The Ecuadorian embassy in Washington, D.C., provides official information at www.ecuador.org. Information about Amerinds and their political involvement can be found at http://www.nativeweb.org/abyayala/cultures/ecuador.

Falkland Islands

The problem that besets the South Atlantic's Falkland Islands concerns who rightfully owns the archipelago. Previously uninhabited, the islands were first settled by the French and the British during the 1760's. France later ceded its settlement to Spain, which recognized Britain's claim to the other major island. In 1816 both Spain and Britain removed their garrisons from the islands leaving them again without permanent inhabitants. Shortly thereafter, newly independent Argentina—the South American country closest to the islands—established a settlement on them, only to be driven out by the British in 1832. When Britain declared its sovereignty over all the Falklands the following year, Argentina refused to recognize its right to the islands. Since then Argentina has consistently claimed that it owns the islands. Argentina pressed its claim through regular diplomatic channels until 1982, when its troops invaded the islands and overran the British garrison. Britain defeated Argentina in the brief war that followed, and the two nations reestablished normal diplomatic relations with each other. However, no agreement was ever reached on the Falklands' sovereignty, which remains a potentially volatile issue.

Also known as Las Islas Malvinas, the Falkland Islands are a group of large and small islands located in the South Atlantic Ocean. The windswept islands lie 320 miles off the southeastern end of Argentina, on almost the same latitude as the Strait of Magellan. The archipelago consists of 2 large islands, East and West Falkland, and more than 340 small islands and islets. Their land area is about 4,699 square miles—slightly smaller than the U.S. state of Connecticut.

Most of the 2,432 people who inhabit the Falkland Islands live on East Falkland, where the capital, Stanley, is located. Virtually all the inhabitants are British by heritage and speak English. Few of them have any roots in Argentina, where Spanish is the official language. The islands' architecture, culture, and lifestyles are distinctly British and thus markedly different from those of Argentina. The people consider themselves British and support the Crown.

Early Exploration. The story of the settlement and administration of the Falklands is one of buying and selling, looting and killing. The islands were discovered in 1592—exactly one hundred years after Christopher Columbus first landed in the New World. English navigator John Davis, of the British royal ship *Desire*, is credited with being the first human being to sight the Falklands. Official Argentine histories of the islands claim that various Spanish and Portuguese navigators, including Ferdinand Magellan, found the islands earlier than Davis, but they do not specify the evidence for these claims.

In any case, about eight years after Davis saw the islands, a Dutch navigator named Sebald de Weerdt was the first person accurately to record his sighting of the Falklands. He established the islands' latitude and longitude, thereby placing them on the world map.

The first actual landing in the Falklands to be recorded occurred in 1690, when British captain John Strong led an expedition there. He spent six days sailing around the two main islands. He named the water separating the two main islands the Falkland Sound, after Viscount Falkland, the head of the Royal Navy at the time. The name Falkland was eventually extended to apply to the entire island chain.

After French navigator Gouin de Beauchene discovered the Falklands' remote outer islands in

1701, the French called the archipelago Isles Malouines. They took this name from Saint-Malo, the French port from which many voyages of discovery set sail. The French became the leaders in investigating the Falkland Islands.

Early Settlements. In 1764 a French nobleman, Louis-Antoine de Bougainville, established a colony of 140 people on the islands. These colonists were well supplied with seeds, hardware, and livestock. However, after Spain—which ruled most of nearby South America—learned of the new French colony, it protested. Two years later de Bougainville agreed to transfer ownership of the small colony to the Spanish government for 25,000 British pounds. The following year possession of the islands was formally transferred to Spain.

While these developments were occurring, British interest in the Falklands was growing. The Royal Navy sent Captain John Byron to survey the islands. A few months later another British captain, John McBride, visited the French settlement on the Falklands and informed its commander that Britain claimed the islands. Both parties were unaware that when de Bougainville returned to France he agreed to sell over France's claims to the islands to the Spanish government.

In 1769 the British and Spanish advised each other to leave the islands. The situation was temporarily resolved when a large Spanish force forced a small British garrison on the islands to negotiate a surrender. The British gave up their settlement and returned to England. By then the Spanish were calling the Falklands Las Islas Malvinas, a variation of the French Isles Malouines.

In 1771 the British returned and established a small force in the Falklands. After only three years, however, they abandoned the settlement. The reasons for Britain's abandonment of its Falkland settlement has ever since remained an issue of contention in the dispute over the islands' ownership. Meanwhile, the Spanish maintained a settlement of their own in the Falklands, but it was never a great success.

Rise of the Argentine Nation. The early nineteenth century was

an era of revolution in South America, and Argentina became one of the first Latin American nations to free itself from the rule of Spain, which was then struggling to preserve its own independence from France. The Napoleonic Wars tearing Europe apart had repercussions around the world. One of these was Britain's brief occupation of Buenos Aires (the future capital of Argentina) in 1806.

When the Spanish governor of the Falklands heard that British troops were occupying Buenos Aires, he fled the islands. He never returned to his post, so Spain's sovereignty over the islands lapsed. From 1806 to 1820 the islands were free of all forms of governmental control and authority. In 1816 Argentina became independent of Spain. Four years later, it proclaimed its own sovereignty over the Falkland Islands. A few years after that the first Argentine governor of the Falklands—which Argentina always called—Islas Malvinas—was appointed.

U.S. Intervention. Louis Vernet, a Frenchman by birth, had established a colony of 90 settlers who were engaged in fishing and dry salting beef which were marketed in South America. Argentina granted Vernet all rights to East Falkland Island and made him governor of the archipelago. Vernet used his authority to stop foreign vessels from hunting seals in the islands. In July, 1831, he seized U.S. sealing vessels.

The United States protested Vernet's actions to the Argentine government, which failed to respond. At the end of 1831 a small U.S. warship took revenge by sacking the Argentine settlement in the Falklands while Vernet was away. The attack was a major blow to the Argentine government.

Profile of the Falkland Islands

Official name: Colony of the Falkland Islands
Status: dependency of Great Britain
Location: off of Atlantic coast of southern South America
Area: 4,699 square miles
Capital: Stanley
Population: 2,432 (1997 est.)
Main language: English
Major religions: Anglicanism; Roman Catholicism
Major exports: wool; hides; meat

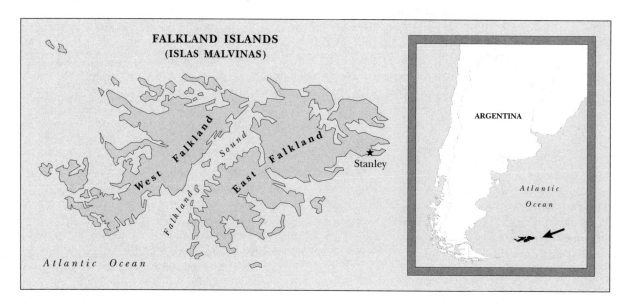

FALKLAND ISLANDS
(ISLAS MALVINAS)

West Falkland

Falkland Sound

East Falkland

Stanley

Atlantic Ocean

ARGENTINA

Atlantic Ocean

Vernet was never to return to the islands.

The following year Argentina sent a temporary governor to the islands, but he was soon killed by mutineers who took over his administration. Confusion and chaos were ruling the islands when a British warship arrived. Its captain, John Onslow, delivered a letter to the Argentine commander informing him that Britain held sovereignty over the islands. The Argentine commander left the islands but did not strike his flag—a gesture that would have symbolized formal surrender.

The British acted quickly, fearing that the United States might have seized the islands because of Vernet's belligerent actions against American vessels. Americans thus unwittingly caused the Falkland Islands government to change hands. From that time only the British flag flew over the islands. In early 1834 Lieutenant Henry Smith was made governor of the Falkland Islands, beginning a long and uninterrupted string of British administrators.

Formal Colonial Status. From 1834 through 1842 the Falkland Islands were administered by naval officers. Their task was to keep law and order and take care of routine administrative matters. In 1842 Governor Moody established his administrative offices in the new village of Stanley. He tried to manage the port as he felt it should be run, but British government support was minimal. The home government's view was that Moody should lead the Falkland settlers by example. However, his work was held back by lack of funds and the general unruly nature of the local seafaring community. After decades of almost no government at all, Falklanders needed time to adjust to being governed.

Governor Rennie followed Moody and continued the effort of stabilizing the community. His attempts to enforce the islands' laws nearly brought Britain and the United States to war.

By the mid-nineteenth century the Falklands colony was well established. However, its official status was not well known, and its laws were generally ignored by the many foreign fishing, whaling, and sealing ships that worked the Falklands' waters. In 1853 the British government notified the United States that it intended to post a naval force in the Falkland Islands to enforce its laws. Soon thereafter two American whaling captains were arrested and imprisoned for killing livestock on the islands. American and British navies nearly collided over this incident. However, the captains eventually paid their fines and were released. The matter was not officially closed for years, but the issue was eventually forgotten.

With vast quantities of seals and whales in the waters around the Falklands, their settlers became largely self-sufficient. Earlier settlers had done well with imported hogs and cattle, but a significant change occurred when sheep were introduced under British rule. The islands lacked natural predators, and the weather was perfect for sheep production. Sheep soon became the mainstay of the agriculture industry in the Falklands.

As the Falklands became self-supporting, the British government officially granted them colonial status in 1892. This status officially certified that all islanders were British subjects.

United Nations Enters the Picture. Argentina never formally gave up its claims to the Falklands. In 1964 it laid its claims before the United Nations, where the issue was debated by the U.N. Committee on Decolonization.

Argentina based its claims to the islands on a Papal Bull dating back to 1493 and the Treaty of Tordesillas of 1494. Under those early documents the Roman Catholic Church recognized a formal division of New World lands between Spain and Portugal. As a former Spanish colony, Argentina claimed it had inherited Spain's sovereignty over the Falklands. It also stressed its own nearness to the islands, as well as the need to end a colonial situation for the people of the islands.

Britain countered Argentina's claims by pointing out that it had had open, continuous, and effective possession of the Falkland Islands since 1833. It also asserted its determination to apply to the Falklander people the principle of self-determination as recognized in the U.N. Charter. Britain further asserted that, far from ending a colonial situation, Argentine rule and control of the lives of the Falklanders against their wishes would, in fact, create one.

The U.N. General Assembly approved a resolution inviting Argentina and Britain to hold serious discussions to find a peaceful solution to the dispute. Those discussions were still proceeding in a cordial and diplomatic fashion shortly before the 1982 Falklands War began.

Argentine Occupation of the Falklands. In March of 1982 the actions of the Argentine government suggested that its cordial discourse with Britain was at an end. Britain had asked Argentina to intervene in the matter of raising the Argentina flag on the island of South Georgia—another British possession about a thousand miles east of the

The surrender of Argentine troops to the British at Port Stanley effectively ended the Falklands War. (AP/Wide World Photos)

In the aftermath of Argentina's defeat in the Falklands War, President Leopoldo Galtieri—who launched the invasion of the islands—was forced to resign, making possible the restoration of democratic government to Argentina. Galtieri was later called to account for his actions in Argentina's so-called "Dirty War." (AP/Wide World Photos)

Falklands. There was no response. The Argentine military junta had already decided to invade the islands and was in no mood to negotiate such a trifling matter as a flag raising.

At that time the Argentine government was in deep trouble with its national economy. Throughout 1981 prices were rising at a rate exceeding 600 percent. Gross domestic production (GDP) was down more than 11 percent. Manufacturing output was down 23 percent, and real wages were also down by 19 percent. Significant unrest was also caused by the mass disappearances of people who had been secretly arrested by the military junta.

General Leopoldo Galtieri, the third dictator to hold the presidency since the army's 1976 coup, launched a military invasion of the islands. The invasion was planned by Argentina's naval commander, Admiral Jorge Anaya. The launch date for the attack, whose code name was OPERACION

ROSARIO, was set for either May 25 or July 9—the dates of Argentina's most important national holidays.

The junta hoped that mounting a successful military operation on one of those days would help divert public attention from the distressing internal problems and restore public support of the government. However, continued public unrest and pressure on the government, combined with mass union demonstrations in late March, caused the junta to move up the date of the planned invasion.

On April 2, 1982, in an act of desperation, the Argentine navy landed thousands of troops on the Falklands. The small detachment of British Royal Marines on the islands put up a futile resistance. British governor Rex Hunt ordered the Marines to lay down their arms. He and the British troops were then flown to Montevideo, the capital of Uruguay. Meanwhile, Argentine troops also seized the outer islands.

During the first segment of the war only four troops were killed, when an Argentine helicopter crashed. General Mario Menendez was named military governor of the islands. As General Galtieri had predicted, the invasion proved popular in Argentina, where mass public demonstrations in support of the invasion erupted in major cities.

The U.N. Security Council immediately passed Resolution 502 calling for the withdrawal of Argentine troops from the islands, along with the immediate cessation of hostilities. Britain placed its own military on war alert. Meanwhile, Argentina drafted thousands of young men and sent them to the islands with no basic training. Within a matter of days Argentine troops on the islands numbered more than ten thousand.

British Counterattack. On April 5, three days after the Argentine invasion, the British government headed by Prime Minister Margaret Thatcher designated a war zone extending two hundred nautical miles out from the Falklands. Britain assembled a naval task force and made a plan to retake the islands. Long-range air strikes were be-

Falkland Islands

1592	English navigator John Davis is earliest human being to sight Falkland Islands.
1600	Dutch navigator Sebald de Weerdt makes earliest undisputed sighting of islands.
1764	First permanent human settlement is established on islands.
1765	Great Britain establishes first settlement on West Falkland island.
1767	Spain buys out French settlement on East Falkland Island.
1774	Great Britain withdraws from Falklands, while Spain maintains its own settlement.
1816	Spain and Britain remove their garrisons from islands.
1820	Newly independent Argentina proclaims its sovereignty over Falklands.
1828	First Argentine settlement is established on islands.
1831	U.S. warship destroys Argentina's settlement in reprisal for Argentina's illegal seizure of three U.S. ships.
1833	Fearing that United States has seized islands, Britain returns to Falklands and expels Argentines.
1834	(Jan.) Britain appoints Henry Smith governor of islands.
1892	Britain grants colonial status to Falklands.
1964	Status of Falklands is debated in U.N. Committee on Decolonization.
1965	U.N. General Assembly invites Britain and Argentina to establish dialogue on sovereignty issue.
1982	(Apr. 2) Argentine troops invade Falklands to expel British forces.
1982	(Apr. 3) U.N. General Assembly passes resolution calling for Argentina to withdraw its troops.
1982	(Apr. 5) British prime minister Margaret Thatcher declares a war zone around Falklands.
1982	(Apr. 25) British commando force recaptures outer islands.
1982	(May 1) British and Argentine troops have major clashes.
1982	(May 2) President of Peru presents peace proposal that is rejected by Argentine junta.
1982	(May 18) U.N. secretary general presents peace proposal that is rejected by Great Britain.
1982	(May 21) British forces begin amphibious assault on islands.
1982	(June 14) British defeat Argentine garrison at Port Stanley; Argentina surrenders.
1990	Argentina and Britain resume normal diplomatic relations.
1993	New Argentine constitution reiterates country's claims to Falklands.
1998	(Oct.) Argentine president Carlos Menem visits Britain.
1999	(Mar. 9) Great Britain's Prince Charles begins state visit to Argentina, where he pays homage to Argentine troops who died in Falkland Islands war.

gun to cut off the flow of supplies from Argentina to Argentine forces on the islands.

Over the next several weeks various nations tried to persuade the two antagonists to negotiate a peaceful settlement. U.S. secretary of state Alexander Haig visited the capitals of both countries to serve as a liaison. After his mediation talks collapsed, he returned to Washington. The British

Foreign Office advised all British nationals living and working in Argentina to leave the country.

On April 25 a small British commando force retook one of the outer islands, where Argentine troops surrendered without firing a shot. Meanwhile, the main British task force was still 8,000 miles from the Falkland Islands.

On April 30 Alexander Haig's mission to both countries was officially called off. U.S. president Ronald Reagan declared that the United States would support the British government and that economic sanctions against Argentina were to be established.

On May 2 Peruvian president Belaunde Terry presented a peace proposal to Argentine president Leopoldo Galtieri. Galtieri appeared inclined to accept the proposal. However, before his junta could ratify the proposal, a British submarine sank the Argentine cruiser *Belgrano* outside Britain's designated war zone, killing more than four hundred Argentine sailors. The Argentine junta then rejected the Peruvian peace proposal.

The War Continues. Over the next several days Argentina and Britain continued fighting, with both sides losing aircraft and men. On May 5 Peru drafted a new peace plan. Two days later the United Nations entered the peace negotiations, but they soon stalemated. Over the next five days Argentina suffered new loses, including the destruction of fourteen aircraft, and the sinking of two ships. U.N. secretary general Perez de Cuellar presented the British government with a peace proposal that Prime Minister Thatcher promptly rejected.

On May 21 British troops made an amphibious landing on the northern coast of East Falkland. From this beachhead the British infantry drove south to capture several settlements before turning toward Stanley. Over the next three days Argentina lost twenty-six aircraft, and the British lost three ships. The bloodiest fighting of the war occurred on May 28 and 29, when British warships and aircraft bombarded the Argentine positions, killing 250 troops and capturing 1,400. The British lost only 17 men killed in combat. Over the next two days the British surrounded Port Stanley and demanded that the Argentines surrender.

On June 4 the U.N. Security Council presented a new proposal for a cease-fire to the British, but Britain rejected it. Two days later the Versailles Summit supported the British position in the Falk-

lands. The peace negotiations continued on all fronts. Meanwhile, British air attacks continued and two more British ships were hit by Argentine missiles. Finally, on June 14 the Argentine garrison at Port Stanley surrendered, effectively ending the war. General Mario Menendez agreed to end the fighting, and 9,800 Argentine troops put down their weapons.

Britain formally declared an end to hostilities on June 20, and reduced the two-hundred-mile war zone around the Falklands to a Protection Zone (FIPZ) of 150 miles. Britain was still wary of Argentine military activities even though they had won the war.

The undeclared Falklands War lasted seventy-two days, claiming nearly one thousand lives, with Argentina suffering about three-quarters of the losses. The war cost Britain the equivalent of at least US$2 billion—a figure equivalent to nearly US$1 million for each resident of the Falklands. Nevertheless, it secured Margaret Thatcher's re-election as prime minister.

The opposite occurred for the Argentine president. General Leopoldo Galtieri resigned shortly after the surrender. His resignation paved the way for restoration of democracy in Argentina.

Aftermath of the War. After the war the Falklands remained in Britain's hands. The British felt that the war was just because they were defending principles of home rule, and that they stood up to aggression and protected the wishes of the islanders who wanted to remain loyal to the Crown. The islanders themselves were clearly hostile to the idea of becoming Argentinean.

The Argentine government has continued to believe that the Falklands will revert to its control. They base their belief on two important considerations. Since 1982 there have been changes in both British and Falkland Islands leadership. Also, the Argentineans see a parallel in Britain's returning Hong Kong to China in 1997. Argentina remains convinced that British capitulation is a real possibility and that the fight for the Falklands can be won.

Recent discoveries of oil in and around the Falkland Islands may change the picture regarding Argentina's claim of ownership. One look at the impressive change in the new Falkland Islands community shows that the local economy is very healthy. Before the 1982 war, the islanders depended exclusively on livestock and wool production. Nearly all the islands' farms were owned by British-based companies that did not re-invest their profits. The islanders had to work for these companies or leave.

The war transformed the islands' economy. The British government gave the Falklands nearly US$100 million to rebuild the local economy. For the first time, islanders found it easy to get loans. With borrowed money they bought out absentee-owned farms and became their own masters. They also sold fishing licenses worth US$50 million per year. A new port complex was built and provided valuable employment.

Tourism in the Falklands also rose dramatically, and new hotels were constructed to accommodate visitors. These gains alone have been considerable. Meanwhile, test drilling has indicated that large oil and gas reserves surround the Falklands. Experts believe that the Falkland petroleum fields may be almost as large as the North Sea oil fields. If the region does prove to be oil-rich, the potential revenue could amount to billions of dollars. Britain would consequently be more determined than ever to keep the Falklands under its control, and thus less willing to consider Argentina's claims to the islands.

In 1993 the Argentine government reiterated its claim to the Falklands by inserting a statement to that effect into their new constitution. British forces remain stationed on the islands, and warships remained on constant patrol.

Meanwhile, the physical impact of the 1982 war is still felt in the islands. When Argentine forces occupied the islands they laid large numbers of antipersonnel and antitank land mines. They es- tablished 120 mine fields with more than 30,000 active mines. Since the end of the war only 4,300 of these mines have been cleared. The mine fields still cover more than twenty square miles of land, and have all been fenced off and are considered "no-go"-areas.

The Falklanders themselves have expressed mixed feelings about mine clearance for they seem to feel that if the Argentineans help in extracting the mines they will gain access to the islands. Mine clearing is no easy matter, because the peat soil moves as it regenerates, and so the mines actually travel out of their original locations.

Earl R. Andresen

For Further Study

A valuable guide to the Falklands sovereignty issue is Fritz L. Hoffman and Olga Mingo Hoffman's *Sovereignty in Dispute: The Falklands/Malvinas, 1493-1982* (1984). An additional broad perspective is Ian J. Strange, *The Falklands: South Atlantic Islands* (1985). Insights into U.S. interests during the Falklands War can be found in State Department bulletins issued in 1982. A readable book on conflict resolution can be found in Wayne S. Smith's *Toward Resolution? The Falkland/Malvinas Dispute* (1991). An interesting book dealing with British opinions regarding ownership of the Falklands is Cecil Woolf and Jean Moorcroft Wilson's *Authors Take Side on the Falklands* (1982). Information on the Falkland Islands on the Internet is limited. However, it is expected that as the issue of Argentine sovereignty becomes more prominent, more information shall also be available on the World Wide Web.

Peru

Peru is the oldest political entity in South America, and its landscape, a breathtakingly beautiful variety of ecological zones, is perhaps the most bloodied. The coastal plains, mountain plateaus, and Amazon jungle have been fought over by pre-Inca civilizations, Incas, Spaniards, independence fighters, rival political and military factions, foreign armies, drug traffickers, and domestic rebels. Rebellions have especially plagued Peru, fostered in large part by a long-standing, deep inequality between the ruling white minority and the indigenous Indian (Amerind) majority. The ruling white elite, centered in Lima, the capital city, held nearly all the political and economic power until the 1990's, while the various Indian groups living in the central highlands and the rain forest were desperately poor. The government lost control of some mountain regions to rebels during the 1980's, and in 1992 the nation came close to disintegrating. By the late 1990's a fragile stability was reemerging.

Peru, the third-largest South American nation in territory and the fourth-largest in population, occupies a mid-continent section of the Pacific Coast. It is bordered by Ecuador and Colombia to the north, Brazil and Bolivia to the east, and Chile to the south. These borders have caused conflicts with Peru's neighbors throughout its history, during which it has both lost and regained territory.

Peru's land is rich in natural beauty and resources. The country is divided into three parallel regions, running north-south, of differing landscape and climate. The coast is a strip of desert. With little agriculture, its economy is based upon fishing. Because more than twenty major rivers cross it from the highlands and it is lined with bays, the coast is the center of transportation and political power. Among its many seaports is Lima, the national capital, home to about one-quarter of the country's people.

The central highlands are a broad band of the Andes Mountains—which contain the highest mountains in the Western Hemisphere—plateaus, and forested foothills. The highlands have produced the nation's wealth throughout most of its history because of agriculture in its fertile valleys and gold and silver mining and wool production in the mountains.

Profile of Peru

Official name: Republic of Peru
Independent since: 1824
Former colonial ruler: Spain
Location: western South America
Area: 496,223 square miles
Capital: Lima
Population: 25,573,900 (1997 est.)
Official languages: Spanish; Quechua; Aymara
Major religion: Roman Catholicism
Gross domestic product: US$92 billion (1996 est.)
Major exports: copper products; fish meal fodder; zinc products; coffee
Military budget: US$998 million (1996)
Military personnel: 125,000 (1996)

Note: Monetary figures rendered as "US$" are U.S. equivalents of values in local currencies.

Increasing exploitation of natural resources, mainly oil, in Peru's jungle region after the mid-twentieth century gave the long-underdeveloped area greater importance to the economy. The jungle's principle features are the Amazon River and its tributaries and the surrounding rain forest. In addition to being a source of earnings from tourism and oil, the Amazon system is the primary transportation route to northern South America and the Atlantic Ocean.

Peru's population was about 25.5 million in 1997. Although about 45 percent of the residents are indigenous Indian and 37 percent are of mixed Indian and white heritage (mestizos), the 15 percent who are white traditionally controlled the political system and economy. There are also small Asian and African ethnic groups. The racial and economic division between the majority indigenous peoples and descendants of white colonists from Spain has been the source of deep bitterness and frequent violence throughout Peru's long history.

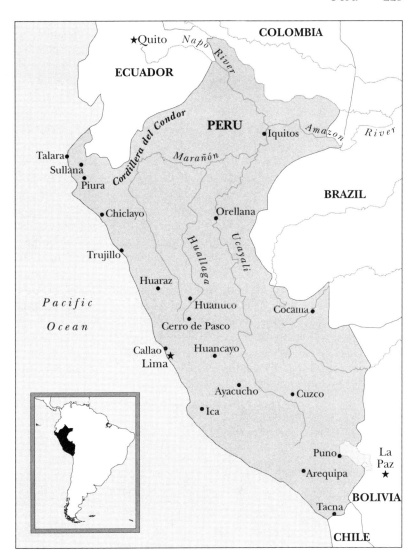

Inca Empire and Spanish Conquest. According to archaeologists, the first villages in South America were built in Peru about 2500 B.C.E. Two thousand years later, region-wide civilizations developed on the coast and in the highlands. The last of these, the Inca Empire, was also the most sophisticated, wealthy, and powerful. Acquiring territory by conquest, it steadily expanded from its base in the city of Cuzco until it controlled the mountains and coast from the modern Ecuador-Colombia border south to mid-Chile early in the sixteenth century.

In 1528 a civil war broke out between Atahualpa and his half-brother Huáscar, both rivals for the title of Inca emperor. In 1532 Atahualpa defeated the forces of Huáscar and was on his way to Cuzco to complete his victory, when he encountered the first band of Spanish conquistadores, led by Francisco Pizarro, at Cajamarca in northern Peru.

Atahualpa expected his army to defeat Pizarro and his 180 followers easily. Curious about the strangers, however, he allowed himself to be lured into a meeting inside the city walls. There, the Incas, frightened by the thirty Spanish horses and the soldiers' muskets, were massacred. Atahualpa was captured. By enlisting the aid of Huáscar's faction, Pizarro later defeated the imperial forces, strangled Atahualpa, captured Cuzco, and installed Manco Cápac II as a puppet emperor. The Spanish held the real power, even though Manco

Cápac successfully rebelled in 1536 and fled to the remote Andes, where he ruled an Inca stronghold at Vilcabamba.

The Spaniards quarreled among themselves for control of Peru and its wealth in gold, silver, and land. Pizarro was assassinated in 1541, and his younger brother and successor was executed in 1548 after he rebelled against royal authority. By then Lima, founded by the elder Pizarro, had become a major port and the capital of the viceroyalty of Peru, from which the Spanish king's personal representative, the viceroy, ruled most of Spanish South America.

During the next 250 years the Spanish retained strict control of the economy and government. Indians were forced to work in mines or on large ranches owned by either Spaniards or their native-born descendants, called Creoles. Constant strenuous labor and diseases introduced by the Spaniards devastated the Indian population, which fell from an estimated 16 to 20 million at the height of the Inca Empire to about 2.7 million in 1570.

Spanish-born colonists continued to hold the highest political and military posts until late in the colonial period. The Peruvian-born Creoles increasingly resented their second-class status. Identifying with them and sharing the resentment was the expanding population of mestizos. Nevertheless, both groups tended to support the king of Spain, upon whose authority the extensive privileges enjoyed by the Creoles depended.

Independence and Border Conflicts. Peru's campaign for independence did not begin until late in the general South American independence movement. Rebel leader José de San Martín captured Lima in 1821, but Spanish royalist forces continued to be a threat until Simón Bolívar defeated them in the Battle of Junín in 1824 and General Antonio José de Sucre finished them off at Ayacucho later in the year. Peru declared its independence from Spain on December 9, 1824.

Bolívar ruled until 1826, when Peruvian Creoles rejected his idea of a confederation with Gran Colombia and Bolivia and started the Republic of

Young members of Shining Path pose for a photographer in the Andes in 1985. (Reuters/Abilio Arroyo/Archive Photos)

Under heavy security, the Peruvian government moved captured Shining Path leader Abimael Guzmán (inside cage) to a maximum security prison in early 1993. To make Guzmán look foolish, the government clothed him in a comical striped prison suit. (AP/Wide World Photos)

Peru instead. Through the early eighteenth century, a succession of generals held the presidency. Military officers almost continuously struggled among themselves for power or engaged in outright civil war. Peruvians did not elect a civilian president until 1872.

Other nations affected Peru's stability as well. A border dispute with Gran Colombia erupted in 1829. In 1836 Bolivian general Andrés Santa Cruz invaded Peru and established the Peru-Bolivia Confederation. Three years later Chile, alarmed at the confederation's power, defeated Santa Cruz's forces and separated Peru from Bolivia again. However, Peru did not achieve political stability until the mid-1840's, when its economy improved dramatically from exports of guano, a natural fertilizer.

From 1859 to 1860 Peru fought a war with Ecuador over land north of the Amazon. Peru won the war and gained a large section of southeastern Ecuador, but the two countries failed to reach a lasting agreement about the exact location of their border. The dispute continued to create tensions until late in the twentieth century, periodically erupting into skirmishes and small wars and dominating the foreign policies of both nations. In 1866 Peruvian forces won another important victory, repelling a naval raid by Spain to capture the Chincha Islands, center of Peru's guano industry.

Another area rich in fertilizers was the coastal Atacama Desert. Parts of the region were claimed by Peru, Bolivia, and Chile, but none exerted unquestioned control. In 1879 the Chilean navy captured Antofagasta from Bolivia and blockaded the

Peru

1438-1524	Inca Empire reaches its greatest extent.
1532	Francisco Pizarro's capture of Inca emperor begins Spanish conquest of South America.
1535	Viceroyalty of Peru, based in Lima, is established; it administers all of Spanish South America except Venezuela.
1824	(Dec. 9) As part of Gran Colombia, Peru wins its independence from Spain.
1829	Peru briefly fights Gran Colombia over disputed border.
1836-1839	Peru and Bolivia join in confederacy.
1859-1860	Peru wins brief border war with Ecuador over disputed Amazon territory.
1866	Peru wins Guano War, defeating Spain's attempt to seize Chincha Islands.
1879-1883	Peru, allied with Bolivia, loses to Chile in War of Pacific.
1914	Coup led by Colonel Oscar Raimundo Benavides inaugurates military's alignment with conservative landowners.
1930	Marxist intellectual José Carlos Mariátegui founds Peruvian Socialist Party.
1941	Peru wins border war with Ecuador, acquiring large tracts of Amazonian jungle and highlands.
1942	(Oct. 29) Peru and Ecuador sign Rio Protocol, an agreement sponsored by United States, Brazil, and Argentina.
1968	General Juan Velasco Alvarado leads coup that makes him president, and he begins sweeping liberal reforms.
1980	After Peru adopts new constitution, civilian Fernando Belaúnde Terry is elected president.
1980	Shining Path rebels launch campaign to win political control by intimidation and violence.
1981	After several days of skirmishes, Peru wins renewed border dispute with Ecuador.
1990	(June 10) Alberto Fujimori is elected president.
1992	(Apr. 5) Fujimori stages "self-coup" by suspending constitution and disbanding congress and members of judiciary.
1992	(Sept. 16) Shining Path leader Abimael Guzmán Reynoso and about two hundred of his commanders are captured, crippling his movement.
1995	Peru and Ecuador fight to stalemate in month-long border war.
1997	Tupac Amaru Revolutionary Movement members occupy Japanese embassy in Lima, where they hold high-ranking political hostages for four months.
1998	(Jan.) U.N. human rights mission inspects Peruvian prisons holding four thousand alleged terrorists.
1998	(Mar.) Ravaged by El Niño-caused flooding, Peru and Ecuador conclude mutual aid pact.
1998	(Aug. 7) Javier Valle Riestra resigns as premier two months after appointment by Fujimori.
1998	(Oct. 26) With help of Argentina, Brazil, Chile, and United States, Ecuador and Peru resolve forty-three-year-old border dispute.
1999	(Jan. 3) President Fujimori appoints Victor Joy Way Rojas premier in major cabinet reshuffle in apparent attempt to strengthen Peru's sagging economy.

coast. Invoking a secret treaty, Bolivia drew Peru into the war. Peru was ill prepared for it. Chilean warships soon disabled one of Peru's two large vessels, and Chile controlled the coast thereafter. The Chilean army invaded Bolivia and southern Peru later the same year. In 1880 the Chileans captured Lima. There were about twenty thousand casualties before the Treaty of Ancón was signed in 1883, bringing peace by ceding most of the desert region to Chile, although the province of Tacna was returned to Peru in 1929.

Twentieth Century Political Conflicts. Peru entered the twentieth century relatively stable and prosperous. In 1914, however, a quarrel erupted over a series of social issues between President Guillermo Billinghurst, a reformer, and Peru's congress, which had a majority of wealthy conservatives. When congress began impeachment proceedings, Billinghurst threatened to close congress—by force if necessary. The armed forces came to the aid of congress. For the next fifty years the armed forces remained closely aligned with the wealthy elite, occasionally seizing power directly to prevent reformers or socialists from holding office.

The father of radical left-wing politics and Marxism in Peru was José Carlos Mariátegui. He founded the Peruvian Socialist Party in 1930 and helped start *indigenismo* (nativism), a movement seeking to return to values from the age of the Incas and to improve the lives of Indians. His ideas influenced subsequent leftist political parties, particularly the Shining Path. In 1932 the government brutally suppressed a revolt in Trujillo by another left-wing party, the American Popular Revolutionary Alliance (APRA). The party went underground, and violence between its members and government forces continued until 1945.

Wars with Ecuador. In 1941 Ecuador's army occupied Zarumilla in an effort to win access to the Marañón and Amazon Rivers, which it had lost in the 1860 war. Peru's army counterattacked, defeated the Ecuadorians in ten days, and advanced deep into Ecuador. The following January, the United States, Brazil, and Argentina negotiated the Protocol of Peace, Friendship, and Boundaries in Rio de Janeiro, Brazil. The treaty favored Peru: It acquired 109,483 square miles of Ecuador's rain forest, an area the size of Tennessee.

Unhappy with the treaty, Ecuador renounced it in 1960. Thereafter, border skirmishes of varying intensity regularly broke out every January near the anniversary of the Rio Protocol. In 1981 the two countries fought a four-day war in the eastern foothills of the Condor Range. A forty-eight-mile section of the border there lay at the heart of the dispute; Ecuador wanted the area because it held the headwaters of the Cenepa River, which flowed into the Marañón River and on to the Amazon.

On January 27, 1995, war again broke out in the Condor Range area when Ecuador captured Peruvian border posts. With mixed success Peru tried to retake the posts with infantry attacks backed by helicopter gunships and mortar barrages. To slow the Peruvians, Ecuador mined roads connecting the countries. Peruvian and Ecuadorian jets bombed each other's strongholds along the border as about ten thousand troops moved into the battle areas and refugees crowded the roads to escape the fighting. Each side accused the other of starting the war in order to increase the popularity of its president or to justify spending money on its armed forces.

Diplomats from the United States, Brazil, Chile, and Argentina met to negotiate a cease-fire with Ecuadorian and Peruvian officials in Rio de Janeiro on February 2. On February 14 both sides signed a cease-fire agreement, but eight days later the truce was broken by the heaviest fighting of the war. A second cease-fire agreement, signed on March 1, succeeded. Military observers from the mediating nations entered the battle zones to make sure the truce held. Together Peru and Ecuador suffered seventy-eight dead and more than two hundred wounded. Peru lost five helicopters and three jet aircraft but was less harmed economically and strategically than Ecuador.

In January, 1996, the two armies again exchanged gunfire after Ecuador bought Israeli-built fighter-bomber jets, which angered Peru. There were no casualties, and tensions eased afterward. In January, 1998, the countries pledged mutual aid to recover from devastating storms caused by a severe El Niño weather system.

On October 26 the newly elected president of Ecuador, Jamil Mahaud, and Peru's President Alberto Fujimori signed a peace treaty in Brasília, Brazil. The treaty precisely defined their border. It also gave Ecuador a small plot of Peru's territory on which to build a war monument and the right to open two ports with access to the Amazon. The

Using a map of Peru and Ecuador, President Alberto Fujimori explains the situation along the two nations' border areas in August, 1998. (AP/Wide World Photos)

verts underwent spiritual ecstasy in the name of gods who, it was promised, would drive out all Christians. The movement, and the Inca stronghold at Vilcabamba, threatened Spanish authority until the city was finally captured in 1572 and the last ruler and spiritual head of the Incas, Túpac Amaru, was executed.

A series of native rebellions took place in the late eighteenth century, culminating in an uprising led by a wealthy mestizo, José Gabriel Condorcanqui, who called himself Túpac Amaru II. It lasted two years. Its army of thousands of Indians and a few Creoles controlled the southern plateau around Cuzco and Lake Titicaca before the Spanish caught and executed Condorcanqui and other leaders.

Throughout its history, Peru was never long without coups and guerrilla movements. In 1968 a reform-minded mestizo army general, Juan Velasco Alvarado, seized power, ending more than fifty years of military support for the conservative elite. For the next ten years the military-controlled government tried to improve conditions for the poor by increasing peasant ownership of land, improving wages, and protecting workers.

Quechua, the largest Indian language, was made an official national language along with Spanish to increase Indian loyalty to the nation. However, by the time Peru composed a new constitution and elected Fernando Belaúnde to the presidency in 1980, a worldwide recession, inflation, and large-scale borrowing by the government had gutted the economy, and the average Peruvian was even poorer. As late as 1992, many Peruvians earned less in one year than most Americans earned in one week.

During the 1980's Túpac Amaru inspired yet another group of rebels, the Túpac Amaru Revolutionary Movement (MRTA). It wanted to drive all foreign influences out of Peru, especially those

two countries supplemented the treaty with plans to share electrical grids and oil pipelines.

Rebellions and Coups. The two presidents reflected the profound political changes in the region during the 1990's. President Mahaud, of Middle Eastern heritage, and President Fujimori, the son of Japanese immigrants, were far from typical politicians. Fujimori's election in 1990 and reelection in 1995 showed that the traditional white elite no longer monopolized power in Peru. Yet the greater access to power by nonwhites came too late to prevent the gap between the privileged rich and the desperate poor from inciting violent rebellion.

In fact, Peru has had a long history of large-scale rebellions, beginning with Emperor Manco Cápac II. During the 1560's a cult called Taki Onqoy attempted to revive the Inca religion. Its con-

from Europe and the United States. It battled both government forces and other rebel groups for control of the highlands, unsuccessfully for the most part. The MRTA grabbed world headlines in 1997 by occupying the Japanese embassy in Lima and holding seventy-two hostages. The guerrillas demanded the release of its members who had been imprisoned. After a four-month standoff, Peruvian special forces stormed the embassy, killed all the guerrillas, and rescued all but one hostage.

The Shining Path. The most famous and feared Peruvian guerrilla organization during modern times was Shining Path, a radical offshoot of the Peruvian Communist Party. It drew its inspiration from the writings of Mariátegui, Karl Marx, and the founder of the Chinese Communist Party, Mao Zedong. Led by a philosophy professor in Ayacucho, Abimael Guzmán Reynoso, Shining Path recruited many Quechua-speaking peasants in the Andes, teaching them to look with pride to their fierce Inca ancestors.

Shining Path taught that the Inca reliance on communal work could be the foundation for social equality based upon Marxist-Maoist principles. However, many of the leaders, such as Guzmán, were middle-class intellectuals who were frustrated with social and economic injustice and hated the widespread corruption in the government.

Although begun in 1970, Shining Path did not gain public notice until 1980 when it forcibly prevented people from voting in a mountain village. Violence began soon after, spreading dramatically through the southern highlands in 1983. Through propaganda, assassination of government officials, skirmishes with the Peruvian army, and bombings, Shining Path eventually took control of large areas. President Belaúnde eventually gave control of twenty-seven provinces to the military in order to fight the guerrillas, but military authority was weak or nonexistent outside the cities.

Shining Path created a "state within a state," or an insurgent state, which it financed by bank robberies, extortion, and taxes imposed on the growing of coca or the manufacture of cocaine. More than thirty thousand people are believed to have died in the struggle, and the violence cost Peru more than US$20 billion between 1980 and 1990 alone. Moreover, hundreds of thousands of Andean residents fled to Lima, which was already swelled by the rural poor from other areas seeking jobs. Shining Path began a campaign of bombings and assassination in the capital as well.

Although it had only about five thousand members, by 1992 Shining Path was so successful that Peru's government was in danger of collapsing. In a drastic, unorthodox move, President Alberto Fujimori dissolved the national legislature and suspended the high courts, both thought to be corrupt or indecisive. In part he staged this "self-coup" to reform the economy, but it also helped him battle Shining Path more efficiently.

Later in 1992, a special police unit captured Guzmán in Lima, along with two hundred other commanders. In prison Guzmán renounced violence and told his followers to stop fighting. These events crippled Shining Path, but one splinter group denounced Guzmán as a traitor and continued the violence. In July, 1995, for instance, sixteen soldiers and twenty rebels died in a battle in the Huallaga Valley, a rebel stronghold. In 1996 another major leader, Elizabeth Cardenas Huayta, was also captured, and Shining Path's influence declined sharply.

Drug Lords. After mid-1970, drug traffickers, sometimes protected by Shining Path units or the Peruvian military, became an increasing source of conflict, principally in the Upper Huallaga Valley in the west-central highlands. Peru became the world's leading producer of raw cocaine. Drug lords, many headquartered in Colombia, exported the cocaine for processing and smuggling into the United States and Europe, the biggest markets. To maintain the supply, the traffickers bribed, terrorized, or killed local government officials.

The United States gave Peru millions of dollars to destroy coca plants, from which cocaine comes. It also sent advisers to train special paramilitary antidrug units, who often fell into firefights with traffickers and rebels. The efforts were largely unsuccessful. Cocaine production remained a major export industry, adding billions of dollars to the economy yearly.

Fighting internal and external enemies wounded Peru during the 1980's and 1990's. It spent nearly 2 percent of its gross domestic product on the military, which strained the economy. Meanwhile, the loss of life, political chaos, human rights abuses, and terror damaged the nation psychologically.

Roger Smith

For Further Study

Edwin Williamson's *The Penguin History of Latin America* (1992) relates the early history of Peru against the background of the Spanish Conquest of the South American continent in detail; passages about modern Peruvian history and culture are sketchy. In *Peru: A Guide to the People, Politics, and Culture* (1998), Jane Holligan de Díaz-Límaco summarizes the ancient and modern history of Peru, including sections about Shining Path and other revolutionary groups.

Mark Thurner examines the political and guerrilla groups among the people of the central highlands in *From Two Republics to One Divided: Contradictions of Postcolonial Nationmaking in Andean Peru* (1997). *Death in the Andes* (1996) is an engrossing fictional account of life among Andean workers and the tactics of Shining Path by Peru's most celebrated writer, Mario Vargas Llosa. Well-written essays about Peru's ancient civilizations, Spanish Conquest, republican revolution, modern politics, Shining Path, cocaine industry, economy, neoliberalism, insurgency wars, and culture appear in *The Peru Reader* (1995), edited by Orin Starn, Carlos Iván Degregori, and Robin Kirk.

John Simpson, a British Broadcasting Corporation (BBC) journalist, gives a dramatic first-person account of drug traffickers and rebels in his *In the Forests of the Night: Encounters with Terrorism, Drug-Running, and Military Oppressions* (1993). Simon Strong explains the military and social policies of Shining Path guerrillas, as well as the Peruvian government's response, in *Shining Path: Terror and Revolution in Peru* (1992). *Peru: A Country Study* (1993) was prepared by the Federal Research Division of the Library of Congress for the Department of the Army and provides an abundance of information about Peruvian history, economy, and politics, accompanied by many photographs.

Several Web sites provide information for travels, and the Library of Congress posts information from *Peru: A Country Study* at http://lcweb2.loc.gov/frd/cs/petoc/html. Two useful sources for general information and current news are http://www.citi.net/ home/richardg/peru1.html and http://ekeko.rcp.net.pe (the Peru Home Page).

Suriname

The tiny South American nation of Suriname received its independence from the Netherlands in 1975. Since then, its struggle to develop a healthy democracy, while trying to establish its identity in the world, has led to recurring economic and political problems. After independence many skilled Surinamers and teachers moved to the Netherlands, where they felt their futures would be more secure. As a result, Suriname's industries and major operations were less efficiently run, and the nation's economy struggled. Because of teacher shortages, the nation's once-high literacy rate declined. The challenge of maintaining harmony among its diverse population that includes Africans, American Indians (Amerinds), East Indians, Javanese, Chinese, Europeans, and Middle Easterners poses numerous difficulties, since each group wants representation in the government. Pressure from different ethnic groups for improved living and economic conditions has led to frequent political unrest and periodic skirmishes among civilian-led governments and military groups for control of the country.

Located on the northern coast of South America, Suriname is bordered on the east by French Guiana, on the north by the Atlantic Ocean, on the west by Guyana, and on the south by the giant nation of Brazil. Suriname's terrain consists of a northern swampy coastal plain, a central plateau region with broad savannas and forested areas, and a densely forested, mountainous region in the south. The latter region isolates the ethnic groups living in the interior from those living along the coast, thereby enhancing ethnic friction in the country as a whole. Most Surinamers live in the narrow, northern coastal plain, where Paramaribo, the country's capital, largest city, and chief seaport, is also located.

There was no active hostility between Suriname and other countries in the late 1990's. However, Suriname has been involved in continuing border disputes with both French Guiana and Guyana.

People of Suriname. Although Suriname is home to less than a half million people, its population is one of the most ethnically varied in the world. Moreover, each ethnic group preserves its own culture. The official language of Suriname is Dutch, but the numerous languages spoken there reflect the diversity of ethnic backgrounds. Most Surinamers also speak

Profile of Suriname

Official name: Republic of Suriname
Independent since: 1975
Former colonial ruler: Netherlands
Location: northeastern coast of South America
Area: 63,039 square miles
Capital: Paramaribo
Population: 424,600 (1997 est.)
Official language: Dutch
Major religions: Hinduism; Roman Catholicism; Protestantism; Islam
Gross domestic product: US$1.4 billion (1996 est.)
Major exports: aluminum; rice; shrimp
Military budget: US$14 million (1997)
Military personnel: 1,800 (1997)

Note: Monetary figures rendered as "US$" are U.S. equivalents of values in local currencies.

Ethnic Composition of Suriname

Ethnicity	Percentage of Population
Hindustani	37.0
Creole	31.0
Javanese	15.3
Maroon	10.3
Amerindian	2.6
other	3.8

Sranang Tongo (Surinamese), a local language that includes elements of English, Dutch, Spanish, Portuguese, and several African languages.

Approximately a third of Suriname's people are Creoles, a people of mixed African, European, and American Indian descent. Another third are Hindustanis, descendants of people from India. The next two largest groups, the Javanese and so-called Bush Negroes, or Maroons, constitute a quarter of the population.

Many Surinamese organizations, including political parties, tend to follow ethnic lines, which sometimes leads to friction and disputes among ethnic groups. For example, the National Party of Suriname finds its support among the Creoles, the Progressive Reform Party from among the Hindustani population, and the Indonesian Peasant's Party from the Javanese. The upper classes of all ethnic backgrounds tend to mix together freely. However, among other classes, social relations tend to remain within ethnic groups.

Historical Background. Before Christopher Columbus sighted the coast of present-day Suriname, the area was inhabited by Arawak, Carib, and Warrau Indians. Spain officially claimed the region in 1593, but gave it little attention. The Portuguese also explored the area in the late 1500's, while the Dutch began settling there in 1616. In 1651 the British built the first permanent European settlement in what is now Suriname. They established cotton and sugar cane plantations, which were worked by slaves imported from Africa.

Suriname became a Dutch colony, known as Dutch Guiana, in 1667. However, because of Dutch neglect, violent conflicts among European settlers and local peoples, and frequent uprisings by the imported slave population, Dutch Guiana did not thrive. The slaves were often treated with extraordinary cruelty. Many slaves fled to the interior, where they maintained a West African culture and established five major "Bush Negro" societies that are still in existence.

In 1863 the Dutch abolished slavery and brought laborers from India and Indonesia—primarily from the island of Java—to work the plantations. As labor costs rose, plantations steadily declined in the early 1900's. As a consequence, many people moved to urban areas along the northern coast.

After World War I, Suriname's economy was transformed when an American firm, the Aluminum Company of America (ALCOA), began exploiting aluminum ore (bauxite) deposits in the eastern part of Suriname. During World War II, more than 75 percent of aluminum ore imports into the United States came from Suriname. As late as 1998, mining sites at Moengo and Paranam were estimated still to have another ten to fifteen years of bauxite reserves remaining. Moreover, other bauxite reserves that have been found in Suriname remained to be developed.

Since World War II, the poorer Hindustanis have become increasingly insistent in their demands for a greater share of Suriname's resources, and the rivalry between them and the Creoles has often become bitter.

Independence and the Struggle for Democracy. In 1951 Suriname began acquiring a growing measure of independence from the Netherlands. It became a self-governing territory in December, 1954. During the 1970's, the Creoles led a movement for full independence, but the Hindustanis opposed this effort. Their opposing views led to many conflicts between the two groups.

The Netherlands finally yielded and gave Suriname its independence on November 25, 1975. Not trusting the fate of an independent Suriname, thousands of prominent Surinamers began emigrating to the Netherlands for security and economic stability. The emigration caused a shortage of skilled labor that greatly restricted economic development in Suriname. It also created a shortage of qualified teachers, which caused the once high literacy rate of Suriname to decline.

Meanwhile, the new nation adopted a democratic form of government, in which the people elected a parliament. Creole leader Henck Arron became the first prime minister. He was again elected in 1977. However, declining economic conditions led to the overthrow of Arron's government by a band of army men in February, 1980. The rebels were led by Lieutenant Colonel Desi Bouterse.

Bouterse's coup was welcomed by the majority of the population. Most people expected that the new government installed by the army would end corruption and improve the standard of living in Suriname. However, the military-dominated government suspended the constitution, dissolved the parliament, and formed a regime which ruled by decree. Throughout 1982 pressure grew for a return to civilian rule. In response, military authorities arrested and killed fifteen prominent opposition leaders, including journalists, lawyers, and trade union leaders.

Following the murders, the Netherlands and the United States suspended cooperation with Suriname. The Bouterse regime increasingly followed an erratic political course, including restricting the press and limiting the rights of the citizens. With the suspension of economic aid from the Netherlands and the United States, economic decline spiraled, the inflation rate started to rise, and increasing pressure built up for political change. In 1982 a democratic opposition movement was brutally suppressed by Bouterse. Several guerrilla wars broke out during the 1980's, further disrupting the nation's economy.

In July, 1986, Maroons led by former soldier Ronnie Brunswijk began attacking economic targets in the country's interior. The Surinamese army retaliated by ravaging villages and killing suspected supporters of Brunswijk. Thousands of Maroons fled to nearby French Guiana.

In 1987 Bouterse finally agreed to free elections,

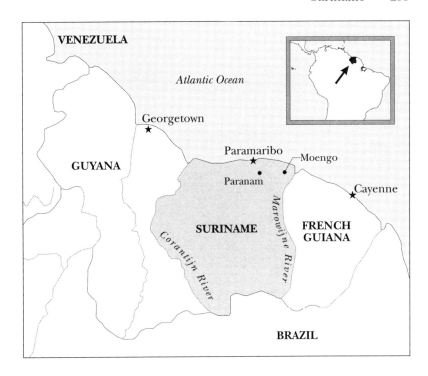

a new constitution, and a civilian government. The constitution established a fifty-one member national assembly with the power to select the president. In 1988 Ramsewak Shankar, a former agriculture minister, was elected president by the assembly. Former prime minister Henck Arron became vice-president. Bouterse, however, continued to hold real power, and he ousted the Shankar government in December, 1990.

Faced with mounting pressure from the United States and other nations, as well as the Organization of American States (OAS) and other international organizations, the government held new elections in 1991 that brought victory to a coalition of the principal Creole, Hindustani, and Javanese political parties. Ronald Venetiaan, the Creole choice, was elected president by the national assembly and Jules Ajodhia vice-president. The new coalition government announced it would change the constitution to end the political role of the army.

Stability Under Civilian Presidents. After the Venetiaan government negotiated a peace treaty with the Maroons and the Amerind insurgents in August, 1992, the major guerrilla groups announced they were disbanding. Bouterse himself resigned as head of the military. Arthy Gorre re-

President Ronald Venetiaan is mobbed by supporters during Suriname's May, 1996, elections, which were won by the party of Jules Wijdenbosch, whom the national assembly elected president in September. (AP/Wide World Photos)

placed Bouterse as commander of the military forces. He brought the armed forces under the control of the civilian government. Meanwhile, Suriname and the Netherlands signed a treaty restoring Dutch economic aid, and economic reforms instituted by President Venetiaan eventually helped curb inflation and unify the official and unofficial monetary exchange rates.

Despite these successes, the governing coalition lost support and failed to retain control of the government in the subsequent round of national elections. This charge primarily came about when many Hindustanis encouraged several political parties to join forces to oust Creole-supported President Venetiaan. In September, 1996, Jules Wijdenbosch was elected president of Suriname by the national assembly. Pretaapnarian Radhakishun became vice-president.

Although friction persists among Suriname's diverse ethnic groups, for the most part they are living harmoniously together while preserving their own languages, religions, and cultural traditions in the face of modernization. The country's interior remains remote and sparsely populated by Maroons and Amerinds, but a few political leaders from these groups have emerged on the national scene.

The Wijdenbosch government has attempted to broaden its economic base, establish better contacts with other nations and international financial institutions, and reduce its dependence on Dutch assistance. Suriname is embarking on development projects in petroleum production, gold exploration and exploitation, as well as extensive development of a tropical hardwoods industry and possible diamond mining. The will and determination of all the Surinamers to build their country on the base of national unity and cooperation under the leadership of a democratic government will determine the future success of Suriname.

Alvin K. Benson

For Further Study

Readable works for young people on Suriname's people, history, government, resources, and the transition to democracy are Sandra Stotsky's *Suriname* (1997), as well as *Suriname* (1995), by Carolyn S. Lieberg.

A more scholarly treatment of these same topics can be found in Rosemarijn Hoefte's *Suriname* (1990). Insights into Suriname's politics, government, racial relations, and conflicts associated with restoring its democracy are well documented in Edward M. Dew's *The Trouble in Suriname, 1975-1993* (1994). Nigel Sizer and Richard Rice discuss Suriname's economic struggles and conditions, along with its policies on natural resources, in *Backs to the Wall in Suriname* (1995).

Surinam Resources of Suriname has hired a New Zealand company to develop an Internet site

Suriname

1498	Christopher Columbus sights Suriname coast during his third voyage of discovery.
1621	Holland establishes small trading settlement in Suriname.
1651	British establish first permanent European settlement.
1667	Holland takes Suriname from England.
1863	Holland abolishes slavery in Suriname.
1914-1918	World War I stimulates aluminum ore mining in Suriname.
1948	Spelling of "Surinam" is officially changed to "Suriname."
1949	All Surinamese residents are allowed to participate in politics.
1954	(Dec.) Suriname is granted self-government.
1975-1980	One-third of Surname's people emigrate to Netherlands.
1975	(Nov. 25) Full independence is granted to Suriname, with civilian government under Prime Minister Henck Arron.
1980	(Feb.) Army under Desi Bouterse overthrows civilian government.
1982	Bouterse government kills fifteen prominent opposition leaders.
1982-1987	Bouterse survives several unsuccessful coup attempts.
1986	(July) Maroon revolt begins in interior.
1987	New constitution and civilian government are established.
1990	Military again takes over government.
1991	Ronald Venetiaan is elected president and makes positive economic reforms.
1992	Peace agreement is reached between government and various guerrilla bands.
1992	Netherlands restores economic aid to Suriname.
1993	Military is brought under civilian government control.
1996	(Sept.) Jules Wijdenbosch is elected president.

for general information about the country (see http//www.surinam.net). The U.S. State Department has compiled a profile of Suriname's geography, people, government, economy, history, and foreign relations (http//www.state.gov/www/background_notes/suriname). An excellent summary of Suriname's history by Peter Troon, a former Surinamer living in the Netherlands, is available (http//www.sr.net/srnet/InfoSurinam/history.html). Important statistics about Suriname, along with a map, the flag, and outlined sketches of the geography, people, government, economy, natural resources, transportation, communications, and military defense are maintained by the U.S. Central Intelligence Agency (http//www.infoseek.com/suriname).

World Conflicts
and
Confrontations

List of Articles by Types of Conflict

This list of major themes running through the volumes identifies essays most pertinent to each theme. Additional references to these and related themes can be found in the general index.

Border Conflicts
Introduction
Afghanistan
Asia
Bulgaria
Central America
Central Asian Republics
Ecuador
El Salvador and Honduras
Eritrea
Ethiopia
Iran
Mali
Morocco
Pakistan
Palestine
Peru
Russia
South Africa
South America
Tibet
Vietnam

Civilizational Conflicts
Introduction
Bosnia
Central Asian Republics
China
Israel
Pakistan
Palestine
Russia
Turkey
Ukraine

Crime and Corruption
Introduction
Afghanistan
Africa
Baltic Republics

Caribbean
China
Colombia
Georgia
Ghana
Italy
Japan
Kenya
Mexico
Nicaragua
Nigeria
Panama
Russia
South Africa
South America
United States

Drug Trafficking
Introduction
Afghanistan
Caribbean
Central America
Central Asian Republics
Colombia
Iran
Mexico
Panama
Peru
South America
Turkey
United States

Economic Conflicts
Introduction
Africa
Baltic Republics
Bulgaria
Burkina Faso
Cambodia
Cameroon

Central Asian Republics
China
Colombia
Comoros
Cuba
Ecuador
Egypt
El Salvador and Honduras
Indonesia
Iraq
Korea
Liberia
Mali
Mexico
Pakistan
Panama
Romania
Russia
South Africa
South America
Tanzania
Ukraine

Environmental Problems
Introduction
Bhutan
Brazil
Central America
Chad
Egypt
Kenya
Niger
North America
Pacific Islands
Yemen

Ethnic and Linguistic Conflicts
Introduction
Afghanistan
Africa

List of Articles by Types of Conflict

Current, Former, and Variant Names of Countries and Regions

Words in **boldface** are names used in article titles in this reference set. The volume numbers in which the articles appear are in parentheses.

Abyssinia → **Ethiopia** (2)
Africa (2)
Albania (4)
Algeria (2)
Anglo-Egyptian Sudan → **Sudan** (2)
Angola (2)
Argentina (1)
Armenia and Azerbaijan (4)
Asia (3)
Bahrain (3)
Baltic Republics (4)
Bangladesh (3)
Basutoland → **Lesotho** (2)
Belgian Congo → **Congo (Kinshasa)** (2)
Belgium (4)
Bhutan (3)
Bosnia Herzegovina → **Bosnia** (4)
Brazil (1)
British Somaliland → **Somalia** (2)
British East Africa → **Kenya** (2)
Buganda (2)
Bulgaria (4)
Burkina Faso (2)
Burkina Faso → **Upper Volta** (2)
Burma → **Myanmar** (3)
Burundi (2)
Cambodia (3)
Cameroon (2)
Canada (1)
Canada → **Quebec** (1)
Caribbean (1)
Catalonia → **Spain** (4)
Central America (1)
Central and Eastern Europe and Former Soviet Republics (4)
Central Asian Republics (4)
Ceylon → **Sri Lanka** (3)
Chad (2)

Chechnya → **Russia** (4)
Chiapas → **Mexico** (1)
China (3)
China, Republic of → **Taiwan** (3)
Colombia (1)
Communist bloc → **Central and Eastern Europe and Former Soviet Republics** (4)
Comoros (2)
Congo (Brazzaville) (2)
Congo (Kinshasa) (2)
Congo (Zaire) → **Congo (Kinshasa)** (2)
Congo Free State → **Congo (Kinshasa)** (2)
Corsica → **France** (4)
Croatia (4)
Cuba (1)
Cyprus (4)
Dutch East Indies → **Indonesia** (3)
Dutch Guiana → **Suriname** (1)
East Germany → **Germany** (4)
East Pakistan → **Bangladesh** (3)
Ecuador (1)
Egypt (2)
El Salvador and Honduras (1)
England → **Great Britain** (4)
Eritrea (2)
Estonia → **Baltic Republics** (4)
Ethiopia (2)
Falkland Islands (1)
Falklands Islands → **Argentina** (1)
Federation of Rhodesia and Nyasaland → **Zambia** (2); **Zimbabwe** (2)
Fiji (3)
Flanders → **Belgium** (4)
Former Yugoslav Republic of Macedonia → **Macedonia** (4)
Formosa → **Taiwan** (3)
France (4)
French Congo → **Congo (Brazzaville)** (2)

French Somaliland → **Somalia** (2)
French Sudan → **Mali** (2)
Gambia (2)
Georgia (4)
German Democratic Republic → **East Germany** (4)
German East Africa → **Tanzania** (2)
German Federal Republic → **West Germany** (4)
Germany (4)
Ghana (2)
Gold Coast → **Ghana** (2)
Great Britain (4)
Guatemala (1)
Haiti (1)
Hispaniola → **Haiti** (1)
Honduras → El Salvador and Honduras (1)
Hong Kong → **China** (3)
India (3)
Indonesia (3)
Iran (3)
Iraq (3)
Israel (3)
Italian East Africa → **Eritrea** (2)
Italian Somaliland → **Somalia** (2)
Italy (4)
Jamaica (1)
Kampuchea → **Cambodia** (3)
Kazakhstan → **Central Asian Republics** (4)
Kenya (2)
Khmer Republic → **Cambodia** (3)
Korea (3)
Kosovo → **Albania** (4); **Yugoslavia** (4)
Kuwait (3)
Kyrgyzstan → **Central Asian Republics** (4)
Latin America → **Caribbean; Central America; South America Lebanon** (3)
Latvia → **Baltic Republics** (4)
Lesotho (2)
Liberia (2)
Libya (2)
Lithuania → **Baltic Republics** (4)
Macedonia (4)
Malaya → **Malaysia** (3)
Malaysia (3)
Mali (2)
Mali Federation → **Mali** (2)
Malvinas, Las Islas → **Falkland Islands** (1)
Mexico (1)
Middle Congo → **Congo (Brazzaville)** (2)
Middle East (3)

Moldova (4)
Montenegro → **Yugoslavia** (4)
Morocco (2)
Mozambique (2)
Myanmar (3)
Nazi Germany → **Germany** (4)
Nicaragua (1)
Niger (2)
Nigeria (2)
North America (1)
North Korea → **Korea** (3)
North Yemen → **Yemen** (3)
Northern Ireland (4)
Northern Rhodesia → **Zambia** (2)
Ottoman Empire → **Turkey** (3)
Pacific Islands (3)
Pakistan (3)
Palestine (3)
Panama (1)
Persia → **Iran** (3)
Peru (1)
Philippines (3)
Portuguese East Africa → **Mozambique** (2)
Prussia → **Germany** (4)
Puerto Rico (1)
Rhodesia → **Zimbabwe** (2)
Romania (4)
Ruanda-Urundi → **Burundi** (2); **Rwanda** (2)
Rumania → **Romania** (4)
Russia (4)
Rwanda (2)
Sainte Domingue → **Haiti** (1)
Salvador, El → El Salvador (1)
Saudi Arabia (3)
Scotland → **Great Britain** (4)
Senegambia → **Gambia** (2)
Serbia → **Yugoslavia** (4)
Sierra Leone (2)
Slovak Republic → **Slovakia** (4)
Slovakia (4)
Somalia (2)
Somaliland → **Somalia** (2)
South Africa (2)
South America (1)
South Korea → **Korea** (3)
South Yemen → **Yemen** (3)
Southern Rhodesia → **Zimbabwe** (2)
Soviet Union → **Russia** (4)
Spain (4)
Spanish Sahara → **Western Sahara** (2)

Sri Lanka (3)
Sudan (2)
Suriname (1)
Syria (3)
Taiwan (3)
Tajikistan → **Central Asian Republics** (4)
Tanganyika → **Tanzania** (2)
Tanzania (2)
Tibet (3)
Trinidad and Tobago (1)
Turkey (3)
Turkmenistan → **Central Asian Republics** (4)
U.S.S.R → **Soviet Union** (4)
Uganda (2)
Ukraine (4)
Ulster → **Northern Ireland** (4)
Union of South Africa → **South Africa** (2)
Union of Soviet Socialist Republics → **Soviet Union** (4)

United Arab Republic → **Egypt** (2)
United Kingdom → **Great Britain** (4)
United States (1)
Uzbekistan → **Central Asian Republics** (4)
Vardar Macedonia → **Macedonia** (4)
Vietnam (3)
Wales → **Great Britain** (4)
Wallonia → **Belgium** (4)
West Germany → **Germany** (4)
West Indies → **Caribbean** (1)
Western Europe (4)
Western Sahara (2)
Yemen (3)
Yugoslavia (4)
Zaire → **Congo (Kinshasa)** (2)
Zambia (2)
Zanzibar → **Tanzania** (2)
Zimbabwe (2)

Index

This index lists the most important personal names, political bodies, places, and other subjects discussed in the essays. Most entries stand alone, but readers will find many subjects listed under broader headings, such as the names of countries and regions. Readers should note that because of the great variety of languages and cultures from which many names appearing in this set come, allowances should be made for variations in both spellings and forms. For example, Western conventions in differentiating between surnames and given names are not followed in all cultures. A Chinese name such as *Mao Zedong*, for instance, will be found below under *Mao*, not *Zedong*. Moreover, name conventions in many cultures are constantly evolving, making it difficult to know precisely where to look for a name. Many cross-references are provided below to assist readers, but it may be necessary to look in more than one place for some names.

A page range in **boldface** type indicates an entire entry devoted to that topic; *italicized* pages indicate photographs.

American Samoa, 794

Amerinds, 1, 11-12, 18; in Central America, 112-115; in Cuba, 70; in Ecuador, 205-207, 211-212; in El Salvador, 121-122; in Guatemala, 116, 130, 132-133, 138; in Mexico, 32, 34, 37; in Nicaragua, 141; in North America, 11, 18; in Panama, 150; in Peru, 222-224, 227-228; in South America, 160, 162-164, 166, 168, 172; in Suriname, 231-234; in United States, 48, 51

Amin, Hafizullah, 526

Amin, Idi, 1, 478, *483*; and Libya, 385, 484

Amnesty International, 5; and Brazil, 190; and Iran, 708; and Libya, 389; and Myanmar, 629; and Nepal, 543, 545; and Northern Ireland, 881-882; and Romania, 1014

Amr Ibn Al-As, 320

Anatolia, 780-781

Anaya, Jorge, 218

ANC. *See* African National Congress (South Africa)

Andes Mountains, 195

Andorra, 894

Andreotti, Giulio, 871

Angkor Wat, 546-547, 551

Anglo-American Caribbean Commission, 106

Anglo-Burman Wars, 622. *See also* Myanmar

Anglo-Egyptian Condominium. *See* Sudan

Angola, **258-265**; army, 260-261, 265; banditry, 263; and Berlin Conference, 258; civil war, 315, 498; and Cold War, 259; communism, 259; and Congo (Kinshasa), 263, 265, 306, 315-316; corruption, 247; and Cuba, 258-260; election fraud, 273; elections, 260-261; ethnic groups, 258; independence, 242; literacy, 258; and mercenaries, 263; oil, 259, 262, 265; and Organization of African Unity, 259; and South Africa, 258-260, 262, 265, 456; and South West Africa People's Organization, 259; and Soviet Union, 258-259; U.N. missions in, 5; U.N. peacekeeping force, 3-4; and United Nations, 260-263, 265, 273; and Zambia, 497-498

Angola, Democratic People's Republic of, 259

Anguilla, 65

Anjouan, attempted secession from Comoros, 296-297

Ankrah, Joseph, 352

Annan, Kofi, in Angola, *263*; and Cyprus, 833; in Ethiopia, *342*; in Rwanda, *431*; and Western Sahara, *491*

Anti-Semitism, 688-689; in Argentina, 168, 182; in Europe, 727-728; in France, 689, 728; in Germany, 726, 851-852; in Romania, 1016. *See also* Jews

Antigua, independence, 65

Antigua and Barbuda, 107; Barbudan secessionism, 67

Antilles Islands, 60-61

Antonescu, Ion, 1016

Aozou Strip, 287, 289-290, 385

Apartheid, 7, 456, 459, 461, 464; institutional basis of, 459-460; legacy of, 459-461, 463-464; opposition to, 454-457, 459, 461; and South African Police, 460

Aquino, Benigno, 645; assassination of, 648

Aquino, Corazon, 646, 648

Arab Federation and Lebanon, 747

Arab League, 3; establishment of, 771; and Iraq, 717, 722; and Kuwait, 737; and Lebanon, 747; and Saudi Arabia, 766; and Syria, 771

Arafat, Yasir, 4, 694, 697, 734, 748, 752, *756*, 758-759, 894; and guerrilla warfare, 758; in Lebanon, 734; in Morocco, *399*; in Spain, *894*; negotiations with Israel, 734; and Palestine Liberation Organization, 691, 730, 750; and Palestinian Authority, 734, 759; strategy of, 758

Aral Sea, 964, 970

Arawaks; in Caribbean, 61; in Haiti, 83; in Hispaniola, 83; in Jamaica, 93; in Suriname, 232; in Trinidad and Tobago, 104

Arbenz, Jacobo, 131, 134, 142; overthrow of, 131

Ardanza, Jose Antonio, 891

Ardito Barletta Vallarina, Nicolás, 153; resignation of, 155

Arellano, López, 123

Argentina, **174-183**; anti-Semitism, 168, 182; and Brazil, 165; and Chile, 2, 174-175; corruption charges, 181; currency, 181; death squads, 175, 182; democratization, 220; disappearances, 171, 175, 178, 180, 218; economic advances, 182; elections, 175, 178, 181; human rights, 180; independence, 215; inflation, 175, 181-182, 218; international grievances against, 180; and International Monetary Fund, 181; Jewish immigration, 182; and MERCOSUR, 182; military government, 175-178, 180, 182; Mothers of the Plaza de Mayo, 175, 180; National Genetic Data Bank, 180. *See also* Falklands Islands; Falklands War

Sudan, 472; in Uganda, 483-486; in Yugoslavia, 903, 905, 1055

Hume, John, 884

Hun Sen, *549*, 553

Hungary, 899-900, 902, 915, 943, 1034, 1037-1038; and Austria, 848; communism, 849; and Croatia, 977, 981; and North Atlantic Treaty Organization, 937; and Romania, 1011-1012, 1014; Slovaks in, 1037; Soviet troops in, 901-902

Hunt, Rex, 218

Huntington, Samuel, 9

Husák, Gustav, 904

Hussein (Jordan), 748

Hussein, Saddam, 10, 696, 711, 713, 717-719, *718*, 721-722, 724, 734, 739, 741, 775; defection of sons-in-law, 724; execution of political enemies, 720; and Ruhollah Khomeini, 721; reelection, 724; reputation for ruthlessness, 719; and secret police, 719-720

Husseynov, Surat, 927-928

Hutu; in Burundi, 271-274; in Rwanda, 427-432, 434-435; Rwanda refugees in Congo (Kinshasa), 316, *430*

Ibarra, Ernesto, 44

Ibo, 2, 418-420; attacks on, 421; secession from Nigeria, 421; and slave trade, 419

Ibrahim, Anwar, 616

Ibrahim, Barre Mainassara, 415

Idris al-Sanusi, 382-384

Ifni. *See* Sidi Ifni

Iliescu, Ion, 1013-*1014*

IMF. *See* International Monetary Fund

Imperial British East Africa Company, 482

Incas, 162; conquest of, 162, 206, 223-224; empire of, 162, 206, 223; modern descendants of, 166, 229; religion, 228

India, **569-582**; and Afghanistan, 529; Ahmedabad riots, 572; Assamese in, 572; Ayodhya mosque, 572-573; and Bangladesh, 534, 538; Bharatiya Janata Party (BJP), 572-573, 576, 581; and Bhutan, 541-544; border disputes, 512, 563, 580, 670; Buddhism, 573; caste system, 569, 572-574; and China, 513, 563-564, 576, 578, 670; Christians in, 573; coalition governments, 570, 572-573; constitution, 5, 572, 574-576, 581; dominion status, 533; economic change, 521; elections, 533, 572-573, 581; ethnic diversity,

571; and Fiji, 808; Gorkhas, 572; government organization, 572; and Great Britain, 857; Hindu nationalism, 3; independence movement, 574; Islam, 515, 574; Jainism, 573; and Kashmir, 577-578, 580, 633-634; language conflict, 574-575; Mizo National Front, 572; Moghul Empire, 574; nuclear power, 575; nuclear weapons, 522, 563, 575-576, 631, 634; Official Languages Act (1963), 575; and Pakistan, 3, 631, 633-634, 636; partition of, 574, 577, 631, 633-634; postindependence wars, 569, 574, 577-578, 581; regionalism, 569, 575; religious conflict, 569, 572-574; Sikhism, 515; Sikhs in, 569, 572-573, 581, 633; and Soviet Union, 575; state of emergency, 572; Tamils in, 515, 572-573. *See also* Kashmir; Punjab

India-Pakistan wars, 532, 534, 574, 578, 631, 633, 635

Indian National Congress; and Bangladesh, 533; and India, 572-573; and Nehru family, 572; and Pakistan, 631-632

Indians; in Malaysia, 612-615; in Pakistan, 636; in Uganda, 482. *See also* Amerinds; Native Americans; *individual societies*

Indochina, French colonization of, 547, 622. *See also* Cambodia; Laos; Vietnam

Indonesia, **583-591**; army, 586; Buddhism, 583-584; and China, 561; Chinese in, 514, 561, 584, 587-588, 683; Christians in, 583; communism, 585-587; currency depreciation, 588; declaration of independence, 585; early history, 584; economic change, 517; elections, 588; ethnic composition, 583; ethnic conflict, 584, 587; Hinduism, 583-584; independence, 586; Indonesian Democratic Party, 588; Indonesian Nationalist Party, 585; inflation, 588; and Irian Jaya, 794; Irian Jaya separatism, 587; Islam, 516, 583-584, 586-587; Japanese occupation of, 585; Java War, 585; languages, 583; Malays in, 583; and Malaysia, 587, 617; and Netherlands, 583-587; and Papua New Guinea, 587, 795; and Portuguese traders, 584; and secessionism, 5; Social-Democratic Association, 585; student demonstrations, 588; and Timor, 516; Timor separatism, 587-588; and Vietnam, 682; and West New Guinea, 586. *See also* Aceh; Irian Jaya; New Guinea; Timor

Inflation, 8; in Albania, 915, 918; in Argentina, 175, 181-182, 218; in Brazil, 185, 187-188, 192;

Lissouba, Pascal, 303, 305; overthrow of, 305

Literacy, 10; in Angola, 258; in Baltic republics, 933; in Cambodia, 549; in Congo (Brazzaville), 300; in Cuba, 75; in Egypt, 327; in Haiti, 87, 90; in Italy, 865; in Libya, 383; in Mexico, 34; in Nicaragua, 144, 147; in Niger, 414; in Saudi Arabia, 764; in Slovakia, 1039; in Suriname, 232; in Western Sahara, 492; in Yemen, 790

Lithuania, 931-941; book smuggling, 935; crime, 936; democracy in, 941; elections, 941; first independence, 934; and Gambia, 346; government corruption, 941; independence, 935; inflation, 940; and North Atlantic Treaty Organization (NATO), 937; and Poland, 933, 940; Poles in, 940; poverty, 940; Roman Catholics, 932; and Russia, 933, 940; Russians in, 936, 940; "Russification," 933; and Ukraine, 1042-1043

Liu Ming Chuan, 660

Liu Shaoqi, 558-*560*

Livingstone, David, 496; explorations of, 306

Lloyd George, David, 876, 879

Lockerbie, Scotland, *386*-387

Lombardy League, 6

Lon Nol, 550

Longowal, Singh Harchand, 581

Lonrho, 409

López Portillo, José, 41-42; currency devaluations, 42-43

Lorraine, 836-837

Lovejoy, Thomas, 193

Low Countries, 821

Luanda, Angola, 258, 261

Lucinschi, Petru, *1007*

Ludwig, Daniel, 187

Lugard, Frederick, 419; and Uganda, 482

Lukashenk, Alexander, 967

Lukowiac, Ken, 180

Lumumba, Patrice, 309-313

Lusaka Accords (1984), 259, 262

Luther, Martin, 848

Lutheran World Federation, 6

Luwero Triangle, 484

Luxembourg, 811, 821, 868

Lyautey, Louis, 397

Lynch, Jack, 879

Mabote, Miguel, 407

Macão, 584

MacArthur, Douglas, 604, 606, 643

McBride, John, 215

McCaffrey, Barry, 44

Macedonia, **993-1001**; agriculture, 1000; and Albania, 995-996, 998, 1000; Albanians in, 917, 993-994, 997-998, 1000; applications of name, 993; arms embargo, 998; and Bulgaria, 993, 995-997; and Byzantine Empire, 994; communism, 997-998, 1000; constitution, 998; and Croatia, 997; early history, 994-995; early independence movement, 995; economic transformation, 1000; emigration from, 997; ethnic composition of, 993; ethnic violence, 998, 1000; and Greater Macedonia, 993; and Greece, 993-995, 997-998, 1000; Greek appropriation of name, 997; and Greek Macedonia, 997; independence, 997; inflation, 1000; Islam, 993-995, 998; Kosovo refugees in, 920; literary language, 996; and Macedonian Orthodox Church, 997; and Ottoman Empire, 994-995; partition of, 995; political parties, 998; poverty, 997; and Roman Empire, 994; secession from Yugoslavia, 946; and Serbian Orthodox Church, 997, 1000; Slavs in, 993-998; and Josip Broz Tito, 996; tourism, 1000; Turks in, 994; U.N. mission in, 5; unemployment, 1000; and United Nations, 997; and United States, 997, 1000; and World War II, 995-996; in Yugoslavia federation, 1050

Machado, Gerado, 73; ouster of, 73

Machel, Samora, 405-407

Mack, Myrna, 134

McKinley, William, and Cuba, 71

Macmillan, Harold, 107

McVeigh, Timothy, 57

"Mad Cow" disease, 861

"Mad Mullah," 444

Madagascar, 294

Madrid, Miguel de la, 42

Mafia, Italian, 6, 865-866, 869, 871; in Albania, 917

Mafia, Mexican, 44

Mafia, Russian, 1023

Magellan, Ferdinand, 214, 796

Magloire, Paul, 85

Magoon, Charles E., 72

Magsaysay, Ramon, 644

Mahathir Mohamad, 617, 619-620

Mahaud, Jamil, 227-228

Mahdi. *See* Muhammad Ahmad